Empire, Industry and Class

Presenting a new approach towards the social history of working classes in the imperial context, this book looks at the formation of working classes in Scotland and Bengal. It analyses the trajectory of labour market formation, labour supervision, cultures of labour and class formation between two regional economies – one in an imperial country and the other in a colonial one.

The book examines the everyday lives of the jute workers of the imperial nexus, and the impact of the Dundee School of Scottish Mechanics, Engineers and Managers who ran the Calcutta jute industry. It goes on to challenge existing theories of imperialism, class formation and class struggle – particularly those that underline the exceptional nature of the Indian experience of industrialisation – and demonstrates how and why the Empire was able to provide an opportunity to test and perfect ways of controlling the lower classes of Dundee. These historical debates have a continued relevance as we observe the impact of globalisation and rapid industrialisation in the so-called developing world and the accompanying changes in many areas of the developed world marked by de-industrialisation. The book is of use to scholars of imperial history, labour history, British history and South Asian history.

Anthony Cox is currently involved in teaching at the Centre of Continuing Education at Dundee University, UK. His research interests include comparative labour history and eighteenth century Scottish radicalism.

Routledge/Edinburgh South Asian studies series
Series Editor:
Crispin Bates and the Editorial Committee of the Centre for South Asian Studies
Edinburgh University, UK

The *Routledge/Edinburgh South Asian Studies Series* is published in association with the Centre for South Asian Studies, Edinburgh University, one of the leading centres for South Asian Studies in the UK with a strong interdisciplinary focus. This series presents research monographs and high-quality edited volumes as well as textbooks on topics concerning the Indian subcontinent from the modern period to contemporary times. It aims to advance understanding of the key issues in the study of South Asia, and contributions include works by experts in the social sciences and the humanities. In accordance with the academic traditions of Edinburgh, we particularly welcome submissions that emphasise the social in South Asian history, politics, sociology and anthropology, based upon thick description of empirical reality, generalised to provide original and broadly applicable conclusions.

The series welcomes new submissions from young researchers as well as established scholars working on South Asia, from any disciplinary perspective.

Gender and Sexuality in India
Selling sex in Chennai
Salla Sariola

Savagery and Colonialism in the Indian Ocean
Power, pleasure and the Andaman Islanders
Satadru Sen

Sovereignty and Social Reform in India
British colonialism and the campaign against Sati, 1830–1860
Andrea Major

Empire, Nationalism and the Postcolonial World
Rabindranath Tagore's writings on history, politics and society
Michael Collins

The Guru in South Asia
New interdisciplinary perspectives
Jacob Copeman and Aya Ikeman

Princely India Re-imagined
A historical anthropology of Mysore
Aya Ikegame

Empire, Industry and Class
The imperial nexus of jute, 1840–1940
Anthony Cox

Empire, Industry and Class

The imperial nexus of jute, 1840–1940

Anthony Cox

Routledge
Taylor & Francis Group

LONDON AND NEW YORK

First published 2013
by Routledge
2 Park Square, Milton Park, Abingdon, Oxon OX14 4RN

Simultaneously published in the USA and Canada
by Routledge
711 Third Avenue, New York, NY 10017

Routledge is an imprint of the Taylor & Francis Group, an informa business

British Library Cataloguing in Publication Data
A catalogue record for this book is available from the British Library

Library of Congress Cataloging in Publication Data
Cox, Anthony.
Empire, industry and class: the imperial nexus of jute, 1840–1940/
Anthony Cox.
      p. cm. – (Routledge/Edinburgh south asian studies series)
      Includes bibliographical references and index.
      1. Jute industry workers–India–Bengal–History. 2. Jute industry
      workers–Scotland–History. 3. Jute industry–India–Bengal–History.
      4. Jute industry–Scotland–History. 5. Jute industry workers I. Title.
      HD8039.J82I4833 2012
      331.7′6671309541409034–dc23   2012024223
ISBN: 978-0-415-50616-8 (hbk)
ISBN: 978-0-203-07675-0 (ebk)

Typeset in Times New Roman
by Wearset Ltd, Boldon, Tyne and Wear

Fir ma mither, Isobel, Helen, Wilson, Falconer

'I'll bury nae heid like an ostrich's,
Nor yet believe my een and naething else.
My senses may advise me, but I'll be
Mysel' nae matter what they tell's…'

Contents

Figures and tables

Figures

Tables

Preface and acknowledgements

I come from Arbroath, where jute, alongside fishing and engineering, used to be a predominant influence. My maternal family arrived in the town in the eighteenth century, the Falconers arrived from their home in the Mearns to take up hand-loom weaving, and generations of my female relatives worked at the jute and the flax. As a 15-year-old schoolboy, I was also sent by my school to work amidst the stoor and din of the preparing sheds at 'Franny Webster's' Burnside mill, but left after a few months on the advice of my grandfather who, even in the late 1970s, knew the end was drawing near for the once mighty staple industry. I was encouraged to become an apprentice engineer, but little did I, or indeed my grandfather, suspect that time was also running out for this other local staple industry.

In the early 1990s, after spending most of the 1980s as an activist and full-time organiser with the Militant Tendency, jute very unexpectedly came back into my life when I became a student at Edinburgh University. I quickly gravitated towards Indian history, which was taught by Crispin Bates, an enthusiastic young academic recently arrived from Cambridge, who encouraged me to become an 'Indianist' despite my initial scepticism regarding my lack of obvious qualifications. Without Crispin's perseverance, and that of the other accomplished tutors on the exemplary 'Rise and Demise of Imperialism' history course, this book would never have been conceived let alone written. It was Crispin who first suggested the idea of doing a Ph.D. comprising a comparative history of jute labour and who encouraged me to persevere with the project after I left Edinburgh University without being able to secure funding. During this time, I conducted research at the University of Dundee archives and was taken under the wing of Professor David Swinfen who arranged funding for me and who supervised my work during the first year of research. After many years I have become re-acquainted with Professor Swinfen who has again proved to be methodical and constructive in his criticisms of various drafts of this work. In my second year of research I transferred to Trinity College, Cambridge, where I was supervised by the late Rajnarayan Chandavarkar. Before meeting Raj I knew and admired him as a formidable historian of Indian industrial labour, and in the course of being supervised by him my admiration for his keen intellect increased. I know that if Raj were still alive that he would have been able to make this a better book. I would like to thank the Fellowship Committee of Trinity College, Cambridge, for electing me as a Fellow in October 1997. I benefited enormously from the first rate facilities at Trinity, and from the advice of many Fellows at the college who listened patiently to my theorising. Particular thanks are due to Professor Ian Glynn who provided me with assistance and guidance, and to Andy Green and Mika De Jong who made me feel welcome. I also benefited enormously from the excellent seminars hosted by the Centre of South Asian Studies at Cambridge, which allowed me to hone my ideas and to benefit from the knowledge of the many keen minds I met there, amongst who I must mention Sanjoy Bhattacharya, Ben Zacharia, Carey Watt and 'Toto'. Many historical and political issues were thrashed out and numerous cups of coffee and pints consumed in search of the solutions.

In the course of my extended field trips to Calcutta, during the mid and late 1990s, I fell in love with the aptly named 'city of smiles'. I will always have happy memories of those times and the many stimulating evenings spent in the company of Chinod, Maneek, Binod and the rest of the regulars at the Sunday night addah. Whilst in Calcutta I also became re-acquainted with Parimal Ghosh who I first met in 1994 while he was conducting research at Dundee University archives. Parimal encouraged me to try my luck in Cambridge, and he was a mine of information on the culture and history of Calcutta. I hope to return there one day so that we can meet up again in the 'Oly' for an ice cold bottle or two of beer and finally sort out the problems of the world. Thanks are also due to Henrike and Henrika Donner for their company and friendship during my time in Calcutta. I would also like to acknowledge my debt to another formidable intellectual who, like Raj Chandavarkar, is no longer with us. Ranajit Das Gupta was a dedicated communist and a historian who pioneered the study of Indian jute labor. I always found him willing to share his ideas and to listen with the utmost patience, even when such patience was far from warranted. I am thankful that by engaging in this study that I had the opportunity to meet such a fine Babu and exemplary comrade.

Subho Basu has continued the proud tradition of Bengali Marxist historiography. I first met him at Cambridge and was immediately drawn to him. Our views on Indian labour history are quite similar, but I could never compete with his breadth of knowledge and deep understanding of Indian labour and the theory of history. I thank Subho for his comments and suggestions for changes to this work in his role as an academic referee. I would also like to acknowledge my debt to John Foster who acted as the other academic referee for this study. I have long admired his work, and I valued his well thought-out suggestions as to how the manuscript could be improved. I cannot let the occasion pass without mentioning Ian Duffield, the senior 'politbureau' member of the 'gang of four' at Edinburgh University. Ian became a friend as well as a mentor, and he has continued to take a close interest in my work, and provided invaluable criticism of earlier drafts of this book.

The present book draws on work that I completed at Cambridge, comprising the 1997 fellowship competition at Trinity College, Cambridge and the Ph.D.

thesis I submitted at the University of Cambridge in October 1999. Despite this, the present study is, it is, to all intents and purposes, a very different kind of work, which draws on additional research that I have conducted since my return to Dundee in 2003. I have come to admire the forthrightness and generosity of Dundonians, an appreciation that has only increased during the course of researching their remarkable history. I am particularly indebted to the ex-jute wallahs and jute workers who I interviewed for this study, and I would also like to thank Sandy Constable and Mike Arnott for putting me in contact with some of Dundee's veteran communists who shed an enormous amount of light on life as a 'bolshie' between the wars. My students on the courses organised through the Centre for Continuing Education at Dundee University have served as invaluable sounding boards for ideas that found their way into the present study, and have also been a mine of information on the history of everyday life in Juteopolis.

Ian Flett, Richard Cullen and the rest of the staff at Dundee city archives have always provided me with excellent service and advice. I also received fulsome assistance from the staff at Dundee central library, the West Yorkshire library and archives, the Scottish national archives and Dundee University archives. Dorothea Schaefter and Jillian Morrison, my editors at Routledge, have been assiduous in their duties and have shown an enormous amount of enthusiasm for this project even when deadlines came and went. When Crispin Bates first approached me nearly four years ago with the idea of turning my Ph.D. thesis into a book, I foolishly believed that I could complete the project in six to nine months. The intervening years have presented many challenges, not least of a financial nature. I have often struggled to keep my head above water, and without the help of my close friends and family this project would never have reached completion. The long hours of writing and re-writing can take their toll, and I am grateful to Jim Anderson for dragging me out from behind my desk in order to sample Dundee's wonderful music scene, while another close buddy Arron Finnon also leavened the loneliness of long-term research by insisting on my occasional presence in the Balmore. Raymond Mennie, Jim Hutchison and Alan Hinnrichs have also become 'muckers', comrades and occasional sparring partners over the last few years, while my return to the north-east coast of Scotland has also enabled me to resume my love affair with Arbroath FC, a passion I have shared with my fellow 'Smokies' Jim Anderson, Arthur Pritchard and Steve and Simon Reynolds.

I must give a special mention to Sarah Glynn. I am grateful that my time in Cambridge allowed me to meet someone who has become my closet comrade, confidante and life partner. When I returned to Scotland in 2003, I was accompanied by Sarah and her daughters Becky and Dassy. I am delighted that my wonderful family of bonny southron quines now regard this beautiful area as their home too. Sarah has been an incisive critic of my work, an unequalled friend in moments of self-doubt and an eident copy-editor. It is undoubtedly the case that this study would have been much poorer without her considerable input, although she cannot be held responsible for the shortcomings and mistakes that remain.

Abbreviations

AEU	Amalgamated Engineering Union
AGM	annual general meeting
AITUC	All India Trades Union Congress
AJSM	Association of Jute Spinners and Manufacturers
BCC	Bengal Chamber of Commerce
BCMU	Bengal Chatkal Mazdoor Union
BJWU	Bengal Jute Workers' Union
BNCL	Bengal National Chamber of Labour
BP	Benthnall Papers
BSP	British Socialist Party
CP	Communist Party
CPGB	Communist Party of Great Britain
CPI	Communist Party of India
CSAS	Centre of South Asian Studies, Cambridge
CSP	Congress Socialist Party
CSSC	Centre of Social Sciences, Calcutta
CUG	Communist Unity Group
DCA	Dundee City Council Archives
DCC	Dundee Chamber of Commerce
DCL	Dundee Central Library
DCPR	Dundee Communist Party Records
DDJFWU/JFWU	Dundee and District Jute and Flax Workers' Union
DSU	Dundee Social Union
DUA	Dundee University Archives
DYB	*Dundee Year Book*
EDMP	E. D. Morel Papers
EIC	East India Company
FAR	*Factory Act Reports*
FFUTW	Forfarshire Federal Union of Textile Workers
FICCI	Federation of Indian Chambers of Commerce and Industry
FLCB	Fairbairn, Lawson, Combe and Barbour
GFTU	General Federation of Trade Unions
GOB	Government of Bengal

GOI	Government of India
IFC	Indian Factory Commission
IFTU	International Federation of Trade Unions
IJMA	Indian Jute Manufacturers Association (later known as the Indian Jute Mills Association)
ILO	International Labour Organization
ILP	Independent Labour Party
ILU	Indian Labour Union
INC	Indian National Congress
IOGT	Independent Order of Good Templars
IOL	India Office Library
IWMA	International Working Men's Association
IWW	International Workers of the World
JFWU/DDJFWU	Dundee and District Jute and Flax Workers' Union
JGA	Jute Goods Association
KLU	Kankinarah Labour Union
KPP	Krishak Proja Party
LC	Lamb Collection
LP	Labour Party
LPC	Local Party Committee
LRC	Labour Representation Committee
LSE	London School of Economics
MFOU	Manufacturing and Factory Operatives Union
MFWPA	Mill and Factory Workers' Protective Association
ML	Muslim League
MRD	Managers Report to Directors
NAI	National Archives of India
NFWW	National Federation of Women Workers
NLS	National Library of Scotland
NMLH	National Museum of Labour History
NMM	National Minority Movement
NMML	Nehru Memorial Museum and Library
NPRP	National Prohibition and Reform Party
NUWCM	National Unemployed Workers' Committee Movemement (later known as the National Unemployed Workers Movement)
NUWM	National Unemployed Workers Movement (formerly the National Unemployed Workers' Committee Movemement)
PLP	Parliamentary Labour Party
RCLI	*Report of the Royal Commission on Labour in India*
RILU	Red International of Labour Unions
SB	Special Branch (Government of Bengal)
SDF	Social Democratic Federation
SLL	Socialist Labour League
SLP	Socialist Labour Party

SPP	Scottish Prohibitionist Party
STUC	Scottish Trades Union Congress
TDP	Thomas Duff Papers
TUC	Trades Union Congress
UP	Uttar Pradesh (formerly United Provinces)
UWA	University of Warwick Archives
WBSA	West Bengal State Archives
WPP	Workers and Peasants Party
WRID	Weekly Report on Industrial Disputes
WWLI	Workers' Welfare League of India
WYLA	West Yorkshire Library and Archives
YCL	Young Communist League

Introduction

[I]t is this attitude of the Jute Baron to the Indian coolies that has always been the reality in Dundee, and the majority of Dundonians know it. They know too that the present desperate plight of the chief industry is due to the employment by the Jute Barons who so long battened upon them – and whose mansions in the environs of Dundee contrast so strangely with the general slumification of most of the city – of still cheaper Indian labour.... Dundee is a great industrial cul-de-sac – a grim monument to 'man's inhumanity to man'. In Glasgow the horrible slums are masked by the multifarious activities and bustle of a great city, and Glasgow, moreover, badly hit though it has been, had never 'all its eggs in one basket' to the extent that Dundee had. There is nothing in Dundee to mask its utter degradation.

(Hugh MacDiarmid, 'Dundee', 1934)[1]

When Hugh MacDiarmid wrote his poison pen letter to Dundee, the city's jute-dominated economy appeared to be near collapse. In 1930, the local unemployment rate had reached over 50 per cent, and it remained well above the national average throughout the 'devil's decade'. The city's housing infrastructure, too, was in a state of crisis through years of underinvestment and neglect, prompting Scotland's rebel *Makar*[2] to claim that Dundee's 'utter degradation' exceeded even that of Scotland's more famous 'city of dreadful night'.[3] The 'industrial cul-de-sac' of Juteopolis, where the 'attitude of the Jute Baron to the Indian coolies has always been the reality' was, according to MacDiarmid, created and sustained by a British imperial nexus that enabled the mill owners of Dundee and Calcutta to profit by pitting one set of workers against the other. While Lancashire was also buffeted by Bombay, Dundee was opened up to Indian cheap labour competition – with the complicity of the British state – to an extent without precedent in the annals of imperialism. Dundee's parlous condition at this time appears to upset accepted views as to how Empire functioned, as the British imperial state allowed into existence and encouraged the growth of a colonial industry that was, apparently, destroying a regionally important 'home' industry.

The impact of the imperial nexus of jute on Dundee has led Gordon Stewart to claim that the city's relationship with Calcutta was one of reverse colonialism, whereby 'the conventional wisdom about imperial exploitation of the colonial periphery is made to stand on its head.' For Stewart, 'jute presents an unusual example of a powerful industry emerging in a colonised setting which almost destroyed the rival industry back in Britain even while the empire was still flourishing.'[4] This apparently radical view of the Dundee–Calcutta relationship does seem compelling, but it actually obscures more than it reveals about the nature of imperialism, and its costs and benefits to industrial development and the living standards of British workers. Imperialism should not be understood by its own self-serving propaganda as a system fundamentally geared to protect and enrich *all* sections of British society. If, however, we reject this circumscribed view, then jute is not such an 'unusual example' as it first appears, which enables the emergence of a much more nuanced and challenging picture of imperialism's impact on Britain – and India – to emerge.

The notion of 'reverse colonialism' is drawn from the core–periphery concept of industrial organisation. In this theory the core of an industry is represented by the major firms whose size and power allows them to set the price of their goods, while the periphery is made up of many small firms that are too small to influence the markets for their goods, which they are forced to sell at prices dictated by the larger core firms. According to Stewart, Calcutta emerged as the core of the imperial jute nexus while Dundee functioned as the periphery. The explanatory value of the core–periphery model as an example of industrial organisation in the real world is, however, limited. In contrast, this study employs the dual-economy model, whereby each branch of industry or group of firms producing related goods can be divided into two sectors; the primary sector (akin to the core) employs the most technologically advanced division of labour and supplies the stable component of demand within the market; the secondary sector (akin to the periphery) uses fewer product-specific techniques of production and satisfies the fluctuating component of demand, but during boom periods the secondary sector will commonly supply the primary firms with goods that they themselves cannot produce.[5]

Examples of the dual economy proliferated during the nineteenth century as industrialisation spread and an increasing number of textile centres competed furiously for markets. In the late nineteenth and early twentieth centuries, the silk industry of Lyon, faced with serious competition from Britain and the USA, re-organised itself towards specialised production by developing new dyes and artificial fibres. During the same period, the Swiss textile industry, which was faced with rising international competition and only a modest domestic market, also turned towards the production of high-quality, customised goods.[6] Dundee's jute mill owners, in a similar situation to their European counterparts, responded in like manner. The rise of jute manufacturing in Calcutta during the 1880s and 1890s, fuelled by cheap migrant labour and huge runs of low-cost sacking and hessian, forced Dundee into opening up new consumer-oriented uses for jute, encouraged by expanding consumer markets in Europe and the USA. At this point the positions of Dundee and Calcutta were indeed reversed, with Calcutta becoming the primary producer and Dundee being relegated to the position of secondary producer within a re-made imperial nexus of jute. However, this did not amount to 'reverse colonialism', but to a re-ordering of the relationship within the wider imperial system, thus enabling Dundee to continue as a major jute manufacturing centre, long after the rise of Calcutta should have reduced it to a mere historical footnote.

The re-making of the imperial nexus of jute was also crucially encouraged by the wider needs of the British imperial system, as Gordon Stewart demonstrates in his own work. The revenue provided by the growing Calcutta jute industry was an important contribution to 'home charges', levied on India to pay for the upkeep of British rule, which, in turn, were used to balance British trade deficits with rising industrial rivals such as the USA and Germany.[7] It was this stark reality that bound the re-made imperial nexus together, ensuring that the 'home' industry's attempts to gain government protection would inevitably founder. It would be wrong, though, to think that the re-making of the imperial nexus did not benefit Dundee's juteocracy. Calcutta became, in the words of a leading Calcutta jute wallah in the late 1930s, 'an umbrella over the heads of the mills in Dundee',[8] by checking the emergence and subsequent growth of jute industries in Europe and the USA. The Calcutta industry also benefited the Dundee jute barons in another more indirect manner. The home industry, through the lobbying efforts of the Dundee Chamber of Commerce, consistently used the largely mythical threat of Calcutta competition to justify their low wages policy in meetings and negotiations with government as well as with labour organisations, which had long-term consequences for Dundee. In the absence of the impulse provided by rising wages, economic diversification was conspicuous by its absence. Instead, a sizable proportion of the profits gleaned from jute manufacturing were exported via Dundee's burgeoning investment trusts, and the city and its people were plunged into a long and turbulent era of jute dependency.

The making of 'paternal despotism'

The last two decades have seen the appearance of a plethora of monographs examining aspects of the world of Indian jute workers. Many of these studies have broadened our understanding of the Indian experience of industrialisation, but the impact on workers of linkages between the two major centres of the imperial nexus has never been examined.[9] The one monograph that deals with the relationship between Dundee and Calcutta, Gordon Stewart's *Jute and Empire*, focuses on matters at the level of the boardroom and government conference chamber and never really touches the world of the factory floor and mill district.[10] This study seeks to fill that vacuum by investigating the worlds of the jute workers of the imperial nexus as these workers responded to, and impacted on, the strategies of capital and state. This approach also makes possible a re-examination of the claims made by scholars of class formation, who have previously limited the scope of their investigations to one or other of the jute working classes of the imperial nexus.

This will also allow an interrogation of Edward Said's, still influential, view that imperialism was exclusively involved in the creation of 'otherness', represented by the stark contrast that was thought to exist between the privileged position of the metropolitan worker and the inferior, backward nature of the colonial subject.[11] At the material level, the British worker benefited from jobs secured through imperial preference and contracts in the colonies. At the level of consciousness, he (the worker is always assumed to be male) was able to feel superior to the degraded colonial worker. A characterisation such as this ignores the more complex reality of the impact of colonialism on the development of the British industrial economy and working class formation. Imperialism was not something that only impacted on far distant lands to people of a different colour, as claimed by Said, as well as the Subaltern School of Indian historians.[12] The *golden fibre*[13] created huge fortunes for those who guided the imperial nexus of jute, but it also brought misery in its train for many who laboured on the killing floors of Camperdown, as well as of Champdany.[14] What is also striking in the contemporary accounts of our period is the blindness of employers, social reformers and officials towards the conditions and experiences of both sets of workers caught within the folds of the imperial nexus of jute. They are glimpsed as through a glass darkly – the form of the image is clear, but the picture is dull – though different writers all categorise the mill workers as beyond the pale.

Dipesh Chakrabarty is a leading proponent of the Subaltern School, and one of the most influential – though by no means unchallenged – scholars of Indian jute mill labour, whose seminal study, *Rethinking Working Class History*, has had a major impact on the field of study.[15] Chakrabarty evokes Foucault and Fanon when he describes the 'paternal despotism' that characterised manager–worker relations within the Bengal jute industry. For Chakrabarty, drawing on Foucaldian motifs, colonial rule was imprinted on the body of the Indian jute mill labourer, as the British developed a 'master–servant' mode of authority where 'the lash remained more important than the fine book'.[16] In *Provincializing Europe* Chakrabarty develops this argument further by explaining that while European citizens reaped the fruits of the Enlightenment project – including democracy, social justice, scientific rationality and civil society – the 'European colonizer of the nineteenth century both preached this Enlightenment humanism at the colonized and the same time denied it in practice'.[17] What was deemed essential to the peoples of Europe was withheld from the colonies through a specious form of philosophical justification based on the historicist stance of many Enlightenment thinkers. John Stuart Mill, in particular, is taken to task for asserting that 'Indians and Africans were *not* yet civilized enough to rule themselves', thus consigning them to an imaginary waiting room of history, an approach that was also used to justify oppressive rule in the colonies while 'Europe' moved towards universal suffrage, a developing equality of opportunity and greater social mobility. In presenting Mill in these simple orientalist terms Chakrabarty ignores his views on Europe. Mill also believed that Ireland was incapable of self-government and in need of 'a good stout despotism', very similar to that practised by the British in India, and that the Greeks were 'too Oriental' to govern themselves.[18] These two countries were joined in the, increasingly crowded, 'waiting room of history' by all of the nations of southern Europe whose populations were wedded to 'inactivity' and 'envy'. According to Mill, even France was marked by the 'double education of despotism and Catholicism', and was thus also barred from his, fundamentally Anglo-Saxon and Protestant, 'community of the free'. Mill's 'Orient', then, was not a phenomenon limited by geography, but rather a state of mind and a way of being that was evident within what he regarded as the cradle of so-called Western civilization as well as the very forcing house of political modernity itself. Mill also excluded large parts of the British population from the 'community of the free'. In 1848, against the backdrop of a Europe-wide revolutionary movement, he wrote that:

> the lot of the poor, in all things which affect them collectively, should be regulated *for* them, not *by* them. They should not be encouraged to think for themselves, or give to their own reflection or forecast an influential voice in the determination of their destiny.... The rich should be in loco-parentis to the poor, guiding and restraining them like children. Of spontaneous action on their part there should be no need. They should be called on for nothing but do their day's work, and to be moral and religious.[19]

This classical statement of the paternalist ethos from the father of British nineteenth-century liberal progressive thought is almost identical in tone, content and language to that of the allegedly 'traditional' Indian concept of *ma-baap*[20] that Dipesh Chakrabarty draws on in order to establish that the Calcutta jute wallahs 'were in *loco parentis* to the workers' – and which Chakrabarty claims fundamentally differed from the experience of western workers who 'belonged to a society where the bourgeois notion of equality was ingrained in culture'.[21] The truth is a little more complex than is allowed for in Chakrabarty's bald characterisation of the British experience of Enlightenment and industrialisation. In 1834, the same year that slaves were emancipated in the British colonies, the 'New Poor Law' effectively introduced another form of slavery on British shores in the shape of the punitive incarceration of the poor through the provision of so-called 'indoor relief'. Frederick Engels described these new 'Poor Law Bastilles' as 'the most repulsive residence which the refined ingenuity of a Malthusian can invent.' Paupers were 'handed over, helpless and without redress, to the caprice of the inspectors', and were forced to complete 'useless tasks', such as stone breaking for males and oakum picking for females, in order that their labour would not compete with those of 'outside concerns'. Those who did not finish their task got nothing to eat and all inmates wore a 'workhouse uniform' that marked out their wretched status. Families were broken up in order to 'prevent the "superfluous" from multiplying, and "demoralised" parents from influencing their children'.[22]

It was not just the vulnerable and marginal who were subjected to legalised forms of coercion. For the working poor, and not so poor, the law offered little protection from forced labour or, indeed, corporal punishment. The 1823 Scottish 'Act of Master and Servants' spelt out the cost to a servant involved in the breaking of a contract of employment: it was 'lawful for any Justice of the Peace

... to commit every such Person to the House of Correction, there to remain and be held to Hard Labour for a reasonable Time, not exceeding Three Months, and ... to punish the Offender by abating the Whole or any Part of his or her Wages.'[23] This legislation would become the subject of a celebrated legal case that revealed the existence of a Scottish form of *ma-baap*. In April 1846, six Dundee factory girls at Baxter Brothers Works, aged between 17 and 20, asked that their wages of 5s 6d be increased by a half-penny per day. The request was refused and, in protest, the girls left the mill during their dinner hour and took the afternoon off. When they returned to work the next morning, one of the Baxter brothers had them arrested and marched through the streets under a police escort. The girls were then tried in a private office by a magistrate and received a sentence of 10 days' hard labour for their act of defiance.[24] Following a defence campaign on behalf of the operatives, a petition was sent to Parliament, but the motion demanding an inquiry into the case was lost by a majority of 25. An account of the case was published in the USA, where it was used, along with similar cases, by the pro-slavery lobby in order to castigate the hypocrisy of British abolitionists who refused to acknowledge the extent to which elements of slavery existed in an industrial society notionally based on 'free' labour.[25] The Law of Master and Servant was modified in 1867, and in 1875 the Employers and Workmen Act made the contract of employment a purely civil engagement. However, employers and foremen still retained extensive powers over workpeople, which the new labour laws did little to nullify; and the sometimes brutal mistreatment of female and child workers – a hallmark of the early British factory system – continued right up to the end of the nineteenth century. Commenting on a rape case in 1886, a Dundee Sheriff claimed that there 'were foremen in the factories who abused their position in a most abominable way, and indulged in practices which were assigned to the American slave-owners.'[26] While the twentieth century would see an end to overt sexual exploitation, encouraged no doubt by the coming of industrial unionism, the patriarchal attitudes that gave rise to such outrages continued, albeit in a less open and more circumspect manner.

The Baxter Brothers controversy erupted at the end of a long period of almost endemic industrial and political unrest. During the 1830s Dundee became a stronghold of Scottish Chartism, and the town's emerging linen lords were not only threatened by an organised labour force, but also by a developing revolutionary working class ideology that was taking shape amidst the rising swell of industrial and political conflict. In 1842, many of Dundee's artisan radicals and leaders embraced insurrectionary politics and praxis as they sought to organise a workers' rising encompassing the textile towns of Forfarshire. Although dubbed the so-called 'Pilgrimage of Folly', and largely dismissed by historians as an ill-judged and farcical adventure, it was actually part of an unprecedented strike movement of textile workers encompassing Scotland and northern England.[27] Despite its lack of success, the events of 1842 underlined the support for revolutionary politics that existed amongst Dundee's craftsmen and textile workers during this stormy period of working class formation.[28]

Artisans in trades such as weaving and heckling provided a disproportionate number of the organisers, leaders, and activists of the emerging working class. Peter Carmichael, the foremost mechanical genius of the Dundee linen industry, described the hand hacklers as:

> [A] peculiar class of men with strongly marked characteristics. As a rule they were great politicians and the 'heckling shop' was frequently the arena of violent harangue and fierce debate. They had an eager desire for news and information and one of their number was usually told off to read while the others worked and listened. This gave them the habit of thinking and acting in concert, for they had a wonderful faculty for combining to enforce their own terms. They were under no law but came to their work and left it as they pleased.[29]

The long war waged by the manufacturers against the hand hacklers, and hand loom weavers, shaped and defined Dundee's emerging modern history. The position of these leading groups of artisan labour was initially undermined through anti-trade union campaigns and the opening up of their trades to greater numbers of recruits, which fatally compromised organisational capability and cohesion. During the 1840s and 1850s technological innovation further undermined the hand hacklers and almost completely removed the hand loom weavers from the production process.[30] They were replaced by a largely female complement of power loom weavers drawn from the Angus hinterland, the Perthshire Highlands and Ulster, including the unfortunate girls at Baxter Brothers who suffered 'hard labour' for their impertinence in demanding a wage increase.[31]

The first recruits amongst the Dundee School who made the long sea journey to Calcutta in the 1850s were foremen, time-served engineers and managers who had come of age during the 1830s and 1840s. 'Paternal despotism' was forged against this background of industrial conflict and social transformation before later forming a template for the evolving labour control mechanism in Calcutta. Similar methods of labour control were perpetuated and reinforced in both centres through the agency of these men who often, following success in Calcutta, returned to finish their working lives within the 'home' jute industry. They became the living exemplars of paternal despotism in both Dundee and Calcutta. Empire thus provided an opportunity to test and perfect ways of controlling the perpetually obstreperous lower classes of Dundee who refused the promise of 'enlightenment' through 'moral upliftment' and the work ethic.

The coming of the up-country men

Bengal was the base and launching pad for British imperial ambitions on the sub-continent during the eighteenth century, and their Indian capital, Calcutta, hacked out from malarial swampland, became known as the 'second city of the British empire'. As a major trading hub and imperial administrative centre, it also became the staging post for the shipment of indentured labour to the far-flung posts of Empire, and for new recruits to India's burgeoning colonial enterprises. This rising tide of humanity was set in motion by pressures exerted during the first half of the nineteenth century. During this period, encompassing the consolidation of British rule in India, a fundamental restructuring of South Asian society and economy was underpinned by the 'traditionalisation' of Indian property laws, swingeing revenue demands, and the monopolisation by British interests of the most valuable areas of commerce.[32] This was backed by coercive force, exemplified by the 'Permanent Settlement' of Bengal in 1793, which was perceptively, and acerbically, described by Victor Kiernan as 'a curiously atavistic repetition of [the] earlier treatment of Ireland.'[33]

This huge process of economic restructuring resulted in de-urbanisation and by 1840, Montgomery Martin, one of the earliest historians of the British Empire, was railing against the 'decay and destruction of Surat, Dacca, of Murshidibad and other places where native manufactures have been carried on', a process that Martin felt was due not to the free play of 'neutral' market forces but to 'the power of the stronger over the weaker'.[34] The linked processes of de-urbanisation and de-industrialisation were compounded by the after-effects of the so-called 'Indian Mutiny' of 1857, leading to an acceleration in the 'peasantisation' process as former artisans and professional soldiers were forced into agriculture in order to meet the escalating demands of British industry and commerce for raw materials and cash crops, such as cotton, hemp, indigo, sugar, opium and jute.[35] The peasants of eastern Bengal, encouraged by rising prices and a growing demand from Dundee manufacturers, increasingly shifted from rice cultivation to jute sharecropping, but they would have done well to heed the prophecy of the Bengali folk-poet, Abed Ali Mian, when he warned that you 'will have to eat the stem of your jute, mark my words/You think you will make money/That is but an empty promise/You will end up drowning in debt.'[36]

The massive expansion of the Calcutta jute industry was crucially dependent on the creation of a major new source of labour supply. This was achieved, as in Dundee, through the recruitment of migrant workers, and the reserve army of labour thus created was used as a potential check on wage demands and worker militancy. While migrant labour in Dundee eventually settled permanently in the mill districts, the up-country Indian migrants retained a link with their home areas, returning at regular intervals to visit their wives and families and sometimes staying for several months at a time before embarking on the long journey back to Bengal. According to Arjan De Haan, this pattern of circular migration means that the 'unsettled' up-country jute workers should not be viewed as a working class.[37] They were not rooted in the urban milieu, but, instead, entertained ambitions of a return to the land. They, quite literally, did not know their place. For Arjan De Haan, echoing Dipesh Chakrabarty, nothing could point up more the differences between the colonies and the modern industrialised world of the metropolis. The village link is seen as exemplifying the immaturity and difference of the east, and this argument was also assiduously used by the British managing agencies in Bengal as a justification for their long-term failure to introduce reforms such as service rules, standardised wage structures and pension schemes for the mass of jute workers. What this view ignores is that, in the context of a low-wage industry with little or no welfare provision for those workers who became unemployed, sick or injured, the village link functioned as a valuable support, while also sparing jute capital the responsibility for the costs of the reproduction of labour in the urban environment.

The jute workers of Bengal were, and are, not alone in eschewing the conventional pattern of working class formation. A whole number of very different societies, at varying stages of economic development, have witnessed the emergence of migrant workforces that have also used their rural home base as an important support to far-flung industrial employment. The miners of the Ruhr valley, during the nineteenth and early twentieth centuries, were predominantly migrant labourers, as were the building workers of Paris, and the possibility of rural living and a return to the land exerted a strong appeal on a large section of French workers up to the post-Second World War period.[38] In present day South Africa, circular migration between the bantustans and the gold mines exists within a highly developed economic infrastructure, and migrant workers played a leading role in the establishment of militant trade unions.[39] In Indonesia, a migrant working class retaining links with their home villages also provided an impetus both for the Indonesian miracle of economic growth during the 1960s and 1970s, and the political convulsions that came in the wake of the 'Asian Crisis' of the late 1990s. It is also certain that the peasant-worker will remain a reality for some time yet as the world-wide industrial revolution continues apace on an unprecedented scale, particularly in China and India. These recent global developments highlight the need to re-interrogate our conception of working class formation.

Class formation in a comparative context

While the Bengal jute industry has given rise to a plethora of studies, no published monograph dedicated to Dundee has appeared since William Walker's ground-breaking *Juteopolis* in 1979. This was followed in 1991 by Eleanor Gordon's *Women and the Labour Movement in Scotland*, which analysed the Dundee jute industry within a broader Scottish context. Gordon drew on a feminist theoretical framework to make a long-overdue challenge to conventional views regarding the organisational apathy of women workers and the division between workplace and domestic ideologies, but her conclusions have encouraged the growth of widespread assumptions – now amounting to holy writ for many Scottish labour historians – regarding the separate worlds and interests of women workers.[40] For Gordon, and other feminist historians, patriarchy is a primary part of the social relations of production, a form of social organisation and control that pre-dated the arrival of industrial capitalism, whilst subordination along class lines is of only secondary importance. In this view, gender divisions, flowing from patriarchal forms of labour organisation and control, played a key role in preventing the emergence of – that 'holy grail' of 'vulgar Marxism' – the ideal or homogenous working class, which in turn prevented the developing working class from posing a revolutionary threat to emergent industrial capitalism.[41]

The truth is, however, more complicated than is suggested in the dualism between a fundamentally divided working class and a homogenous, unified and contained working class. We should not be forced into a conceptual straitjacket that ultimately narrows our understanding of social processes. The search for an 'ideal' working class produces only a chimera. The reality of class formation, be it within the imperial metropolis or the colony, is much more complex, challenging and colourful than the search for this perennially grinning Cheshire cat, whose incorporeal smile constantly mocks our attempts to discover in fact, what exists only in the minds of social theorists.

The social and political convulsions that accompanied the rise and fall of the imperial nexus of jute demonstrated, sometimes in spectacular fashion, the transformative possibilities created by differences in ethnicity, religion and gender that marked both workforces, calling to mind Charles Sabel's challenging view that 'the very diversity of economic experience, which in the determinist and essentialist view marks the immaturity of the world' actually becomes 'a precondition for its transformation'.[42] It is also important to bear in mind that the diversity of the emerging working class in both centres was accompanied and complemented by marked continuities in social and cultural practices, which themselves were threatened, and often re-shaped, by the development of the imperial nexus of jute. The attempts by jute mill owners to reform or remove these practices often gave rise to serious and widespread strikes in both centres. What we might term revolutionary moments of time involving mass strikes, political organisation and – often violent – community mobilisation, were made possible by the coming together of this diversified and, apparently, divided working class.

This study employs a flexible understanding of capitalism, industrialisation and comparative working class formation, influenced by Ira Katznelson's ground breaking project on comparative working class formation in Europe and the United States.[43] Katznelson's model comprises four connected levels that are designed to overcome the inherent deficiencies within structural conceptions of class formation, particularly their omission of 'family patterns, demography, cultural traditions, inherited practices, state organization and policies, geopolitics, and other factors'.[44] While the first level, 'structure', conventionally relates to the structure of capitalist economic development, the second level, 'ways of life', is not only 'determined in part by the structure of capitalist development', but also by 'the social organization of society lived by actual people in real social forms'.[45] At the third level, 'dispositions', 'classes are formed groups sharing dispositions', but not necessarily speaking class dispositions, who 'may view the current situation as the outcome of circumstances that cannot be altered or as posing the possibility of something better.'[46] The fourth level encompassing 'collective action' is differentiated from 'disposition' when formed groups are 'organised and act through movements and organizations to affect society and the position of the working class within it.'[47]

In this study class formation is not viewed as a 'one off' phenomenon that naturally follows from the existence of a capitalist mode of production and that goes through a series of necessary stages. Instead, class formation is seen as comprising a constant process of making, unmaking and re-making, freed from developmental assumptions, which allows an appreciation of the ways in which workers were centrally involved in the creation of their own history. My primary aim is to reveal the connections that existed between different phases of class formation in Dundee and Calcutta as a result of the central role played by the development of jute dependency and the imperial nexus of jute. The different, but linked, worlds of the jute workers of the imperial nexus will be examined in ways that take due account of the quotidian experience of the workplace and mill district, and the extent to which workers were able to forge and maintain methods of struggle, organisations, and alliances with other sections of the working class.

In both centres, migrant workers transformed the areas that they poured into. In the absence of meaningful social welfare policies by the state or employers, social networks came into being that helped to sustain body and soul in often unforgiving urban environments, while the close relationship between community and workplace was of central significance in the process of class formation and affected wider culture. The *oary* tongue, markedly different from the spoken Scots of its Angus hinterland, became an unmistakable Dundonian badge.[48] In Calcutta, the mill areas that grew up to the north of the city similarly gave rise to a distinctive form of pidgin Hindi that was found nowhere else. The imperial nexus of jute also created gender imbalances in both centres, giving rise to family and household structures that were markedly different from those that were the norm within their respective wider societies. Jute dependency brought two very different areas and cultures into collision and collusion, and imparted shared characteristics in working class formation that, in large part, flowed from the nature of the industry, the character of the *golden fibre* and the products fashioned from it.

Instability was woven into the very fabric of this imperial nexus. Periods of high profitability encouraged new entrants into the industry in both centres, while irregular bursts of expansion by existing firms also encouraged a tendency towards overproduction and unstable markets. This was further compounded by the speculative conditions regulating output and profits, whereby a 'successful year's trading depends very largely on hitting the right time to buy the fibre, and, when the demand for the manufactured article depends so largely on the results of wheat, sugar, coffee, and other harvests in various parts of the world, hitting the right time to buy must always be to some extent a matter of luck.'[49]

Jute workers bore the brunt of pressures exerted not only by volatile international markets but also by the often unpredictable movements in the market value of the raw material as it made its way from the fields and streams of Bengal to the jute *godowns* of Calcutta and on to Dundee. If unprofitable working was expected as a result of short orders and high raw material costs, and workers resisted wage cuts, employers always had recourse to the lock-out or temporary closure of their works, which would lead to a lower level of losses than if they kept the mill open and completed their orders. Owners in both centres could also claim insurance payments, designed to protect them from long-running disputes, and some strikes were engineered by employers in order that they could claim insurance during periods of poor or uncertain trade. For the jute lords of the imperial nexus it was an article of faith that the trade could not bear any large increases in wages, and that serious or long-term recessions could only be overcome through recourse to often drastic wage cuts, which created endemically volatile industrial relations.

For management and employers in both centres, the act of questioning and challenging authority by workers was viewed as tantamount to rebellion or revolution. However, while paternal despotism was a reality for jute workers in both Bengal and Dundee, it was not unchanging, and nor would it go unchallenged. It was a harsh teacher, and its lessons were taught to all workers at the point of production within the imperial nexus of jute, irrespective of age, gender, religion, caste or 'race'. It taught workers hate as well as fear, and taught them what to fight against as well as what to submit to.

Because this is a comparative study of class formation, there are very few comparable texts that can serve as a guide to its organisation and structure, which is challenging, but also potentially liberating. I have adopted a chronological narrative structure, allowing the main themes to emerge and to build into a clear and coherent argument, regarding the centrality of the imperial nexus on class formation and wider social relations in Dundee and Bengal. Chapter 1 lays the basis for the study as whole by focusing on the evolution of the imperial nexus of jute following the establishment of links between Dundee and Calcutta based on the exploitation of the jute fibre. The central role of Scots in the rise of the managing agency system in India will be outlined and explained, as will the emergence of the so-called 'Dundee School' of engineers, foremen and managers within the early Bengal jute industry. Chapter 1 will also examine the ways in which Dundee jute firms attempted to maintain their position through the development of new 'speciality' jute goods and the increased exploitation of their labour resources. Chapter 2 looks at the Indian experience of class formation during the period of the remaking. It analyses the move towards the recruitment of a migrant up-country workforce and the stresses that were created in industrial relations during the shift towards hessian production by the Calcutta 'jute wallahs', and the central role of the Dundee School as an unwitting agent for the development of workers solidarity in Bengal. Chapter 3 looks at the social consequences of jute dependency in Dundee following the remaking of the imperial nexus of jute: focusing on the emergence of the female headed household, the central role played by child labour on the economy and wider society of Juteopolis, and the impact of these developments on the position of male workers in Dundee. The chapter will explain how and why the remaking of the imperial nexus spawned a city that became an 'industrial cul-de-sac' and a byword for everything that was retrograde about the Victorian and Edwardian experience of industrial development and urbanisation.

The second part of the study represents a thematic shift towards an examination of the emergence of working class politics in the imperial nexus of jute. Chapter 4 examines and explains the rise of socialist millenarianism in Dundee from the early 1900s onwards and the central role played by child labour in workers militancy and the emerging politics of class in Juteopolis, while Chapter 5 examines the impact of nationalism, Khilifat and the coming of the communists on workers struggle and class formation in Bengal from the immediate post-First World War period up to the late 1920s. Chapter 6 looks at the rise of communist influence in Dundee during the 1920s and the central influence of the imperial nexus on the evolving conflict between labour reformism and the more militant politics of class championed by the communists. The final chapter examines the forces that led to the breaking of the imperial nexus of jute during the 1930s. The changes to work processes in the Bengal jute industry and workers' bargaining power that came in the wake of the depression will be analysed, as will the change in production strategy signalled by the move towards the, hitherto Dundee-controlled, markets for speciality goods, sparked by the increasing competitive threat to Anglo-Scottish capital by so-called 'outside mills' controlled, in the main, by Marwari interests. The far-reaching implications of these changes on the imperial nexus and on industrial relations within the Bengal jute industry will be discussed and explained. The final chapter also examines the implications of the new Indian production strategy on the Dundee jute industry. The 1930s witnessed the beginnings of a major rationalisation of the Dundee jute industry, through the increasing introduction of high speed spinning, which had important consequences for manning levels and the gender balance of the workforce within the 'home industry'. This shift towards the increasing employment of male labour in Dundee will be explained as will the increasing removal of women workers in the Bengal industry. Finally, Chapter 7 analyses the impact of policies fashioned by the British home and imperial governments on the changing nature of the Dundee Calcutta relationship during the 1930s, and their role in breaking the century long imperial nexus of jute.

1 The making and re-making of the imperial nexus of jute, 1840–1900

> You used to think your 'Cutty' small and poor,
> See now, how I've grown by great Sirmure.
> Nigger Sam, Birkie,[1] Victoria, and Champdany,
> Have spent upon me many a British penny.
> At home we're all now on the newest plan,
> The Electric lights things spick and span.
> Thousands of dusky serfs to do our bidding.
> Mrs J[uteburgh]. (laughs)
> Don't laugh, you know I am not kidding.
> Our servants never strike, least if they do,
> For one that goes away, we can get two.
> I've taken away all your old colonial people,
> That used to swear by Dundee and the Old Steeple.
> For our Yankee cousins a strong bid will make,
> And give your Frisco bag trade a great shake.
> (D. H. Nicoll, *Ten Years of Conflict and Mrs Juteburgh*)[2]

Although the above excerpt is undated, its title indicates that it was written around 1895–6 at the height of the furious trade struggle between Dundee and Calcutta that laid the basis for the re-making of the imperial nexus of jute. Relations between the two centres had taken a serious turn in 1885, with the creation of the Indian Jute Manufacturers Association (IJMA, shortly therafter renamed the Indian Jute Mills Association) and their adoption of an output control policy that undermined Dundee's position in the foreign markets for 'standard' jute goods. The references to electric lighting and 'thousands of dusky serfs to do our bidding' points to the impact of shift-working and the expansion of the Bengal jute industry that took place during the early 1890s, which in turn led to a determined campaign by Dundee's jute lobby to curb night shift working in Bengal during 1895–6.

The unfolding competitive war between the jute industries of Calcutta and Dundee was waged, on both sides, by Dundonians, as the destiny of the Bengal jute industry was guided by Dundee's 'old colonial people' who had foresworn 'the Old Steeple'.[3] The bitterness widely felt in their home city at this time towards the Dundee School of Calcutta-based managers, supervisors and engineers is underlined by the reference to 'Nigger Sam', a crude, racist play on the name of the Samnuggur jute mill, established by the Dundonian Thomas Duff, which had spearheaded the move into the US 'Frisco bag trade' for burlap.[4]

The impression given by *Ten Years of Conflict and Mrs Juteburgh* is that the fight was all over bar the shouting. The poem also captures the sense of confidence of the Calcutta 'Cutty' (the 'winsome wench' and nubile witch conjured out of the drink-addled brain of Tam O' Shanter in Burns' celebrated poem),[5] portrayed as an ungrateful daughter glorying in her own mother's ruin. Indeed, the poem seems to detail an act of slow matricide. But, how far is the poem a true reflection of the changing nature of the relationship between Dundee and Calcutta? Was the humiliation of Dundee as complete as is suggested in the poem, or is there another more complex story to be uncovered from between its lines?

The genesis of jute dependency

Jute and Dundee were made for one another. Manufacture of coarse hemp and linen dated back to the late Middle Ages, but during the eighteenth century Dundee's linen industry underwent a transformation as it benefited from government-led economic development, which aimed to undermine growing support for Jacobitism and to tie the Scottish junior partner more firmly into the Union with England.[6] While other areas such as Dunfermline, Leeds and Belfast catered towards the manufacture of finer linen products, Dundee, drawing on its tradition of coarse textile production, thrived on orders for military and naval supplies such as sailcloth, hammocks, sheetings, as well as osnaburg cloth,[7] destined for the slave plantations of Virginia and the Caribbean. The Napoleonic Wars laid the basis for the emergence of firms such as Baxter Brothers who, encouraged by low-interest loans from a vibrant local banking sector, transformed themselves from modestly sized merchant manufacturers into the future lords of Linenopolis.

Before the widespread growth of the factory system in the nineteenth century, the linen industry was conducted on a domestic basis. In centres such as Dundee and Forfar, spinning and weaving was commonly combined with ordinary crafts, and in the towns and villages on the Fife coast weavers also turned to fishing in times of slack trade. The move towards mechanised spinning led to the wiping out of the Scottish cottage linen industry, and Forfarshire became one of the cockpits of Scottish industrialisation. By the late eighteenth century, there were no less than 23 centres of linen production along the north-east coast of Scotland, with the main development located in and around Dundee.[8] By 1822, even before machine-spinning had become general, the area was producing no less than 60 per cent of the total Scottish output of linen manufactures.[9]

The Dundee merchants and linen firms of the late eighteenth and early nineteenth centuries were involved in a trading network stretching from the flax growing areas of the Baltic and the Low Countries to the important cloth markets of North America and the West Indies. With one foot in trade and shaped by a ruthlessly competitive market, the emerging linen lords tenaciously fought any threat, whether real or imagined, to their own narrow interests. In 1823 the Dundee-controlled Forfarshire Chamber of Commerce opposed a reduction of sugar duties on the grounds that 'the interests of the linen trade of this country are intimately connected with the prosperity of the West Indian planters as your petitioners supply Osnaburghs for the whole of their negroes clothing.'[10] The linen manufacturers were ardent supporters of slavery, which they viewed as integral to their trading relationship with the plantations, and they fought furiously against its abolition. In the event, however, emancipation was not the disaster that many predicted, and sales and profits soon exceeded those during the era of slavery, fuelled by the steady expansion of new markets. The early Scottish linen industry was also reliant on child labour, and the linen lords jealously guarded their right to continue this exploitation, so that while the 1833 Factory Commission led to pioneering legislation aimed at prohibiting the employment of children, Dundee's linen manufacturers successfully appealed for exemption.[11] The coming of jute would strengthen the close association between Dundee and child labour, and the linen lords' blinkered attitude towards labour legislation would also become a defining characteristic of the future jute barons.

The expansion of power spinning created a rapidly increasing demand for handloom weavers that was only partially satisfied by increasing migration from Dundee's hinterland of Angus, Fife and Highland Perthshire, and the town's metamorphosis into Juteopolis would only be assured with the opening up of migratory links with Ulster. The Irish were a familiar sight in and around Dundee during the late eighteenth century, comprising handloom weavers, flax dressers and seasonal harvest workers, but during the 1830s they started arriving in larger numbers, prompted by adverts in the Irish press promising good wages and the availability of cheap steamship travel, which made the short sea passage to Scotland easier following its introduction in the late 1820s. Thereafter emigration to Dundee by single women and family groups, with men seeking work in heckling and weaving and women and children in the spinning mills, increasingly fed on itself as immigrants wrote back to their families with news of job opportunities and wages in excess of those available in southern Ulster.

Like Scotland, Ulster had witnessed a phenomenal growth in linen manufacturing during the eighteenth century, which guaranteed rising living standards for many labourers, cottiers and small farmers who took up handloom weaving, while hand spinning also provided an important supplement to family income and a vital source of support for poor single women. By the 1830s, however, Ulster's domestic linen industry, like many of the traditional textile areas of India during the same period, was in a state of near collapse due to the mass production of cheap Lancashire cottons, which also depressed the price for competing linen goods, while the rise of Belfast as a major centre of power-driven wet spinning thoroughly undermined hand spinning as a paying occupation.[12] It was during these turbulent times that Thomas Beggs, an Ulster weaver-poet, wrote that 'the guid auld times are gane out o' sight/An' it mak's the saut tear start to mine e'e/For lords o' the Mill and Machine hae' decreed/That bodies like me maun beg their bread'.[13] The advent of the Irish Famine during the 1840s turned Irish emigration from a stream into a tide. By 1851, approximately 50 per cent of the labour force of the Dundee linen industry was Irish born.[14] Ten years later it was estimated that the proportion of Irish in Dundee and Glasgow was almost identical, at around 15 per cent of their respective populations. By 1871, nearly two-thirds of first generation Irish immigrants in Dundee were female, a much larger proportion than in Glasgow, Edinburgh or Aberdeen.[15]

Female participation in the emerging jute industry was greater than any other British textile industry as a result of the systematic removal of male labour from weaving and heckling during the 1840s and 1850s, a process amounting to a social as well as an industrial revolution. In Lancashire, by contrast, many male artisan workers retained their position, and their wider social status, following mechanisation, thus paving the way for the emergence of a large male labour aristocracy within the cotton industry.[16] In sharp contrast, the male labour aristocracy in the Dundee jute industry was drawn from a much narrower layer of skilled engineers, foremen and tenters, which, as we shall see, would have major consequences for the subsequent socio-economic development of the town.

Although anti-Catholic and anti-Irish riots occurred in the 1830s, the succeeding decades were marked by a remarkable lack of sectarianism in Dundee, despite the continuation of large-scale Irish immigration. According to William Walker, this was due to the fact that the vast majority of incomers were young females, while Dundee, unlike the west of Scotland, did not experience high levels of Protestant Irish immigration.[17] However, anti-Irish feeling was also limited through the ability of the burgeoning Irish population, along with native Scottish Chartists, to forcibly prevent the establishment of the Orange Order in the town. In July 1841, an attempt by the Orange Order to celebrate the anniversary of the Battle of the Boyne was stymied when a vast mob assembled to prevent the march from taking place. The marchers had to be protected by local police, and by Catholic clergymen who, unsuccessfully, called upon the 'infuriated mob' to refrain from violence.[18] This represented a major setback in the attempt to establish the Orange Order north of the Tay, and while the organisation did grow in Dundee during the 1870s, religious sectarianism remained a minor cause for concern, which markedly differed from the situation in Glasgow and Lanarkshire where sectarian tensions escalated during the later nineteenth century.

The coming of jute

The East India Company (EIC) were using and trading jute rope, *gunnies*[19] and canvas throughout India as early as the 1740s, but the wider commercial possibilities of the fibre were not seriously appreciated until the end of the eighteenth century, when the possessions of the burgeoning British Empire were being systematically scoured for raw materials that could be turned to commercial account. In 1792, the EIC directors ordered enquiries to be made in Bengal regarding hemp substitutes and in 1803 experimental farms were established and a scientific officer, a Dr Roxburgh, was appointed to take charge of them.[20] Consignments of farmed jute were sent to Kew Gardens in London and then distributed to British textile centres, but early attempts to raise interest amongst manufacturers failed due to the coarse nature and appearance of the 'disreputable fibre'.[21] In 1822, however, parcels of jute made their way to Dundee and, following a decade of experiments, the fibre was successfully spun at the Chapelshade Works of Balfour and Meldrum.[22] Enterprising Dundee linen masters increasingly turned to Indian jute as a low-cost substitute for rough bagging made from coarse tow, a waste product of linen manufacturing, used for the packing of cotton wool.[23] A more humble origin for the future *Golden Fibre* cannot be imagined.

It was the threat of war between Britain and Russia in the 1830s that prompted many Dundee linen manufacturers to use jute in the place of Russian flax, and the Crimean war of the 1850s that launched it towards becoming the world's premier packaging material. As supplies of Russian flax were being systematically cut off, an increasing number of Dundee mill owners switched to the cheaper Indian fibre. Many made the move unwillingly, given the early reputation of the 'disreputable fibre', and the quality of linens was often underlined through a – often disingenuous – promise that they were free of jute.[24] In 1834, the year that really marks the beginnings of the importation of jute into Britain on any appreciable scale, one ton of jute was selling for between £12–14, whilst the cheapest grade of flax was quoted at £26. By 1854, flax was selling for £46–£48 per ton, and jute for between £20–£25, and by 1860 the price differential had increased, with the cheapest variety of flax quoted at between £42–£43 per ton whilst jute was selling for as little as £15 per ton.[25]

The year 1860 also witnessed the removal of the export tax on raw jute following incessant prompting from the Dundee Chamber of Commerce (DCC). In 1866, the town's favoured position during the early period of the emerging imperial nexus of jute was further underlined when an attempt by the Government of India to re-impose the jute export duty was vetoed by the Home Government – encouraging large increases in jute imports from 37,000 tons in 1860 to 103,000 tons in 1871, and further strengthening the town's long-standing association with low-cost textile manufacturing.[26] Whilst Dundee's commercial and industrial interests benefited from this developing trade, so too did the colonial state in Bengal through the receipt of large, and increasing, revenues from the growing cultivation of jute, which filled a vacuum created by the slow demise of indigo as a cash crop, thus serving an important political, as well as economic, purpose. Jute *gunnies* became a humble, but integral, component for the growth and maintenance of *Pax Britannica* and, by marking out the killing fields of Sebastopol, Gettysburg, Sedan, Ladysmith, Mukden and Flanders, also became a major icon of modern warfare.

In 1843, the legal prohibition on the export of British textile machinery was lifted, which encouraged the international dissemination of British manufacturing technology and expertise.[27] Jute manufacturing was quickly established in northern France, and by the 1860s jute industries had also taken root in Germany and Belgium, which, given these countries' long association with linen manufacturing and their developed industrial infrastructures, bode ill for the emerging Juteopolis. Thus, the Dundee jute industry, unlike the Lancashire cotton industry, did not have a long period of development before the appearance of international competition, which was further demonstrated in 1855 with the establishment of jute manufacturing in Bengal. Drawing on Dundee expertise in management and machinery, George Ackland, a former East India Marine officer and failed tea planter, floated a small spinning mill, with a daily output of eight tons of yarn, at Rishra to the north of Calcutta, utilising machinery manufactured at the Douglas foundry in Dundee under the supervision of John Kerr, who also selected Robert Findlay, a former manager at James Neish's Coldside Mill, to oversee the establishment of the new Indian mill.[28]

Although Dundee expertise was essential to the establishment of jute manufacturing at Rishra, this would have been impossible without the financial aid of Bysumber Sen, a Bengali *banian*.[29] Another early Bengal mill, the Soorah was run for a number of years by a firm of Marwaris,[30] while the Rustomjee mill was established by the Bombay businessman Chunder Ramjee in 1874.[31] However, as the industry emerged in the 30 years following the opening of the Rishra mill, it became more and more a preserve of Anglo-Scottish capital, a situation that would remain until the rise of Marwari industrial capital following the First World War. Once the pattern of Anglo-Scottish ownership was established, it became increasingly difficult to breach the unofficial colour bar that became the industry's hallmark – in contrast to the Bombay cotton industry, which witnessed substantial Hindu and Parsi involvement.[32] There were, though, other reasons why, for a long period, many Indians declined to make the move into industry. The late 1840s had seen increasingly lurid examples of breaches in British business etiquette, involving the exploitation of 'loop-holes in law, over-trading, over speculation, advances to plausible merchants without capital and fraud and failure of the principals in London.'[33] As a result, suspicion of British business morals became a part of Indian thinking at a time when the colonial economy was being integrated into the fast-expanding world capitalist system, through the development of the railway, the telegraph and the steamship.[34]

Britain's burgeoning eighteenth-century empire provided opportunities for a growing stream of Scots who, frustrated by the relative lack of profitable opportunities in their homeland, came to dominate the East India Company (EIC), particularly during the period of the so-called 'Dundas Despotism'.[35] Their influence in India increased following the ending of the EIC's monopoly of Indian trade in 1813 and the so-called 'Indian Mutiny' of 1857.[36] Kinship links proved central to their business success with cousinship being recognised 'as a kind of family obligation, as well as providing the basis of loyalty and discipline.'[37] The commercial and manufacturing firms (termed managing agencies) that some of these ambitious young Scots founded during this period ultimately became economic power brokers of the British Raj. Jardine Matheson & Company began trading in 1832 – their rise to prominence founded on their central involvement in the Chinese opium trade. Another Scottish firm, Mackinnon Mackenzie and Co., established by the Glasgow cotton trader William Mackinnon, built a shipping empire encompassing India, Burma, Australia, the Persian Gulf and east Africa. This vast area became ringed with other Scottish merchant houses, while the Indian sphere of operations broadened for the managing agencies as new opportunities presented themselves in tea growing, mining, and jute manufacturing.[38]

Although they evolved into powerful and wide-ranging business organisations, many managing agencies were 'hatched out in the premises of agency houses' amongst close groups of 'business associates who decided upon the project and floated the enterprise.'[39] They controlled these new enterprises, despite minimal ownership of their shares, by dominating the boards of directors and appointing their own managing agency to look after the interests of the company, which then received often large commissions on gross profits or sales and a generous share of dividends. The massive benefits that accrued to the directors of the managing agencies is demonstrated in the case of Andrew Yule & Co., which went on to control 10 jute mills in Bengal despite owning less than 30 per cent of the equity of any of these firms.[40] Thomas Duff & Co., the sole Dundee based managing agency in Bengal, also emerged as one of the 'big four' of the Indian jute industry following its establishment in 1883.[41] The success of its founder underlined how an enterprising Scot born under the shadow of the 'Old Steeple' could scale the business heights by using his knowledge of, and close contacts in, both centres of the imperial nexus of jute. In 1859, Duff became the first manager of the Borneo mill, and set about the successful re-organisation of its shop floor and machinery in close consultation with machinery manufacturers in Dundee.[42] In 1869, Duff returned to Britain and, after being involved for a short time in the management of a jute mill in Barking, retired from business. However, in 1872–3 he was tempted out of retirement by fellow Dundonians the Nicol brothers and J. J. Barrie, and became involved in founding the Shyamnagar jute mill on the northern outskirts of Calcutta.[43] The Shyamnagar example also underlined the advantages of connections with British capital markets in London, Glasgow and Dundee.[44] The partners set about raising the capital in Dundee, where Thomas Duff's achievements were well known. They found little difficulty in securing shareholders as the city was awash with spare capital following the dramatic expansion of the jute industry during the American Civil War and the sometimes spectacular returns from US investments. The experience, reputation and international trade and business connections of figures such as Thomas Duff played an important part in enabling Bengal to break into international markets in the 1870s and 1880s. Bengali and Marwari merchant capital lacked the international business connections – if not the financial means – that would have encouraged their greater involvement.[45] In stark contrast, the expansion of the Bombay cotton industry was dependent on breaking into the Indian market, and the knowledge and connections of Parsi and Hindu merchant capital encouraged their greater involvement in mill management and ownership.[46]

The managing agencies moved towards the recruitment of Scottish supervisors from the very outset of the establishment of the Bengal industry, again in contrast to Bombay where Hindus and Parsis were commonly employed as supervisors alongside British colleagues.[47] The small Baranagore mill in the far north of the jute belt, with a complement of 200 power looms and 40 hand looms, employed no less than 17 Scottish assistants.[48] D. R. Wallace, writing in the 1920s, wistfully commented that 10 of the Baranagore assistants 'were over 6 ft. in height. They were nearly all men who had been drafted when young from country districts to supply the demand for the jute and flax mills in Dundee and other Forfarshire towns.'[49] Below the Dundee School was a layer of native supervisors known as sirdars,[50] while every Scottish assistant also had an English speaking babu[51] attached to his department, who acted as a time-keeper and as a medium of communication.[52] The position of head sirdar was as far as an ordinary Indian worker could proceed up the hierarchy of the mill, and while, formally at least, it represented only the second lowest rung of the supervisory hierarchy, informally it became an increasingly powerful position. There were several sirdars within each department (the number depending on its size). Line sirdars oversaw around 20 workers, and were under the command of the head sirdar of each department who, in turn, answered to the Scottish supervisor.[53]

Figure 1.1 Baranagore Mill Staff, 1862. Bottom row, far left, Thomas Duff; second bottom row, centre, facing camera holding cane and with left hand on lapel, D. B. Wallace, father of R. C. Wallace.

Calcutta was the headquarters of the colonial economy developed by the Anglo-Scottish managing agencies, but jute manufacturing was carried out at its margins, and was a world away from the sophisticated clubs and salons of the colonial elite.[54] By the early 1900s, the jute belt stretched in a thin ribbon, hugging both sides of the Hooghly, from Bansberia, situated approximately 30 miles to the north of the city on the Howrah side of the river, to Budge-Budge, on the opposite bank, around 10 miles south of the city. By 1900, jute mills had been established in several localities, including, from north to south, Bansberia, Jagatdal, Kankinarah, Bhadreswar, Barrackpore, Titaghar, Rishra, Howrah, Calcutta city, Budge-Budge and Chengail-Bauria, which soon became industrial towns in their own right. Industrial growth was disproportionately concentrated in the north, exploiting the lower land prices on the outskirts of the city and existing rail links with both Calcutta and northern India. The mills in the Calcutta-Howrah conurbation were few in number and were erected in the first period of sustained industrial growth in the 1870s and 1880s. As a result of the pressures of urban location, the expansion of these mills became a problem, as was the provision of housing lines, which were established by the vast majority of Indian mills in order to attract, and to control, the increasing flow of migrant labour, which markedly differed from the situation in Dundee where workers relied solely on private rented housing.[55] Mills in the south of the jute belt were not only less numerous and more isolated than those in the north, they also relied on a mainly Bengali workforce, and were, with notable exceptions, smaller than the northern mills due to the business strategy of Andrew Yule & Co., which had a number of mills located in the Budge-Budge area.[56] In effect, there were three highly distinctive sectors within the Calcutta jute belt, distinguished by the multiform character of the labour employed, the size of the mills, and the pattern of mill clustering. As we shall see, these structural differences would also have a marked impact on the ways in which jute workers in the different mill districts mobilised and organised resistance to jute mill management and the colonial state.

Inside the mill

The technology of jute manufacturing was borrowed almost wholesale from the linen industry, with the production process divided up between six main departments: batching, preparing, spinning, weaving, finishing and sewing.[57] The first preparatory process of 'softening', involving the application of an oil and water emulsion to the raw fibre, draws attention to an important difference between the jute industry and other textile industries, such as cotton and linen. Jute fibre is very hard and woody and more preparation was required to make it ready for manufacture, which in turn meant that many more workers were required in the jute industry than in textile industries that relied on materials more malleable than the 'disreputable fibre'. The large, bulky machines involved in preparing the raw material also meant that much more room was required in a jute mill than in a cotton mill.

The next operation, carding, was completed in two stages breaking and finishing, which reduced the jute fibres into a more or less parallel formation in the form of a long, continuous ribbon or sliver. The sliver was then moved onto the drawing process, making the jute fibres more uniform, parallel to one another and free from external impurities, through the slivers being passed between pins and becoming increasingly stretched. Next, the loosely twisted slivers were spun, which drew the rove to the required yarn size and imparted the necessary twist required for the particular count spun.[58] Badly spun yarn meant regular breaks at the weaving stage. Though perceived as skilled work, spinning was a much dirtier job than weaving, due to the clouds of dust that were thrown up during the spinning process. Snuff and chewing tobacco were widely used by mill workers in Dundee in an attempt to counteract the effects of the dust, while *paan* served an equivalent purpose in the Bengal jute industry. Spinners were normally time paid workers, and were less well paid than weavers in both centres.

Conditions within the weaving department were usually in stark contrast to those in other departments. Weaving was cleaner work, due to the absence of dust, which in Dundee formed the basis of a perceived division in respectability between weavers and spinners. Weavers often wore hats, whilst spinners commonly wore shawls or went bareheaded. Although weaving was better paid, less dirty and more highly regarded work, the weaving department was the noisiest of any within the industry, which made verbal communication between workers over any distance impossible. This gave rise to the development of a sign and lip language amongst Dundee weavers that enabled them to converse above the hubbub of the looms.[59] Weaving required the close and constant attention of the operator who, being paid on the piece system, often ignored the safety procedures that slowed down production and affected earnings, so that industrial injuries in weaving were far more common than in other work processes. Following weaving, the cloth was cropped, then cleaned through brushing, and finally ironed – calendered to give its trade name – at high speed. The different grades of cloth were then separated. Hessian cloth was lapped and folded, and sacking – which was sold as gunny bags – was cut and stitched in the sewing department.

Segmentation was central to the organisation of labour within the Dundee jute industry. The supervisory and management levels within the industry were almost the sole preserve of men, apart from a few 'shifting mistresses'. These women were invariably ex-spinners who were employed to recruit and supervise juvenile and child labour, and were possessed of a fiersome reputation.[60] The male overseers and assistant overseers were normally promoted from the ranks of the mechanics or tenters and wielded an enormous amount of power on the shop-floor, being responsible for recruitment and discipline and having the authority to sack workers on the spot.[61] Occupations requiring a mechanical knowledge such as maintenance and tenting were only for male workers, and maintenance work could only be secured following an apprenticeship. Tenting involved the setting up and 'tuning' of looms, and tenters in some works shared in the bounty system applied to weavers, paid on production over and above a certain quantity, which caused a fair level of antagonism between them and weavers. Apart from menial secretarial work, women did not impinge on the clerical side of the industry. The ratio of women to men within the Dundee jute industry was roughly 3 : 1. Skilled production occupations such as spinning, weaving and winding were, for a long time, the sole preserve of women, although the inter-war period would witness the increasing recruitment of male spinners, weavers and winders.[62]

The sexual division of labour within Dundee jute industry was at its most rigid within the factory (or weaving). Here, male workers were employed as beamers and dressers, as supervisory and maintenance workers (such as over-seers, tenters and mechanics) and, by far the largest grouping, unskilled labour-ers. Within the mill, there were occupations that engaged both men and women, but these were mostly confined to the batching house and to shifting, which was carried out by young boys and girls in the spinning flats where they were employed in replacing full bobbins for empty ones on the frames. Where males and females performed the same tasks they were generally paid similar wages. In the mill, spinners were almost always women, with adult males confined to supervision and maintenance work. The work of 'piecing', or 'fixing up' the loose ends dropped by the spinners, was undertaken by young women, many of whom would themselves become spinners. While shifting and piecing often served as an informal apprenticeship for female spinners and preparers, male shifters would be 'let go' when they reached the age of 18, which qualified them for an adult wage.

The Dundee jute worker very often had little knowledge regarding the differ-ent work processes outside his or her immediate department. According to one weaver:

> I was never in a mill in my life, I'd never even seen the inside o' the mill. When you went into your work the factory was on one side, the mill was on another side and you'd no occasion – maybe you were allowed, maybe you weren't, I don't know, but I was never in the mill in my life. Just my own factory bit.[63]

Most mills and factories in Dundee, in contrast to the single-storey Calcutta mills, were multi-storey and the different departments were often in separate buildings, which militated against industrial efficiency on the one hand, but on the other, by physically dividing workers, allowed for more efficient supervision. Trade unions were conspicuous by their absence in the early jute industry although unorganised and 'spontaneous' strikes were relatively common. While strikes were limited to single departments or mills and were of very short dura-tion, many were successful in the context of booming trade conditions and regular shortages of labour.

In 1863, the British Social Sciences Association noted that the introduction of power looms had 'virtually compelled a general advances in wages', suggesting that jute workers shared, at least to some degree, in the boom times of the 1850s and 1860s.[64] Improvements in diet and clothing were, however, limited by steadily rising prices, and the already large earnings gap between the wages of male skilled jute workers, such as foremen, engineers and tenters, and the lowest paid jute workers widened even further.[65] The earnings gap between jute workers and other Scottish workers was even greater. In the mid-1860s, when jute weavers were earning 13s, shipwrights in Glasgow were earning 36s, masons 32s 6d and painters 26s.[66] In Lanarkshire, skilled foundry workers, who were amongst the highest paid Scottish workers, were earning wages of 10s per day, and even foundry labourers were earning wages of 2s a day, just short of those paid to jute weavers.[67]

The boom times that marked the era of *Pax Britannica* suddenly juddered to a halt with the emergence of the so-called 'Great Depression' of 1873–96,[68] and the limited gains made by the jute workers were quickly snatched away through successive wage cuts, a situation that was replicated in many trades across Dundee.[69] In 1872, the gathering offensive by the employers provoked widespread strike action, amongst 'lumpers' at the docks, slaters, pipemakers, blacksmiths, joiners, calender workers, rope and twine makers, hacklers and even domestic servants, and a marked growth in trade union formation.[70] The jute workers also caught the mood of the times. The close kinship and community links within many mills departments ensured that perceived slights from employers and management could spark spontaneous and sometimes long-lasting departmental disputes into life, which, with the onset of depressed trade conditions from the 1870s, provided a springboard towards mill and even industry wide disputes. Writing many years later, the Dundee jute workers' leader, Henry Williamson, remembered these years when 'never a week passed by without presenting the … same sad familiar scene – a band of tousled, loud voiced lassies with the light of battle in their defiant eyes gathered together in the street and discussing with animation and candour the grievances that had constrained them to leave their work.'[71] During the course of a power loom weavers' strike in the north-east of Dundee during the New Year celebrations of 1872, following the withdrawal of holiday pay by the employers, the workers' representative was 'told by the head of the firm that the workers were getting the beef and he the bones'. When this was communicated to them one of the girls replied, 'very weel, I'll gie him my beef, if he gies me his banes'.[72] Rising working class militancy in Dundee was further underlined, and encouraged, with the formation, in the early 1870s, of a local section of the International Working Men's Association (IWMA), a development that probably owed its impetus to the gathering campaigns around trade union formation and reduced working hours.[73]

In the last two months of 1874, thousands of jute workers downed tools and staged large-scale demonstrations in protest at the amendment of the 'Mundella' bill, which fixed the maximum working week at 56 rather than 54 hours.[74] In August 1875, wage reductions provoked another wave of jute strikes, leading to the formation of the East of Scotland Mill and Factory Workers' Protective Association (MFWPA), but six years later the new union was effectively bankrupted as a result of having to provide large amounts of strike pay during the course of a drawn-out dispute at the Camperdown mill of Cox Brothers.[75]

Becoming Juteopolis

From the 1850s up to the early 1870s, Dundee's jute industry underwent a marked process of vertical integration, giving rise to a handful of massive industrial enterprises that existed alongside a plethora of much smaller producers specialising in processes such as preparing, spinning and weaving. The biggest of the giant complexes and one of the earliest firms to realise the potential of jute manufacturing was Cox Brothers of Lochee, situated a few miles to the west of Dundee. Established in 1841, the firm began mechanised weaving in 1845 and by the 1860s its Camperdown Works was the largest jute mill in the world, employing around 3,000 workers who completed every process in jute manufacturing, including weaving, bleaching, and dyeing. A branch railway line was constructed in order to connect the Camperdown Works with Dundee docks and the Dundee–London railway line, while the firm also established their own fleet of ships, a fully staffed branch office in Calcutta, alongside a massive jute warehouse, and – the first of its kind – a steam press to facilitate baling, which guaranteed the firm regular supplies of jute fibre.[76]

The boom times continued into the early 1870s, and the profits gleaned from fratricidal conflict in America and from the short but profitable savagery of the Franco-Prussian War were re-invested, fuelling a doubling in spindles and looms between 1870 and 1874 alone.[77] While growth was encouraged by the expansion of existing jute mills and the establishment of new mills, these years also witnessed a decisive switch from linen to jute production in Dundee and Angus, with major long-term consequences for the area's subsequent socio-economic development.[78] Investment that could have been used to encourage greater industrial diversification, as was happening in central Scotland, was instead channelled towards jute. As a result, engineering, shipbuilding and machinery manufacture all remained secondary industries, despite some growth through servicing and supplying the expanding jute industries of the imperial nexus – a failure that was, however, by no means due to a shortage of investment funds.

The period during and following the American Civil War presented Dundee investors with a unique opportunity to buy America on the cheap. The theatre of war provided massive orders for gun-carriage covers, wagon covers, sand bags and tenting, and Dundee firms were also granted massive tracts of land by the Union government in lieu of payment. Robert Fleming, an employee of Baxter Brothers, was sent to the USA in 1870 to keep a check on the firm's investments, where he also pioneered Dundee's interests in real estate through the establishment of Dundee and US-based investment trusts, making a fortune for himself and his employers in the process.[79] The American west contributed in another more poignant way to the rise of Juteopolis, through the utilisation of buffalo hide in the making of the aptly named buffalo picker, an instrument used to separate the strands of weft when weaving jute cloth. However, this practice had to be discontinued following the near-extinction of the once enormous herds, which was partly done at the behest of US army strategists determined to cut off the staple food supply of the native plains tribes in the 1870s and 1880s. Once the plains were cleared of buffalo, and the native tribes, the investment trusts quickly moved in to establish cattle ranching on a massive scale.[80] The burgeoning investment trusts were popularised in the Dundee area where almost all of their capital was raised. The original directors of the Oregon and Washington Trust included members of Dundee's prominent textile dynasties.[81] The returns to those who invested in these trusts could be enormous. In the 1940s, it was calculated that if £1,000 had been invested in the Scottish American Trust Co. Ltd in 1873, it would have been worth £70,000, and earning £3,000 per year, by 1929.[82]

Despite large-scale investment, in the first Tay bridge project as well as jute manufacturing, the large, and increasing, funds held by the city's booming investment trust funds were never devoted to local economic diversification. Indeed, it is unlikely that the investment trusts, which were largely controlled by linen and jute interests, would ever have encouraged new industries that might have endangered the low wage economy spawned by jute dependency. It was certainly the case that George Lowdon's pioneering attempt in 1876 to establish an electrical engineering firm in Dundee foundered through a lack of funds, despite the local investment mania of this time.[83]

The decade of the 1870s was a roller-coaster ride for the Dundee jute industry, as feverish trade during and immediately following the Franco-Prussian war gave way to an erratic cycle of peaks and troughs in demand and increasing labour troubles. This situation worsened in the second half of the 1870s as the economic consequences of delayed rains, drought and raging famine in China, India and South America became apparent in the balance sheets of firms reliant on the carrying trade.[84] The 1870s, however, would not be chiefly remembered for troubled economic conditions and labour disputes. On 28 December 1879 the much-lauded and recently constructed Tay railway bridge – a vaulting symbol of Victorian ambition and confidence – collapsed during a howling gale. The New Year's festival, normally a time of warm conviviality, gave way to mourning as the harrowing details of the disaster were revealed. It was a terrible way in which to close a decade, and many must have hoped that it was not in fact an awful portent.

By the 1880s, Dundee was investing around £500,000 annually in investment trusts, and while Edinburgh invested more in absolute terms Dundee had a much higher proportion of its total resources devoted to US investments.[85] As world trade struggled to recover from the depression of the 1870s, new further-flung investment opportunities were sought out. Funds raised, chiefly through the endeavours of the textile industry, made their way to destinations as varied and exotic as Australia, New Zealand, Canada, Hawaii, Ceylon and the Bengal jute industry. Following the establishment of the Titaghar and Victoria mills, between 1882–5, one-eighth of the Calcutta capacity was controlled by Thomas Duff & Co, the sole Dundee-based managing agency in Bengal. Foreign investment in jute was, though, not limited to India. In 1884, the Arbroath firm of flax spinners and sail makers, Douglas Fraser & Sons, along with Mr Etchegaray, an Argentinian merchant, established the *Sociedad Anonima Fabrica Argentina de*

Alpargatas on the outskirts of Buenos Aires, which manufactured the *alpargata*, or rope-soled shoe, made from jute fibre.[86]

The close inter-relationship between the jute industry and the investment trusts during the 1870s and 1880s provided fortunes for the few, and a modest income for innumerable middle-class 'coupon clippers'. There was, though, a growing conviction that the accelerating investment mania could have potentially disastrous consequences, which the *Dundee Year Book* of 1885 reflected when it urged caution on the part of local investors:

> The amount of money already called, and which has yet to be called on Companies recently constituted, is so large that the possibility of raising it in Dundee would have been questioned not many years ago. We do, therefore, think it advisable that some time should be given for the digestion of these investments before more are crowded on our local market.[87]

The advice was not heeded, and by 1888 more than 75 per cent of Scottish capital invested in US cattle companies had been lost and four out of eight public companies had gone bankrupt. The crisis intensified with the development of the Baring crisis in 1890 and the subsequent depression of 1893–4, which threatened Scottish enterprises who had not heeded the warning and repatriated their investments. Volatility in the financial markets also impacted on labour relations in the Dundee jute industry, as wage reductions and other cost cutting measures became the order of the day for mill owners who, in addition to substantial losses on their American investments, also faced increasing Indian competition and the loss of important markets through the imposition of protective tariffs by a growing number of European countries. These developments were also accompanied by furious denunciations from an expanding and increasingly confident socialist movement. In July 1897, Tom Mann, the revolutionary socialist and labour leader, visited Arbroath where he launched a bitter tirade against 'coupon clippers' who he accused of earning income from rents and interest whilst giving 'nothing in return, and [living] at other people's expense.'[88] For socialists like Mann the financial crises of these times were but a reflection of the mounting contradictions within capitalism, a message that increasingly resonated amongst already low-paid jute and linen workers who were facing wage cuts, speed-ups and regular bouts of unemployment.

The rise of the 'Calcutta cutty'

During the 1870s, the Bengal jute industry was enormously stimulated by the continuing development of the Indian railway system, the opening of the Suez Canal, and the increasing importance of Calcutta as an international trading hub. Between 1858 and 1878, exports of jute goods from India expanded from 969,724 cwt. to 5,362,267 cwt. per year.[89] In 1874 and 1875 alone, eight new Indian mills were started, bringing the total number of looms up to 3,500.[90] In contrast to many of the smaller and older mills in Dundee, the jute mills of

Bengal were mostly of one storey and built on a large scale, and, through a system of sky lighting, were both well ventilated and well lighted. Bengal's rapidly expanding jute industry also provided a bonanza for the Dundee engineers, machinery manufacturing firms and building specialists who played a pivotal role in the construction of the new single-storey mills, and in supplying them with machinery and plant.

During the 1870s, the Bengal jute industry was still predominantly geared to the manufacture of sacking and Dundee firms increasingly avoided Calcutta competition by concentrating on the production of finer grade hessian cloth.[91] In the process, the Dundee–Calcutta relationship developed apace, with Bengal emerging as the secondary sector within an evolving imperial nexus. The 1870s were also, however, marked by a major new development within the Bengal jute industry that had far-reaching consequences for the imperial nexus of jute. In the last years of the decade, the Shyamnagar and Hastings jute mills both successfully produced hessian cloth and opened up business links with American buyers, supplying wheat pockets and burlap cloth.[92] As a result, the number of hessian looms doubled in quantity, from 910 in 1877 to 1,800 in 1885.[93] Stricter attention to quality also enabled Calcutta jute producers to secure regular British orders for twills, flour bags and other finer quality bagging, a development encouraged through the development of links with London-based commercial firms, such as Messrs Walter H. Hindley.[94] By the mid-1880s, Calcutta firms had captured further markets for Levant grain sacks and other twill goods, and expanded their market share in wheat bags, Australian bran bags and Egyptian cotton packs, which led to a steady increase in the production of hessian cloth.[95]

For many historians of the Bengal jute industry, it is difficult to conceive of a time when the industry was anything other than a lumbering colossus, marked by poor productivity, outmoded machinery and myopic management.[96] During the 1880s, however, the Bengal jute industry was expanding on the basis of 'best practice' in relation to the utilisation of machinery, mill construction and effective management, to a degree only available to a few of the more successful and larger firms in and around Dundee.

At the end of 1884, disquieting reports reached Dundee regarding the formation of the Indian Jute Manufacturers Association (IJMA). D. R. Wallace, who was himself a leading figure within the Bengal jute industry, described the reasoning behind the establishment of the IJMA as follows:

> During the years prior to 1884, attempts had been made at intervals to fix selling prices by so-called bona fide agreements. Efforts had also been made from time to time in the direction of curtailing production to assist the markets. But the difficulty of arriving at unanimity rendered these good intentions only partially successful. Hence, in 1884, the question of combination began to take shape.[97]

Faced with a potentially powerful combination of Bengal manufacturers, a rising challenge from Bengal-made hessian cloth and a developing problem with overproduction, Dundee's mill owners responded with a policy of short-time working, which, though, ended abjectly. When this failure was debated by the local Chamber of Commerce (DCC) J. H. Walker, a leading figure within the local jute trade, pointed out that:

> [Y]ou cannot compare Calcutta with Dundee for the simple reason that the mills in India are all new and run on exactly the same lines. In Dundee we have old and new mills, and the difficulty in securing unanimity in the adoption of a short time movement was due in great measure to the differences between the old and newly constructed mills.[98]

The newer and smaller firms in Dundee did not have the amassed reserves enjoyed by the larger established firms and were compelled to work the maximum hours in order to keep overhead costs as low as possible, a situation that, as we shall see in Chapters 6 and 7, would be repeated on a much bigger scale in Bengal during the inter-war period, following the emergence of largely Marwari-controlled 'outside mills'.

In Dundee, the failed working time agreement was also accompanied by an unprecedented industry-wide strike wave, following the attempt to impose wage cuts on an already hard-pressed and increasingly defiant workforce. Writing many years later, the Unitarian minister and labour leader, Henry Williamson, described being approached by a number of male trade unionists who asked him to intervene at a mass strike meeting. Williamson urged the strikers to return to work and to form a union, and a short time afterwards the Manufacturing and Factory Operatives Union (MFOU) was established, with Williamson as its honorary president, but de facto leader.[99] Williamson also claimed that the employers welcomed the formation of the union as they felt it would help check the development of 'spontaneous' or 'wild-cat' strikes, and this conciliatory approach towards the employers would form the *modus operandi* for Williamson and the MFOU in the following decades.[100] Williamson was a classical 'outsider', with no family links in Dundee or with the jute industry, and was regarded with suspicion by the local Trades Council, which refused to affiliate the new union because it was not formed and led by workers.

The strike wave and unionisation of mill workers in 1885 pointed to the very real and growing impact of Calcutta competition on Dundee's staple trade and social stability, which many feared would only grow more serious with the formation of the IJMA, and its commitment 'to protect the members of the Association against competition'. In June 1889, at a rally of jute workers in Arbroath, Williamson denounced the impact of foreign competition, which, he maintained, had reduced 'many poor creatures in Dundee' to a condition 'as degraded as that of the slaves in the Southern United States'.[101] During the 1880s, wages in the jute and flax industries had fallen by around a quarter, and Williamson was characteristically eager to echo the employers' claim that growing foreign competition was largely responsible for this state of affairs, but, as we shall see, other trade union figures would increasingly challenge this view.

The re-making of the Dundee–Calcutta nexus

By 1892 Bengal was producing hessian in ever larger quantities and the following year increasing international demand was such that there was a great rush to increase output. In 1894, many Bengal mills installed electric lighting and worked 14 to 15 hours per day, which increased productive capacity by around one-sixth by November 1895, leading a Calcutta-based correspondent to admit that no 'one who knows anything about the jute industry can visit the jute mills here without coming to the conclusion that as regards the common run of hessians and sackings Dundee's position is seriously threatened'.[102] Dundee's situation appeared even more serious when the stark difference in working costs was taken into consideration. In 1894, one of the earliest attempts to compare the two centres found that Dundee wages, including managers and clerks salaries, came to £6 5s per ton. In Calcutta they were estimated at £2 19s 7d. It was also calculated that a ton of jute could be turned into hessian in Dundee for an average cost of £11 10s, while in Calcutta the cost was £5 19s 2d. Total manufacturing costs for sacking in Calcutta was thought to be Rs65 per ton, or £3 10s 5d, whilst Dundee's costs were almost double this figure.[103]

Although many commentators, perhaps inevitably, viewed these figures as proof of the incredible cheapness of Indian labour, a significant part of the difference in working costs was actually due to movements in the exchange rate between the rupee and sterling.[104] In 1881–2, the wages of 'skilled workers', including weavers, in the Bengal jute industry were thought to be Rs25 per month, or between 11 and 12s per week, at the exchange rate of that time, while the wages of Dundee weavers were, at between 10s to 11s 1d., remarkably similar.[105] Between 1882 and 1895, however, the steady devaluation of the rupee against sterling effectively created a gap in the wages bill between the two centres of over 100 per cent in favour of Calcutta, while a further 20 per cent would also need to be added to take account of Calcutta's longer working week.[106] Devaluation did provide Dundee with some short-term relief, with regards to raw material prices, but this was effectively wiped out as a result of the rising price of raw jute, from Rs28.4 per bale in 1894 to Rs58.4 in 1906, due to growing demand and the speculative activities of middlemen.[107]

The re-making of the imperial nexus, encompassing the 1880s and 1890s, also witnessed a radical change in opinion regarding the comparative skill levels of Scottish and Indian jute workers. Up to this time the products of Calcutta's looms were almost universally derided, but by 1894 it was found that Calcutta cloth was 'very much stronger than the heavily glazed Dundee article, and they now sell on equal terms.'[108] In spinning, too, there were also big improvements. The increasing speciality production of Dundee meant that yarn quality had to be high, which in turn meant that spinning frames were run at lower speeds thus allowing the spinner to tend more spindles than was the case in Calcutta, where sacking remained a higher percentage of total production. As the Bengal mills turned towards the production of hessian, however, there was a steady increase in the number of spindles tended by the spinners.[109] Although the number of looms in Bengal increased from 1,180 to 9,330, or seven times, between 1872 and 1894, the number of spindles went from 13,000 to 185,600, or 13 times, during the same period. And, while it required the yarn from 11 spindles to keep a loom going in 1872, by 1894 this had increased to 20 spindles per loom.[110] Between 1870 and 1890, Dundee's ratio decreased from 25.2 to 19 spindles per loom, which produced a rough parity between the two centres.[111]

Evidence from the *Report of the Textile Factories Labour Commission* of 1907, which is detailed in Table 1.1, also indicated that manning levels in the two centres were nearing parity. The difference in manning levels in the Bengal industry, however, did not refer to the number of workers who were needed to operate machinery at any given time but to the large numbers of 'spare hands' or 'floating' labour who were commonly employed on a daily basis by the Calcutta mills. The use of 'floating' labour' has been seen as a central characteristic of the Bengal jute industry, and its coming into being and continued existence into the post-colonial period has also been connected to the migrant character of the greater part of its labour force.[112] In fact mills in both centres carried a large percentage of 'floating' labour. When trade was brisk, workers would be recruited at the mill gate and would be hired on a daily basis. This 'floating' labour moved between different mills in the same locality, chasing available work, higher wages and better conditions.[113] Most workers in Dundee had as little security of employment as their counterparts in Bengal, and in some respects they were much more vulnerable to the unstable conditions of the jute trade because, in contrast to the migrant Indian workers, they had no village link that they could

Table 1.1 Number of workers engaged at different machines in jute mills in Dundee and Calcutta, *c.*1907

Machine	Dundee jute mill	Calcutta jute mill
Jute softener feed end	3 women and 1 man = 4	2 men
Jute softener delivery end	3 men	2 women
Breaker card fed end	2 women	2 women
Breaker card delivery end	1 woman or 1 man	1 woman
Roving frames	1 woman, sometimes 1 woman attends to 2 machines	1.25 workers per machine
Spinning frame (sacking)	1 spinner per frame of 60 spindles	1 spinner per frame of 36 and 60 spindles
Spinning frame (hessian)	1 spinner per frame of 60 spindles	1 spinner per frame of 90 spindles
Loom	1 woman attends 2 looms, except with wide looms where she attends to 1 loom = 0.5	1 man at each machine
Calender	2 men	5 men
Total	15.5	16.25

Source: Compiled from *Report of the Textile Factories Labour Commission*, Appendix B, London, 1907, pp. 66–9.

fall back on during trade depressions or strikes. The casualisation of labour was a strategy grounded in the realities of producing for volatile international markets, and whether labour was, or was not, migrant mattered little to the employers, who were more concerned that labour should be both 'flexible' and plentiful. The settled proletariat of Dundee, divorced from any real or meaningful connection to the land, proved to be just as flexible as their, predominantly migrant, counterparts in Bengal. Indeed, in some regards, Dundee jute workers proved to be more flexible. For example, Dundee mill owners rarely faced the kind of seasonal labour supply problems commonly experienced in Bengal, and they were also able to introduce double-loom working when similar efforts conspicuously failed in Bengal.

The question still remains – why did the Calcutta mills carry so much spare or 'floating' labour compared with Dundee? The widespread system of shift working, then in vogue in India, necessitated the employment of 30 per cent more workers than was required for normal working, while additional 'spare hands' were also employed to relieve hard pressed production workers, particularly in the weaving department, owing to the long working hours occasioned by night working.[114] The increasing use of multiple shifts from the mid-1890s, following the introduction of electric lighting and night shift working, also encouraged an increase in so-called 'sharp practices' involving the 'cooking of wages books'. In 1909, the chief factory inspector in Bengal admitted that the operation of the shift system meant that 'neither the inspector, the manager, nor his assistants will be in a position to state the exact number of hours worked by different classes', thus leaving the system open to abuse by corrupt Scottish supervisors, sirdars and babus who engaged workers, and who sometimes accrued large amounts of wealth from the employment of so-called 'fictitious labour'.[115] Twenty years later D. H. Buchanan, an American industrialist and businessman, recounted the experience of a mill manager in Bengal:

> who decided to distribute the pay envelopes himself and in order to avoid the giving of two or more envelopes to the same man or to men not working, he took along a bucket of red paint with which he marked the bare foot of every person paid. The result was that, at the end, he had a considerable number of uncalled-for envelopes.[116]

Labour supply was also adversely affected by the famines and epidemics that reared their heads during this time, compelling mill managers to retain the services of workers who may not have been required to work immediately but who may have been needed at short notice when new or urgent orders for goods were made.

Mill managers often used the poor work ethic of local Bengali labour as a justification to replace them with, what they viewed as, more willing workers from the up-country tracts of Uttar Pradesh (UP) and Bihar. However, during the period of re-making, the dilatory habits of up-country workers and their poor productivity, when compared with Dundee, also became a source of complaint, particularly in order to justify opposition to government labour legislation. This was underlined by the 1907 *Report of the Textile Factories Labour Commission*, which argued against the restriction of working hours in Indian mills and factories because:

> No legislation can alter the natural and ingrained habits of Indian workers. They have been in the habit of leaving their work at odd and uncertain periods throughout the nominal working hours. They go into the mill compounds which generally speaking are large and open for taking food, bathing, drinking water, and necessary purposes. In some mills efforts have been made to prevent such unauthorised stoppages, but workers prefer them to fixed longer periods. Unlike the English the Indian mill hand takes frequent holidays, for up to 1–3 months.[117]

This view was furiously attacked by a member of the Textile Factories Labour Commission in a 'Minute of dissent'. For Dr Nair it was:

> a very old argument which has been repeated times without number and nearly everyone seems to be inclined to attribute the whole phenomenon of loitering to the ingrained habit of Indian workmen.... [I]t is not an ingrained habit at all but only a manifestation of the adaptive capacity which all human beings possess more or less. Intense and concentrated labour ... for 13 or 14 hours per day, week after week, and month after month is beyond the physical endurance of ordinary human beings.... A system more likely to bring about degradation of labour is impossible to conceive.[118]

In 1906, the British government official B. R. Foley, during the course of investigations into the reasons for seasonal labour shortages in the Bengal jute industry, had also found that:

> the shortage of labour during the hot weather has only been experienced since the introduction of electric lights into the mills, since this has enabled the hands to earn more by working longer hours. They are in consequence better off, more independent, and able to take longer and more frequent holidays.[119]

The heat and particularly the humidity during the summer months in Bengal is excruciating, particularly for workers involved in manual occupations in those older mills that often lacked proper ventilation. Foley found that shortage of labour was commonly experienced during the period from 15 March to 15 June, the hottest, most humid time of the year. But Foley also discovered that Bengali workers were just as likely as up-country workers to absent themselves from work during the hot weather.[120] The holidays taken by up-country workers were not a consequence of the indolent, immigrant character of labour, but flowed from the 'adaptive capacity' of the jute mill worker, both Bengali and up-country. Following the introduction of electric lighting, many jute workers sought to maximise their earnings during the cooler periods of the year, in order to avoid the discomfort of summer time working, while the pattern of circular migration also enabled up-country migrant workers to extend their working lives, the visits to their home village serving as recuperation from the rigours of industrial employment.

As a result of the various factors affecting manning there were 650 workers per 100 looms in Bengal in 1894, as against the 1890 Dundee worker-loom ratio of 307:100.[121] The Dundee worker-loom ratio had, however, been greatly reduced from the mid-1870s, when it was estimated at 455:100.[122] The higher manning levels in Indian mills not only provided physical and monetary relief for Indian workers, as well as perquisites for sirdars, babus and Scottish supervisors, it also relieved the pressure on the Dundee jute industry regarding comparative working costs. Indeed, without the inflated Indian costs that followed from factors such as the shift system, fictitious working, the carrying of 'spare hands', and the enervating climate, it is difficult to see how the Dundee jute industry could possibly have remained a paying proposition.

Jute and empire

During the 1880s and 1890s, the competitive war between Dundee and Calcutta was conducted against the background of increasingly vociferous demands, from the powerful Lancashire cotton lobby, that British factory legislation should be fully implemented in India. During the first half of the nineteenth century India emerged as a major market for Lancashire made cotton piece-goods, but by the late nineteenth century the expanding Bombay cotton industry was increasingly threatening British exports to the sub-continent. However, while determined campaigning by Lancashire, with Dundee involved as a junior partner, led directly to the passing of the Indian Factories Act of 1891, this did little to slow the growth of Indian industrialisation.[123]

When the Bengal jute mills began extensive night-shift working in the early 1890s, Dundee's embattled jute barons turned to Sir John Leng, the recently elected Liberal MP, who drew the attention of the Secretary of State for India to the 'fact that a large jute mill in the neighbourhood of Calcutta, fitted with electric light, is now working 22 out of the 24 hours daily, and that women and young persons are reported to be regularly employed through the night.' He further enquired whether it was 'lawful, under the Indian Factories Act, for mills owned by English [*sic*] capitalists, and competing with similar mills in the UK, to be worked night and day with three shifts of hands.'[124] Leng's questions were batted off, and Dundee hopes of remedial action seemed dashed following the failure of the Lancashire cotton lobby to support them. An attempt to elicit the support of the UK Associated Chamber of Commerce also failed in March 1895 when it warned of 'the dangers of intermeddling with the largest population subject to the British Crown.'[125] It was against this background that Sir John Leng travelled to Bengal to see for himself the consequences of the apparently unequal contest between Juteopolis and the *Calcutta Cutty*. When Leng returned in March 1896 he immediately received an invitation to address the Dundee Chamber of Commerce and began his peroration by explaining that:

> Ever since I knew Dundee I have heard predictions of impending ruin, which have been generally followed by periods of great activity of local trade, large extensions of works and rapid increase of population. In this connection it was satisfactory for me to learn during my recent visit to India that, notwithstanding the extraordinary development of the industry there, more jute had been imported into Dundee than ever before, showing that the merchants and manufacturers have not altogether lost confidence in the future of the local trade.[126]

Leng, however, went on to admit that he 'was impressed more than anyone who has not visited that country is likely to be with the great advantages the Calcutta jute mills possess'. Leng reported that six 'new mills are being erected ... and 12 previously established are being extended. Within 12 months upwards of 3,000 new looms and 60,000 new spindles are to be added to the 10,000 looms and 200,000 spindles now working.'[127] Leng also confirmed the earlier reports that women and children were involved in night working, but, rather than lambasting the practice, he declared himself 'satisfied that the Indian method of working by shifts is adapted to the climatic conditions and the habits of the people, and is not open to attack on humanitarian grounds, since the hours of any of the women and children employed not only do not exceed but are often fewer than in our own mills.' Leng's *volte-face* was compounded when, instead of underlining his earlier call for protection for the 'home' industry, he presumed to 'advise' his audience of jute barons:

> to travel more and see more of the world, and to see what the markets of the world required and then attempt to meet those requirements. Most of all, the new order of things required new methods and the challenge facing Dundee was to transform its commercial practices and marketing techniques in order to meet these new challenges.[128]

Leng was treading a fine line between criticism and insolence when he reproached his audience for their limited knowledge of the wider world. After all, Dundee's jute merchants and mill salesmen were very familiar with the exotic and far-flung outposts of the world markets. Leng's refusal to support the call for protection of the 'home' industry was probably a reflection of his understanding of the central place of jute to the British imperial system of trade and finance. He concluded (surely echoing the official government view) that this situation would force Dundee to accept its new position as the secondary sector within the imperial nexus of jute.

The rise of Germany and the USA as manufacturing powers during the late nineteenth century fuelled a growing British trade deficit with these two countries and adversely affected the British balance of payments. But, as a result of Britain's balance of payments surplus with India, it was possible to make good between two-fifths and one-third of this deficit.[129] Because both raw and finished jute goods comprised a significant, and growing, proportion of Indian exports, jute was a central component in this British system of deficit financing – and especially so following the devaluation of the rupee in 1894–5. The expansion of Indian textile production also provided a bonanza for British machinery manufacturers, accounting for nearly a quarter of British exports of general engineering products in 1913. This situation meant that Dundee's jute interests were fated to successive failures in their attempts to elicit government support to remain the primary centre within the imperial nexus of jute, but if we view Dundee's lobbying as an attempt to buy time and to limit damage rather than to stop the clock then their efforts begin to make sense.

The Dundee response to Calcutta competition

John Leng believed that the threat of growing foreign competition provided an opportunity for the Dundee jute industry to embrace product diversification:

> [W]hile the heavy end of the trade must more and more centre in Calcutta, there will always be room for Dundee if its manufacturers develop to the utmost the finer classes of goods, and aim at supplying the specialities which the markets of the world continually require.[130]

Many Dundee jute firms had, in fact, already turned towards new uses for jute and hessian other than the most widely produced length of jute cloth, 'the common ten-and-a-half'. The international markets for jute products were still growing, encouraged by the inherent cheapness of the raw material, its increasing use as a substitute for dearer fibres, such as cotton and flax, and the inexorable rise in the international carrying trade. This situation formed the basis for a new nexus between Calcutta and Dundee whereby each area catered to widely different markets and developed production strategies that fundamentally differed from one another. Dundee secured major openings when jute displaced flax in the manufacture of coffee bagging, along with the increasing use of jute yarns for use as cords, twines and ropes. Dundee also became a major source of sugar bags, meaning that more attention had to be paid towards creating a 'clean product' for use in transporting this perishable and valuable commodity.[131] Above all else, it was the growth of mass markets for linoleum in Britain, Europe, and particularly the USA that ensured a future for Dundee as a major textile centre, after jute replaced flax as a backing material.[132]

The drive to open up new markets along with the increasing problems faced by the city's investment trusts also pushed mill owners towards a more intensive exploitation of labour resources. Jute workers who appeared as witnesses before the 1893 Royal Commission for Labour complained that a 'bounty system' (which was widely referred to as 'blood money') was used to speed up machinery and to pay workers at a lower rate, meaning that they had to work harder in order to earn the same as formerly. Piece rates were also commonly applied within alternate work processes, encouraging some piece workers to set a frantic pace that time-paid workers in the following processes were forced to keep up with, but without an increase in wages.[133] The employers sought to justify this cost-cutting mania by pointing to the impact of rising Calcutta competition, but some trade union and labour activists, with the conspicuous exception of Henry Williamson, were starting to challenge this emerging consensus. In April 1896, the Dundee Trades Council leader John Mann addressed a local meeting of textile trade union activists where he:

> referred to the question of competition with India, and said in the articles which were appearing in a local paper on the question they did not really get the whole facts. It was not shown in these articles how many individuals had to be employed to turn out the same amount of work as one individual did in this country. Besides, if they took the market rates current in Dundee at the present time, there was no doubt that a profit was being made, and, while the profits might not be so large as they once were, they were sufficient to permit of some concession being made to the workers.[134]

The inference in Mann's words was clear: the Dundee mill owners were using the whole question of 'foreign competition' as a smoke screen to justify swingeing wage cuts, a claim that was given some credence by the fact that wage cuts and speed ups affected workers who were involved in the production of 'speciality goods', which were not in direct competition with the products of Calcutta mills.[135] The fundamental problem facing the 'home' industry at this time was over-production, particularly with regards to 'standard' jute goods, but while wage cuts encouraged overproduction (because piece workers, such as weavers, strove to increase their output), they did bring about an immediate and easily calculated reduction in working costs, and so remained in favour as a cost-cutting tactic throughout our period.[136]

From the 1880s onwards, Dundee's move towards the production of specialities and the increasing stress on quality created further strains for many workers as cost cutting and intensification of the labour process became the order of the day. In the event, this attempt by sections of Dundee jute capital to counter Indian competition was largely successful so that, notwithstanding the doom-laden outpourings of some contemporary observers, the balance sheets of many jute firms remained remarkably healthy throughout, and indeed beyond, the period of the so-called 'Great Depression', of 1873–96. Baxter Brothers, which despite the frequent claims of company representatives was involved in jute production, posted losses only twice between 1878 and 1900, while the medium sized jute firm, James Scott and Sons, witnessed an increase in turnover from £40,000 to over £300,000 between 1877 and 1899.[137] Another even smaller Dundee jute firm, William Benvie, was able to ride out the storms of the 1870s by diversifying into calendaring, and by the 1880s the firm was thriving.[138]

An erratic but generally rising level of output was maintained by the Dundee jute industry up to and beyond the First World War. Indeed, according to one estimate output grew two and a half times over between 1870 and 1907.[139] Exports of jute yarn increased from 17 million lbs in 1880 to over 47 million lbs in 1903, and exports of piece goods also increased from 183 million to 211 million yards during the same period.[140] The estimated value of all this increased production more than doubled from £3.1 millions to £6.8 million, which is not the kind of performance associated with an industry facing extinction.[141] Nevertheless, the impact of Calcutta competition in the export markets for sacking was striking. Between 1880 and 1903, exports of sacking from Dundee declined by 50 per cent, with income from this source plummeting from £1,452,446 to £519,333.[142] Profit levels did, however, stabilise as a result of the second Boer war of 1899–1902, and further improved with the outbreak of the Russo-Japanese conflict in 1905.[143] Although Calcutta was the chief beneficiary of the war-fuelled prosperity, the level of demand was such that Dundee was called upon to render assistance, which, by forcing it back towards the production of gunny bagging on an enormous scale, slowed the progress of product diversification. An additional fillip for the 'home' industry was, though, provided with the continued expansion of cotton and sugar production, and in the growing US market for linoleum backing cloth of hessian outside the staple 40 in.[144]

By the early 1900s, the Dundee jute industry employed more jute workers and produced more goods than at any point during its history, but the pay packets of jute workers still remained lighter than in any other sector of British industry.[145] Indeed, by this time the jute workers' living standards were probably lower than they had been in the early 1870s.[146] Juteopolis became a low-wage 'industrial cul-de-sac', not because of an organic crisis within the staple trade but as a direct consequence of the successful attempts to avert such a crisis. Chapter 3 will demonstrate the high price that was paid for this success, as the working poor of Dundee were forced to bear the sometimes brutal consequences of jute dependency and the re-making of the imperial nexus.

2   The coming of the up-country men

Labour conditions and class formation in the Bengal jute industry, 1875–1910

> Hastings Mill … has made more money than any other mill here. The manager, John Finlay, who is the Nestor[1] among the mill men now … has tact, mother-wit, and a common sense in the management of the workers. He is intimately acquainted with their language and character, and the consequence is that things go on smoothly. There are no better workers in the world than those in the Indian jute mills. A *paternal despotism* [emphasis added] suits them exactly. Whenever they get to believe in their manager as one who will be kind though firm with them, who, while demanding absolute obedience, will give them absolute fair play, their loyalty is secure. They look up to him as a sort of God. There are no strikes at Hastings Mill.
>
> ('The Calcutta Jute Mills', *Dundee Year Book* of 1894)[2]

The above quotation has been utilised by Dipesh Chakrabarty, a leading proponent of the Subaltern School of historiography, as a means to characterise the nature of the labour control mechanism within the Bengal jute industry as being founded on the traditional Bengali notion of ma-baap (literally mother–father), which offered a stark contrast to the less personalised forms of labour control within more industrialised societies.[3] The impression given by the *Dundee Year Book* article is of the Scottish supervisor as an all-powerful omnipotent presence within the Bengal jute mills. The paternal despotism practised by them demanded 'absolute obedience', but, in return, the native worker received 'absolute fair play', thus ensuring his loyalty to the firm. While this characterisation can be seen as an orientalist conception of colonial industrial relations *par excellence*, it hardly functions as an adequate description of labour relations at this time. Not only was the whole nature of the relationship between the Dundee and Calcutta jute industries being turned on its head during the 1890s, but the Bengal jute industry had already begun to experience rising labour discontent during 1894, and the following year would witness the eruption of strikes the length and breadth of the jute belt, with some of the most serious being waged over the issue of the mistreatment of native workers by 'God-like' Scottish supervisors.

The condition of Indian jute workers during the early phase of industrialisation

Between 1879 and 1881 alone, the number of Indian jute workers increased from 27,494 to 40,551, and many – probably a majority – of these workers were natives of Bengal.[4] Even by 1886, and despite a growing stream of up-country recruits, it was still thought that the majority of jute workers were from districts adjoining or near to Calcutta, such as Howrah, Hooghly and Nadia, who commonly returned to their villages following the long working day. Thus in 1908 a group of four Budge-Budge weavers informed the Indian Factory Labour Commission that 'As most of us live in villages at a distance of two to four miles from the mill, it means we have to get up in the morning between 3 and 4 am, and do not get home till 8.30 or 9 pm.'[5] Other workers took up temporary residence near to the mill and rejoined their families at weekends and during the harvest and marriage seasons. Majoo Maithi, a 25-year-old rover at the Bowreah cotton mill in Calcutta, who appeared before the Indian Factory Commission (IFC) in 1890, was born in the Cuttack district of Orissa and had 'a home there and land, bullocks and cows'. He had worked at the Bowreah cotton mill for about 11 years, but returned home regularly 'after a year and a half or two years' where he stayed for 'eight or ten months'.[6] There was also longer-distance migration from within Bengal itself. Taroni, a 20-year-old female worker on the drawing frames at Baranagore mill, had a home in Midnapore, to which she returned in order to see her uncle and aunt, 'sometimes once a year, sometimes twice a year'.[7]

Early accounts of labour conditions within the Bengal jute industry often drew attention to the 'dilatory' habits of local workers, which were invariably contrasted with the 'highly disciplined regularity of attendance' of British factory operatives.[8] In 1880, the manager of Bowreah cotton mill complained that, 'The whole day you will see the workers come out of the mills, go to the tanks to wash their hands and feet, then to some place set apart in all the mill compounds to smoke, and then to the water deliverer of their own or some superior caste to drink water; this in the most leisurely manner possible.'[9] As long as the Bengal jute industry remained a small affair, comprising a few mills, these 'dilatory' habits were tolerated by management. Official acceptance of such behaviour was probably the price that British jute mill owners paid for relatively stable labour relations. Similar problems were also experienced by the Dundee mill managers of the early nineteenth century in their attempts to habituate labour to the new ways of working associated with factory production. In the 1820s the pioneering linen master, William Brown, complained that many of his 'hands' were 'continually sighing after something they have no business with and rendering themselves uneasy.'[10] The less than 'Protestant work-ethic' of many Dundee mill workers was still a problem by the later nineteenth century, particularly amongst *halflins*.[11] Bob Stewart, during his time as a half-timer, 'devised a few tricks' in order that the cleaning out of jute waste from under the spinning frames was done during working time, rather than during the break, as was company policy, 'One of the tricks was to set the waste on fire while the frame was running. The spinner would think the frame was on fire and put the power off. I became adept at these tricks, and after getting the cleaning done would dash off in the break on my own ploys.'[12]

A major cause for concern for the managers of Bengal's early mills was the proliferation of religious festivals, which led to problems with temporary, and often large-scale, absenteeism. Many festivals were lavish affairs with participation not limited by religious or regional affiliation, with some lasting many days and involving the consumption of narcotics – particularly opium and *hashish*.[13] The Durga Puja of 1894 was accompanied by complaints from a Dundee reporter that the week long closure of mills did not seem to satisfy the Indian worker, who 'thinks that if he works nine or ten months in the year he works enough and deserves two or three months rest.'[14] The reporter from Dundee seemed oblivious to the fact that many mill owners in his home town also faced similar, and long-term, problems with the *Hogmanay*[15] and New Year celebrations: a mid-winter festival, of pre-Christian origin, which remained a more popular Scottish custom than Christmas up until the post-war period. When William Brown attempted to commence night working on 2 January 1821 he found that at

> the hour appointed I and my superintendents waited the arrival of the hands. Till eight o'clock not one appeared and report went that most of them were drunk owing to the money I had lent them, and the New Year revel not being over.[16]

Absenteeism during *Hogmanay* and New Year long remained a problem in Dundee and Irish migrants showed no inclination to forego the Scottish festival, which they participated in with some gusto. In 1918 the local press opined that, 'The start in the mills and factories this morning was very varied. Probably the west end [where Irish labour was particularly concentrated] was the worst of the two, though in the east there were likewise a few delinquents.'[17]

Despite the presence of the ubiquitous *toddy*[18] shop in and around Indian mill compounds, Scottish observers commonly contrasted the workers peaceable social habits with those of their, apparently, more rumbustious and less deferential counterparts on the banks of the Tay.[19] The *Dundee Year Book* of 1894 described, in Sylvan tones, a visit to a mill compound:

> I walked round the native village in connection with the Kamarhatty Mill on Saturday evening, where John Lawrence is Governor-General, and was amazed at the perfect quiet which reigned, although it was a community of 2,000 to 3,000 persons. A perfect contrast to a Saturday night at home amongst a similar number of mill workers.[20]

This idealised view of Indian workers would, however, give way to its frightening – and just as overdrawn – opposite when Calcutta was rocked by so-called communal disturbances in 1895 and 1896. Despite the orientialist conception of Indian labour relations painted by the *Dundee Year Book*, strikes and other forms of worker protest were not unknown in the early Bengal jute industry, particularly during the 1870s and 1880s when the industry was expanding at a rate faster than the supply of labour. In 1875, in one of the earliest references to labour troubles in the Bengal jute industry, the Divisional Commissioner of the Burdwan district noted that:

> The jute and cotton mill industries are enlarging, and the coolie population is beginning to acquire factory characteristics, and to need the special attention of the Police and Excise Departments. A case of rattening occurred in Serampore since the close of [last] year, when the coolies demanded the punishment of a factory *jemadar*, and not obtaining that, stopped the spinner boys going into the mill to work.[21]

The reference to 'rattening' in this quotation is highly interesting. Unfamiliar and now rarely used, the term is derived from the Scots word *ratten* (also *ratton* or *rattan*), referring to a 'sly person', which gives a clue as to the kind of acts of industrial sabotage associated with the practice.[22] That Bengali jute workers were also capable of open, organised, and large-scale protest is evidenced by the reference to the successful picketing that 'stopped the spinner boys from going into the mill to work', while another leading British colonial official also noted in the 1880s that 'strikes are by no means unknown'.[23] Strikes and other forms of organised protest rarely transcended the level of the department, let alone the mill or district, and very rarely lasted more than a few days. The rising demand for labour during this period also enabled workers to pick and choose their employment options. In 1882, the Senior Magistrate of the 24 Parganas district complained that, 'Here the workers are masters of the situation. So far from the labour market being overcrowded … the hands command their own terms, are excessively independent, and at the least attempt to coercion they migrate at once to another establishment.'[24]

Labour supply conditions during the early period of the Bengal jute industry enabled local workers to successfully defend patterns of work involving frequent short breaks and temporary absenteeism, but the establishment of the Indian Jute Mills Association (IJMA) in 1885 ushered in short-time working and lower wages, prompting some jute workers who appeared before the IFC in 1890 to remember better times. Taroni, who we have already met, complained that she now earned less as a result of short-time working and that in 'the old days when the mills were working full-time, [the workers] got Sunday holidays.'[25] Rajoni, a weaver who had been employed in the Union jute mill for 19 years, complained that formerly the workers 'always got Sunday holidays. In those days she earned 2–8 [rupees] a week, and now she earns only 1–10 for four days'. Shama Charan Samuth, a 34-year-old weaver at the Budge-Budge mill, complained that he was 'suffering loss of income by this present arrangement and would prefer to work six days.' As a result, Shama worked 'in his fields on the days the mill is not at work', and also frequently went 'out as a hired labourer' in order to supplement his income.[26] During the second half of the 1880s, competition intensified with Dundee in the export markets and pressure mounted on mill managers up and down the Hooghly to meet rising production targets and more stringent quality requirements for hessian cloth. The long-established working patterns of Bengali labour were still being frowned on, but the complaints of managers and officials now had a sharper edge.[27] If Bengali labour would not adhere to the new ways of working then mill managers were now increasingly in a position to replace them with workers who were.

The coming of the up-country men

Seasonal migration to Bengal from northern India was long established as families and communities travelled in groups in order to supplement their income, from small landholdings and labouring, in search of harvesting work, a form of seasonal migration that was also followed by Irish harvest workers in Scotland during the late eighteenth and early nineteenth centuries. By the last two decades of the nineteenth century, however, migration from UP and Bihar (the so-called 'cow belt') was assuming unprecedented proportions, and the promise of regular work and wages drew many within this developing river of humanity to the mushrooming jute industry of Bengal.

Although the labour that was attracted to the jute belt during this time was predominantly migrant this has to be qualified. The large distances and expense involved in visiting their home villages, and the low wages paid in the jute mills, ensured that workers could go only once every two or three years – possibly more for better paid workers such as weavers. These visits could last up to six months or even longer, depending on the worker's financial and personal situation, leading to a pattern of 'circular migration' that is still in evidence today.[28] Many migrant workers came from areas of UP and Bihar that had been textile centres in the eighteenth and nineteenth centuries, before their local economies were undermined by the growing importation of Lancashire-produced cotton cloth. The weavers of Lucknow, an important centre of fine cloth production, were faced with the steady erosion of their trade, and responded by shifting production towards coarser and cheaper varieties of cotton, but, from the 1850s onwards, the coarse cloth trade also increasingly succumbed to competition. Between 1860 and 1863 alone, imports of raw cotton into Ghazipur district almost halved and it was reported that many 'of the Julahas[29] of this district have of late migrated to Mauritius and elsewhere.'[30] In Allahabad the number of looms at work declined from 10,000 in 1860 to 4,000 by 1863, when it was reported that 'the unemployed operatives may be seen seeking for service as *bhisties*[31] or *coolies*'.[32] Although economic restructuring was responsible for laying the basis for the creation of a migrant workforce in the up-country tracts, it was famine and plague that triggered the large-scale migrations of the 1890s. The similarity with Dundee's earlier experience of immigration, in this regard, is striking. From the 1830s onwards, the town's linen masters were able to tap an available source of Irish migrant labour as Ulster's cottage linen industry struggled to compete with factory-produced goods. Above all else, though, it was the eruption of the Irish Famine of the 1840s that provided a dramatic cue for large-scale Irish emigration.

Like their Scottish and Irish counterparts, the hand loom weavers of northern India looked wistfully back to a 'Golden Age', before the advent of machine-made cloth, plague and, predominantly Marwari, moneylenders. In 1888, during an interview with the District Collector of Ghazipur in UP, a 70-year-old weaver complained that 'fifty years ago he was far better off than he is now', prompting his interlocutor to confirm that cheap imports of British-made cloth was a major 'cause why the weaver has to a great extent found his occupation gone'.[33] In textile districts, such as Gaya in Bihar, impoverished weavers turned to one of the few avenues of alternative employment now left open through migration to the fast-expanding industrial belts around Bombay and Calcutta – to the extent that by 1893 a Gaya district official was able to observe that the 'Howrah mills are full of Gaya Julahas.'[34]

During the 1890s, rising in-migration led to a rapid change-over to a predominantly up-country workforce in large parts of the Bengal jute industry, with an industrial census of six jute mills revealing that while local labour had slumped from 18,770 to 7,740 between 1895 and 1897, up-country labour had increased from 10,500 to 15,727.[35] While Bengali workers became the exception in the northern sector of the jute belt, they still comprised the majority of the workforce in the southern sector, particularly around Budge-Budge.[36] Migrant workers were overwhelmingly young males, travelling without female relatives who remained back in their home villages, giving rise to a marked gender imbalance within the fast-expanding mill districts on Calcutta's outskirts, which was a reverse image of Dundee's gender imbalance. Between 1872 and 1911, the proportion of females to males in Bengal's industrial towns declined from 789 to 582 per thousand.[37]

According to Arjan De Haan, the pattern of circular migration followed by up-country jute workers demonstrated that they were not committed to the industry.[38] Dipesh Chakrabarty, too, underlines the 'unstable' and 'migratory' characteristics of Indian jute workers, arguing that this meant that the jute working class in Bengal was 'born spastic'.[39] The pattern of circular migration was also used by jute capital as a justification for the long-term and conspicuous failure to introduce reforms such as service rules, standardised wage structures and pension schemes for the mass of employees within the jute industry. Large-scale circular migration also meant that a significant part of the costs associated with the social reproduction of labour were transferred to the migrants' areas of origin, which allowed the managing agencies to set wages at a much lower level than would otherwise have been the case.[40] The burgeoning Indian jute industry was, in effect, subsidised by the poverty stricken up-country tracts, a process that, through the creation of a vast reservoir of extremely cheap labour, also laid the basis for the remaking of the imperial nexus of jute.

What is striking is not the lack of commitment of the migrant jute workers but their ability to remain within the industry for so long given the sometimes appalling working and living conditions they encountered. To underline this point even further we may point to the fact that the pattern of circular migration was also followed by the Dundee School. In their case, however, this pattern was given a contractual form. Dundee supervisors commonly signed a four or five year contract that included six months' 'home leave', granted in order that they could 'recuperate and return to their work in India as fit as it is possible for them to be.'[41] The fact that Indian workers also chose to use the village link in order to recuperate should not be invoked to explain 'failure' (of proletarianisation) but as a successful strategy that allowed them to stay alive on the killing floors of Bengal's jute mills for as long as possible.

The fast-increasing migrant wave resulted in a mass incursion into Bengali society of a semi-permanent army of 'outsiders' who were, initially at least, closed off from the culture and politics of their adopted homeland. Another prominent feature of the Bengal jute industry was the predominance of Julaha Muslims in weaving departments, particularly, but not exclusively, in the northern sector of the jute belt. During the late nineteenth century, British colonial writers increasingly pointed to the communal character of the Julahas within the eastern districts of UP, which became the basis for the creation of a stereotype that was used to characterise all Julaha weavers, irrespective of their geographical location.[42] In Bengal, the Julaha weavers also fell victim to this process of stereotyping as evidenced in 1906 when the government investigator, S. H. Freemantle, observed that they were 'notoriously ignorant and superstitious people and took the lead, I am informed, in the Calcutta plague riots.'[43] As Gyan Pandey has pointed out, this 'construction of communalism' ignored the fact that religious conflict was encouraged, if not created, by the stresses that accompanied British commercial penetration of northern India during the nineteenth century, and also ignores 'the many acts and institutions that were perceived as a common threat by all the people of a locality in which these same weavers participated.'[44]

Once established in the Bengal jute industry, the Julaha weavers were able to prevent the incursion of other groups into their occupation. By the time of the 1921 Census, it was estimated that Julaha and Sheikh Muslims constituted 41 per cent of the 'skilled workers' within the jute labour force, with 72 per cent of skilled Julahas concentrated in weaving.[45] A recent recruit in the weaving department would, crucially, have to rely on the goodwill and compliance of established weavers in order to learn trade secrets, and Muslim weavers were in a position to limit the recruitment of other groups through a collective reluctance to accept workers who were not of their religion or from the same area. In reality, though, little effort was probably needed to prevent an incursion. Recruits to the jute industry from the up-country tracts were likely to gravitate towards those mills and occupations where their kin or regional group were already established.[46] Weavers were also employers in their own right, which enabled them to introduce patrimonial recruitment practices into the weaving departments, thus further bolstering their position. In 1905, B. R. Foley, noted that the 'weavers were mostly Muhammadans from up-country and they were the best weavers; they would not learn their boys spinning, as it was not so highly paid, but took them into the factory with them and taught them weaving.'[47] Whilst their wages were never sufficient to support a family within the mill district, weavers' wages were commonly twice that of other workers. They were not only the best paid section of the workforce: in 1930 an IJMA representative noted that, 'Those workers who come from up-country are usually sturdier than the Bengalis, or people who have been permanently settled in Bengal for a long number of years. *The weavers, in particular, have a very good physique*' [emphasis added].[48] Although many mill managers and colonial officials referred to the 'ignorance' and 'superstition' of the Julahas, labour organisers often had a very different view. Writing in the 1950s, the communist leader Indrajit Gupta drew attention to the literacy of weavers as well as their reputation for militancy, while Saroj Bandophadyay, a communist volunteer in Shyamnagar in the 1940s, also discovered that many up-country weavers were literate.[49]

Julaha weavers were also noted for their militancy, a reputation which, as we shall see, derived from the leading role they played in the unprecedented strike waves of the 1890s. In effect, the jute weavers functioned as the main organising centre of Bengal's emerging working class, but, despite their ability to provide a lead that other workers were prepared to follow, the struggle was never evenly matched. The British managing agencies had vast resources at their disposal, and their close links to the colonial state also enabled them to impose what Subho Basu has described as a 'Manager Raj' in the mill districts.[50] The power of the jute wallahs was, though, most keenly felt inside the tightly controlled mill compounds.

When labourers gathered at the gate of a jute mill in Bengal in order to get a job for the day, they hoped to catch the eye of a head sirdar, who, like his 'blackcoated' Dundee counterpart, was responsible for the hiring and firing of workers within individual departments. The sirdar was an important presence and influence within the mill and the mill areas beyond the compound walls, and was, along with the Scottish supervisor, an essential bulwark of paternal despotism. Although their influence within the early Bengal mills was limited by the more direct role the Dundee School then played in labour supervision, the small complement of Scottish supervisors were increasingly unable to run the later, much larger, mills without native assistance, particularly following the advent of the multiple shift system. The Scottish complement continued to grow in number, but by the 1890s they were a much smaller proportion of the total workforce than formerly, a trend that would continue up to the end of our period.[51] The increasingly isolated Scottish supervisors had little knowledge of the growing number of workers under their charge, of their different personalities and abilities, and by the end of the nineteenth century their main role involved supervising the sirdar and babu cadre. By this time, too, the technical role of the Dundee supervisors had, at least to some extent, been taken over by Bengali engineers, who were recruited in large numbers to undertake maintenance work, and whose skills had been noted, and praised, by Karl Marx. As well as being the eyes and ears of the mill managers, the Dundee School was also a reservoir of talent that was used to replenish and freshen up the ranks of higher management, as had been the case with many of the pioneer jute wallahs.

By the inter-war years, it was calculated that the ratio of sirdars to workers in the Bengal jute industry was 1:20, in stark contrast to the 'home' jute industry where a foreman commonly supervised 50–70 workers, while managers in some of the smaller Dundee mills and factories undertook the task of labour supervision.[52] The sirdar was also a powerful figure within the mill districts, where he often cast a long shadow within community panchayats.[53] The wealth and power of some sirdars was such that that they were able to become philanthropists by making substantial gifts at times of religious festivals and by financing the construction of mosques and temples.[54] They also commonly kept cows and buffaloes and some became *kistiwallahs*, or moneylenders, as well as shopkeepers and property holders.[55] According to the government investigator B. R. Foley:

> It is a common thing for the sardars, however, who are working in these mills, to rent land nearby on which they build houses, where they lodge operatives working in the mill. The mill thus obtains labour without any trouble, since it is in the interest of the sardars to keep their houses full, and in some of these bustis thus formed there is overcrowding and a serious neglect of sanitation.[56]

It is important to stress that the sirdar cadre was not a monolithic or homogenous category. They were the most numerous single section of the supervisory cadre, comprising innumerable line sirdars and also the much less numerous, but much more influential and powerful, departmental head sirdars. In 1942, I. L. Tripathi, who had recently been engaged as a trainee assistant in the Birla mill, was given an impromptu demonstration of sirdar power when the head sirdar and the Scottish overseer of the weaving department became involved in a dispute. In Tripathi's recollection, the sirdar made a motion with his hand and within seconds the entire weaving department had ground to a halt. Being young and from a privileged Marwari background, Tripathi was curious about the enigmatic figure who, whilst he showed respect to the 'young sahib', was treated with near veneration by the workers. The Muslim head sirdar that Tripathi remembered cut a very impressive figure. He was bearded and stout with a ram-rod straight posture and tall with it, and was always dressed in a dhoti and black dress coat. He was never without his cane and the machinery would be started and stopped only at his sole command, after he had checked the time on his gold pocket watch.[57]

By the beginning of the twentieth century, there were no less than five different grades of supervisory personnel between the manager's office and the worker on the shop floor of the mill, comprising, in descending order of rank, the assistant manager, the departmental supervisor, the babu, the head sirdar and the line sirdar. The basis of sirdar power rested on his patron–client relationships with the workers, and his ability to secure them regular employment as well as reasonable wages and working conditions. His ability to confer patronage depended on the state of trade, as well as other factors such as the way that working hours were organised and allocated, and the wider political climate. During the earlier period of the Bengal jute industry, when the sirdar's authority was curbed by regular labour supply problems, he was chiefly concerned with retaining the services of the most capable workers and avoiding stoppages that could potentially halt or harm production. During this time, the ability of the sirdar to extract perquisites from workers was more limited than it would become following the rapid growth of the Bengal jute industry during the 1890s.

While wages and working conditions were superior to those in many other sectors of the colonial economy, such as coal mining or tea picking, being a jute mill worker was never a soft option. The constant pushing of the sirdar and the urge to maximise income ensured a steady stream of sometimes horrific industrial accidents. Work had to be conducted at speed (particularly when there were immediate and important orders to be completed), in conditions of high humidity, which was a particular problem for up-country workers who were used to a far drier climate, forcing some workers to 'contrive a fan arrangement on a rotating shaft or machine, which, though it meets his needs, is generally a most inefficient instrument.'[58] Migrant workers who were anxious to maximise remittances to their families also commonly forced themselves into working long hours, while cutting back on their food intake.

Although most up-country workers did not bring their female relatives with them, some formed temporary marriages with women in the jute mill towns, meaning that they had two different *samsars*, or households, one based in the mill towns and the other based in their native village, a practice that served to weaken the hold of caste and religion in the mill districts.[59] In 1923, the government investigator, Curjel found that up-country workers predominantly selected their partners from amongst Bengali women, many described as widows, who commonly worked as sack sewers and feeders in the carding department.[60] Bengali Hindu women who formed temporary marriages with up-country workers normally put a vermillion mark on their forehead, which was a mark of marriage.[61] The household structures formed from these temporary marriages could be highly complex and rarely comprised conventional family groupings. They were also marked by a lack of security and permanence, and could break up as a direct result of enforced unemployment, industrial accidents or sickness, when male up-country workers would retreat to their home villages in order to recuperate or to access support within their direct kin groups.[62]

Male circular migration also had far-reaching consequences on social and gender relations in the up-country area of origins. A folk song, still sung by the women of Gorakhpur, recounts the grief and sense of loss felt by the wives of the migrants who made the long journey to Calcutta. A woman is given a parrot as a parting gift by her husband before he leaves for the east. Following his departure the parrot becomes a proxy for her husband as she sings to it, 'By day I will feed you, parrot, with milk and rice in a dish. And at night I will take you to sleep between my breasts.' Finally, she sends the parrot to her husband in Calcutta and perched on his head it responds to his questions about the condition of his family at home, 'Thy wife weeps daily and hourly (Ah Ram!) thy mother weeps; yes thy mother weeps the whole year through.'[63] Another poem, 'Bidesiya', by the early twentieth century poet Bihari Thakur, further captures the distress felt by the women left behind in the up-country tracts, in which Calcutta became a metaphor for the husband's mistress, 'Railroads are not our enemy, nor are the steamships. Our real enemy is *naukri* (service away from home).'[64]

The vast majority of migrant workers during the 1890s were drawn from Bihar and UP, but the early twentieth century would witness considerable migration from other areas, by groups that commonly travelled as a family unit. Madrassi labour arrived in often large family groups and their numbers increased 'tremendously' from the early 1900s onwards, particularly in the Titaghar mills where the women commonly found work as feeders on softening machines.[65] Some up-countrymen also settled into long-term relationships with local women, and by 1930 government officials were of the view that these settled groups were dependent 'entirely on the mills' for their support. They were now regarded as 'landless, and as a rule … employed entirely in the mills', which thus provided the basis for 'the genesis of a specialised population which is now the rule of the west.'[66] This assumption, that industrialisation in Bengal was following a path based on the British model, would, however, prove very wide of the mark.

The recruitment of migrant labour: causes and consequences

The question still remains – why did jute capital not attempt to tap the vast hinterland of Bengal for their labour needs, instead of opting for the recruitment of a further flung and largely migrant workforce? It has been suggested by Parimal Ghosh that Bengal's changing land–man ratio, which followed successive and serious famines and plagues during the last decades of the nineteenth century, discouraged local rural labour from embarking on industrial employment.[67] The statistical evidence that would back up Ghosh's view is, however, lacking, as only three out of 13 of Bengal's districts showed a decrease in the mean density of population between 1881 and 1891.[68] Another explanation is outlined by Ranajit Das Gupta, who suggested that successive outbreaks of famine, plague and 'Burdwan fever' during the course of the second half of the nineteenth century had a thoroughgoing 'devitilising' impact upon Bengali workers. In effect, a whole layer of chotalok[69] society within Bengal was 'rendered incapable of performing hard and strenuous labour even in agriculture.'[70]

During the 1860s the value of raw jute exports increased from Rs4.1 million to 20.5 million, before running up against a major slump during 1872–3, when prices plunged by nearly 50 per cent.[71] This downturn demonstrated that jute dependency could suffocate those who came within its ambivalent embrace, and led to growing conflict between the increasingly hard-pressed ryots and the landlords over the level of rents, which culminated in the formation of a peasant agrarian league in Pabna in May 1873. The 'revolt' simmered on through 1873 and 1874, as famine conditions appeared in some districts of Bengal, prompting a move back to rice on the part of many hard-pressed peasants.[72] Bengal was hard hit by the impact of economic depression in the early 1870s, but other less fortunate areas were devastated. El-Niño combined with the depression and with official reluctance to challenge the precepts of liberal political economy to produce a famine of biblical proportions in the Deccan and around Bombay.[73] The grave misfortune of the famine actually came to the aid of the Bengal jute ryots, as the demand for gunnies to export grain to the affected areas helped pull the jute sector out of slump during 1873–4.[74]

The increasing demand for industrial labour coincided with a further large expansion in the growing of jute. As international demand for raw jute, and the returns to the ryots, spiralled, this created a growing demand for rural labour, thus undermining Ranajit Das Gupta's claim that Bengalis had been 'rendered incapable' of undertaking physical labour. By the late nineteenth century, the prospect of opening up the eastern parts of Bengal to industrial recruitment had receded, as these areas were being further developed for cash crops, and their relative affluence, compared to the western parts of the Province was increasing. The growing demand for cash crops such as jute not only lessened the push factor in eastern Bengal. If Anglo-Scottish jute capital had made efforts to draw its labour force from eastern Bengal, this would have affected the land–man ratio in the province, and could have provided the basis for a growing bloc between the ryots and the jute workers. Not only would industrial wage rates have been affected, but too close a relationship between industrial and rural labour could have strengthened the organisation of the ryots and their ability to raise the price of the raw material. By relying on a migrant industrial workforce, drawn from Bihar and UP, jute capital successfully avoided creating over-close regional, religious, kin and village links between the mills and the growing areas.

It is also interesting to note the conjuncture between the advent of migrant recruitment on the part of British jute capital, and the emergence of the stereo-type of the 'feckless' and 'disloyal' Bengali. Although the Permanent Settlement of 1793 closed off an avenue for the emergence of a Bengali industrial bourgeoi-sie, it also created a vast rural rentier class, thus providing the basis for the emer-gence of Calcutta's urban bhadralok. Due to the small scale of their holdings many amongst the bhadralok were forced to increasingly supplement their rural income by professional or clerical jobs, which often required a basic grasp of English education, and it was from this social layer that radical and nationalist mass politics in Bengal emerged. The establishment of reform organisations such as the 'Young Bengal' movement and the Brahmo Samaj in the first half of the nineteenth century gave way to the adoption of more overtly political move-ments later in the nineteenth century.[75] From the late 1850s, the increasing price of jute, as a result of the expansion of the jute industry in Scotland, combined with the rising costs of indigo production to push the patience of ryots forced to grow indigo at the behest of European planters to breaking point, which culmi-nated in the so-called 'Blue Mutiny' of 1859–60. Wide sections of 'respectable' and popular opinion, including – for the first time – the bhadralok rallied to the support of the ryots, and the Bengali 'pleader' made his first auspicious appear-ance as the 'Blue Mutiny' entered the hagiography of Indian nationalism.[76]

The bitterness that accompanied the confrontation between the British indigo planters and Bengali nationalist opinion would, however, be eclipsed by an issue that effectively foreclosed the possibility of the British authorities ever driving a wedge between Bengal's middle classes and emergent Indian nationalism. In February 1883, Sir Courtenay Ilbert, encouraged by the liberal policy of Ripon, the Gladstonian Indian Viceroy, moved an amendment to the Criminal Procedure Act of 1872 that allowed Europeans to be tried, for the first time, by Indian judges. For many within the British community the Ilbert Bill challenged 'the cherished conviction which was shared by every Englishman in India, from the highest to the lowest ... that he belongs to a race whom God has destined to govern.'[77] The furious response of the British community to the Ilbert Bill gave rise to increasing racial tensions and a counter-response from the nationalist minded bhadralok. Even the moderate nationalist newspaper *Amrita Bazar Patrika* concluded that 'friendship between the races ... has become utterly impossible.... We must agitate'.[78]

In 1894, the widening gulf between the Bengali and British communities was given literary expression with the publication of *The Jungle Book*. Rudyard Kipling effectively transformed the 'feckless' and 'disloyal' bhadralok into a stock literary figure when the 'Bander-Log', the monkeys, were juxtaposed with the 'true Jungle people', such as the wolves, bears and panthers, representing barely concealed characterisations of the British in India. Baloo the bear warns Mowgli that the:

> Monkey People are forbidden ... to the Jungle People.... They were always going to have a leader, and laws and customs of their own, but they never did, because their memories would not hold over from day to day, and so they compromised things by making up a saying: 'What the *Bandar-Log* think now the Jungle will think later.'[79]

By the end of the nineteenth century, bhadralok radicalism was becoming a mounting cause for concern for the British authorities as cultural and social concerns gave way to a growing interest in politics, encouraged by the formation of the Indian National Congress (INC) in 1885, and a growing determination, influenced by the work of figures such as Surendrenath Banarjee, to emulate the more militant forms of organisation and activity associated with Irish republicanism. In addition, India witnessed gathering movements of Hindu and Muslim religious revivalism that directly impacted on the Bengal jute industry.

The 1894–7 labour up-surge

By the early 1890s it had become the established view of mill management that migrant workers were 'more submissive, more malleable, more hard-working, more steady and more regular in their work than the local Bengali labour.'[80] This had also been the reasoning behind the increasing recruitment of a youthful, predominantly female, immigrant workforce in Dundee's early linen mills. In both cases, mill management and owners were guilty of an over-determined view of the racial, class and other characteristics of the different workforces. In reality, there were no innate differences between Bengali and up-country men, as there were none between the Scots and Irish, but the prejudice of management undoubtedly became a factor in the move away from the recruitment of local workers in both cases. Thus, a typology of labour emerged that mimicked the typology of race upon which the civil standing and political representation of the subject Indian populations was based. However, as we shall see, the views of management regarding the qualities of different groups of workers would undergo far-reaching changes during the long period with which this study is concerned. Over time, the cheap and quiet female jute worker in Dundee would give way, in the eyes of jute capital, to the recalcitrant and amoral 'mill-girl', whilst the 'malleable' up-country labourer in Bengal would quickly transmogrify into a potent threat to law and order and even to the existence of British rule itself. Indeed, as we have already seen, this transmogrification of the up-country worker was coincidental with the first sustained waves of emigration from Bihar, UP and Orrisa.

By the early 1890s, the Bengal jute industry had outstripped the Dundee industry in terms of size, with 27 mills, over 9,000 looms and a workforce of 67,000.[81] The growth of the Bengal jute industry also meant increasing opportunities for the Dundee School of supervisors and managers, and by 1894 they probably numbered 300–400.[82] Their presence was, though, not without its problems. During the 1890s the emerging mill districts, to the north of Calcutta and in the fast-developing industrial cul-de-sac of Howrah, witnessed increasing strikes and riots, which followed the frequent confrontations between the Dundee School and an increasingly assertive Indian workforce. In 1894, 'brick batting' of Scottish supervisory staff was experienced at Baranagore and Kamarhati jute mills as Muslim workers demanded paid holidays on the occasion of Bakr Id, and, in early 1895, Muslim and Hindu workers at the Kankinarah jute mill jointly demonstrated for paid holidays during the Bakr Id, Muharram and the Rathajatra festivals.[83] The demonstration at Kankinarah seemed to be a signal for the development of unrest on a wider scale when a similar demonstration took place at Gourepore jute mill.[84] The Gourepore mill manager informed the government investigator Pratt that 'agitators are about, possibly old hands, who teach the younger ones their rights, or supposed rights.'[85] This is the first recorded mention of labour 'agitators' in government records in Bengal, and the reference to 'old hands' indicates that they were workers, either more experienced and older up-country migrants or possibly, but less likely, local Bengali workers.

In April 1895, further trouble broke out at the Titaghar mill when management stopped the pay of Muslim workers who had absented themselves on the day of Bakr Id. When, following threats by workers to the manager of the mill, Scottish supervisors resorted to the use of firearms, serious rioting broke out, resulting in numerous assaults on police officers who were called in to restore order. The trouble died down following the arrest of the 'ringleaders', but further unrest flared up at Kamarhati jute mill in June when the pay of Muslim workers was stopped after they had taken time off for Muharram. Scottish supervisors again armed themselves to 'resist a possible outbreak', but order was restored when management conceded to the workers' demand for a recognised holiday in order to attend future Muharram festivities.[86] Trouble continued through 1895, with a strike against a reduction of spinners' wages at the Kankinarah mill, and another calling for the removal of an unpopular sirdar at the Budge-Budge mill. Both strikes were marked by serious *gheraos*, or mobbing, of Scottish staff, which included attacks on the European quarters. An interesting feature of this strike wave was the emergence, for the first time, of child labour as a major factor in the development of action at the Champdani mill in February 1895, when the shifting squads within the spinning department put forward a demand for a wage increase that was refused. As a result, the adult workers joined the strike and the mill was shut down for three days.[87]

The 1895 strike also led to the establishment of the Mahommedan Association at Kankinarah, in the far north of the jute belt. According to its first President, an up-country mill clerk, Kazi Zahir-ud-din Ahmed, speaking in 1908, the organisation was established 'with the object of attracting more Mahommedans to jute mills, but since then Hindus had been admitted to membership, and now the association looked after the interests of the operatives generally.'[88] As a result, the Mohammedan Association succeeded in re-inventing itself as the first trade union type of organisation in the Bengal jute industry, albeit one limited to a specific locality.[89]

The 1895 upsurge would be firmly put in the shade during June and July 1897, as strike action encompassed large swathes of the jute belt for the first time in the history of the industry. During the last two days of June, the 'Talla riots' effectively paralysed Calcutta, as Muslim mobs, including some 'mill-hands', attacked police constables and Europeans following the demolition of a mosque. Whilst the authorities were at pains to characterise the upsurge as a communal riot, it was significant that the Muslim mobs did not target Hindus and that Hindu 'bad characters' joined the predominantly Muslim rioters.[90] Shortly after the riots, Rabindranath Tagore wrote that:

> [A] group of lower class ignorant Musulmans, brickbats in hand, tried to create trouble on the streets of Calcutta. What was surprising about their attempt was that the English were made special targets of it.... These lower class Musulmans neither read newspapers nor do they write in them. What happened was after all a matter of some importance, yet we know nothing of what went on in the minds of these inarticulate people.[91]

Order was only restored in the centre of Calcutta with the deployment of the Gloucestershire infantry regiment, but trouble started to spread to the jute mill areas. On hearing of the Talla incident, the workers of six jute mills in the Kank-inarah, Jagatdal and Shyamangar areas, to the north of Calcutta, struck work and military detachments had to be despatched to restore order. From 2 to 7 July serious trouble continued, particularly in the Barrackpore area, where a large mob of workers, estimated at around 2,000–3,000, broke through the gates of the Alliance compound, surrounded the mill and attacked the engine house. The Scottish supervisors responded by firing 'a few rounds of snipe shots' which forced the mob to retreat, but the trouble only died down when military and police detachments were deployed.[92]

The 1894–7 labour upsurge represented a defining moment for industrial relations along the banks of the Hooghly. In the immediate aftermath of the 1895 strike wave, the IJMA believed that Muslim workers 'would be a constant source of anxiety unless the former order of things could be established whereby the Hindu element would preponderate'.[93] In 1898, the IJMA executive decided to halt the recruitment of Muslim mill-hands: an order that was, however, more honoured in the breach than the observance.[94] For many British colonial officials and contemporary observers, the Talla riots demonstrated the deep-seated religious fanaticism of the Muslim labouring poor in general and the Julaha weavers in particular, but this view of the riots as 'communal' did not really add up. Although elite Muslim politicians and reform organisations distanced themselves from the riots, ordinary Hindu workers – characterised as *badmashes*[95] and *goondas*[96] – participated with some gusto and also took an active part in the demonstrations and *gheraos* that swept through the mill areas around the demands for paid holidays for both Muslim and Hindu religious festivals.

The roots of Julaha militancy did not lie solely in their outraged religious feelings, as claimed by mill managers and colonial officials. Table 2.1 details the growth of the Bengal jute industry between 1877 and 1915. With the move towards the increasing production of finer hessian cloth the demands of customers for uniform and better-made products increased, which placed mounting pressure on the recently recruited migrant workers, reflected in the consistent lowering of the worker/loom ratio that took place during this period of the re-making of the Dundee–Calcutta nexus. While the pressure on all grades of labour was increasing, particular problems were experienced by the Julaha weavers who were being compelled to compete with Dundee's female weavers, who had been producing hessian cloth since the widespread introduction of power looms in the 1850s. The increasing stress on these, often very recent, recruits was tremendous, and was further exacerbated with the move towards night-time working from 1895 onwards. Mill machinery was now kept running for 15 hours per day, six days a week, and weavers, unlike other workers, were expected to be on duty for 15 hours, in order to ensure 'regularity in the cloth' that they produced, and in some cases this was 'extended to 15½ or 16 hours.' Although the weavers were relieved by one helper for four to seven looms, thus allowing time for meals and a little rest during the day, the helpers were so few 'unless the weavers chose to pay for them out of their own wages – that these hours were very long.'[97] The move towards hessian production, combined with long hours, required increased 'concentration of mind and alertness of the eye', leading to greater physical strain and the 'additional danger of these workers likely to loose [*sic*] their eyesight by constant work in the bright glare of electric

Table 2.1 Growth of Bengal jute industry, 1877–8 to 1914–15

Year	Sacking looms	Hessian looms	Total looms	Exports of cloth (in million yards)*	Exports of bags (in millions)*	No. of workers employed	Worker/loom ratio
1877–8	2,948	948	3,858	3.59	24.89		
1885–6	4,900	1,800	6,700	15.34	75.56	47,640	7.1
1895–6	6,584	3,117	9,701	182.01	171.23	77,618	8.0
1900–1	8,613	6,600	15,203	427.20	206.35	110,051	7.2
1905–6	10,805	12,756	23,561	697.98	257.76	143,429	6.1
1914–15	15,751	22,603	38,354	1156.11	667.66	230,627	6.0

Source: For loom statistics, R. C. Wallace, *Romance of Jute*, p. 95; figures for exports of cloth and bags, both gunny and hessian, from ibid., p. 99 (* figures for export of cloth and bags refer to average exports for the years, 1874–8, 1884–8, 1889–93, 1894–8, 1899–1903, 1904–8, 1914–18 respectively); for number of workers employed, Ranajit Das Gupta, *Labour and Working Class in Eastern India*, Appendix A, p. 46.

light, and thus being early incapacitated from earning their own livelihood.'[98] The issue of 'bad yarn' also became a particular issue of concern to weavers as it affected the smooth running of the loom leading to bouts of 'down time' and a reduction in earnings. Weavers, as in Dundee, were paid on a piece-rate basis, determined by 'various factors, such as the width of the cloth produced, the width of the loom used, variations as regards porters and shots, the weight of the cloth produced, etc.'[99] The introduction of shift working also allowed mill managers the opportunity provided by the change-over to alter piece rates to the workers detriment.

The further attempt by mill managers to prevent workers from attending festivals not only hurt their religious feelings but also deprived them of much needed recuperation. The demand for paid holidays to attend these festivals also underlined that the recent up-country recruits were rapidly learning 'the rules of the game' in their new industrial environment, particularly so when we consider that paid holidays would not become a reality within the Dundee jute industry until the late 1930s. The Talla riots also demonstrated the rapid radicalisation that affected many up-country workers as they grappled with the problems and complexities of their new environment. In part, this growing militancy was encouraged, if not fostered, by notions of fairness and honour held by Indian workers. The period encompassed by the re-making of the imperial nexus witnessed a developing collision between the 'world view'[100] or 'moral economic'[101] outlook of Indian workers – drawn from concepts of customary right, fairness and social honour – and the interests of management.[102] These concepts comprised the notion of *Dasturi*, which can loosely be defined as a customary right, whilst the related concept of *Insaf* referred to a sense of fairness. The third central notion, *Izzat*, can be defined as a sense of social honour.[103] For many contemporary British, and Indian, observers the jute workers were an amorphous mass, with basic needs and wants that appeared to be barely above the level of livestock. The idea that workers might possess an intellect or something approaching a 'world view' would have appeared preposterous. However, the Indian worker's world view played a fundamental part in the ways in which he attempted to understand and negotiate his world. In the context of working in a low-wage industry, it was important for individual workers to retain a sense of dignity. For many Julaha weavers, the imposition of night working and the attack on their rights of worship, as well as challenging concepts such as *dasturi* and *insaf*, also challenged their sense of honour as Muslims and must have underlined the alien, colonial character of the mill managers and supervisors, thus making them more receptive to the nationalist and Pan-Islamic rhetoric of Indian nationalism and Muslim reform organisations respectively. The militancy of the workers, though, went much further than was thought politic by many nationalist and Pan-Islamic leaders.

Paternal despotism was founded on and in turn strengthened the patriarchal character of industrial and social relations in Bengal, but during the late 1890s it became a double-edged sword as workers increasingly challenged Scottish supervisors, who demanded 'absolute obedience' not through being 'kind but firm' but through the use of violence.[104] Indeed, the strike wave of 1894–7 began with a dispute at the Shyamangar Mill, in the north of the jute belt, started by spinners protesting against the assault on a worker by a Scottish supervisor; and, between 1894 and 1897, another five disputes (in the Kamarhati, Titaghar, Budge-Budge, Baranagore and Alliance mills) involved serious attacks on Scottish mill personnel.

The reaction of many supervisors and managers to the ferment was one of barely concealed panic, most clearly demonstrated by their increasing use of firearms. During 1895, the Lt. Governor of Bengal responded strongly to the new phenomenon of gun-toting Scottish supervisors by stating that

> the occasions on which recourse to such weapons is really necessary are of the rarest possible occurrence, and that there are few crowds of native workers who would not yield to firm and reasonably conciliatory action on the part of European managers and assistants.[105]

In contrast to the earlier dismissive attitude of the Lt. Governor, however, the period following the 'Talla Riots' of 1897 witnessed an extensive reform of the policing arrangements in the jute mill areas, following insistent requests from the IJMA for greater military protection. Additional companies of the Bengal Military Police were established and stationed along the river Hooghly near to Barrackpore, from where they could be easily and swiftly moved to any trouble spots in the northern sector of the jute belt, whilst the existing police outpost in the south of the jute belt, at Budge-Budge, was strengthened and a British Inspector was appointed to co-ordinate police operations in north Calcutta and the 24 Parganas.[106] The actions of the Government of Bengal were endorsed by the Government of India on the grounds that:

> These people [i.e. the millhands] are occasionally a danger to the metropolis as well as to their employers. There is a tendency for them to increase in numbers and in power of combination with the increasing industrial activity of this part of Bengal. It is unlikely that their excitability or fanaticism will decrease. A strong police force is necessary to control them when they misbehave.[107]

Although government observers and the mill authorities commonly characterised the strikes of this period as primarily communal disputes, many actually arose out of the workers' growing resistance to the attempts by employers to inculcate discipline and the 'right of management to manage'. During the period 1894–7, of the 17 major disputes that were reported in Bengal 16 occurred in jute mills. Of these 16 strikes (involving a total of nine mills), 12 were concentrated in the northern portion of the jute belt, while two were recorded in the Howrah area and a further two at Budge-Budge in the south. Many mills and factories were also affected by the Talla controversy over June and July 1897, and most of these strikes were again concentrated in the north of the jute belt and involved mainly up-country workers.[108]

The swadeshi agitation, 1905–8

While local labour appeared to be relatively quiescent during the 1890s, they would play a leading role in the wave of strikes that accompanied the swadeshi agitation between 1905 and 1908, which was sparked by the partition of Bengal. Although partition was officially justified on the grounds of administrative efficiency, Curzon's home secretary was more forthright, 'Bengal united is a power; Bengal divided would pull in different ways ... one of our main objects is to split up and thereby weaken a solid body of opponents to our rule.'[109] In the early stages of the movement, programmes of boycott and national education proliferated and moderate nationalist politicians were forced into supporting new methods of struggle and a more militant nationalism that sought full independence from British rule. 'Bande Mataram' (I bow to you Mother), the patriotic song written by the Bengali poet and novelist Bankim Chandra Chattopadhyay, became the rallying cry of the swadeshi activists who sought to challenge British rule through a tactical embrace of the principle of passive resistance.[110] On 16 October 1905 a national day of agitation against the partition was widely observed in Calcutta. It was reported that shops in the 'native quarters were almost universally closed', most offices were forced to close down after 2 pm and 'there was not a single cart or a coolie near any of the four goods termini of the Eastern Bengal State Railway.' *Amrita Bazar Patrika* also reported that 12 jute presses, along with sugar, shellac and gun factories, were forced to close. The shutdown in the jute industry was thought to be almost total.[111] While many mill managers closed their mills in order to avoid trouble, the workers of Sibpur mill, in the southern sector, forced management to shut the mill. At the Fort Gloster mill, also in the southern sector, another strike occurred on 16 October when Bengali clerks were disciplined by management for exchanging *rakhis*, thread wristlets, with Muslim weavers as a token of Hindu–Muslim unity. In December 1905, the Fort Gloster mill was again affected by strike action, which further underlined the impact that the Dundee School was having on the growing anti-colonial mood amongst jute mill labour. The Fort Gloster strike was sparked into life when the mill manager objected to the raising of the 'Bande Mataram' slogan at closing time. The cry was then 'taken up by one department after another', and when the Scottish mill assistants intervened, they were assaulted by the workers and the mill manager was also forced into defending himself with his fists.[112] Following the arrest of two 'ringleaders' the workers took solidarity strike action, angrily stating that they were 'all brothers in the mill, all brothers in Bengal; that in arresting the two men they had all been insulted.'[113] In the same month, three other serious strikes broke out over the issue of the ill-treatment of Indian workers. Two of these, at the Gourepore and Lower Hooghly mills, were of short duration and were amicably settled, but the third dispute involving workers at the government printing press was more serious and of longer duration. The government-appointed managers locked out the workers and dismissed the 'ringleaders' in a dispute against a reduction in the *Puja* advance, which escalated into a bitter strike against service conditions and the ill treatment of workers at the hands of 'European officers'. The following year similar disputes also encompassed the East Indian Railways and the Clive jute mill.[114]

It was becoming increasingly apparent to jute mill managers up and down the Hooghly that these protests, against the physical manifestation of paternal despotism, were no 'flash in the pan'. The 'race question' was now something that could not be ignored. It had become an important issue for workers encouraged by the separate, but linked, movements encompassing Hindu and Muslim revivalism, the rise of Indian nationalism and the move towards more militant forms of struggle against British rule, as well as the pressures that came during the remaking of the imperial nexus. In effect, paternal despotism had now become an urgent political issue.

It should come as no surprise, then, that the first serious attempt to establish an industry-wide trade union organisation for jute workers occurred during the course of the swadeshi agitation. The founding meeting of the Indian Millhands Union took place at Budge-Budge on 19 August 1906, at a meeting of over 2,000, overwhelmingly Bengali, operatives. The union was the brainchild of A. C. Banerjee, a swadeshi activist and barrister, who would shortly after represent defendants in the Talla riot case. What was surprising was the fact that the union received the blessing of Andrew Yule & Co. in their efforts, but this is a little less surprising when consideration is given to A. C. Banerjee's opposition to 'hasty and injudicious strikes'. The further, barely concealed, attempt to buy off Banerjee suggests that the union was viewed by management as a possible bulwark against the type of spontaneous strike action that had affected mills in the Budge-Budge area from the 1890s onwards.[115]

By 1907, the union was attempting to extend its influence and had adopted the ambitious sounding title of the Indian Labour Union (ILU). In June 1907, the union was mediating a strike at the Burmah Oil Company depot at Budge-Budge, and a further union branch was established across the river at Howrah following a strike at the Delta jute mill in September 1907, while A. C. Banerjee was also involved in disputes at the, nearby, National and Belvedere jute mills in January 1908. Such was Banerjee's growing reputation that requests for assistance and intervention started to arrive from areas as distant as Monghyr in Bihar, where Indian workers were reportedly suffering 'under forced labour' by the American owned Peninsular Tobacco Company. In January 1908 A. C. Banerjee, as President of the ILU, also produced 16 weavers and spinners of the Budge-Budge jute mill as witnesses before the Factory Labour Commission.[116] However, from the middle of 1908, nationalist interest in the 'labour question' declined sharply and there is not a single reference to such issues in the Banerjee papers after the end of 1908. As a result, the ILU withered on the vine and many radical young nationalists turned towards revolutionary terrorism.

The 14-year period between 1894 and 1908 represented a watershed in the formation of the jute working class of Bengal. During this time, the jute workers had been transformed, in the minds of capital and government, from an amorphous mass of 'quiet, peacable, and docile beings'[117] into a fast-expanding and distinctive social group imbued with the 'power of combination' that had become 'a danger to the metropolis as well as to their employers.'[118] We have already seen how the move towards the increasing recruitment of migrant labour in Dundee was, in large part, undertaken by the Scottish linen lords in order to remove and exclude more organised and militant local male workers from the production process. The resulting diversification of the workforce that followed from this move also laid the basis for the later emergence of a militant labour force that became increasingly associated with spontaneous and wildcat strike action on a constantly widening front. A very similar process took place in the Bengal jute industry from the late 1880s onwards, but the development of learning through collective struggle took place over a far shorter space of time than in Dundee. In large part, this was due to the telescoping effect that followed from the rapid and unprecedented opening up of the up-country tracts to industrial recruitment. Between 1890 and 1905, employment in the Indian jute industry grew from 60,600 to over 143,000, leading to the emergence of a more diversified workforce along ethnic and religious lines.[119] This diversity, which in determinist and essentialist views of class formation 'marks the immaturity of the world', actually amounted to a necessary precondition for a radical transformation in workers' consciousness.[120] The strike movements of 1894–7 and 1905–8 involved workers drawing on central elements within their old identity, particularly those relating to communitarian ideas of solidarity and fair exchange, which were re-interpreted in the light of the, for many workers, very different experience of industrial labour and struggle. Unexpected layers of meaning in old concepts such as *dasturi* and *izzat* were revealed to the point where their meanings became transformed, and the dominance of 'paternal despotism' was seriously challenged.

The 1880s and 1890s was a formative experience for those recently recruited migrant workers who dreamed of returning permanently to their landholdings and a secure existence, but who, peering around the edges of their preconceptions, began to catch a glimpse of the reality of their position.[121] Economic circumstances conspired to trap them in the mill areas for far longer than they had intended, where they worked long hours and were under almost constant surveillance, particularly where they were housed in the mill lines. The Dundee–Calcutta relationship not only concerned shareholders and industry magnates, but also acted as a driving force in the process of class struggle and formation in both centres as workers were pushed into challenging the dominance of 'paternal despotism' through recourse to new methods of organisation and struggle that appeared to be constantly widening in scope and scale.

An interesting, and far from accidental, coincidence in the timing of major industrial struggles in both centres is also evident. As we saw in Chapter 1, the formation of the IJMA in 1885 led directly to attempts by the Dundee mill owners to institute short-time working, which sparked the strike wave that ushered in the formation of the MFOU. In 1895, wage reductions, following the adoption of night working, led to widespread strikes in both Dundee and Calcutta as the employers slashed wages, against the background of a competitive war between the two centres of the imperial nexus. In 1905–6, strike action led to the formation of unions in Dundee and Calcutta and in both cases the impetus for organisation came from 'outsiders' who were motivated by a concern to effectively harness, and control, the jute workers militancy. This task proved to be beyond the 'responsible' trade unionism of A. C. Banerjee and, as we shall see, the more militant brand of communist and nationalist inspired trade unions that later emerged would fare little better.

3 The imperial nexus and the making of Juteopolis, 1875–1910

There's a Juter[1] and a Battener[2]
Sailing up the Tay,
And a' the wives in Foondry Lane
Are singing blithe the day.
There'll be pennies for the bairnies,
A pint for Jock and Tam,
Money for the picters,
The auld fowk get a dram.
We'll gie the secks the go by,
We canna sew and eat,
And fivepence for twenty five
Will no buy *muckle*[3] meat.
We'll hae steak and *ingins*[4] frying,
Lift oor claes a' oot the pawn,
We'll gaither *wulks*[5] and boil them
in a corn beef can.
(Mary Brooksbank, 'Foondry Lane')[6]

Mary Brooksbank was a jute mill worker and revolutionary socialist, whose first flat, when she married in 1924, was a garret in 'Foondry Lane, a 'little narrow thoroughfare that ran from Blackscroft to Seagate.' Such was the condition of her new matrimonial home that she later admitted that 'when I first saw it I wept.... It could only be described as an outsize Dog Kennel.'[7] Brooksbank, therefore, knew of what she wrote. 'Foondry Lane' was home to 'dockers, mill workers, trawlermen and shipyard workers', but the song focuses on the wives who would turn to sewing sacks when better paying work had dried up. It was an occupation carried out in the home, away from the prying eyes of factory inspectors, where the very young and the very old would be pressed into service for pitiably low wages.

The dockers' wives 'kent[8] mair aboot the ships movements than the stevedores', and 'could be heard calling out the information about the *hammie*,[9] the *liverie*,[10] and the battens, as they were coming up the river.'[11] There was a good reason for this. The ships that brought their cargoes of *pucca*[12] jute from Bengal ensured work for the wives of 'Foondry Lane', and 'this meant at least brief periods of prosperity for them and their bairns.'[13] The sacks and needles would then be put aside and for a short time they could enjoy 'steak and ingins', 'money for the picters', a 'wee dram' and they would be able to lift their best 'claes a' oot the pawn'. 'Jock and Tam' would also enjoy their pint and 'would sing into the wee sma' oors'.[14] Inevitably, however, the Juters and Batteners would take their leave of Dundee, the work would dry up and the wives would return to the *secks* and the needles and their 'best claes' would go back to the pawnshop, as they found themselves, yet again, working away to the darker rhythm of jute dependency.

The re-making of the imperial nexus and the labour aristocracy of Dundee

The 1840s and 1850s was marked by an increasing feminisation of Dundee's textile workforce, a process that accelerated even further during the later nineteenth century and the re-making of the imperial nexus of jute. In 1851, the percentage of males within the local textile industry was nearly 48 per cent, but between 1891–1901 the percentage of men involved in the jute industry was estimated to be around 27 per cent.[15] Opportunities for male workers within the wider local economy were not much better. Although the mechanisation of the linen industry from the 1820s onwards encouraged the development of an engineering industry its growth was modest, and by the 1860s it employed no more than 3,000 workers.[16] By 1901, those engaged in engineering and machine making comprised 4,666, the increase being due – at least in part – to the expansion of the textile machinery manufacturing industry, following the emergence of foreign jute industries, but especially the Calcutta jute industry. Shipbuilding showed no long-term growth and by 1901 employed a workforce of only 1,376. The major employer of male labour by a considerable distance was the jute industry, which, despite being held responsible for creating a 'woman's town', employed over 9,000 adult male workers in 1901. Employment opportunities for young male workers under the age of 20 were also concentrated in jute. Of the 10,252 males between 12 and 20 years of age in employment in 1901, some 3,937 were employed there, whilst engineering and machine making employed 880 and shipbuilding a paltry 174 male workers under the age of 20.[17]

Even if a young male worker was able to gain admission to a recognised apprenticeship, this did not provide a secure wage, as it was not just the jute industry that was prone to downturns in the business cycle. Dundee's building industry struggled due to a contraction in house-building in the late nineteenth and early twentieth centuries, while the city's small shipyards struggled to compete with the much larger yards concentrated along the Clyde, and were subjected to frequent rationalisation, cost-cutting and lay-offs, particularly of younger workers.[18] As a result, temporary, and sometimes long-term, migration was a familiar experience for Dundee's younger skilled workers. After finishing his apprenticeship as a carpenter in Gourlay's shipyard in the late 1890s, Bob Stewart, a founder member of the Communist Party of Great Britain, took to 'tramping' in search of wages higher than the 10 shillings per week he was offered as an 'improver'. His 'tramping' took him along the Clyde, to England and even to South Africa.[19]

Within the jute industry, skilled male workers such as mechanics, firemen, tenters, foremen, clerks and managers only ever made up a small proportion of the total workforce. Whilst male workers as a whole comprised just over a quarter of the workforce, the proportion of boys to men was about three to one, and most men were concentrated in unskilled and semi-skilled occupations. As a result, managerial positions within the jute industry were only open to the 'aristocracy of labour' amongst the tenters, mechanics and foremen.

The mechanic enjoyed a high status within Dundee's early textile industry. In the 1820s the pioneering linen manufacturer, William Brown, advised the Directors of his East Mill that 'Any person you may employ as a manager should be a regularly bred mechanic, [and] experienced for several years in the management of some known mill in the neighbourhood'.[20] In the course of a working day the manager regularly consulted with the mechanic, who was, in terms of background and culture, often identical to the managerial cadre, and was thus well placed to rise through the ranks and eventually command a position at the very summit of the industry. By the end of the nineteenth century, however, the 'heroic' period of the jute industry was long past and most mechanics had to be content with a regular wage and the status that went with being part of the male aristocracy of labour within an overwhelmingly female industry. But new opportunities were starting to emerge in India, and by the beginning of the First World War the Dundee School of supervisors, managers and mechanics in Bengal numbered upwards of 1,000, underlining the growing importance of the imperial nexus with regards to the creation and perpetuation of Dundee's labour aristocracy.[21]

The holding of a City and Guilds certificate and the recognition of skilled status were necessary preparations for employment in the Bengal jute industry. Typically, the men of the Dundee School began their working lives as apprentice mechanics or tenters, where they came in contact with the rough and tumble culture of the Dundee mills, an experience that left its mark on many.[22] Alex Scott became a supervisor in Calcutta, and his experience highlights the difficulties faced by the young worker and his family during the period of training. In 1928, at the age of 16, he became an apprentice mechanic at Caird's mill, where his mother worked as a weaver and his father as a yarn dresser. Alex was an only child and, with two wages coming into the home, his parents were able to subsidise his arduous five year long apprenticeship.[23] In addition to a full day's work, Alex attended night school at Dundee Technical College from 7.15 pm to 9.15 pm four nights a week. On Fridays, the evening was spent performing overtime at the mill, while the weekend was normally occupied with writing up notes and working out calculations. The apprentice would spend a proportion of his time in each department of the mill and factory, including calendering, spinning, winding, the low mill and the engineering department, where he worked alongside, and learned from, a time-served mechanic. The wages that Alex earned as an apprentice were minimal: 10s in the first year, 12 in the second, 14 in the third, 18 in the fourth and 21 in the fifth year, and the scholarship charges of £10 per term were paid by his parents.[24]

Within the ranks of the mill managers, formalised training ended when a man finished his apprenticeship, either as a mechanic, engineer or clerk, and even well-to-do families associated with the jute trade expected their sons to begin their adult life in the mill or the office rather than at college or university. Alfred Tosh was the nephew of Charles Tosh, a leading figure with Thomas Duff & Co in the years before and during the First World War, and his father had been a jute broker in Calcutta but returned to Dundee in 1919 to become a 'gentleman farmer'. At the age of 17 Alfred entered the jute trade as a clerk with a local accountancy firm, a 'family tradition' that he was expected to follow because 'university [was] not seen as important for a career in business. ... If you weren't in the jute business, then you weren't accepted shall we say.... [Y]ou wouldn't see a job advertised, you had to be told about it and recommended.'[25] The enterprising and talented could, with a little luck, make their way through to the top, but personal connections counted for much. Alistair Martin, who started work at the Kinnison Mill in Bengal in 1947, had first been made interested in the prospect of 'going east' when, as a schoolboy, he caddied for returning jute wallahs at Arbroath golf course.[26] Alex Scott, who started work in the Baranogore mill in 1939, admitted that it had 'always been in the back of my mind' to go to Calcutta because his grandfather had worked in the industry there and stories told around the fire at New Year had fuelled his imagination of the exotic life 'in the east'.[27]

The importance of 'personal connections' was also evident in the home industry. In 1927, the Committee on Industry and Trade reported in relation to the job prospects of graduates from Dundee Technical College that unless 'the home student has relatives or friends to assure him of a suitable post in jute manufacture on completing his course, he runs a serious risk of finding himself without one.'[28] For unskilled male workers, the jute industry provided employment prospects, but at low wages compared with many other occupations. In 1886, women jute workers were earning 9s 7d per week, whilst male wages were 19s 4d.[29] Although these figures suggest that men were paid much more than women, the average male wage was inflated by those of employees in supervisory and ancillary occupations, and only 8 per cent of male workers in Dundee received a wage in excess of one pound per week in 1886.[30] This relatively well-paid section of the labour force included foremen, tenters, mechanics, joiners, engineers and firemen. The wages of the vast majority of male jute workers were much lower, and many earned less than the best-paid female workers. In 1886, women in double-loom power weaving earned more than adult male softeners, preparers, rove and bobbin carriers and hand loom weavers, and their wages were equivalent to the better-paid male workers such as cutters and selectors.[31]

Table 3.1 Wages of selected groups of workers in the Dundee jute industry, for 1886 and 1904

Occupation	1886	1904
Male overseer	*33/–	*34/–
Weaver (female)	11/1	19/–
Spinner (female)	8/3	10/4
Shifters (male)	5/11	9/4
Shifters (female)	5/9	9/–
Rover (male)	8/3	11/–
Rover (female)	8/6	11/11

Source: Figures for 1886 taken from D. Lennox, 'Working Class Life in Dundee, 1878–1905', unpublished Ph.D. thesis, St Andrews University (n.d., prob. 1906), Appendix; Figures for 1904, Dundee Social Union, *Report on Housing and Industrial Conditions*, Dundee, 1905; * Average wages, calculated from Lennox.

By 1906, the average wage of women workers in the jute industry was 13s 5d, representing a 40 per cent increase from 1886 wage levels. During the same period, the average male wage rose to 21s 7d, an increase of 12 per cent, but around half of all male jute workers still earned less than one pound per head, and 10 per cent earned less than 15s.[32] Low wages in the jute industry were exacerbated by Dundee's high cost of living, which, in 1905, was calculated by the Board of Trade as being almost on a par with London.[33] The wages of male workers in the jute industry were consistently recorded as the worst in British industry, and almost half of male jute workers earned less than the minimum required to sustain the 'physical efficiency' of a family comprising a husband, wife, and three children.[34]

There was an even greater gulf between the earnings and status of the male aristocracy of jute labour and some unskilled male jute workers than there was between the labour aristocrats and the better-paid female workers. Foremen and mechanics were also much more likely to be regularly paid, and to emulate the social values of their managers, if not always their employers. They attended church more regularly than their less privileged workmates, and were also more likely to have smaller families, to take regular holidays, to belong to clubs and societies and to be involved in formal politics. Some mechanics and foremen lived in company properties, but where foremen and skilled workers resided in the same street as ordinary workers an informal hierarchy was often observed – to which Bob Stewart's autobiography testifies. The tenements on the other side of the street from where his family lived 'were a bit more classy. They did not have the middens and had a W.C. on the stair landing. This we called the syrup side and our side the treacle side.'[35]

Eric Hobsbawm has argued that the Dundee jute industry's very narrow layer of affluent male workers should not be viewed as important as the more numerous labour aristocrats in occupations such as engineering and cotton manufacturing. For Hobsbawm, the male skilled workers in these industries amounted to a 'super aristocracy'.[36] However, the level of differentiation between the income of the upper layers and the lower layers of workers is at its narrowest in precisely those trades that Hobsbawm considers the preserve of the 'super aristocrat', and at their widest in the jute and linen industry, which Hobsbawm sees as less characterised by the existence of a powerful labour aristocracy. An 'aristocracy' is by its nature drawn from a very narrow base and it should be self-perpetuating and difficult to join, so that it could be argued that the labour aristocracy of Dundee were the true 'super aristocrats'. But, whilst emerging as a super-aristocracy of labour in a descriptive sense, Hobsbawm is quite correct to point to the limits of their influence on the wider working class of Juteopolis, in political, social and cultural terms.

Half-time labour and the remaking of the imperial nexus

The remaking of the imperial nexus resulted in the often barefooted *halflin* becoming as emblematic of Juteopolis as belching mill chimneys and coarse tongued spinner lassies. Between 1870 and 1885, Scotland's jute workforce grew from nearly 15,000 to just over 36,000, or around two and a half times, but, during the same period the number of children aged between 10 and 14 within the jute industry increased more than seven times over, from 574 to 4,123.[37] In the Scottish flax industry, the increasing reliance on child labour was also striking. Between 1870 and 1885, the number of children increased by 58 per cent, from 1,970 to 3,125, whilst the industry-wide workforce dropped by 22 per cent, from 49,917 to 39,086, as indicated in Table 3.2.

By 1891, children comprised 18 per cent of Dundee's textile labour force, the largest of any Scottish industrial centre.[38] In numerical terms, only Glasgow had more children at work, but the difference was only a few hundred more out of an industrial workforce that was around four times greater. Dundee's mill owners used every opportunity at their disposal in order to defend their reliance on child labour. In 1884, Dundee Chamber of Commerce (DCC) launched a campaign 'arguing that the city's practice of employing children should be treated as a special case'.[39] The campaigning efforts of the DCC had the desired effect, but child labour was again an issue in 1891, when government was considering raising the minimum age of half-timers. On this occasion, the DCC successfully

Table 3.2 The employment of children under 13 years of age in the Scottish flax and jute industries

	1870	1874	1878	1885
Flax workers	49,917	45,816	37,476	39,086
No. of children	1,970	3,421	2,753	3,125
Jute workers	14,911	30,893	30,401	36,269
No. of children	574	3,620	2,877	4,123

Source: *Dundee Year Book, 1885*, Dundee, 1886, pp. 32–3.

pressed their local MP to support 'the views of the deputation to the Home Secretary in regard to keeping the limit of age for employment of half-timers at ten as at present.'[40] Aside from local clergymen and some trade union and socialist activists, support for the continuation of the half-time system in Dundee was more or less general at this time, encompassing not only the jute mill owners but also many working class parents and even union figures – such as Henry Williamson who claimed that he was employed as a half-timer during his childhood in the USA. Indeed, Williamson was such a keen supporter of this issue that he went so far as to establish a Parents League in 1904 in order to oppose legal restrictions regarding child labour.[41]

John Leng, who became a Dundee MP in 1889 as a self-proclaimed champion of working class interests, also exhibited what might charitably be called an ambiguous attitude towards the issue of child labour. During the course of the general election campaign of 1895, the Tory-supporting Dundee *Courier* reported that although he had indicated his support for raising the age of half-timers, he had also introduced a deputation of Dundee employers to the Royal Commission on Labour, while the Dundee Trades Council also accused Leng of going back on his commitment to the eight-hour day.[42] Leng's pragmatic – not to say cavalier – approach to the 'labour question', and particularly to the issue of child labour, helped assuage the anger of the jute mill owners following his failure to support the cause of protection for the home jute industry.[43] The continuing appeal of child working for hard-pressed families lay in the comparatively high wages that could be earned by young jute workers: in 1903, the *Dundee Advertiser* claimed that, 'the female millhand early earns wages much larger then the milliner or housemaid in other Scottish towns.'[44] Children's wages in the jute industry also compared favourably with their adult workmates. In the late nineteenth century, half-timers in the Victoria Spinning Company were earning around a third of the pay, while working only half of the hours, of spinners, and adolescent workers between the ages of 14 and 17 were earning wages not far short of those paid to many adult workers.[45]

Child labour was predominantly drawn from households headed by unskilled and semi-skilled male workers. With larger numbers of dependents, compared to households headed by female or male skilled workers, they relied on the wages of children, as well as adult women, for their viability and long-term sustainability. Children, particularly females, were co-opted into the industrial workforce where, as with Mary Brooksbank, they 'very early ... learned the habit of self-discipline', with 'wishes, desires, hopes, ambitions ... dutifully suppressed in the interests of those I loved, my father, mother and brothers.'[46] They often found work in the jute mills through family and kin and community links, and the address of the young would-be worker also had a bearing on their chances of securing long-term employment. In Baxter's mill, more noted than most for their paternalist employment practices, 'to get a job in the batching house ... you had to come from Todburn Lane, Dens Brae or King Street', which were all in proximity to the massive Dens Road mill complex in the east end of the town.[47] 'Spare' or *orra* hands were also 'occasionally "taken in" from the gate', but 'they were mainly transients' whilst those 'who were "asked in" were the elite.'[48] Young workers would often begin work in the same mill, and often in the same department, as their mother or other members of their family. This was the experience of Lizzie Duncan, who began her working life in 1916:

> I was also thirteen years old when I started in the spinning department, the oldest of the family, and my mother had six at home.... I got my exemption from full-time education and started work as a shifter,[49] and had to go to the night-school until I was fourteen for three nights a week ... and she used to come and meet me, because I was scared in the dark. If she didn't meet me I stood at the end of Taits Lane and shouted.... My mother got me beside her so she could keep an eye on me, it was the biggest mistake she ever made. Anything I did, they were going and telling my mother.[50]

By the turn of the twentieth century, the Dundee School Board was granting more exemptions for child workers than Glasgow, Edinburgh, Aberdeen, Govan and Paisley combined – and these were all areas that also contained textile industries. In 1900 nearly 5,000 children under 14 were still working in the Dundee jute industry. Of this total, 2,800 worked as a result of the granting of exemptions, and in 1910 the factory inspectorate openly criticised the Dundee School Board for increasing the number of exemptions by 100 over the figure for the previous year.[51] Indeed, the same inspector's report pointed out, 'that in Scotland for girls and boys of 13 a 12 hours day ... is legal, while for such children in India a working day above seven hours is forbidden by law.'[52] It is remarkable that a Scottish factory inspector was compelled to draw such an unfavourable contrast following nearly a century of British labour reform and regulation. Indeed, even by the late 1920s, D. R. Wallace was still able to claim that Indian child workers enjoyed greater legislative protection than their British counterparts.[53]

The period following the First World War did witness a contraction in the number of child workers within the jute industry, but the wages of children still remained important to many families headed by unskilled and semi-skilled male workers, and legal exemptions to families in need allowed them to send their children to work. Oral testimony and the autobiographies of former jute workers, such as Bob Stewart, also suggest that forged birth certificates, or 'false lines', were widely used by families, who, due to force of circumstance, were compelled to flout legislation on child labour.[54] Whilst there is little evidence that employers actively co-operated with this practice, there appears to have been little desire on their part to stamp it out.[55]

The close confinement of the working week encouraged an appetite for entertainment, particularly among adolescent labour, which, before the coming of the cinema and the dance hall in the twentieth century, was provided by the 'monkey parade'. Large groups of young people congregated in Dundee city centre at weekends, which induced panic amongst the more respectable denizens of the burgh. In March 1875, a deputation of prominent citizens approached the Town Council:

regarding the state of the Nethergate and Perth Road on Sunday evenings. It was pointed out that these streets were then frequented by crowds of people, and that a practice had sprung up on the part of a number of young lads from 16 to 18 years of age, who paraded in bands and rudely jostled and attacked with foul language those they passed, particularly young girls, which had become unbearable.[56]

The half-timer and adolescent jute workers were an important, and growing, fraction of Dundee's late Victorian workforce, and an exuberant presence and influence on the city's evolving working class culture. As we shall see in Chapter 4, they were also capable of defending their own interests, both at the individual level and through organised mass action – to a degree that has never been fully appreciated.

Social conditions in Juteopolis

The Dundee property market for rented accommodation – like that in Edinburgh and Glasgow – was predominantly controlled by shopkeepers and small businessmen.[57] This guaranteed a modest but regular income for the city's middle classes, and particularly middle-class spinsters who were often provided with a small number of tenancies by fathers concerned with bolstering the social position of their daughters in the absence of suitable marriage partners, particularly in the years immediately following the First World War. The consequences for many of the working class tenants who financed this private form of middle class social insurance were often catastrophic.[58]

By the first years of the twentieth century, Dundee's slum quarters presented an urban and social disaster, but most middle-class Dundonians were blissfully unaware of the real conditions facing the poorest sections of the city's population. The respectable middle classes could go about their business and remain oblivious to the poverty that lay sometimes little more than a stone's throw from the city centre and the roads along which omnibuses and trams carried them to social and business engagements, cultural events and their places of work. The appalling housing conditions of Juteopolis would, though, prompt an unprecedented act of mapping of the city's dark places. In 1905, the publication of the Dundee Social Union (DSU) *Report on Housing and Industrial Conditions in Dundee* uncovered 'certain social evils' that were described as a 'disgrace and national peril'.[59] Realistic remedies were, however, in shorter supply, and the social conditions so graphically illustrated by the DSU *Report* would linger – and in some cases worsen – as the new century progressed, prompting even Winston Churchill to admit in 1921 that 'if you saw the kind of lives the Dundee folk have to live, you would admit that they have many excuses'.[60]

Bob Stewart was a product of the Dundee slums and the half time system. His father had been a grieve in the Parish of Eassie in Angus, but, with 10 children and only a small income, the family was forced to move to Dundee in 1879:

Our first house in Dundee was at 21 Lawrence Street, in a block of tenements, built like all the others, in close proximity to the jute factories. These tenements were built in flats or platforms very similar to the construction in most prisons. There were four 'houses', usually a kitchen with one or two rooms, on each 'plat'. There were no lavatories, no baths or other essential amenities, but there was running water, naturally only cold.

We entered by a covered entry called a close, which led to a stair winding up the 'plats', again in the best prison design. There was a ground floor and three stories which meant sixteen families to a block, many of them large families like the Stewarts. In the courtyard stood an open midden for rubbish which was used by the males as a dry closet. The women used a pail indoors and later emptied the midden weekly, wheeled out the muck and emptied it on the street to wait for a cart to take it and its perfume for disposal.[61]

It is indicative of the slow rate of progress in slum clearance and improvement, that when Stewart revisited Lawrence street in 1962, the 'original tenements complete with "plats" were still standing. The only change was that the midden had gone and one lavatory had been installed for each "plat". That is one lavatory for four families.'[62] The large Stewart family occupied a tenement flat comprising three rooms, with the male children bedding down in one room, the female children in another, and the parents in the kitchen. As Bob Stewart ruefully commented, 'the privacy was somewhat restricted' as 'both rooms led off the kitchen.'[63] As bad as these conditions were, the DSU *Report* revealed that the situation was much worse for many other families who commonly had to make do with one or two rooms making any kind of sexual segregation of sleeping arrangements impossible.

By the last years of the nineteenth century, the city's housing stock was subject to a degree of degeneration that was at its most marked in and around the major mill districts, which were starting to become even more overcrowded as the demand for labour increased in response to war-fuelled boom following the outbreak of hostilities in South Africa in 1899. Whilst the 24 year period between 1867 and 1891 saw the building of an estimated 12,811 houses for working people, the following 23 year period between 1891 and 1914 produced only 7,756, as Dundee shared in the UK-wide crisis in working class housing that followed from rising building costs.[64] The period from the 1890s did witness a slowing down in Dundee's rate of population growth, but conditions actually worsened during this time as the housing built in the second half of the nineteenth century began to deteriorate. Local authorities were given sweeping powers, through national legislation, to close the worst of the slum housing, but this was only slowly replaced, leading to a continuous worsening of overcrowding.

A principle reason for the lack of house building, particularly at the lower end of the market, was that it had become less and less of a paying business. Whilst, as we have seen, this was part of a UK-wide phenomenon, there were local factors that further aggravated Dundee's housing situation. The financial prosperity flowing from the success of the investment trust movement, particularly in the USA, attracted money away from private housing investment at a time when the development of, and financial support for, public housing in Dundee was almost non-existent. The disincentive to invest was further strengthened when rent controls were introduced following the election of Labour Party and Scottish Prohibitionist Party town councillors in 1905.[65]

In 1905, James Thomson, the highly active Assistant Burgh Surveyor of Dundee, revealed that 'the density of the congested districts was … from 380 to 882 persons per acre, and 32,897 persons were said to occupy 66 acres, or at the rate of 498 persons per acre.'[66] The extent of overcrowding in Dundee actually exceeded that in Calcutta in 1901, where by far the most crowded ward was Colootolla with 281 persons per acre.[67] Whilst the vast majority of working class Dundonians, in contrast to their counterparts in Calcutta, lived in four-storey tenements, the extent of overcrowding per room was still remarkably high, with 49 per cent of the city's population living 'more than two persons to one room in houses of less than five rooms', compared with 33 per cent in Edinburgh and 48 per cent in Glasgow.[68] In the UK as a whole, in 1901, the extent of overcrowding was estimated at 8 per cent, whilst Gateshead and Tynemouth, both with 31 per cent, represented the worst English examples, with London at 18.6 per cent.[69] The figures for overcrowding in Dundee, and Glasgow, were actually more comparable to Calcutta, where it was thought that 'more than half the inhabitants have less than half a room per head, and 90 per cent have three quarters of a room or less'.[70]

Perhaps the greatest indictment of the industrial hellhole created by jute dependency and the imperial nexus is to be found in the DSU statistics regarding infant mortality. Investigators found that of 20,095 children, within the 4,384 families studied, 7,492 or 37 per cent had died, while the rate of mortality amongst babies up to one year of age born to jute workers was 59 per cent.[71] This incredible figure, which bears comparison with the mortality rates for infants born to working mothers in the Bengal jute industry, demonstrates the struggle for existence endured by Dundee's labouring poor.[72]

Mary Walker, the DSU's leading investigator, blamed the jute industry's 'over-employment of women', and especially married women, for Dundee's exceptionally high rate of infant and child mortality. It was not the employment of women per se but more the nature of women's employment acting in combination with appallingly low wages and foetid social conditions that spawned this massacre of the innocents. Few women jute workers received the extra nutrition necessary for pregnant and lactating women. Low nutritional standards were, and remain, one of the principal causes of infant mortality, meaning that many, if not most, women subsisting on diets deficient in milk, butter, eggs, green vegetables and fruit were particularly at risk.[73] Rickets, which was endemic in Dundee, particularly amongst adults who had been half-timers, often led to a contraction of the pelvis, making childbirth difficult. An Aberdeen study of the 1940s also found that the foetal mortality rate of underweight and small (5ft 1in and under) women was twice that of women over 5ft 4in.[74] Women jute workers were often seriously underweight and small in stature: of 27 women jute workers whose heights were recorded following their arrest for drunkenness between April and December 1905, only one was over 5ft 2in.[75] Dundee's high rate of infant mortality was also encouraged by the fact that, along with cotton workers in Preston, jute workers commonly 'worked longer into their pregnancies – 14 per cent up to one week before delivery than the better paid textile workers of Paisley'.[76] In addition, many babies were delivered by untrained midwives in cramped, overcrowded and dirty housing conditions that encouraged endemic gastro-intestinal diseases amongst infants. Indeed, it is a wonder that so many of Dundee's infants survived given the unforgiving environment that they were born into.

During the first years of the twentieth century, there was an unprecedented shift in the regional balance of British infant mortality rates, as demonstrated in Table 3.3. Up to that time, English infant mortality rates had always been higher, but thereafter Scotland's infant mortality rate fell at a far slower rate than England's, and in the decade 1906–16 the Scottish rate actually increased. For Dundee, the rise in infant mortality during this time was even larger than for Scotland as a whole – meaning that the city was the most dangerous place to be born in Britain, if not Europe. The explanation for Dundee's rising infant mortality rate may well be connected to the slowing rate of population growth in the city during this time, which meant that a higher percentage of babies were being conceived and carried by mothers who had spent most, if not all, of their lives in the increasingly toxic atmosphere of Juteopolis.[77]

Mary Walker, quite correctly, felt that the root cause of Dundee's appalling social conditions lay in the 'unequal contest' whereby Dundee had 'to compete in the world's markets with the product of the native labour of Calcutta.' Although this situation had 'gone on for the past thirty years, with the advantage always in favour of Calcutta', Walker felt that the future prospects of Dundee's jute workers were even bleaker:

> It is true that efficient labour and cheap labour are not interchangeable terms, but it is an open question whether in the ordinary processes of jute manufacture the white workers have any special advantage in brain or skill in a contest with the Indian workers.[78]

Table 3.3 Infant mortality rates, 1901–20 (per 1,000)

	England	Scotland	Dundee
1901–5	138	120	154
1906–10	117	112	156
1911–16	110	113	164
1917–20	90	99	129

Source: Corporation of Dundee, Notes by Medical Officer of Health on the Report of a Sub-Committee of the Scientific Advisory Committee on Infant Mortality in Scotland, February 1944, p. 3.

Mary Walker, in contrast to many other contemporary observers, saw no fundamental differences between the skill levels of jute labour in Dundee and Bengal,
leading her to conclude that Dundee's jute workers 'must, in time, yield place to
the cheaper workers, unless a way is found to develop aptitudes in the white
workers for more specialised forms of production.' Reading Walker's comments,
it seems as though nothing had changed in the 20 years since the formation of
the Indian Jute Manufacturers Association and the fears regarding foreign competition that were being increasingly expressed at that time. In fact, as we saw in
Chapter 1, many Dundee jute firms had successfully diversified production
towards speciality goods, but the late 1890s witnessed the development of conflict in South Africa, which, in response to rising war needs, propelled a widespread move back to the production of the most primitive of jute goods, the
gunny sack.

Patriarchy, the female headed household and class formation in Juteopolis

It is perhaps not surprising, given the central role of women, that feminist labour
historians have turned their attention towards labour relations in the Dundee jute
industry. According to Eleanor Gordon, gender relations in Dundee were bitterly
fought over and indeed superseded class conflict:

> Even in a town such as Dundee, where female employment was widespread
> and many women were the major or sole contributors to the family income,
> the yoke of patriarchal authority and control hung heavily, defining the
> nature of their work, earnings, modes of supervision, and codes of
> behaviour.[79]

In Eleanor Gordon's view, 'women's entry into social production did not release
them from male domination or replace gender subordination with exploitation as
waged labour, but rather their experience as workers was premised upon their
subordination as a gender.'[80] Gordon also argues that a patriarchal bloc existed
between male workers and employers, thus ensuring that women's position was
fundamentally undermined even by the trade unions that claimed to represent
them:

> The notion of the male provider and protector reinforced the claims of
> skilled, semi-skilled, and unskilled trade unionists to a prior right to work
> and a demand for a family wage.... [T]he response of the trade union move-
> ment ... was to view women's low pay as a consequence of their inability to
> organise and as a threat or a problem to be overcome by excluding them
> from the labour market or at least controlling their entry.[81]

While Gordon's overarching view of patriarchy, as an interlocking system of
social relations benefiting males irrespective of their social position, may reflect

conditions within some other British industries (but even there it may well be open to challenge), it is untenable as a description of gender and class relations in Dundee. There, patriarchy was not so all encompassing, as claimed by Gordon, and was situated within a network of labour practices and attitudes that equated with the rule of the father over the rest of the family.[82] Female *and* male workers were both subject to the control of senior males who were concentrated in supervisory, management and ownership roles.

We should also remember that skilled male workers in the Dundee textile industry were largely removed from the production process altogether during the first half of the nineteenth century, so that the city's experience of industrialisation and mechanisation was, in many respects, more akin to that in the German and French textile industries than it was to other British textile industries. For example, in the Lancashire cotton industry the male spinner was able to retain his leading position within the division of labour, and the relative degrees of status associated with it.[83] In the Dundee textile industry, by contrast, the male labour aristocracy was drawn from a much narrower base, and represented a smaller proportion of the workforce, which had major repercussions for class formation and social relations in the city. Dundee was also markedly different from Paisley, its most comparable Scottish counterpart, where the feminisation of the textile workforce was accompanied by a spectacular expansion in engineering in Renfrewshire and Clydeside.[84] In Paisley, many men were thus able to find skilled work at higher wages than those paid in the cotton mills and the town did not experience a gender imbalance in its population as occurred in Dundee, where by the beginning of the twentieth century there were almost three women to every two men between the ages of 20 and 40.[85] In addition, female operatives in Paisley were generally single and left work when they married, meaning, according to Catriona MacDonald, that gender roles underlining the 'governing duty of woman and wife and mother' imposed tighter restrictions on Paisley's female population than was the case in Dundee.[86] The widespread availability of work for women in Dundee, despite low wages, allowed working women a degree of economic independence that, allied to a dearth of male job opportunities, seriously undermined the position of many men as the main provider and head of the family, thus severing a central link in Eleanor Gordon's patriarchal chain.

The increasing feminisation of the jute workforce created by jute dependency and the remaking of the imperial nexus also encouraged into existence complex family and household structures. In 1871, 'many factory girls' were said to have kept 'independent households for themselves', but female-headed households started to become even more widespread in Dundee from the 1880s onwards, a time when Indian competition was starting to cause mounting anxiety.[87] By 1891, 32 per cent of all households in the city were headed by women and by 1904 this figure had risen to 35 per cent, 'the largest [proportion] in any Scottish town'.[88] In 1912, Mary Walker described the circumstances that often encouraged the formation of female-headed households:

When two working women live together their circumstances are comfortable. Some of the most attractive little homes in Dundee are those of women and girls living as companions. The friendship begins in their youth, often persists till old age, and is only broken by death. It is a frequent complaint that young girls leave home when they begin to earn good money, simply from the love of independence, breaking loose their family ties in a thoughtless and callous manner.... [S]ometimes her parents are dead; sometimes they drink, and the girl with an instinct for better things can endure no longer the squalor and misery of the two-roomed house. In such cases she leaves her home, sometimes taking some of her brothers and sisters with her, sometimes setting up joint house-keeping with a companion of her own age and sex.[89]

The female-headed household tended to contain fewer members overall and fewer dependent children, and was much more likely to contain women than men, meaning that there were 'fewer demands on household income than those experienced by male headed households with larger numbers of dependent children and adult males.'[90] They were also 'much more capable of sustaining themselves than male headed households, a situation reinforced by the high levels of irregular employment amongst men.'[91] It is interesting to note that whilst women in the same broad occupational groupings, such as weavers, tended to stay together, over one-fifth of female-headed households contained workers from both mills and factories, undermining the widespread assumption that there was a serious social divide between weavers and spinners.[92] Female-headed households also commonly offered refuge to extended kin and were more likely to have siblings (particularly sisters) and parents (particularly mothers), as well as nieces, nephews and even cousins living with them, and thus served as a more important source of kin support than conventional families.[93] The pressures of appalling living conditions in the family home also meant that many girls who did not have the resources to set up a home of their own drifted into lodgings, or into the hostels and boarding houses that were established by agencies such as the Sisters of St Vincent de Paul, whilst for those in desperate straits there were lodging houses such as the Metropole, which were reserved 'for the very poor, for the casual worker, the homeless woman, the tramp.'[94]

Graham Smith has demonstrated how the growth of the female-headed household in the late nineteenth century, along with the upsurge in strike action during the 1880s and 1890s, promoted awareness amongst Dundee women of their status.[95] His research reveals a 'hidden matriarchy', which was based upon the central role of poor urban women in the survival and regulation of the families and communities of which they were a part. They acted as unofficial midwives and doctors and knew how to take care of themselves in street fights and family feuds, and, because they were often employed outside the home, they enjoyed a degree of independence and self-respect that was very different from the dependency exhibited by married women of the upper layers of the working class and of the middle classes.[96] In the context of a 'woman's town', spinsterhood did not connote failure, 'nor were widows isolated, nor were wives and mothers without husbands necessarily abandoned women.'[97] Working women, through the female-headed household, were able to draw upon, participate in, and extend the collective community of Dundee's working class. Indeed, the openness of the female-headed household to kin and non-kin facilitated 'a wider solidarity, socialising youth, including boarders, enabling co-residents to combat high rents', whilst also providing 'a basis for the mobility between workplaces that was used to resist the most oppressive employment conditions.'[98] In the process, the female-headed household contributed towards the emergence of a network of relationships that, as we shall see in Chapter 4, would also have important implications for working class formation in Dundee.

The male-headed household

Although the female-headed household emerged as a defining characteristic of Juteopolis during this time, the male-headed household actually remained the predominant form of household structure. There were, though, major differences between households headed by skilled workers and those headed by unskilled and semi-skilled workers. Between 1891 and 1911, skilled males headed around a third of Dundee households, and their situation throws into contrast the difficulties facing the much larger grouping of unskilled and semi-skilled males.[99] Skilled male workers, with better wages and greater job security, were seen as 'a good catch' by young women and were thus much more likely than their less skilled counterparts to marry and to become the head of a household. Although they formed a much larger proportion of the total population of Dundee, unskilled and semi-skilled male workers, including labourers, porters, carters, hawkers and mill workers, made up only a quarter of all the heads of household within the city between 1891 and 1911.[100] Inevitably, the jute industry, as the single biggest employer of male labour, provided many of the heads of household from this unskilled and semi-skilled male cohort: these men were often married to, or cohabited with, women who themselves worked in the jute industry, so that whilst 9 per cent of tradesmen's wives worked in 1891, over 36 per cent of the wives of semi and unskilled workers were in employment.[101]

In 1907, a Report of the General Assembly of the Church of Scotland found that 5 per cent of registered marriages in Dundee were classed as 'irregular'. While this total was the lowest of any major town or city in Scotland, many Dundee couples did not bother to register their informal forms of co-habiting.[102] Within these households, domestic and sexual relations tended to be more equal than in more 'respectable' households associated with the 'cult of domesticity', with men sharing in some of the domestic duties such as caring for children and preparation of meals, particularly, as we shall see, as a result of enforced idleness through unemployment.

For social commentators from the late nineteenth century through to the end of our period, the more democratic households headed by unskilled and semi-skilled male workers were wrongly seen as underlining Dundee's position as a 'woman's town'. During 1889 James Connolly, the future Irish but Edinburgh-born socialist and republican leader, lived and worked in Dundee. In a letter he penned to his fiancée during this time we have the first documentation of his interest in social issues. He described Dundee as a city where women worked whilst their husbands were unemployed, claiming, wrongly, that there were 11 women working for every two men.[103] In so doing, Connolly provided an early reference to what became known as the 'kettle boiler', the male unemployed worker who stayed home to tend house whilst his wife or unmarried partner went out to work. Writing in the 1920s, H. V. Morton, a noted British travel writer, described the following encounter with a Dundee 'kettle boiler';

> I heard the Irish brogue, and saw Pat smoking his pipe at the cabin door:
> 'Out of work?' I asked one man.
> 'I am'
> The place looked neat and clean. He explained that his wife worked in the mill, while he was nurse, cook, and housemaid! He looked extraordinarily incompetent. This unnatural domestic life, is I believe, a characteristic of Dundee when the shipyards are idle.... I asked him how it felt to be dependent on a wife. He appeared unconscious of any humiliation. He said it was a good day's work to look after two children, and he would rather do a day's work than wash one baby! But his wife knew how things were. She gave him beer money, and sometimes took him to the pictures![104]

For Morton, the fact that Pat received 'beer money' from his working wife graphically illustrated the 'unnatural domestic life' followed by many Dundee households, which, for many other social commentator, was also emblematic of the social degradation and emasculated condition of many of the city's male population. In fact, what was being played out within these households was not some sort of matriarchal imperative, but a deeply pragmatic and democratic domestic arrangement that was a response to the nature of Juteopolis itself. More than this, the coming into being of the 'unnatural domestic life' of Dundee, whereby the patriarchal Victorian domestic ideal was turned on its head, was due to the imperatives of imperialism, which brought about the re-making of the Calcutta–Dundee nexus in the last decades of the nineteenth century.

The 'undersized' and 'underfed' male jute worker became as much a token of Juteopolis as was the sharp-tongued spinner or the barefooted *halflin*. By the last years of the nineteenth century, the normal diet for many of Dundee jute workers represented a significant departure from earlier culinary habits. White bread, tea, margarine and sugar were increasingly used instead of the more traditional – and more nutritional – oatmeal, bone broth, potatoes and suet.[105] Whilst the 'broth pot' remained a common feature in some households, where the wife remained at home, the often heavy nature of work and the long hours of many women jute workers meant that little time or energy was left to oversee the lengthy preparation of wholesome meals, and the convenience foods of the day, such as soup and pies bought from 'cook shops', became a staple for many working class families.[106] But the major reason why the families of jute workers were not able to enjoy an adequate diet had less to do with the inconvenience and lack of time caused by high rates of female participation in the local economy – instead it was fundamentally economic at root. Diets were poor for many families, whether or not wives had time to market and cook properly, and for the lowest paid of the working class the situation was even worse. In 1904, DSU investigators interviewed a sack sewer, with two children, who received 5d or 6d per bundle of sacks, which would be spent on a loaf at 2½d, tea at 1d, and sugar at ½d. The woman managed to avoid paying rent as she was living in a house that had been condemned, but the factor was going to turn her out. The furniture in her small single room consisted of a bed with sacks on it, and a chair and table.[107] That this was not an isolated case was demonstrated in 1911 by the Royal Commission on the Poor Laws and Relief of Distress, which calculated that 30 per cent of children in Dundee subsisted on a 'third class' diet largely made up of tea, 'piece',[108] porridge and the occasional piece of meat or fish, a percentage unequalled by any other Scottish city. Only 11 per cent of Dundee's population enjoyed a first class diet comprising milk, regular meat or fish, vegetables, eggs and pudding.[109]

In effect, the coming of jute dependency and the remaking of the imperial nexus created a race of stunted mill workers in Dundee who bore a closer resemblance to their Indian counterparts than to any comparable group of British male workers. As Table 3.4 demonstrates, while the average weight of a spinner in Bengal was estimated at 107.93 lbs in 1908, it was calculated that Dundee's male textile workers weighed only a little more, at 111.83 lbs.[110] Even more remarkable was the fact that Indian and Scottish textile workers were both lighter in weight than the inmates confined within the walls of the state prison of the United Provinces. Influential members of the Indian Factory Labour Commission were infuriated by the claim, made by Dr Nair who also served on the Commission, that industrial employment in a highly profitable colonial industry may have been worse for physical well being than penal servitude. Nair's calculations

Table 3.4 Average weight of adult males in selected occupations in Dundee, United Provinces and Bengal, 1905–8

Occupation	Average weight (in lbs)
Spinner, United Provinces	107.01
Spinner, Bengal	107.93
Textile worker, Dundee	111.83
Prisoner, United Provinces	115.05
Worker in metals, Dundee	121.81
General labourer, Dundee	130.77

Source: For Dundee figures see David Lennox, 'Working Class Life in Dundee, 1878–1905', St Andrews University, Ph.D. thesis, (n.d., probably 1906), Table 13, Measurement of Men of Artisan Classes Born in Dundee. For Indian figures see Indian Factory Labour Commission 1908, *Report and Appendices*, London, 1909, 'Minute of Dissent by Dr T. M. Nair'.

were dismissed on the grounds that 'every Jail Superintendent makes it a point to feed up and fatten the prisoners under his charge', to which Nair sarcastically replied, 'I know that that is a procedure adopted at many sanatoria for the treatment of consumption. I did not know that Indian prisons were run on the Nordach system.'[111] In a further withering riposte, Nair concluded 'that these figures justify the remark of Mr Bezanji in his evidence before this Commission that "those accustomed to mill life regard it as worse than jail life." '[112] Many of Dundee's jute workers would no doubt have been stunned to learn that they too may have benefited from a period of fattening up in an Indian prison.

While young male workers in the Dundee jute industry could earn good wages for a few years, the DSU *Report* noted that 'the youth who has passed some years in the mill often finds himself at 17 or 18 without occupation, and with no trade or other skilled employment available. He either leaves the city, becomes an unskilled labourer, or develops into a loafer.'[113] Faced with few employment opportunities, many unskilled and semi-skilled male workers took the option of flight from Juteopolis. When a group of Dundee jute workers was transferred to Barrow-in-Furness in the early years of the twentieth century, the northern English town became a 'sort of vestibule through which the young Dundonian passed to the outer world.'[114] Other longer-distance links were created following the establishment of jute manufacturing in the USA. From the mid nineteenth century up to the early years of the twentieth century, increasing numbers of jute workers and their families from Dundee and its hinterland made the Atlantic crossing in search of better prospects, particularly during periods of local trade depression. Many stayed on permanently, but some, including the great grandparents of the writer, returned when economic conditions or personal circumstances improved.[115]

Some of the unskilled male workers who remained in Juteopolis opted for a way of living that flew in the face of middle class – and upper working class – notions of respectability. Long hours of work and low rates of pay often gave way to no pay and long days in pursuit of work or free entertainment. We can quantify the physical toll, measured in pounds and inches, that poverty and lack of work took on the male working class of Dundee, but what about the impact on the mental outlook of those to whom security of employment and decent wages were a pipe-dream? The pressures of low pay, frequent unemployment and over-crowded living conditions took their toll, not only on the physique of many men, but also on their manners and on their sense of themselves. For those at the bottom of a civil society that not only valued but demanded hard work and respectability, the sustained effort required just to get by was often too much. It was often easy, for many living under these circumstances, to give way to fatalism, political apathy, alcoholism and ultimately brutalisation.

A patriarchal culture that underlined the duty and responsibility of the male breadwinner combined with limited economic opportunities for a substantial section of the adult male population to create a massive gulf between the ideal of the male headed family and the ability of many male workers to realise this ideal. The result was outbursts of sometimes ferocious savagery, and levels of

alcoholism and casual violence that resisted all punitive efforts aimed at controlling and limiting such behaviour. With no stake in the system, and with the constant threat of de-proletarianisation, some from the ranks of the male labouring
poor sunk into lumpen forms of behaviour that were indeed animal-like, but
which had palpable social and material roots.

Oary Dundee

Poverty may have induced feelings of pity in some observers and of contempt in
others – and the coarse speech and conduct of the poor may have appalled the
respectable – but it was the violence of the labouring poor that brought the most
extreme reactions from the middle classes. It was from the ranks of the labouring
class that were drawn the drunkards who turned Dundee's streets into battlefields
on Saturday nights and during holidays. The middle classes' fear of, and revul-
sion for, the lower classes of Juteopolis was often bolstered by personal experience. Bruce Lockhart, the British secret agent and author, whilst a boy in Dundee
in the late 1890s, was in the habit of accompanying the assistant master of his
private school on Saturday shooting expeditions up the Tay river. On their way
back to Broughty Ferry from these expeditions the pair often had to pass through
Dock Street, the main red light area situated, as the street name implies, near to
the city's docks:

> in which every second door opened into a public house. 'Drunks' of both
> sexes encumbered the pavement. Brawls were frequent, and on one occasion
> we had to make a wide detour to avoid a bottle fight. Beneath the yellow
> light of the street lamp I saw a man fall, his head smashed open by a broken
> bottle. His opponents were kicking him. I should have liked to rush in to
> stop this brutality, but my knees knocked with fear. And, indeed, to a small
> boy the crash of broken glass, the pools of blood lying on the pavement, and
> the vision of the pale, sodden faces of the men and women, more like
> animals than human beings, were terrifying enough.[116]

This passage by Lockhart is valuable, not only for its descriptive value, but also
because of the sense of horror that it conveys on the part of an impressionable
middle-class schoolboy. And, this sense of horror at the animal-like behaviour
of the lowest layers of the city's population also served as a formidable weapon
in the armoury of those who argued that it was not social conditions that gave
rise to such outbursts of casual violence, but lax morals. An official discourse
was created, devised by employers, policemen, local civil servants and church
groups, which characterised the mill hands as inherently predisposed to violence, thus encouraging the perpetuation of punitive action against the urban
working poor. Returns showing the occupations of persons convicted for breach
of the peace in Dundee between 1 October and 6 November 1903 showed that
31 of the accused, out of a total of 105, were labourers and 41 were mill
workers.[117]

Victorian Dundee became honeycombed by a myriad of voluntary associations, charitable institutions, religious groups and social clubs, almost all of which viewed the majority of the city's population as little more than objects of pity, scorn or admonition, and certainly not as potential members or meaningful participants of civil society. Not surprisingly, given the limits imposed on free time by the long working day, the physical nature of the work and low educational levels, the vast majority of the industry's workforce played little part in what was essentially a middle class dominated civic life. Although working and living conditions were grim for many caught within the comfortless folds of jute dependency, there was another side to the society spawned by jute and the developing imperial nexus. Juteopolis inherited, and developed, a vibrant oral culture from the rural areas of origin of the different streams of immigrants who came to labour in its low mills, spinning mills and weaving sheds. The Angus hinterland, the Highlands and Ulster contributed towards this developing *Oary* culture. Song had long been important for the rural labouring population of these different areas. During Edmund Burt's travels in the Scottish Highlands during the 1720s he observed that:

> where there are any number of women employed in harvest work, they all keep time together, by several barbarous tones of the voice; and stoop and rise together, as regularly as a rank of soldiers, when they ground their arms. Sometimes they are incited to their work by the sound of a bagpipe; and by either of these, they proceed with great alacrity, it being disgraceful for any one to be out of time with the sickle. They use the same tone, or piper, when they thicken the new-woven plaiding, instead of a fulling mill.[118]

From the 1830s these, and many other, work songs accompanied the women who came, in increasing numbers, to carry out harvest work in the Scottish lowlands. Alongside these seasonal migrations, other flows of a more permanent character moved towards Dundee and other Scottish textile centres from increasingly destitute parishes in the Scottish Highlands and islands.[119] On their arrival in Dundee, the migrants encountered an already rich urban culture of work and leisure songs, leavened by high literacy levels, particularly amongst artisan labour, which, by the 1840s, helped produce a veritable 'Republic of Letters'.[120] Every Saturday evening, Dundee's leading weaver-poets would meet in the dingy workshop of James Gow, whose 'four posts of misery' was located in the dark, dirty and dismal environs of Long Wynd in the town centre. This emerging literary circle included William Thom, the 'Bard of Inverurie', who would capture national attention for his poetic efforts. Other luminaries included James Myles, and John Mitchell who fled the country as a result of his political activities during the so-called 'Pilgrimage of Folly'.[121] The rise of the woeful cult of McGonagall has, though, overshadowed the accomplishments of Dundee's 'Republic of Letters', which is now all but forgotten in the popular mind.

The decline of the handloom weavers not only removed an important organising centre for the emerging working class of Dundee, it also hastened the decline

of the 'Republic of Letters'. By the late nineteenth century, Dundee was synonymous with Gradgrind Calvinism and low overall levels of literacy.[122] This is
demonstrated by the fact that, although they were the single largest grouping of
male workers in Dundee, textile workers, including overseers, comprised only
18 per cent of readers in the Dundee Free Library in 1885–6. However, during
the same period, power loom weavers comprised 30 per cent of all female
readers, which strongly suggests that they shared, at least to some extent, the
same inclination for bookishness exhibited by their male counterparts in handloom weaving during the genesis of jute dependency.[123]

By the late nineteenth century, the radical literature of the 'Republic of
Letters' had been replaced by pale *kailyard*[124] imitations churned out by local
magazines and newspapers such as the *People's Journal* and *Dundee Advertiser*,
which exemplified just how far the popular literary culture of Dundee had fallen
from the mid-nineteenth century achievements of poets such as William Thom.
Outside the small, self-regarding, literary circles of Juteopolis, however, a
popular oral and musical culture was forged in the low mills and the factories.
We thus see the development of a cultural interface between the vibrant rural
and semi-rural ballad tradition of the north-east coast of Scotland and the traditions and culture of other immigrant groups. The migrants who came from
Ireland, Angus and the Highlands brought with them their own traditions of
story-telling and song. In Dundee they melded together and were transformed
into a distinctive Scottish urban working class culture.[125]

This is demonstrated in the case of Mary Brooksbank, who was born 'on a
raw-cold winter's day' on 15 December 1897 in Shiprow in Aberdeen, 'one of
the worst slums in the city.'[126] Her mother was 'a fisher lassie ... when she
wasn't being a domestic servant' and her father's family came from the parish of
St Vigeans, in the Arbroath area, which during the late eighteenth and early
nineteenth centuries was a hand loom weaving centre. Here, the auto-didactic
artisan tradition drew on the much longer-lived north-east Scottish ballad tradition. Song and story-telling were therefore a central part of Mary's inherited
culture. She was blind for the first four years of her life and received very little
education. At the age of eight, her family, which included four brothers, moved
to Dundee to seek work. At 11 she started work, illegally, as a shifter before
being discovered and sacked, but she returned to the mills shortly afterwards. As
she grew older Mary began to listen, note down and collect the work songs she
heard in the mills, such as *The Dundee Lassie* and *The Strike Song*,[127] before
taking up the pen herself, particularly following her retirement when she produced many powerful and moving poems in the *oary* tongue.[128] It would be
migrants like Mary Brooksbank, shaped by the ballad traditions of rural Angus
and the fishing communities of the north-east coast, as well as others from the
Scottish Highlands and Ireland, who would develop and forge the *oary* culture
that emerged out of the low mills and tenements of Juteopolis.[129]

The *oary* tongue became the working class voice of Juteopolis, a distinctive
form of Scots that is still widely spoken in the city's housing 'schemes' that hug
the outer fringes of old Juteopolis. It is widely believed, by ordinary Dundonians

as well as by academics, that the *oary* tongue evolved out of the hubbub and noise of the city's mills, re-shaping the conventional Scots affirmative 'aye' into the Dundonian vowel sound 'eh'. The distinctive sound this produced within the city's evolving working class language is well illustrated in the hard bitten 'traditional' song, *Eh'll Awa' Hame*, which also reveals the way in which families were dislocated and the violent reality that attended generational conflict in Juteopolis:

> Eh'll no' bide wi' ma Granny nae mair,
> Eh'll no' bide wi' ma Granny nae mair,
> She skelps ma face an' she pulls a' mi hair,
> An Eh'll no' bide wi' ma Granny nae mair,
> Eh'll awa hame tae mi Mither ah will,
> Eh'll awa hame tae mi Mither ah will,
> She keeps a wee shop at the tap o' the hull,[130]
> An' she sells a wee drappy at sixpence a shot.[131]

Music and song was also a way in which the talented, and not so talented, performer could earn extra money in order to eke out low wages, or the miserable pittance provided by parish relief payments, and their numbers increased dramatically following the First World War, augmented by many disabled veterans, 'some displaying a card stating this, others wearing medals or ribbons; one having his medals set in a frame in his hurdy-gurdy'.[132] The street was a major focus of entertainment, and buskers would also regularly patrol the 'backies' of the tenements and serenade audiences from the 'pletties'. The public house, or pub, and the drink that it provided, was another major medium through which Dundee's *Oary* culture was forged and transmitted. It was where singers and story tellers could succeed, at least for a brief moment, in taking the minds of their audiences away from the cares and worries of the day. The pub also played the role of social club and friendly society, as well as providing opportunities for networking and information on job vacancies in the absence of employment bureaus. The importance of women's work, and the wages they earned, to the local economy meant that the Dundee pub was not a wholly masculine space, although this applied more to pubs at the lower end of the scale. Dundee pubs, as elsewhere, did not conform to one type: there was a major difference between 'Mennies' bar in the Perth road, with its inlaid mahogany fittings, and its clientele of skilled tradesmen, clerks and small business people and the 'John O' Groats' pub frequented by the unskilled and the unemployed. Indeed, many of the meaner sort of Dundee's pubs were little more than basic drinking dens, serving cut price liquor that could ease the path towards oblivion for the more desperate. Bob Stewart, who sold newspapers as a boy, described these drinking dens as 'evil, smelly places', characterised by the 'stench of beer, the sawdust on the floor, the spittoons and the salt fish the publican kept on the counter because it gave the customers a thirst when they chewed it.'[133]

While it was frowned upon for the non-working wives of the 'better sort' of tradesman to be seen in the pub, the working women of Juteopolis could hold their own with the men at the bar as well as on the shop-floor. In fact, women mill workers were amongst the most resolute recidivists when it came to petty crimes such as 'behaving while drunk in a disorderly and riotous manner'. Dundee pioneered a surveillance scheme, whereby the local police authorities kept detailed records, including photographs, of those convicted more than three times under the terms of the Inebriates Act 1898, which were circulated to all licensed premises in Dundee.[134] Table 3.5 is an example from 1905.

A total of 30 out of 41 convictions involved workers within the jute industry, of which 27 were women workers. Of the eight convictions for 'behaving while drunk in a riotous or disorderly manner', seven belonged to women mill workers, including Mary Devannah, whilst the sole man convicted of this charge was John George who was employed as a mechanic in the Bank Street Works.[135] The precarious position of many of the women is underlined by the fact that 10 of the 34 were staying in lodging houses, with one staying at the East Poor House at the time of conviction, while seven were also unemployed. These women seemed to constitute a group whose lives were in the process of unravelling due to the influence of alcohol, poverty and personal misfortune. As they stared into the camera at police headquarters, some, judging by their demeanour, must have known that the abyss beckoned them.

Dundee had more pubs per head of population than Glasgow, but the city consistently had a lower rate of convictions for drunkenness during the period

Table 3.5 Likeness and description of person referred to in Dundee Police Notices, April 1905 to January 1906

Register No. 24	
Date of Registration	29th Day of July 1905
Name and Alias	Mary Devannah
Residence	208 Seagate
Where Employed	Victoria Works, Scouringburn
Age	16 years
Height	5ft. ½in.
Build	Proportionate
Complexion	Fresh
Hair	Brown
Eyes	Grey
Peculiarities or marks	M.N., C.B., Tombstone. & c., left forearm; Heart back of r/h
Occupation	Millworker
Date and Nature of Last Conviction	29 June, 1905 – Contravention of Sect 70(1) of the "Licensing (Scotland) Act, 1903." – Behaving while drunk in a riotous or disorderly manner. Court at which Convicted – Police Court, Dundee.

Source: City & Royal Burgh of Dundee, Licensing (Scotland) Act, 1903, Printed Notices circulated in Police District, Notices from 10 April 1905 to January 1906.

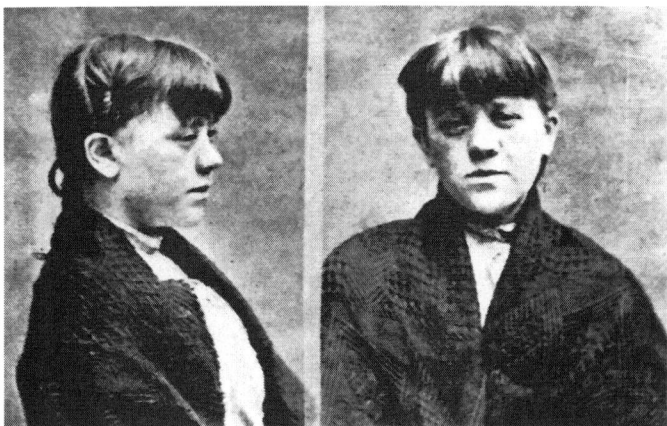

Figure 3.1 The public notice referring to Dundee mill worker Mary Devannah, charged under the Inebriates Act during 1905, gave her age as 16, and her height as 5ft ½in. With permission of Dundee City Archives.

1861–1901, while the rate more than doubled in both centres during this period, in stark contrast to Edinburgh where a sporadic downward trend in the numbers of convictions was experienced.[136] The DSU *Report* revealed 'that the death rate in Dundee was 0.086 per 1,000 of population for the year 1902 ... The corresponding percentage for the whole of Scotland was 0.069 ... [while] 1.2 per cent of the population [of Dundee] were apprehended for drunkenness.'[137] Part of the explanation for the increase in conviction rates may well lie in Bob Stewart's observation that Dundee's reputation as a 'town of drunkards ... really arose from the impoverished lives of the people. They were so poorly fed that a couple of nips of whisky and pint of beer was enough to send them into a drunken stupor',[138] an observation equally applicable to Glasgow where speed-ups, retrenchment, and endemic underemployment also affected an industrial workforce struggling in the face of rising foreign competition and volatile export markets.

An especially interesting feature of the printed notices circulated by Dundee's police authorities is the light they shine on the common practice of tattooing amongst the women of the urban poor, with 17 of the 34 women sporting tattoos including 11 mill workers and three spinners. Most tattoos were initials, probably referring to family relations and sweethearts and were sported by older as well as younger women. Bridget Glancey, a 60-year-old mill worker at the Manhattan works, as well as having a broken nose, sported a blue mark on her brow and the initials E. G. on her left forearm.[139] In 1912, David Lennox also observed that 'tattooing is a common habit in Angus and neighbourhood', and suggested that the practice was a cultural survival from the area's Pictish past, noting that in 'Angus and its neighbourhood ... prehistoric "standing" or "hir-stones" are called "pech-stanes."'[140] The word 'pech' is a local rendering of the term Pict, which derived from the 'Latin "painteds", a Roman nickname arising from an actual tendency amongst the northern peoples to apply pigment to their skin.'[141] However, it is more likely that the practice of tattooing in Dundee was of more recent origin. From the late eighteenth century onwards, the town's seafarers became familiar with increasingly far-flung cultures and this may well have been the route through which tattooing came to be adopted in Dundee. The burgeoning trade with Bengal may well have brought the seamen of the town's clippers into contact with groups such as the women of Banjera in East Bengal, who tattooed their skin 'in such a manner to appear as though the skin was a flowered fabric', while the absence of tattoos on the thighs of young Burmese men was deemed to be emasculating.[142] International connections such as these may well serve as an explanation for the existence of tattooing in and around late Victorian Dundee, but tattooing amongst the women of the area is rarely, if ever, mentioned. Tattoos did enjoy a brief vogue amongst the British aristocracy, following the visit of the Prince of Wales to Palestine in 1862, when he had the Jerusalem cross tattooed on his arm. However, by the early 1900s elite attitudes had shifted.[143] For many amongst the middle class a tattoo, if noticed at all, would have signified the alien and criminal character of its bearer. Havelock Ellis noted in 1890, drawing on research conducted at Derby prison, that of 555 inmates only 41 (including one woman) sported tattoos, comprising 'chiefly soldiers, with a few miners and sailors.'[144] This low incidence of tattooing, and its apparent absence within occupational groupings other than those mentioned by Ellis, marks the Dundee sample as highly unusual. Not only was tattooing practised widely within a female occupational grouping, it was also of long standing, as suggested by the fact that older women such as Bridget Glancey sported them. This is further borne out by the sophisticated nature of some of the Dundee women's tattoos, indicating that they were not self-administered and that tattooing was common, and long standing, enough to have encouraged the development of specialised skills.[145] There were designs that appeared to be common to both men and women (five of the seven men sported tattoos), including spiders' webs, which appeared on the back of the hand between the thumb and forefinger, along with depictions of anchors and bracelets around the wrist. Two of the women mill workers also sported a highly distinctive tattoo, an enigmatic combination, comprising a heart visible on the back of the right hand along with a tombstone on the left forearm. The exact meaning and significance of this design is elusive, but it serves as a potent symbol of the fragility of life, and love, within the often unforgiving milieu of Juteopolis.

Although widespread poverty and appalling social conditions became a hallmark of Juteopolis, the remaking of the imperial nexus also paved the way for the creation of a working class that was relatively unburdened by gender and generational divisions. Chapter 4 will examine how the mill-girls, half-timers and male mill hands of Juteopolis were able to forge a culture of resistance to the rule of the jute barons, which ensured Dundee's emergence as a major Scottish storm centre of working class socialism during the first two decades of the twentieth century.

4 Working class militancy and labour politics in Juteopolis, 1885–1923

> In the second month of 1888 I removed into the city of Dundee, and very soon I became aware of a new spirit hovering over the people. The signs were [there] to those who could read them, and I found myself, without being able to explain how it came about, ranged on the side of the new time.
>
> (David Lowe, *Souvenirs of Scottish Labour*)[1]

David Lowe's arrival in Dundee coincided with an up-surge in local strike activity, trade union organisation, and the re-emergence of revolutionary socialist politics. His belief that 'a new spirit [was] hovering over the people' also echoed the growing optimism of a growing band of socialist activists who, like Lowe, were 'ranged on the side of the new time'; but this task of transformation was by no means a foregone conclusion. Electoral politics in Victorian Scotland was very much an elite pastime. Even with the coming of the Third Reform Act of 1884, which created an electorate encompassing 57 per cent of the Scottish adult male population, many working class men were still excluded as a result of the prohibition against transient workers, lodgers and those receiving poor relief. Dundee, with a population comprising substantial numbers of, often itinerant, Irish and Scots labourers and mill workers had the smallest electorate amongst the four Scottish cities with only 39 per cent of adult males eligible to vote: followed by Glasgow with 42 per cent, Edinburgh/Leith with 51 per cent and Aberdeen with 65 per cent.[2] At the municipal level, the situation was little better, with fewer than half of men and around one in 12 of women in Dundee being eligible to vote.[3] Up until the early 1900s, Dundee Council chamber was controlled by small business interests, and seats were often filled, without the need for an election, by shopkeepers and publicans, leading to frequent press complaints that dealers 'in whisky, property speculators and such like should be kept out of the Council by all means. They are there for their own interests and not for the interests of the ratepayers'.[4]

Despite the 'new spirit' observed by Lowe, it seemed as though the majority of Dundee's working population had little interest in, or indeed use for, formal politics, and it would not be until 1918 that the female workers of the jute industry played any kind of meaningful role in electoral politics, when all women over the age of 30 were enfranchised. Even then, a large proportion of jute workers, of both sexes, still remained outside the electoral process until the franchise was further widened in 1929 to embrace all adults above the age of 21. Those who did have the vote turned Victorian Dundee into a stronghold for the Liberal Party, which appealed to the leading textile dynasties, such as the Baxter and Grimond families, as well as to businessmen, clerks and skilled workers within shipyards, engineering factories and jute mills. Indeed, such was its hold that Winston Churchill gladly accepted the offer to become a Liberal candidate in 1908 for what he presumptuously thought would be a 'seat for life'. Liberal hegemony in Dundee would, however, be increasingly challenged by the rise of independent working class politics. We saw in Chapter 1 how the 1870s witnessed a growing national movement towards trade union organisation, which culminated in parliamentary legislation around working hours and limited legal protection for trade unions. This up-turn in labour activism was part of a wider labour revival in countries such as France, Germany and Italy that had been growing since the early 1860s, which included the formation of the International Working Men's Association (IWMA) – or First International in which Marx and Engels played a leading role – in 1864. The development of the Paris Commune in 1870–1 fanned further interest in socialist ideas and in the status and profile of the First International – despite the limited involvement of its activists in the Paris events – demonstrated perhaps with the establishment of a branch of the IWMA in Dundee during the early 1870s.[5]

The process of working class radicalisation in Dundee continued into the 1880s, with a growing demand by labour and trade union activists for independent working class parliamentary representation.[6] Although many trade unionists, including leading elements in the Trades Council, were firm Liberals, increasing numbers of educated working men were also becoming convinced of the need for meaningful independent working class representation. The early 1880s saw the emergence of the Social Democratic Federation (SDF), which, though small and overly dominated by its jingoistic founder, H. M. Hyndman, successfully nurtured a generation of working class revolutionaries and played a significant role in the founding of the Labour Party.[7] James Duncan, a calenderer who conducted regular outdoor meetings, was an early member of the Dundee SDF and one of a small group of activists who developed a notable position for the party within the city's political street culture during the 1880s.

The SDF was not the only socialist party in Dundee during this time: Desmond Greaves records that James Connolly joined the Socialist Labour League (SLL) in 1889 during his brief working sojourn in Juteopolis.[8] While socialist party politics in Dundee was a minority pursuit, there were also a number of independent socialists, including street vendors, shop-keepers and pub landlords, some of whom had been pushed towards small-scale entrepreneurialism as a result of black-listing. The barber shop of David Fawns, on the south side of the Scouringburn, was 'the rendezvous of Radical thinkers, both in religion and economics', including a handful of socialists and 'Irishmen of the most militant kind' who 'denounced the Government and the "*Times*"'.[9] The major issues of the day were hotly discussed and debated amidst the steady click of scissors and the smell of hair tonic, and anger was raised by the 'milk and water' attitude of the Liberal Party towards Irish home rule: an issue that led to the eruption of major divisions inside the Liberal Party in 1886.

By the late 1880s, the SDF had two Dundee branches, while sales of the party newspaper, *Justice*, were organised through the network of paperboys who plied their trade in the pubs and streets of the city centre, and who received a small commission on every newspaper sold. In the context of rising strike action throughout the city, the SDF party office in the Overgate was a hive of activity as groups of unskilled workers visited to receive advice and encouragement with strike activity and the formation of trade unions.[10] In March 1889, the Dundee SDF came to national prominence when they conducted a campaign against the attempts by local magistrates to ban street meetings. The agitation, which was led by a tailor and a well-known local SDF activist, James Robertson, culminated in a mass street meeting attended by up to 15,000 'curious onlookers', and socialists drafted in from all over the country. Robertson was subsequently obliged to 'find caution to the extent of £10 not to break the criminal law again for six months', but the ban on street meetings was lifted and the local SDF gained a fair amount of notoriety for its determination to challenge Dundee's magistrates.[11] According to William Walker, the Dundee SDF was a 'tiny' and ineffectual presence, and their victory around the issue of free speech was 'not an episode in the class war so much as an interval of street circus' with little more than 'entertainment value'.[12] He continues, that 'it is perfectly impossible to reconcile [Desmond Greaves'] account of socialist courage in the face of persecution with the story told' by the newspapers. It is odd that Walker should take the local newspaper reports at face value, particularly when he admits elsewhere that the Liberal *Advertiser* and Tory *Courier* habitually portrayed socialism as respectively 'lunatic and amusing' and 'dangerous and disreputable'. Walker also seems ignorant of the more balanced account provided by David Lowe, who was an active participant in the SDF demonstration.[13]

In the circumstance of the time, with a major up-turn in strikes, trade union formation and a growing restlessness over the lack of working class political representation, the emergence of a party such as the SDF, despite its small size, was a development filled with potentially ominous consequences for the local elites. Not since the heady days of Chartism had Dundee's streets echoed with such passionate denunciations of Gradgrind capitalism; and the punitive attitude of local magistrates, as well as the dismissive and contemptuous press reports, signalled a gathering determination on the part of sections of the local elite to nip the socialist threat in the bud.

During the 1890s the SDF was joined by the Independent Labour Party (ILP), as the influence of socialist ideas continued to grow. During this pioneering period, socialist politics comprised 'a camp in which there were many tents', with activists often flitting between different parties and belonging to more than one at any given time.[14] There were, though, also increasing attempts to bring Dundee's different socialist groups together on the issue of fielding an independent working class parliamentary candidate, culminating in the establishment of a local Labour Representation Committee (LRC) in the early 1890s (comprising socialists drawn from the SDF, ILP and trade unions).[15] In 1895, the LRC rallied behind the candidature of James MacDonald, a member of the SDF who was standing as a Labour candidate in Dundee for the second time following the 354 votes he had gathered at the 1892 election. MacDonald's stump speeches drew large and enthusiastic audiences, and his vote of 1,313 was respectable, if not spectacular, compared to the 7,602 and 7,592 votes won by the successful Liberal candidates Edmund Robertson and John Leng respectively.

Dundee's infant Labour Party would, however, make a major breakthrough with Alexander Wilkie's election at the 1906 general election. Wilkie was one of two Labour MPs elected in Scotland, the other being George Barnes, a Dundee-born engineer who was elected from Glasgow Blackfriars. Wilkie had earlier sought the Liberal nomination for Dundee, but was rejected in favour of H. Robson, an ageing London-based stockbroker.[16] Despite his rejection by the Dundee Liberal Association, Wilkie personified the type of respectable and moderate trade unionist that had been a bulwark of working class Liberalism since the dawn of *Pax Britannica*. In February 1900, Wilkie and James MacDonald clashed at the inaugural meeting of the Labour Representation Committee (LRC) in London, when MacDonald moved a resolution demanding that working class MP's should form a distinct party based upon a recognition of class war and having as its object the socialisation of the economy. Wilkie countered with an amendment demanding that Labour Party MPs should be allowed a free hand in deciding upon policy and that they should be free to ally themselves with other parties: Wilkie's amendment won.[17] Wilkie and MacDonald exemplified the two major trends within Dundee's early labour movement: one a pragmatic, moderate approach that embraced 'the politics of the possible', and the other a more militant strain that, at least at the level of rhetoric, looked towards radical socio-economic transformation. There were, though, other socialist groups and parties in Dundee that looked to capture the attention of the working class.

The rise of socialist millenarianism and the re-making of the imperial nexus

The belching mill chimney is often seen as the architectural feature that defined the skyline, as well as the economy, of Juteopolis, but it vied for dominance with the steeple spire. Thirty new churches, belonging to the Church of Scotland, the Free Church, as well as the Catholic and Episcopalian churches were built between 1836 and 1900.[18] Although a city of many churches, Dundee was marked by declining rates of church attendance, in common with the other major Scottish urban centres, during the late nineteenth century. In 1851, nearly 27 per cent of Dundonians attended a morning and afternoon service, but by 1881 the percentage had fallen to 22 per cent and by 1891 it was 15 per cent.[19] Catholic attendance was higher, reflecting its importance in providing welfare services to incoming streams of Irish immigrants, and the role of religion in maintaining

Irish identity and links with the 'auld country'. Irish unity of purpose, as William Walker suggests, was also 'directly turned to working class account in the field of industrial militancy.'[20] In effect, the structural diversity of Dundee's emerging working class was accompanied and complemented by strong cultural continuities that were re-shaped by the development of modern industrial society: a process that, as we saw in Chapter 2, was also evident in Calcutta.

Despite the greater religiosity of Catholic Irish workers, the period of study was marked by mounting concerns regarding the lax religious observance of mill workers. Given the penchant of mill owners, managers and foremen for religiosity, and their heavy involvement in church affairs, it should come as no surprise that many jute workers traded time at church on a Sunday morning for the opportunity to have a 'lie in', and recover from the exertions of the working week. While the mill girls may have blanched at the attentions of the established churches, less mainstream Christian temperance groups, such as the Rechabites and the Band of Hope, did succeed in attracting their support.[21] Within the fast-developing industrial society of nineteenth century Dundee, such groups provided not just spiritual comfort but support of a much more material kind in the absence of any ameliorative efforts on the part of the local authorities and elites who oversaw the destruction of the old forms of domestic industry and the support networks that were associated with the immediate pre-industrial period. They also provided a critique of the new society created by gathering jute dependency, which, though it lacked any political perspective, denounced the sin of mammon without fear or favour by revealing the hypocrisy of local elites who lectured the urban poor on the importance of respectability, sobriety and industry. In the absence of an effective labour movement, following the precipitate decline of Chartism from the late 1840s, they were often the only voices questioning and challenging the new world order brought into being by the 'invisible hand of the market'. Radical temperance and popular Christian groups such as the Band of Hope, the Rechabites, and later the Independent Order of Good Templars (IOGT), stood separate and apart from the mainstream Presbyterianism favoured by Dundee's elites and middle classes. These groups, also became an important influence in the development of a socialist party that melded religious and political radicalism, and which captured the imagination, and support, of many mill workers from the early years of the twentieth century through to the nineteen thirties.[22]

Although the Scottish Prohibitionist Party (SPP) emerged alongside the infant Labour Party in the early 1900s, its roots lay in another world, separate and distinct from official labourism. In fact, the SPP was less a political party and more a religious/social movement, which owed its strength to what William Walker described as 'a raw, emotional Christianity heavily overlaid with apocalyptic and ... millenarian yearning.'[23] Edwin 'Neddy' Scrymgeour, the founder and charismatic leader of the SPP, was the son of James Scrymgeour who moved to Dundee from Kirriemuir in 1840.[24] James had been a chartist but on 'coming to Dundee, and getting acquainted with the dangerous classes, and having studied the drifts and currents in the lower strata of society, Mr Scrymgeour became afraid of radicalism.'[25] James became a leading figure within the Band of Hope in Dundee as well as being one of the first members of IOGT in the town, following its introduction from the United States in 1869.[26] While Neddie Scrymgeour's political philosophy was shaped by his family background, his attitude towards political radicalism was in stark contrast to that of his father. J. D. Kemp has commented that 'Edwin Scrymgeour wanted to abolish capitalism rather than encourage capitalists to become more philanthropic', and while his father found that his temperance work opened doors to paid work and patronage from upper class supporters 'Edwin's more threatening attacks on the system of which drink was a part had the opposite effect.'[27]

Neddie Scrymgeour's involvement in socialist prohibitionism came via the ILP, which he joined some time during the early 1890s. In 1895, he was one of two ILP councillors elected to Dundee Parish Council, but he became increasingly disillusioned with the party's reluctance to address the issue of alcoholism, and in 1901 took the step of forming the SPP. Many, if not most, of the new party's founding members were drawn from the IOGT and the Rechabites. SPP meetings were modelled on those of the IOGT, involving Masonic style rituals that were followed at all meetings as well as separate ceremonies for the induction of new members.[28] Meetings were opened with a prayer by the 'branch Chaplain', which was then followed by a lengthy set speech by the branch President underlining the importance of prohibition in abolishing the 'poverty, crime and misery under which society groans.'[29] The SPP enjoyed a close relationship with the IOGT in its early years, but Scrymgeour's strident stance on the issue of prohibition led to increasing tensions, and in 1904 membership of the SPP was made inconsistent with membership of the IOGT, leading to the expulsion of hundreds of members, many of whom promptly joined the SPP.[30] In 1905, there were three Dundee branches of the SPP and nine in Scotland as a whole.[31] By 1911, the SPP had established 18 Scottish branches, but, despite its growing national spread, Dundee continued to be the heartland of the party.

The SPP's leading members and prospective candidates were drawn from amongst skilled workers and the lower middle classes, but the party's appeal was much broader. The antics of the SPP were closely followed by Dundee's mill girls, an appeal attributed to their notorious faddism. Through often rowdy, and always entertaining, street meetings, Scrymgeour and the SPP appealed to Dundee's urban poor in a language that chimed with their lived reality. In stark contrast to Labour and ILP spokesmen, Scrymgeour never stooped to moral sermonising, or attempted to prove his fitness for office by underlining his respectability. Instead he hunted down exemplars of corruption and hypocrisy and called for a thoroughgoing social change that amounted to a veritable 'cleansing of the Augean stables'. In the process his rhetoric often became transformed into a barely concealed form of socialist millenarianism. In a typical outburst in 1912, he thundered against the

> blasphemous organized cannibalism ... insolently defended by cowardice within the Houses of Parliament, alleged houses of God, municipal

chambers, Trades Unions, or at the ballot box [that was] sufficient to warrant a ravagery [*sic*] ... of the whole Vanity Fair as a going concern.[32]

While the large majority of jute mill girls were not church going, the mix of populist politics, public stunts and Biblical prophecy appealed to their more anarchic instincts. The emerging *Oary* culture defined itself by what it was not, as much as what it actually amounted to, meaning that millenarian radicalism and the jute worker were made for one another. They were both seen as marginal, anachronistic and even as ridiculous by their well-heeled betters.

Despite its title, the SSP was never a party that focused solely on the 'drink question'. Although members were required to renounce alcohol, the party extolled a wide-ranging socialist programme, including Scottish home rule, which was almost identical to the programme of the ILP. The SPP, however, went much further in their denunciations of jute dependency than any of their competitors on the left, to the extent that Scrymgeour often had to fend off criticism from irate SPP members that the party devoted too little attention to prohibition and more to socialist rhetoric.[33] The SPP strongly resembled the Labour Church movement founded in Manchester in 1891 by John Trevor, a lower middle-class former Baptist who embraced deism in the 1880s. According to Eric Hobsbawm, the theology of Trevor's Labour Church was difficult to describe because 'it hardly existed.'[34] For Hobsbawm, the chief function of this 'odd movement' 'was to lubricate the passage of Northern [English] workers from Liberal Radicalism to an Independent Labour Party, and having done this it disappeared.'[35] By the end of the nineteenth century, the Labour Church had collapsed into the ILP, which itself always retained 'a whiff of the dissenting chapel in its oratory.'[36] In stark contrast, millenarian socialism in Dundee would retain its mass influence into the 1930s.

In his seminal study, *Juteopolis*, William Walker used the example of the SPP as a stick to batter Eric Hobsbawm's stages theory of historical development. In taking Hobsbawm to task, William Walker pointed out that the

> Prohibitionists ... were more truly a sect in that they resisted assimilation into the broader ranks of the Labour Movement. Nor was the Prohibition Party a precursor of official Labour but a contemporary with it and at times an enemy of it.[37]

Even more unusually, the SPP combined elements of both the labour sect and the millenarian movement;

> Whilst he acknowledged that there is 'no *a priori* reason why they [millenarian movements] should not be urban', and 'no *a priori* reason why religious labour movements should not be revolutionary', Professor Hobsbawm is clearly sceptical of finding what he admits to be theoretically possible.[38]

This underlines the danger of attaching too much importance to the flawed teleology of development inherent within the 'stages theory' of history exemplified by Hobsbawm's notion of 'the forward march of Labour', as well as the equally flawed Whig/liberal view of historical development. While Hobsbawm dismisses millenarianism as a historical anachronism in the world of 'mature' industrial capitalism, Neddy Scrymgeour's socialist millenarianism was very much a creation *of* 'mature' industrial capitalism during the 1890s and early 1900s, represented by the emergence of jute dependency and the social and political stresses that came in the wake of the re-making of the imperial nexus of jute.

Although William Walker was justified in taking Hobsbawm to task, his analysis of the evolution and significance of the SPP represents a highly jaundiced view, heavily influenced by the work of Norman Cohn, which locates the SPP in an ideological chain connecting 'the millenarian groups of medieval Europe with the totalitarian movements of the twentieth century.'[39] For Walker, the utopianism of the SPP, while laudable, was misguided and even dangerous, because 'the Prohibitionist Party in the twentieth century shared a psychology which has its parallel in modern atheistic totalitarianism.'[40] However, the real significance of radical Christian millenarianism lay in its role as the 'heart of a heartless world'.[41] Christianity has always been a salve and prop for the poor and powerless, but it has also provided the germ for the development of powerful political forces that have attempted to re-make the world. The attempt by Cohn and Walker to denigrate utopianism by equating it with totalitarianism ignores a fundamental social and historical reality – that the dream of utopia fulfils a primary human need, and this was as true for a mill worker in Edwardian Dundee as it was for a stocking maker in sixteenth century Bohemia.

In stark contrast to William Walker, J. D. Kemp contends that the characterisation of the SPP as millenarian is based 'on some of the more outrageous utterances of Scrymgeour and one or two other party members'.[42] While Kemp contends that 'Scrymgeour's views on religion were not shared by all of the party',[43] it is the case that Scrymgeour cast a long shadow in his Dundee heartland, and for those who attended the party's, often rowdy, street meetings and who voted for them at municipal elections, he personified the SPP, and that personification was millenarian in key regards. Scrymgeour saw the SPP as a collective charged with establishing a Godly republic on earth, not through a piecemeal programme of reform, but through a moral, and political, cleansing that went far beyond a limited concern with municipal and parliamentary politics.

The appeal of millenarianism was rooted not only in religious enthusiasm but also in material distress, feelings of insecurity and of a dread regarding future prospects, or lack of them. For many, caught within the increasingly comfortless folds of jute dependency, it must have seemed that the Apocalypse had arrived, or at the very least that it was on its way, which allows us to re-interrogate Eleanor Gordon's (and others) notion of the so-called fatalism of the mill-girls.[44] If fatalism it was, then it was a radical fatalism psychologically connected to the material reality created by increasing jute dependency and the re-making of the imperial nexus, which brought in its train inherent insecurity, underemployment and awful housing conditions.

Workers' militancy and the growth of trade unions in Juteopolis

In Chapter 3 we saw how the re-making of the imperial nexus led to the increasing recruitment of children and adolescents into the 'home' jute industry, and one of the most striking features of labour relations during this time was the militancy and organisation displayed by the *halflins* of Juteopolis. This was spectacularly demonstrated in 1889 with the eruption of a Dundee school students' strike for shorter hours and fewer lessons, which rapidly engulfed other schools through the deployment of 'flying pickets'. Within five days, the school strike had spread to Broughty Ferry, Forfar, Swansea, Liverpool and the east end of London,[45] giving rise to what can only be described as a moral panic in the Dundee press:

> It has not yet been ascertained through what medium schoolboys received the signal for united action.... Such movements do not spring up spontaneously. They are always evidence of a deep conspiracy against social order.... It is perfectly evident that schoolboys from Land's End to John o'Groats could not without organisation arrange to strike simultaneously. The doom of the Empire must be near at hand if the country is honeycombed ... with secret societies of schoolchildren.[46]

While these fears were dramatically exaggerated, the scale and planning behind the 1889 school strike was quite remarkable, but it would be surpassed in 1911, when Dundee *halflins* again took a leading part in initiating a school students strike that quickly spread nation-wide. These school strikes took place against the background of serious and widespread strikes at the local and national level. For Stephen Humphries:

> The characteristic features of both these major strikes – notably their nation-wide scale, the widespread use of pupil pickets and street marches and demonstrations – were all derived from the practices of the emerging labour movement. Interviews clearly reveal that working class children learned strategies of collective bargaining and resistance from the parent culture and practiced them at moments when they seemed most likely to succeed – moments when the local working class community was locked in industrial conflict.[47]

Dundee's *halflins* needed no 'parent culture' to play the role of school-master, or mistress, to them. Large-scale protest was a regular occurrence within the city's mills and factories, with *halflins* often featuring as leading protagonists, as was demonstrated when a strike by shifters over wages sparked one of the largest industry-wide stoppages of the 1890s. Henry Williamson had unwittingly laid the basis for the strike at a mass meeting on 15 July 1895 by announcing that 'trade intelligence' indicated that the time was ripe for a 10 per cent wage claim. Williamson, however, also urged his audience to avoid strikes 'for as long as

they could' by keeping a tight rein on the 'great many young people … not ame-
nable to reason [who were] able to do a great deal of mischief.'[48] Four days later,
shifters in a number of mills walked out, and by 24 August they had been joined
by 18,000 workers, with another 10,000 locked out as the employers desperately
tried to break the fast-spreading dispute. On 22 August, encouraged by the
decision of Messrs Grimond & Co. to pay a 5 per cent increase, Williamson
announced his support for the strike, but four days later he called for an uncondi-
tional return to work, writing in John Leng's *Dundee Advertiser* that the strikers
should 'frankly admit they were beaten'.[49] The *Advertiser's* lead editorial article
welcomed this volte-face, but pointedly reminded readers that it was Williamson's demand for a 10 per cent wage rise that had sparked the strike in the first
place. The editorial concluded with the heartfelt hope that the suitably chastened
union leader would now realise 'how much more easy to loosen than to recall
are the elements he works with.'[50]

Faced with a spreading lockout and without any means of support, workers
drifted back to their mills and factories, and by early September the jute industry
had returned to normal working. Despite its failure, the strike, through the widespread support shown by adult workers, underlined the crucial importance of
children's wages to many household budgets in Juteopolis. The 1895 strike also
pointed up the limited influence of the self-styled Moses of the mill girls.
Blinded by an overweening sense of his own importance, and the limited success
that had followed the establishment of the MFOU in 1885, Williamson had
found to his cost that he could not turn the militancy of the jute workers on and
off like a tap. He would not be the last labour 'leader' in Dundee, or Calcutta, to
make this mistake.

The 1895 strike gave rise to increasing anger at Williamson's *ma-baap*
approach to labour relations, from both jute workers and Dundee's wider labour
movement. In 1905, the publication of the Dundee Social Union's *Report on
Housing* created a rising interest and sympathy for the jute workers' plight. The
appalling wages and working conditions that were still the norm in the city's
staple trade, in the context of improving trade conditions, not only produced
indignation amongst progressive opinion, but also a response from jute workers
themselves. In February 1906, another strike and lockout brought the jute industry to a standstill, and the prevarications of Williamson on this occasion drew a
rising crescendo of criticism and abuse from ordinary workers. During a strike
meeting Williamson was unceremoniously 'informed' that he did no know 'what
he was bletherin about', while a critic at another meeting observed 'I would like
to see you haudin up a frame'.[51] The dissatisfaction with Williamson's handling
of the dispute and his repeated calls for workers to end the strike also prompted
a delegation of women jute workers to approach Dundee Trades Council for
their support, an initiative that provided the basis for the establishment of an alternative union to the increasingly discredited MFOU. The following month, the
founder and organiser of the National Federation of Women Workers (NFWW),
Mary MacArthur was sent to a snow-bound Dundee charged with forming a new
jute workers' union.[52] Before setting off Mary had confided to close friends that

she was 'thoroughly frightened' by what she might find in Juteopolis, and shortly after her arrival she openly admitted that she 'did not know of any community where textile workers are largely employed, which can in the least compare with the backward state of matters existing in Dundee.'[53] Despite her understandable trepidation, Mary threw herself into activity, alongside the Dundee Social Union, the Women's Trade Union League, and a plethora of socialist activists.

The 1906 strike provided an unprecedented opportunity for Dundee's small revolutionary left to raise its profile. In 1903, the SDF had lost many of its most able and committed activists, with the establishment of the Socialist Labour Party (SLP). The new party, which would be involved in the creation of the British Communist Party in 1920, was founded by leading SDF activists, most notably James Connolly, who had become increasingly disenchanted with Hyndman's jingoism and increasing authoritarianism. The SLP was, though, hamstrung by its small size. In 1912, it had 28 branches, but by 1914 this had dropped to 15, with an active membership of around 300, the majority concentrated in Scotland.[54] In contrast to the increasingly dismissive attitude of the SDF leadership towards industrial struggle, the SLP was deeply influenced by the syndicalist ideas of Daniel De Leon.[55] With little chance of change through parliamentary channels, despite the advances made by the Labour Party, the industrial sphere provided an opportunity for the SLP to overcome their isolation from the wider working class. The new party threw its meagre resources into the jute strike, organising as many as seven meetings a week, addressed by party leaders such as William Paul, and by the end of the dispute a Dundee SLP branch had been successfully established.[56]

The efforts of Dundee's labour and progressive movement, including the SLP, delivered tangible, and far-reaching, results. On 13 March 1906, the Dundee and District Jute and Flax Workers' Union (JFWU) held its inaugural meeting. New members were enrolled at a modest fee of 6d and weekly dues of 2d and 4d; a 25-strong committee was also elected, comprising 15 women and 10 men. The new union started with an initial membership of around 3,000, but within six months this had increased to 4,242. Women outnumbered men by more than 2:1, but this proportion increased following the decision to exclude skilled male workers from membership.[57] The first President of the JFWU was John Sime, an ex-foreman at the massive Bowbridge Works of Grimond Brothers who had been sacked for his trade union activities. In December 1907, he was appointed as the union's full-time secretary, for which he was paid the same wages as he had earned at Bowbridge. The first years of the union were marked by an often bitter fight for recognition from many employers who regarded any challenge to their right to manage as tantamount to mutiny.

The years preceding the outbreak of the First World War witnessed increasing jute strikes, fuelled by rising problems in the export markets, particularly in the USA, and the return of wage cuts and short-time working. In December 1911, during the course of a national carters' strike, Dundee's local authorities became so alarmed at the prospect of trouble that they requested the help of the military. Three hundred soldiers from the first battalion of the Black Watch were drafted into the city and the police force was strengthened by the addition of 200 constables drawn from other Scottish police forces.[58] As a result of the strike, the mills were forced to close for lack of fuel, and upwards of 30,000 excited textile workers thronged the city's streets, adding to the already heightened atmosphere.[59] Enforced and unpaid idleness so close the New Year festival was a bleak prospect for many jute workers, but the local press reported that many 'entered into the spirit of the struggle', taking up the chant 'Are we down-hearted? No! We're out for the carters oh!'[60] Although not actively involved in the dispute, the rising status of the JFWU was underlined when John Sime was invited to take part in the negotiations that ended the strike in Dundee on 24 December 1911.

The growing importance of the JFWU was further demonstrated less than three months later when, in stark contrast to previous disputes, a strike was planned by the union leadership in conjunction with Trade Union Federation officials at a national level.[61] Five days into the strike, 2,000 workers at the Camperdown Works in Lochee marched to the head office of Cox Brothers shouting their demands. Although the crowd was eventually pacified and dispersed, following the intervention of some of the company's senior directors, 16 Smith and Wesson .38 calibre automatic pistols and 1,500 rounds of ammunition were subsequently ordered for the protection of the Camperdown foremen.[62] The strike came to an end in the middle of April 1912 when the employers agreed to an average scale of wages in preparing and spinning, and the establishment of a labour disputes committee. The outcome of the Camperdown dispute confirmed that the JFWU was now a major industrial and political force that could no longer be dismissed or ignored. In October 1913, the new order of things in Jute-opolis was further underlined when John Sime courteously declined an unprecedented invitation from Malcolm, Ogilvie & Co, Ltd to attend a 'social meeting.'[63]

During the 1912 jute strike, the JFWU leadership responded to employer intransigence and intimidation in kind and with interest. Striking workers were encouraged to identify 'scabs' and 'blacklegs', and fights became commonplace on the picket lines and in the surrounding streets as workmates, neighbours and former friends clashed. For the feminist labour historian, Emma Wainwright, employing a Foucaldian concept of power, the determination of the JFWU to meet force with force was a clear example of 'domination in resistance':

> Through a disciplinary gaze which worked amongst the workers themselves, a self-monitoring of workers through union intimidation attempted to produce an homogenous protesting group. Therefore, whether within the confines of the enclosed work space, or outside, workers could not exist outside of or beyond power. The work gates became sites where conflicting regimes of disciplinary power worked on workers.[64]

According to Wainwright, women workers could never be free from male power, least of all through joining a trade union. She argues that by placing 'women within rigid categories [the JFWU] aimed to regulate and control the transgressive qualities of the working class and wider social relations, and in turn, recreated order – a male order.'[65] This view of power is unmoored from any historical or socio-economic context, so that the violence of strikers and the 'disciplinary project' of the JFWU becomes equivalent to the violence and discipline of the local state and the employers. In reality, conflicts between workers and employers were never fought on equal terms. Most strikes failed, and worker militants were subjected to the very real threats of sacking, arrest and blacklisting. The violence of the strikers was a reflection of the sometimes desperate struggle they were engaged in, and the 1912 strike was in many ways a litmus test for jute trade unionism. The managers of Camperdown were often described as the most despotic in the city, and by challenging the right of management to manage the strikers were assured of a determined response, as the arming of foremen demonstrates. It also appears patronising in the extreme to characterise the mill girls as simple dupes of a male-dominated trade union apparatus. The mill girls were nobody's dupes. The JFWU, like the MFOU, struggled to control them, and most strikes erupted not, as often claimed by the employers, through the manipulation of workers by JFWU leaders, but through 'wildcat' actions that the union was often forced to intervene in.

Emma Wainwright's view that 'working class women were implicated in their own subordination' is of a piece with the work of Eleanor Gordon, who does, however, stress the JFWU's lack of control over the jute workers. Gordon also claims that 'the informal organization of the women and their culture ... reflected a fatalistic acceptance of class divisions and inequality as part of the natural order of things'; and she illustrates her point by quoting the lyrics of *Oh, Dear Me*: 'Oh dear me, the warld's ill divided/Them that works the hardest are aye wi' least provided/But I maun bide contented, dark days and fine/But there's no much pleasure livin' affen ten-and-nine.'[66] This song is widely attributed to Mary Brooksbank, but was probably adapted from a song that was popular amongst mill workers during the late nineteenth century. While it embraced a determination to 'bide contented' in a world that was recognised as being 'ill divided', this is not the only song within the mill girl corpus; and the pre-First World War period of intensified industrial struggle provided new additions to the developing song-book of *Oary* Dundee. The *Strike Song* was collected by Brooksbank some time during the second decade of the twentieth century: 'We are out for higher wages/As we have a right to do/And we'll never be content/Till we get our ten per cent/For we have a right to live/As well as you.'[67] What is demonstrated by the *Strike Song* is not a revolutionary consciousness, but neither is there a hint of the fatalism adduced to mill-girl culture by Eleanor Gordon. The *Strike Song* represents an affirmative demand by the mill girls to take industrial action in defence of their own interests, as well as the 'right to live as well as you.' These words were no doubt directed at the employers and at other better paid workers within the city. It illustrated a demand by the mill girls to be recognised as equals and was an appeal for wider support in their struggle, which was perceived as tantamount to an act of rebellion – if not revolution – by the jute barons.

The period from 1905 up to the outbreak of war underlined the power of class as an organising principle that could neutralise gender, generational and religious divisions amongst jute workers. The 'Irish question' remained an issue of some importance in Dundee, but serious ethnic and religious conflict was largely conspicuous by its absence, in stark contrast to Glasgow and Edinburgh where 'Orangeism' would go on to exert a mass influence during the 1930s with the rise of groups such as the Scottish Protestant League and Protestant Action respectively.[68] In addition, while the early years of the twentieth century saw the rise of female suffrage as a serious political issue, its appeal to the working women of Juteopolis appeared to be quite limited.[69] The JFWU, Labour, the prohibitionists, and smaller socialist groups such as the SLP, all continuously hammered away at the necessity of building and maintaining class unity, and their message found willing ears, as demonstrated by the growth of trade union membership and the increasing influence of socialist politics within the city. The convulsions of the pre-war years would, however, be put firmly in the shade during and immediately following the First World War with the eruption of unprecedented levels of industrial and social struggle, which would see Dundee take its place alongside 'Red Clydeside' as a major Scottish storm centre of working class militancy.

War, workers militancy and rent strikes

The announcement of war in August 1914 was accompanied in Dundee, as elsewhere in Britain, by an atmosphere akin to that of a holiday. As young men rushed to enlist, rising patriotism gave way to anti-German sentiments that spilled over into attacks on, and the looting of, many Jewish businesses and shops with German sounding names. As a result of this looting, and the internment of Germans, Dundee's small, but industrious, Jewish community, which had developed from trade links with the Baltic region, stretching back beyond the eighteenth century, was effectively broken up and dispersed.[70]

In February 1915, against the background of escalating labour trouble in many jute mills, the Fourth Battalion of the Black Watch, known as 'Dundee's Ain', was cheered enthusiastically by huge crowds as it made its way from Dudhope barracks overlooking the city centre to West station in order to board the trains that would take them to France.[71] Many of these recruits were jute workers who had enthusiastically rallied to the flag a few months before, and some of the companies were proudly led by the newly commissioned heirs of the city's textile dynasties, such as George Cox and his brother William.[72] By May 1915, at the same time as 'Dundee's Ain' nervously waited to go 'over the top' at Aubers Ridge,[73] the 'home' jute industry was booming as a result of a government order for four million sandbags and the jute trade unions struggled to keep track of the innumerable trade disputes as workers demanded wage increases in order to counteract rising prices and rents.[74] Official figures showed that retail food prices in the first 12 months of war rose by an average of 32 per cent in the larger industrial towns and that the price of a loaf of bread rose from 5½d to 8d

or more.[75] The employers responded to mounting strikes and labour supply problems through the recruitment of fisher girls rendered idle by the stoppage of
fishing. Despite these efforts the strikes continued, and by July 1915 the employers threatened a 'general lockout'. However, many employers, faced with full
order books, were compelled to give into the workers' demands, and by the end
of July the strikes had ended.[76] Labour shortages and increasing disputes in
important sectors of the war-time economy still continued to exert themselves,
and in July 1915 the government introduced the Munitions of War Act, which
made it a penal offence for workers to leave employment or to take a new job
without their employer's consent.[77]

During the second half of 1915, Glasgow's growing rent agitation was
accompanied by the development of strikes over the Munitions Act, rising prices
and the growing threat of conscription. The linking up and coming together of
rent agitators and worker militants on Clydeside was beginning to worry authorities, already increasingly nervous about the lack of progress in war aims and the
mounting war casualties. Trouble was not confined to the Glasgow area, as the
rent issue also started to exert itself in Dundee.[78] In August 1915, the landlords'
trade association gave notice of their intention to increase rents from 11 November. In September 1915, as thousands of factors' notices dropped through letter
boxes all around the city, a self-styled 'Tenant', in the correspondence columns
of the *Courier*, reflected the mounting anger when he denounced the landlords as
'unpatriotic' for their attempts to increase rents by 15 per cent, before asking
pointedly, 'Glasgow tenants are up in arms. ... Are the Dundee tenants to
knuckle under?'[79] In fact, meetings were taking place all across the city as the
deadline for the signing of the new agreements approached. On 16 October
the *People's Journal* informed readers that 'excitement ... is increasing with the
issue of the [rent] missives, and in many "lands" the housewives are organising
stairhead opposition to the landlords and the rent gatherers.'[80] A few days later,
following the issuing of 'quit notices' by many landlords, tenants 'retorted by
fixing placards in their windows' intimating 'to house hunters that they need not
expect to be allowed to "see the house"'.[81] The 'official' labour movement in
Dundee was slow to recognise the seriousness of the rent agitation, but in September 1915 Dundee Trade Council convened an open meeting in order to
discuss the issue. This led to the establishment of a joint committee, made up of
activists drawn from the Trades Council and Dundee Labour Representation
Committee (LRC), with the aim of introducing 'organisation' into the spreading
dispute.[82] Despite this show of unity, tensions within the city's labour movement
would be brought to the fore when Edwin Scrymgeour was voted down as one of
the speakers at the first 'Indignation' meeting organised by the newly convened
joint committee.[83]

The Dundee rent agitation unfolded against the background of increasingly
disquieting news from the Western Front. In February 1915, the Fourth Battalion
embarked for France with a complement of 900 men, but by September 1915,
and despite the arrival of replacements, it had been reduced to about 420 men.[84]
Much worse was to follow. Over the course of three days, between 25–27

September 1915, 'Dundee's Ain' was effectively decimated when a further 230 men were killed or wounded at the Battle of Loos – including all but one of the battalion's officers, who were easily identified by German snipers due to the gleaming red hackles on their bonnets.[85] In Dundee, news of the losses prompted widespread stupefaction and then a rising sense of anger, which Mary Brooksbank vividly recalled many years later in her memoirs when she wrote that the 'Cameronians, the Black Watch, and the Royal Scots claimed their recruits from Craigie mill, and as the casualty list grew, our Patriotism evaporated.'[86]

It was during this time, too, that anti-war activists, including Edwin Scrymgeour and Bob Stewart, came to prominence and to the increasing attention of the authorities for their denunciations of the mounting slaughter, and of the actions of the city's landlords who were intent on increasing the rents of many families with soldiers at the front. At the end of November 1915, the local courts ordered a soldier's wife and her three children to remove from their tenement within a week. 'Mrs McAdam protested strongly at the decision of the Court, remarking, "When your man's away they fling you onto the street."'[87] In early October 1915, one newspaper correspondent, who wrote under the *nom-de-plume* 'Strafe der Landlords' suggested that tenants should publicly unmask the 'landlord Huns', who were often also shopkeepers whose businesses were in the mill districts.[88] This suggestion was taken up by LRC activists who drew up a blacklist of shopkeepers that was distributed amongst the rent-strikers, which proved particularly effective in bringing a number of hitherto intransigent shopkeepers-cum-landlords to heel.[89] The *halflins* of Dundee also played a leading role in the rent agitation by looking out for the approach of bailiffs and factors,[90] and parading the streets with placards whilst singing the strike song, 'Are we downhearted?', which, as we have seen, had been a popular ditty during 1911 carters' stoppage.[91]

As the Dundee rent-strike grew in scope and scale in the autumn of 1915, the 'official' labour movement struggled to bring it under control. On 11 October an LRC public meeting on the 'rent issue' was swelled to such an extent by a 'considerable number of women' that an overflow meeting had to be held. The anger of the audience was palpable but, in sharp contrast to the approach of Glasgow's labour activists, the LRC did not take the opportunity to establish a tenants' organisation. For J. K. Young:

> It is difficult to avoid the conclusion that Dundee's labour leaders were anxious to avoid any wildcat protest over which they might have little control and wanted to avoid any rival organisation to their own being set up. Their experience of women unionists in the jute mills, where a disciplined response had been difficult to achieve during disputes, may have led labour leaders to avoid harnessing the female fervour which had been evident at the Gilfillan Hall meeting.[92]

Instead of establishing local rent strike committees, the LRC threatened a strike within engineering and shipbuilding in order to force government to intervene in the developing dispute. J. K. Young may well be correct in her surmise that the exclusion of the jute industry from any proposed industrial action was rooted in the labour leaders' fear that they could not properly control the jute workers. With many women workers, and a fair proportion with men at the front, becoming increasingly militant, many labour leaders may well have baulked at involving them in the proposed strike – which would have been akin to holding a tiger by the tail.

J. K. Young does, though, exaggerate the differences between the Dundee 'labour leaders' and ordinary jute workers. Many, if not all, of these 'labour leaders' lived in rented tenement properties, and were themselves seriously affected by the rising cost of living and the prospect of rent rises. John Sime, the secretary of the JFWU, who was facing eviction in early November, informed the Hunter Committee of Enquiry that 'My wife tell me she spends all my wages on food to keep the house going'.[93] The same situation applied to skilled workers such as engineers and shipbuilding workers. The rent issue was increasingly important to even relatively well-paid skilled workers due to the large price rises that followed the outbreak of war. While Sime admitted that jute workers had succeeded in winning wage rises of around 20 per cent in the course of 1915, he also added that the cost of provisions and fuel had increased by an estimated 42 per cent during the same time.[94] It was also the case that the JFWU was in no state to organise an industry-wide strike at this time (as it had in 1912). By the end of 1915, their membership stood at 5,000, compared with 9,000 in 1912, and union funds were not sufficient to finance a large strike of uncertain duration.[95] Under these circumstances it made perfect sense for the Dundee LRC and Trades Council to concentrate strike action in industries, such as shipbuilding and engineering, which, while important, did not encompass the mass of the city's working population, thus enabling the jute workers to participate through street protests, rent strikes and by financially supporting the proposed strike. In the event of evictions on any sort of scale, however, it is unlikely that the labour leaders would have been able to prevent strike action breaking out and potentially encompassing large parts of the jute industry.

As the Martinmas term approached, the attempt to bring rent-strikers before the courts was deplored by the local press, which commented, 'no matter what economics may have to say in such cases, merely to proceed with them is to play with fire.'[96] In the event, Martinmas passed off without the expected scenes of conflict. Very little flitting was reported, as the possibility of trouble seemed to stay the hand of those who may otherwise have been tempted to rent a striker's house, while landlords and tenants alike waited to see how the national government would respond to the mounting crisis.[97] The rent strikes developed into a British-wide agitation at a time when the conflict on the Western Front was resolving itself into a murderous war of attrition, encouraged by the apparent incompetence of government and the Army High Command's disregard for human life. In Clydeside, with its central importance to the war economy, the rent strikes were coming together with mounting conflict over issues such as the Munitions of War Act and 'dilution' in the engineering and shipbuilding trades.

Trouble was not confined to the Clyde. Aberdeen and Fife on the east coast were affected along with Mid-Lanark, Clydebank, Greenock, Cambuslang and Hamilton on the west coast, while Annan and Gretna in south Scotland also saw widespread action by munitions workers. There were increasing fears within government circles that these disputes, if not brought to a speedy resolution, could threaten war production and transform themselves into a political challenge to government authority. As a result, government moved swiftly with the establishment of a committee of inquiry that visited Dundee on 2 November 1915.[98] In the week before Christmas 1915, the government rushed a bill through parliament that restricted British rents to pre-war levels.[99]

Although the rent strikes became a major feature of social and political struggle in Scotland during the First World War, there were important differences between Dundee and Glasgow in the way the rent struggles unfolded and in the manner that resistance was planned. As we have already noted, Dundee, in contrast to Glasgow, did not witness the emergence of a city-wide tenants' organisation. For J. K. Young:

> The unusual structure of household income which existed in Dundee, with its reliance on paid female labour, may in some ways have contributed to the lack of a local network of resistance. With the women tied to a long working day, and yet still responsible for family welfare, there would have been little time or energy left to devote to fighting the factors or marching to the city chambers.[100]

In Glasgow, city-wide coordination through the medium of a central tenants' organisation was an essential prerequisite for the success of the rent-strike there, but Dundee was a much smaller and more compact city. In the event of evictions in one part of Dundee, news would have travelled fast and may well have drawn large and militant crowds from the immediate neighbourhood and from other parts of the city – and would almost certainly have led to the development of strikes within many jute mills. And, while there was no formal organisation in Dundee, aside from that provided by the LRC, this does not mean to say that organisation was absent. J. K. Young herself points to the 'stairhead meetings' that were reportedly taking place all across the city. In the event of a strike, these stairhead and close meetings could have quickly transformed themselves into ad-hoc networks of resistance, which would have been much more important to the course of such a struggle than the LRC committee. Indeed, Young herself admits, it was the 'possibility of trouble, or tenant solidarity that put people off trying to rent a striker's house' and not the demands of the LRC for government regulation of housing policy.[101] It is also worth bearing in mind that 'long working hours' and responsibilities for 'family welfare' did little to prevent women jute workers becoming increasingly militant in the period up to and beyond the end of the war.

Although the issue of rent increases may have been settled by the end of 1915, rising prices along with other issues would come to the fore during the following year against the background of the murderous offensive on the Somme and the development of an Irish Republican insurrection in Dublin that claimed the life of many of the leading figures of the rebellion, including the revolutionary socialist – and one time Dundonian – James Connolly. From March to June of 1916, an industry-wide jute strike, over wages, convulsed Dundee, but the strikers succumbed in the face of the large stocks of finished goods that had accumulated during the months of full-time working prior to the dispute. As the strike raged during April 1916, divisions appeared between the JFWU and MFOU, when the latter union suspended strike pay to its members. Henry Williamson and the MFOU leadership were becoming concerned at the increasing violence and militancy that accompanied the 1916 strike, something that was also beginning to worry Dundee's civil authorities and employers. At Camperdown works the militancy of mass pickets so alarmed Cox Brothers that they applied to the Army High Command for military help to ensure continuous working.[102] In the same month, the newly established *Textile Workers' Guide* pointedly asked, '[w]e do not know whether we have corrupted the Clyde engineers or they us'.[103] In the face of escalating tensions, the MFOU withdrew their support from the 1916 strike, leading to a serious internal rift that effectively sealed its fate as an effective labour organisation. The MFOU started to haemorrhage members, encouraged by a gleeful John Sime who 'hounded the Mill and Factory Operatives' Union out of existence by systematically treating it as a pariah.'[104] By contrast, the JFWU went from strength to strength. In March 1916, membership stood at 5,035, but by April 1917 it was almost 9,000 and by December 1918 it had soared to 19,704.[105]

The First World War became a defining period for the jute workers of Dundee. The huge demand for sandbags and other war materials ensured regular and largely unbroken employment and rising wages. While increasing conscription and the militarisation of war production encouraged trade union militancy at home, the mood of the times also transmitted itself to soldiers on the front line with the eruption of the Etaples mutiny in which Scottish soldiers, including many Dundonians, played a central role.[106] The war also witnessed increasing government intervention with the establishment of the Jute Trade Board, forcing employers to the negotiating table and bolstering the position of the JFWU. Union influence was, though, still limited in one important regard. During September 1918, Dundee mill workers in their thousands, and in the face of employer hostility and lukewarm union support, unilaterally decided to work for no longer than 48 hours per week by refusing to attend work on Saturdays. The jute workers' demand would be realised, underlining again the potency and effectiveness of non-union forms of organisation and the inability of the JFWU to control its membership.[107]

The post-war labour upsurge

The First World War produced a bonanza for the Dundee jute industry as a result of the massive demand for sandbags, which absorbed up to 70 per cent of the industry's production of jute goods. During 1915, 150 million sandbags were sent to the different theatres of war within the space of two weeks, resulting in profit margins that had not been witnessed since the boom years that accompanied the Crimean War.[108] At the end of December 1919, it was reported that Dundee had enjoyed 'a favourable share of the world's jute requirements', while all the talk of 'the threatened interruption of the Dundee trade has so far come to nil.'[109] The continuation of high profits and increasing rates of inflation also encouraged frequent disputes over wage levels. The coming of peace saw a realisation of the long-awaited JFWU demand for permanent Trade Board control, but while the employers could no longer act in the unilateral manner of pre-war Juteopolis, the advent of Trade Board regulation failed to ensure industrial peace.

The employers, galvanised, perhaps, by the success and increasing influence of the JFWU, responded by establishing their own industry-wide organisation, the Association of Jute Spinners and Manufacturers (AJSM). The first major act of this new employers' body, in July 1919, was to oppose the payment of a holiday bonus for the forthcoming 'Peace Celebration'. The AJSM's attitude stemmed from the continuing conflict over the working hours issue, and it was decided that only those workers who had attended work on Saturdays should receive the payment. It proved impossible for the AJSM to hold the line, and when it was discovered that the Victoria Spinning Co. Ltd 'had made a gift of 5/– to their workers in respect of the Peace Holiday', the employer, Mr F. L. M. McGrady, was asked to explain himself. 'I personally gave each worker employed by this company 5/– ... in grateful acknowledgement of the services rendered to their country by over 150 of our workmen during the war, many of whom served under me both at home and in Flanders; also of the services rendered by the women in knitting socks, etc, which the company sent to Flanders.'[110] Despite McGrady's stance, and that of other employers, the AJSM insisted that 'the workpeople, with certain exceptions, should not receive wages for Saturday 19th July'.[111] The AJSM may have felt justified in their opposition to holiday payments for the 'Peace Celebrations', but, as the example of F. L. McGrady demonstrates, it also gave rise to grave misgivings even within their own ranks. In wider society the move was seen as petty and mean-minded, and even as unpatriotic given the war-related work of the jute industry. It also served to underline just how little had changed in the jute industry, despite the advent of the Trade Board system, the creation of the AJSM and the rising influence of the JFWU.

From 1920 onwards, the boom times were starting to come to an end. Deflationary monetary policies, which encouraged potential buyers to postpone purchases and manufacturers to delay production, along with fluctuating exchange rates and the erection of tariff barriers, led to mounting problems for the Dundee jute industry.[112] Further dislocation and rising unemployment was experienced with demobbed men returning to reclaim jobs in an industry that had become even more highly feminised in their absence. In 1921, the *People's Journal* reported that the population of the city had decreased by 8,134 from 1911,

although, following the incorporation of Broughty Ferry within the city bounda-
ries, the official Census figures showed a slight increase from 165,004 to
168,315.[113] The large decrease in population was explained away by the *People's
Journal* with the rather hopeful claim that it was due to the 'transitory movements which took place in June among unemployed workers in the jute industry.'[114] Though shocking, the decrease in Dundee's population may have been
expected to alleviate growing unemployment and the chronic shortage of
working class housing. Instead, it was reported that:

> With a decrease in the population of 8,134 the extraordinary demand for
> homes experienced immediately before and after the armistice would appear
> somewhat of a paradox. But this circumstance is accounted for. The build-
> ing of new homes was largely curtailed, if not wholly suspended, a year or
> two before the war. During the war no new houses were built. It has also to
> be taken into account that before the war and during its progress a large
> number of slum dwellings were closed, rendering the demand for homes in
> other quarters more acute.[115]

Robert Mitchell, Chief Sanitary Inspector for Dundee, found that the worst
examples of overcrowding were in the city centre, particularly in the Overgate
and also in 'certain localities in Lochee', where transitory workers, described as
'birds of passage', drawn mainly from Glasgow 'find it most convenient to con-
gregate', which led to appalling examples of overcrowding, 'some of them of a
very distressing kind'.[116] Although efforts were made to improve housing conditions, progress was slow. By 1928 less than 4,000 new houses had been built
in Dundee, while slum clearance schemes were postponed so that overcrowding
would not worsen. The new houses that were built, such as the pioneering Logie
estate, which was constructed during 1919–20, turned out to be of little benefit
to those most affected by poor housing due to the high rents and their location
away from the main industrial areas. As a result, the tenants of the new housing
schemes were drawn mainly from the 'blackcoated classes, whose better means
and greater influence have placed them in a more favourable position for acquir-
ing the new homes.'[117]

Although the continuation of the Trade Board system strengthened the position of the JFWU, through the establishment of minimum wage rates, the onset
of trade depression from late 1920 onwards led to a series of, Trade Board sanctioned, wage cuts and the development of high unemployment. By late 1920,
upwards of 7,000 jute workers were unemployed out of a workforce of 30,000,
and by August 1921 the unemployed and those on short-time working numbered
18,000. In the same month it was also announced that 12,000 workers on short
time were to have their national insurance 'stopped' following the expiry of the
six week payment period on 15 August 1921.[118] In response, Dundee Parish
Council wrote to the Prime-Minister, the Scottish Secretary of State and the local
MP, Winston Churchill, warning that they 'could not regulate parochial relief as
the proper solution of the situation … is national and not local.'[119] By the end of

August, the local press was reporting 'pathetic scenes in Dundee Sheriff Court' as large numbers of applicants appeared to press their claim for local parish relief, including a married man with five young children who;

> admitted he was able bodied, but stated he was unable to find any work. It was solely for his children that he wanted relief. 'They have had nothing to eat for the past two days', he tearfully remarked, 'and I can do nothing to help them.'
>
> The Sheriff – 'I sympathise with you, but I can only administer the law as I find it, and it forbids me to grant relief in the case of an able-bodied person. I am sorry, but I must refuse the application.'
>
> 'But what am I to do?' appealed the man. 'I cannot sit and watch my children starve. If I steal I suppose I will get caught, and yet if I can get no help there is nothing for me but to steal' ...
>
> All the applications were refused.[120]

The inevitable happened: over the course of the three days between 7 and 9 September Dundee, along with a number of other British cities and towns, was rocked by riots, which, in scope and scale, had not been witnessed since the early nineteenth century. A large crowd numbering hundreds descended on the Lord Provost's house demanding that he reverse the local parish decision. Despite a heavy police presence the crowd repeatedly attempted to break the cordon and besiege the house, and the Lord Provost's daughter was injured by flying glass when the carriage that she was travelling in was stoned. Frustrated in their attempts to raise their grievances with the Lord Provost, the crowd vented their frustration on the shops and offices in their path. The parish offices were sacked by a large mob of unemployed workers chanting the 'Red Flag' and the city centre was looted. Despite the intervention of, the prospective Labour candidate, E. D. Morel,[121] the city was wracked by riots for three days, the local press noting that 'many of the window breakers were young girls.'[122] The Dundee riots were part of a wider outbreak of violence that was greeted with alarm by the government, which pressurised Scottish local parish councils to drop their opposition to payment of local relief, a decision that quickly brought the disturbances to an end.[123]

The period from 1923 saw a gradual but distinct improvement in the fortunes of the city's staple trade, encouraged by a recovery in the US market and the adoption of short-time working in the Calcutta jute industry. Improving trade conditions also acted as the cue for the development of the most serious and far-reaching dispute in the history of the jute industry. In January 1923, trouble broke out in the spinning flats of Camperdown Works, which now belonged to the recently formed conglomerate Jute Industries Ltd.[124] The strike erupted when the employers, with the support of the AJSM, reduced spinners' wages to the minimum Trade Board rates of pay, whilst also requiring them to attend to an increased number of spindles.[125] John Sime was infuriated at this attempt to alter established working practices and on 23 February, after a lengthy and increasingly bitter correspondence with the firm, he instructed the Camperdown spinners to operate only one frame. The following day the entire mill was 'closed down within one hour' on the orders of management, thus paving the way for the escalation of the dispute.[126] On 8 March, the JFWU called out all members employed by Jute Industries Ltd, but when the firm re-opened the gates of their different works in the city on 14 March workers returned en masse, apart from those at Camperdown Works where the strike remained solid. The following day, notices were posted throughout the city announcing an industry-wide lockout from 23 March, which lasted four weeks, while a further one-week lockout also followed. Eventually, after 27 weeks, the strikers were forced back through lack of resources and failing support within the wider city.

The Camperdown strike demonstrated that the jute barons had, according to their own lights, learned the lessons of the past 17 years encompassing the rise of the JFWU. They now understood the need for a more disciplined and central-ised form of organisation. Jute Industries Ltd, and the AJSM, saw the Camper-down strike as a gilt-edged opportunity to curb the power of the JFWU and to undermine the position of John Sime. However, while the Camperdown dispute ended the brief heroic age of the JFWU, the union was not broken as a result of the dispute and nor was Sime's position within the union fatally undermined. The strike did, though, leave a bitter legacy for the future of industrial relations in Juteopolis, which will be examined in Chapters 6 and 7.

The situation facing the Dundee labour movement had appeared to be very different only a few months before the eruption of the Camperdown dispute. In November 1922, Winston Churchill was unceremoniously ejected from his 'seat for life'. It was a bitter and unexpected blow for Churchill who, it was widely believed, momentarily lost his poise, and his dignity, when he responded to the news of his defeat by predicting that in Dundee with his going, 'the grass would grow green through its cobbled streets, and the vigour of its industry [would] shrink and decay.'[127] Neddy Scrymgeour came top of the poll with 32,578 votes in the two-member constituency. E. D. Morel, the Labour candidate, was also elected with 30,292 votes. Churchill was reduced to fourth place in the poll with 20,466 votes, while Willie Gallagher of the Communist Party (CP) gathered an impressive 5,906 votes. The combined vote for left candidates, representing the SPP, Labour and the CP, encompassed almost half the registered voters, which made Dundee the most left-leaning of Scottish cities.[128] It was a stunning result and in the heat of victory John Sime exultantly declared, 'We are naturally elated at … the removal from Dundee of the stigma of returning as its representative, one of the most dangerous men to the peace of the world. Dundee has purged itself, and has made history.'[129]

Dundee's reputation as a Liberal stronghold during the nineteenth century was based, at least in part, on the support provided by the city's large and growing Irish Catholic population – flowing from the party's long-standing support for Irish Home Rule. Following the First World War, however, Scotland witnessed a decisive shift to the left on the part of Catholics, but the sea-change in Dundee was further encouraged by Churchill's support for, and close involvement with, the suppression of Irish republicanism. A growing number of Catholic and Irish figureheads became embroiled in the gathering anti-Churchill bandwagon. In March 1921, the Archbishop of Melbourne visited Dundee and urged Catholic voters to 'find someone who would be in closer touch with the working men and women in Dundee [and] then instead of an enemy of Ireland, we would have ... one who would be likely to have sympathy with Ireland.'[130] In 1918, Edwin Scrymgeour had won the endorsement of the United Irish League and the *Catholic Herald*, and this support was repeated in 1922, while Labour also shared the endorsement of mainstream Catholicism. Although communism was vigorously denounced by the Catholic hierarchy, the new creed enjoyed wide support within Sinn Fein and the IRA circles. In October 1922, *The Dundee Catholic Herald* expressed their concern regarding the number of 'Catholic lads' who could 'rattle off socialistic and communist doctrines better than they can answer questions from the *Penny Catechism*.'[131] These 'Catholic lads' joined a Dundee electorate that had increased more than fourfold since 1908, when Edwin Scrymgeour had first stood for parliamentary office, including many former half-timers who had grown up during the stormy decades of the 1890s and 1900s. It was this new electoral force that spearheaded Scrymgeour's challenge to Churchill as well as to the hegemonic claims of Labour during the 1920s.

In May 1923, a few months following the election of Scrymgeour, and at a time when the Camperdown strike and lockout was still raging, the Kinnaird cinema screened the silent feature film *The Four Horsemen of the Apocalypse*. It was reported that crowded 'houses have witnessed the show at each performance', and that the cinema had 'secured the picture for a second weeks run.'[132] The Dundee clergyman, the Reverend T. S. Taylor, expressed concern at the public reaction to the film:

> The picture, he said, would no doubt have awakened in many minds a kind of wonder as to what the apocalypse was. ... To many the Book of Revelation was a curious epistle. There were those who believed in a fixed future, and those to whom the future seemed dreadful. He had seen posters announcing that 'millions now living would never die' – a type of sensational evangelism which appealed to fear and superstition.[133]

Some among the audiences of *The Four Horsemen of the Apocalypse* may indeed have been overly influenced by 'fear and superstition', but they should perhaps be excused. After all, many were still grieving for sons, husbands, friends and lovers, who had been lost amidst the barbed wire and mud of countless battlefields, while the sense of fresh hope that had greeted the Armistice had quickly dissipated in the face of a gathering economic crisis attended by mounting social and political unrest. To this extent, Scrymgeour's taste for apocalyptic rhetoric echoed the timbre of the times in a more effective manner than the careful constitutionalism and moderate reformism of more mainstream Labour representatives.

5 Challenging the jute wallahs

Non-cooperation, communism and the Marwaris, 1918–30

Earlier in the present year I was beginning to feel uneasy about the increasing number (as it seemed to me) of assaults by Europeans on Indians not all of which appeared, as far as I was able to judge from the newspapers, to have been adequately punished.... But since then there have been several more of these outrages; and the enclosed article in the *Daily Herald* of 30th August indicates feelings of which I am sure we shall hear more before long in the House of Commons.... I [ask] you to do everything in your power to check an evil ... which unless someone from time to time takes a stand against it (as Curzon did) must embitter racial feeling and lower our prestige.

(Letter by the Earl of Birkenhead to the Viceroy of India, September 1926)[1]

In April 1926, John Spence, a Scottish supervisor at the Gourepore mill, was arrested following the death of a weaver called Jagnarayan, who, it was alleged, had been seriously beaten by Spence after protesting the refusal to grant him sick leave. Spence was subsequently cleared of culpable homicide because no witnesses came forward to corroborate allegations that he had assaulted Jagnarayan, and he was hastily sent back to Scotland. News of the acquittal sparked widespread rioting in Gourepore, which led to the death of George Ireland, a Scottish supervisor.[2]

The 'Spence Case' captured international press coverage and, as indicated by the quotation from Birkenhead, prompted growing anxiety within the upper reaches of the British state. It also revealed the extent to which the Dundee School, and paternal despotism, was being challenged by Indian workers. While Scottish supervisors had been the focus of increasing workers' anger during the 1890s and 1900s, it was now apparent that they had become a potent symbol of colonial rule and a prime, and vulnerable, target for those who sought to challenge the British Raj. Even more worrying for the colonial state was the fact that this emblematic conflict united Muslims and Hindus. This chapter will demonstrate how and why the Scottish supervisor became transformed from a 'sort of God' into a totem around which jute workers organised themselves in a unified fight against colonial capital, and the novel challenges to paternal despotism that came in the wake of non-cooperation and the arrival of communism on the subcontinent.

Communalism and class: the Calcutta riots of 1918

The First World War witnessed massive growth in the output and profits of the Bengal jute industry that continued into the immediate post-war period, enabling Thomas Duff & Co. to pay shareholders in three of their Calcutta mills a dividend of 50 per cent in 1919, while it was also reported that some other companies were paying dividends of 300 and 400 per cent.[3] The war-time boom was, though, accompanied by an investment drought and workers' wages remained very low, a situation made all the worse by rising inflation, which was widely attributed to the speculative trading of, predominantly, Marwari merchants in basic commodities such as rice and cloth. During August 1918, rising resentment towards the Marwaris was further inflamed, particularly amongst the labouring classes, following reports that Marwari merchants had successfully prevented the Calcutta Corporation from investigating trading practices in the cloth markets. The extent of official anxiety prompted by this development was underlined when one government Mandarin nervously observed that while the Marwaris had always been 'the object of mob-hatred for much the same reasons that the Jews are in Russia and the Armenians in Turkey [they] have been in particularly bad odour in recent times owing to high prices which are generally attributed to their machinations.'[4]

The Marwaris were a traditional merchant community that hailed from the Jodhpur-Marwar region of Rajasthan. They were marked by a conservative religious outlook and their growing prominence as traders was closely connected with the rise of opium within Britain's imperial economy during the mid-nineteenth century.[5] They also benefited from the structural economic changes that accompanied the consolidation of British rule. In the wake of the 1857 'Mutiny', Marwari grain dealers and moneylenders fanned out across India, and by the late 1860s were established in most of the major commercial and trading centres of the British Raj. In Bengal they were also able to replace *Khatri*[6] and Bengali merchants as *banians* for the emerging British-controlled managing agency houses that controlled the main areas of eastern India's colonial economy. By the beginning of the twentieth century, Marwari traders had firm control of the raw jute market, working either on their own account or as representatives of the managing agencies. Not content with merely controlling the market in raw jute, they turned their attention to dealing in manufactured jute goods. As the Indian Central Jute Committee observed in 1941:

> Early in the present century ... a new feature in gunny trading began to make its appearance. Some Marwari merchants saw prospects of good profit in buying certain classes of goods and holding them until heavy demand caused a rise in prices. Accordingly, they commenced their operations by buying from mills and selling to shippers as soon as they considered that a reasonable profit had materialised. This was the beginning of large scale forward selling by mills, a system which is now a regular feature of trade in gunnies.[7]

Thus was *Fatka* born, and by 1912 it was claimed that it had become so popular that almost everyone, including 'members of the Bar Library, tramway conductors, businessmen, babus and *bhistis* (watermen)' was having a little flutter.[8] As the Marwari dealers' scope of trade grew, so their organisational efforts also increased. A plethora of native trading associations came into being, represented at the top by the Indian Chamber of Commerce. The predominant position of British business was facing a growing challenge, prompting furious denunciations from the Indian Jute Mills Association (IJMA) and individual mill companies, who viewed *Fatka* as responsible for turning 'legitimate trade into a huge gamble.'[9] The fierce reaction of British colonial capital to the growing Marwari challenge was grounded in the realisation that a major new competitor with large resources was cornering the market in raw jute, thereby artificially inflating the price of the raw material, particularly in periods of short-crop.

The commercial opportunities created by the First World War allowed the Marwari merchants to reap a rich harvest, and paved the way for the emergence of G. D. Birla and Sarupchand Hukumchand as jute manufacturers – a development that marked the beginning of a new and turbulent era for the Bengal jute industry. The Marwaris, like their eighteenth and nineteenth century Scottish counterparts in the East India Company, were a closely knit group who used family connections in order to cement and to spread their influence. By 1918, leading Marwari families, such as the Birlas and Bhimanis, had established large mansions in and around central Calcutta on land cleared of their former populations of, predominantly Muslim, small traders and craftsmen. However, the success of the Marwaris came at a price. In 1910, central Calcutta witnessed serious rioting following Marwari attempts to prevent cow slaughter during Bakr Id, which resulted in four deaths and the deployment of troops to central Calcutta and the mill districts. As a result, many wealthy Marwaris dismissed their Muslim coachmen and *syces*[10] and refused to rent out land to Muslim tenants.[11]

During 1918, the rising tensions occasioned by rampant inflation and the violent outburst of anti-Marwari feelings were compounded by a mounting influenza epidemic, or 'war fever' as it was called, which led to a 50 per cent rise in the mortality rate in Calcutta. The worst affected areas included the, predominantly Muslim, dock and industrial suburb of Kidderpore, and the ineffectual attempts by the Calcutta Corporation to contain the epidemic caused growing Muslim anger. Populist Muslim clerics were also making militant forays into the public realm by inveighing against the Marwaris, and denouncing the under-representation of Muslims within the Bengal Legislative Assembly. The development of the Khilifat movement[12] further added to the febrile atmosphere that was building, which, according to the chief secretary of the Bengal government, was 'favourable for the circulation of wild rumours and the apprehension of disturbances.'[13] Matters finally came to a head on 9 September when city-wide riots broke out, triggered by the banning of an All-India rally in Calcutta organised to protest against the *Indian Daily News* for an article they published that described an Arab 'gazing down into a gutter as reverently as if it were his Prophet's tomb.'[14] The rioters were overwhelmingly up-country Muslims of the poorer classes, comprising butchers, carters, coolies and mill workers, although up-country Hindus, described as *benarasis* (hooligans from Benares), were also identified as taking part. Although Marwari houses, businesses and temples felt the brunt of the rioters' ire, 'Europeans', including the two Deputy Commissioners of police and British jute merchants, were also attacked. The following day, 10,000 jute workers from mills in the Garden Reach area struck and a Scottish supervisor was violently assaulted. A procession of 2,000 jute workers, many shouting and dancing to the beating of drums and led by naked 'fanatics' covered in mud and ashes, set off towards Calcutta, but their progress was halted by the deployment of military force, which led to the loss of 24 lives. Attacks on jute mill managers as well as arson and looting also took place during the course of strikes at the Ganges and Lansdowne jute mills in the Howrah area.[15] The mobilisation of Muslims was initiated by non-Bengali, predominantly up-country, preachers and journalists, along with elite Muslims from Bengal, such as Mujibur-Rahman, the Secretary of the Bengal Presidency Muslim League, and prominent members of the Bengal Legislative Assembly, such as Fazlul Huq.[16] As the riots developed over 9–10 September, however, the anxiety of the Muslim elites grew, and the Reception Committee for the banned Calcutta protest meeting appealed to the government to intervene in the spreading crisis.

Bengali historians have questioned the extent to which the events of 1918 were actually communal in character. For Suranjan Das, while communal violence during 'this period provided a channel for an expression of the socio-economic grievances of the lower social orders ... it was only in the 1940s that communal solidarity virtually pushed out the element of class conflict from the consciousness of the rioting groups'.[17] Subho Basu sees even less evidence of communalism acting on the Calcutta riots, arguing that 'workers interpreted the Pan-Islamic programme as an opportunity to protest against the city's traders.'[18] While this was undoubtedly the case with the mass of up-country mill workers, the riots started in those parts of central Calcutta where economic and social tensions were exacerbated by religious divisions between, predominantly lower-class, Muslims and wealthy Marwaris. Issues such as cow protection and attempts by Muslim businessmen to open slaughter houses had fanned communal tensions in central Calcutta, concentrated in and off Harrison Road and College Street, which had lingered since the Bakr Id riots of 1910. While the riots of September 1918 undoubtedly contained an element of communal discord in the early stages, thereafter the disturbances developed a momentum of their own, particularly when the up-country mill workers arrived on the scene. As Subho Basu has pointed out, during these demonstrations and marches the issues of the *Indian Daily News* article and Khilifat were not mentioned, and, when 'shouting slogans against the Marwaris, up-country workers accused the traders of adulteration – an accusation without any communal content whatsoever.' It is equally clear, as Basu also suggests, that 'workers interpreted the Pan-Islamic programme' as an opportunity to protest against the speculative practices of the city's, predominantly Marwari, traders.[19] We thus see the coincidence of class and communal tensions informing one another and producing a protest movement that actually amounted to more than the sum of its parts, so that even where communalism was clearly evident other factors also contributed. In this regard, the attacks on Scottish supervisors and managers by mill workers that preceded the large-scale marches into Calcutta are of particular interest.

Non-cooperation and the Dundee School

In 1919, as European crowned heads toppled and Empires crumbled in the wake of the carnage created by the Great War and the Russian Revolution, the British Raj was rocked by the sudden eruption of the non-cooperation movement, organised to protest at the passing of the Rowlatt Act.[20] Tens of thousands of Indians – comprising the urban middle classes as well as workers in industrial centres such as Bombay, Ahmadabad and Calcutta – were drawn into its wake. At its height, it became more a millenarian uprising than a political campaign as many participants, both Hindu and Muslim, saw it as a means of ending colonial rule and ushering in a new 'Golden Age' for India.[21] The violence that accompanied the movement, despite the efforts of the leaders to channel it along more moderate lines, gave rise to increasing fears that India was on the brink of a convulsion on the scale of the, so-called, 'Indian Mutiny' of 1857.

Launched by Gandhi, the non-cooperation movement was a joint initiative between the Indian National Congress (INC) and the Khilifat movement. The movement started with Gandhi's establishment of a *Satyagraha Sabha*[22] designed to bring together Muslims and Hindus. Despite the fact that organisational preparations were extremely limited, due to the unwillingness of the INC to support the movement in its early stage, the non-violent *hartals* were evidence of a gathering communal unity. A peaceful rally of Muslims and Hindus took place at Calcutta's Nakhoda mosque on 11 April. The following day Marwari and up-country Muslim youth engaged in running battles with the army and police in the same neighbourhoods that had witnessed the looting of Marwari houses and businesses the previous year. As Gandhi's satyagraha gathered momentum, British nervousness was brutally demonstrated by the Amritstrar massacre on 13 April 1919, which saw the killing of hundreds of unarmed demonstrators, thus virtually ensuring that the non-cooperation campaign would spiral into violence. The outrage caused by the Amritsar massacre galvanised the United Satyagraha. Support came from Marwari traders and businessmen, the Muslim Khilifatists and the Congress leadership. The spreading Khilifat agitation and rapidly deteriorating wages and conditions led to rising tensions in Indian industrial centres, which further fuelled the millenarian hopes unleashed by Gandhi's promise of *swaraj* within a year (despite his insistence that industrial labour should take no part in the Rowlatt satyagraha).

In late 1919, an unprecedented India-wide strike wave started in the woollen mills of Cawnpore and amongst railway workers at Jamalpur, before spreading to Calcutta, with a 35,000 strong strike of jute workers between 9 and 18 January 1920. Industrial unrest intensified over the course of the next two years against the background of a developing recession and constantly rising prices. Towards the close of 1920, 13 jute mills in Howrah were affected by a strike wave involving over 30,000 workers demanding wage increases of up to 20 per cent. Although economic demands were to the fore, it was clear that other factors were also at work. The Howrah strikes and street demonstrations all heavily featured Khilifat activists, leaders and slogans, and Julaha Muslim weavers played a prominent role, underlining the extent to which jute workers were influenced by – and in turn influenced – the character and course of the mass movement that lapped around the mill compounds.

The Howrah strike signalled a protracted period of labour struggle. In 1921, 38 strikes took place involving over 200,000 jute workers, while the following year there were 41 strikes involving 164,000 workers.[23] No fewer than 19 of the disputes during 1920–2 involved violent incidents between supervisors and workers, while eight involved assaults on Scottish assistants.[24] Nine disputes gave rise to the demand for the sacking of individual sirdars, while one dispute actually led to the demand for the reinstatement of a supervisor.[25] The 1920–2 strike wave graphically demonstrated the extent to which paternal despotism had failed to adapt to the challenges created by the colonial context in which it operated. The struggle that ensued between the Dundee School and up-country jute workers appeared as a microcosm of the wider struggle that was deciding India's destiny. For educated Indian nationalists, nothing summed up the racism of British colonialism more than the fact that poorly educated, and often coarsely spoken, lower class Scots could be allowed to become such powerful figures within the jute mills. The extent of this power was demonstrated in the late 1920s, when labour organisers alleged that sirdars were often compelled to provide Scottish assistants with a 'cut' of the bribes they received from workers, which, though, rarely took the form of cash:

> [I]t will be sufficient if you supply his table by marketing for him. The 'marketing' is, of course, a comprehensive term for it does not include merely plantains, gourds, cucumbers, cabbages, etc. It is very often an affair of gold and silver in as much as the sardar has to pander to the passions of the Europeans by procuring for them brandy and concubines. Many a mill hand in his inability to procure hard cash for his bribe has to execute a promissory note for the same, which he has to pay off by weekly instalments together with the interest accruing on it.[26]

For increasing numbers of jute workers, labour organisers and the radical bhadralok, the debauched elements within the Dundee School, with their appetite for French brandy and Indian concubines, were not only exemplars of capitalist oppression, they had also become a symbol of British colonial depravity.

Many of the most serious disputes during 1920–2 involved allegations of the maltreatment of women and children. The physical assault by a sirdar or a Scottish supervisor on a woman or child often acted as the final straw for male workers, and as a spur to the development of industrial struggle on a wider basis. In August 1920, in one of the opening actions of the strike wave, the Wellington jute mill in Rishra was closed down for two days following a walk-out by the spinning department protesting against an alleged assault on three 'spinning boys' by the manager. The dispute ended when the manager agreed to pay compensation of Rs10 to each of the boys.[27] The Hooghly mill was also forced to close when the women of the preparing department walked out, and was only able to re-open following the dismissal of the 'European assistant in charge' who, according to the strikers, had been guilty of assaulting one of the women and of 'general improper conduct'.[28] These disputes demonstrate that paternal despotism had become, in effect, a double-edged sword that could actually intensify and widen industrial disputes, both qualitatively and quantitatively, into a full-blooded assault on the racialised basis of power relations. The serious labour disputes involving women and child jute workers that so marked labour relations during the 1920s also provides a partial explanation as to why mill managers appeared increasingly keen to retrench child and women workers during the 1930s.

The patriarchal character of social relations within the jute workforce, encompassing ideas of personal honour or *Izzat*, undoubtedly contributed towards male workers coming to the defence of women and child workers. It is also clear that the heightened political atmosphere that accompanied, and contributed towards, the labour upsurge of this time played a major role in the jute workers' willingness to challenge paternal despotism. During 1920–2, nearly 50 per cent of violent incidents were clustered in the Howrah area, where Khilifat, and nationalist, influence was strongest.[29] There were, though, other, more indirect, factors that contributed towards the scale and seriousness of the violence between the Scottish supervisors and Indian workers during this time.

During the First World War, Scots answered the call of 'King and Country' and fell in greater numbers than their comrades elsewhere in the British Empire.[30] The high rate of Scottish casualties has been viewed as a contributory factor towards the deservedly ferocious reputation of Scottish troops, and their brutal mistreatment of German prisoners of war. Major John Stewart of the Black Watch admitted in a letter to his wife that his battalion 'TOOK VERY FEW PRISONERS' at Loos in 1915, adding that 'the main thing is to kill plenty of HUNS with as little loss to oneself as possible'.[31] Many of the younger 'jute wallahs' had seen active service with the Black Watch, which recruited widely in Dundee and Angus. The close proximity of the First World War and the strict regime under which they worked would have discouraged many Scottish supervisors from spending precious free time on parade grounds or in basic military training, but some of those who enrolled, perhaps still suffering from the traumatic impact of their war-time experiences, may well have been more ready to turn to violence in the face of worker unrest.

The life of most Scottish supervisors in Bengal was dominated by the long hours on the factory floor, and the heat and humidity that increased physical exhaustion, but during periods of political instability strikes could develop suddenly and without any warning. At such times the Scottish supervisors experienced unbearable tension and jangled nerves, brought on by the prospect of trouble. Strikes could very quickly turn the jute mill into a battleground, and the supervisors, in their white suits and topees, presented highly conspicuous targets.[32] Under these circumstances, minor incidents could quickly escalate into major ones through fear-inspired overreaction on the part of the supervisors, so that fear of trouble often became an underlying cause of trouble itself. This was dramatically demonstrated, at the height of the Howrah strike wave in late November 1920, when a Scottish assistant produced a Lewis gun, which sparked widespread rioting and looting that was only pacified following the large-scale deployment of police.[33] A government mandarin angrily observed that he had seen in

> the newspapers that the manager of one of the mills brought out his machine gun yesterday. An incident such as [this] in a moment of excitement would have the most deplorable results. Please see that steps are taken to warn mill managers and all others without delay.[34]

In the charged atmosphere surrounding the Khilifat upsurge the British colonial authorities were very mindful of the dangers involved in giving a free rein to the Dundee School. The Advocate General of Bengal, T. C. P. Gibbons, confirmed that Scottish supervisors would only be protected from prosecution under certain circumstances:

> If [there being no military force present] a Magistrate or an officer in charge of a police station or any police officer of superior rank calls upon any male person (not being a soldier and acting as such) to disperse the assembly and, if necessary, to arrest and confine the members so offending, such male person must obey the order, and, if he acts in good faith, he is protected.[35]

Up to 1920 Europeans had been mobilised in the Indian Defence Force, but with the implementation of the Auxiliary Forces Act on 1st October of that year its place was 'taken by the force created under the Indian Territorial Force Act'. In effect, the new military unit was organised along the lines of the 'old militia' in Britain, consisting of 'batteries which will be embodied annually for 28 days consecutive training, after such preliminary training of recruits not exceeding 28 days as may be required.' The new Auxiliary Force, as it was known, was 'restricted to European British subjects' between the ages of 18 and 30, and enrolment was conducted on a voluntary basis.[36]

These changes increased government control over the use of firearms by Scottish supervisors, but, following the Lewis gun incident, the Auxiliary Force was regarded with scepticism, and the government debate on its use had as its purpose the defining of acceptable reasons for the deployment of military force by the jute mill authorities. Their freedom to act independently of the colonial state was not permitted, and nor would it be at any point during our period. In fact, the mill managers, through their increased appointment as magistrates in the mill areas, were being brought more within the orbit and control of the colonial state so as to avoid the risk of high-handed and arbitrary use of force. The belief that this measure would calm labour relations would, though, prove to be misplaced.

During the 1920 Lewis gun debate, a complacent government official assumed that, 'managers and assistants are nearly all of them members of the Auxiliary Force and, as such, can be called out under Section 18 of the Auxiliary Force Act.'[37] Inquiries actually revealed that 'many mill managers and European mill employees [have] not joined the Auxiliary Force.'[38] A further investigation confirmed that the Auxiliary Force had a total complement of 269 in the 41 jute mills that were detailed, representing – at a rough estimate – one-fifth of eligible supervisors. While some mills were heavily represented, with 105 members concentrated in only eight mills, many mills had few or no members within the Force.[39]

It is apparent that the Dundee School was never seen as a significant potential military force in the face of widespread civil unrest during the inter-war period. The majority of Dundee supervisors evinced little interest in becoming members of the Auxiliary Force, and the colonial authorities always harboured serious misgivings over its deployment during periods of political, communal or industrial tension. Instead, the regular military and police forces, comprising mainly Indian personnel, were commonly deployed. Although private British subjects did play a role, alongside official troops and police, during disturbances, their deployment was always seen as necessarily supplementary, and attended with an expectation of all manner of possible dangers. This raises an important question with regard to the nature of the relationship between the jute wallahs and the colonial state. In prior studies of the Bengal jute industry this relationship has been viewed as one of absolute nexus, with the colonial state sanctioning and even encouraging the use of violence by the mill authorities in the course of industrial action and political agitation.[40] This may well have been the case up to the First World War, but the 1920s saw the emergence of a much more critical attitude towards jute capital on the part of the colonial state. This does not mean that the interests of state and capital became fundamentally different. On the contrary, when the colonial state acted as a regular brake on the, sometimes dangerously reckless, attitude of jute capital towards questions such as labour relations, its aim was to discourage greater resistance by labour, which would have damaged business interests as well as providing explosive propaganda for the nationalists and endangering British rule. As we shall see, however, the coming of the communists would have a critical impact on this evolving strategy.

The post-war growth of trade unions in Bengal

The war years witnessed a dramatic expansion in Indian industrial output, and further growth was expected in the post-war period, while the establishment of the Indian Industrial Commission of 1916–18 also signalled a willingness on the part of the colonial state to ascertain the possibilities for further Indian industrial development.[41] This growing official interest and involvement, representing a qualitative change from the old established laissez-faire policy, was reinforced by the establishment of the Indian Department of Industries in October 1917, while an Advisory Board of Industries was also formed in Bengal.[42] If the colonial state was beginning seriously to address the question of Indian industrialisation, they were also becoming increasingly aware of the attendant social and political dangers that lay behind such a process – something the post-war labour upsurge forcibly underlined. Indeed, such was the impact of the unrest in Bengal that the government of Bengal set up a commission to investigate its roots causes. The resulting *Report of the Committee on Industrial Unrest* of 1921 observed that it was:

> a regrettable fact that, in spite of all that has been done during the last quarter of a century to improve the material condition of the work-people in the jute mills and other large industrial concerns on the banks of the Hooghly, the personal relations between employers and employed are much less intimate and cordial than they were twenty years ago. Unless something can be done to bridge this gulf, the continuance of disputes is inevitable, leading to interruptions of work, engendering ever increasing bitterness and causing material loss to the workers, the employers and the community at large.[43]

The *Report* noted that strikes happened in the conspicuous absence of trade union organisation of any kind, and were 'due as much to a general spirit of unrest as to the specific causes alleged in individual cases.'[44] For the members of the Indian Committee on Industrial Unrest, some form of direct worker representation promised to be a means whereby workers' grievances could be identified and dealt with before industrial struggle assumed serious proportions, but there were potentially serious obstacles in the path of such reforms:

> In the case of the workmen's representatives, there may be difficulties to begin with in finding men whose recommendations will carry weight outside limited bodies of workmen, but these difficulties will no doubt disappear with the spread of proper workmen's organisations and the introduction of duly constituted Works Committees.[45]

We see in these comments the interesting, but erroneous, assumption that 'proper workmen's organisations' would inevitably 'spread', thereby leading to the emergence of a layer of 'workmen's representatives'.

Back in the UK, the British state, too, was involved in an unprecedented intervention into industrial relations. During the war years, a double-pronged strategy had come into being, involving the official encouragement and patronage of 'respectable' trade unionism alongside the waging of obdurate war against the more crimson varieties of worker activist and leftist organiser. This evolving strategy was graphically illustrated by the British 'Report of the Committee of Enquiry into Industrial Unrest', of 1917–18:

Within some unions, in some districts, there exists an element inclined to methods tending to undermine the authority of the duly authorised Executive Councils and District Committees of the unions, and who are desirous of using the machinery of the unions to further their own extremist views. This tends to aggravate, rather than allay, industrial unrest.

Quite apart from this revolutionary element there is another class who perhaps do something to create a form of unrest, not altogether to be deprecated, although the middle of war may not perhaps be the appropriate time to air such views. We refer to the growing class amongst the workers of this country who are taking an interest in economic questions, and are studying the principles of political economy. This class who are not at all in sympathy with the extremists ... are, it is recognised, inspired by a general desire to better the conditions of the workers, by obtaining for them a larger share in the results of industry.[46]

During their hearings in Dundee, the British Committee of Enquiry into Industrial Unrest would come into contact with two men who exemplified these two tendencies. John Sime, the secretary of the Dundee and District Jute and Flax Workers' Union (DDJFWU), personified the 'class who do something to create a form of unrest, not altogether to be deprecated'. The ex-foreman of Grimond's Jute Works had, by this time, become established as Dundee's leading trade unionist. In the cold weather of 1925–6, he would also visit Calcutta in an attempt to encourage into being a functioning trade union after the image of the DDJFWU.[47] While Sime always waged an obdurate war against the jute barons of Dundee, he also turned his considerable bile and organisational abilities against communists within the DDJFWU. During the same hearing, the committee also made the acquaintance of Bob Stewart, a leading figure within the Dundee Labour Representation Committee (LRC), who later became a leading communist activist. Stewart regaled the members, in his own inimitable style, with the Marxist theory of surplus value as a means of explaining the widespread industrial trouble of the war years. It must have been apparent to the members of the committee that men such as Stewart had to be stopped, and just as apparent that men such as John Sime were in many ways more capable of accomplishing this task than the iron fist of the state apparatus.

In India, by contrast, the colonial state was starting, almost from scratch, to guide into existence a constitutional trade union movement that could be used to dampen the social and political effects of expected rapid industrialisation. Some help was provided by the Montagu-Chelmsford reforms embodied in the 1919 Government of India Act, which allowed for a limited extension of the franchise, and for the selection and promotion of labour representatives – at the discretion of the colonial state – to sit in the reformed Indian Legislative Assembly.[48] In addition, the advent of the International Labour Organization (ILO), and the need to nominate Indian representatives, presented a further opportunity for the creation of a layer of 'responsible' labour leaders at the provincial and national level.[49] In Bengal, one such figure was K. C. Roy Chowdhury, a moderate trade union activist of long standing who had served as Keir Hardie's private secretary during his visit to Bengal in 1905–6. With the advent of the ILO and the Government of India Act of 1919, Chowdhury came to national and international prominence as an Indian labour representative. He was viewed as a benevolent spirit by the jute wallahs and the colonial state, to the extent that he was dubbed '*Jo Hukum*', or 'Yes Sir', by more militant labour activists.[50] Figures such as Chowdhury, who had been involved in local and small-scale constitutionalist trade union activities, often in the face of bitter opposition from employers, now found themselves representing millions of wage labourers on the national and international stage.[51] Through forums such as the ILO they came in contact with, and were assiduously wooed by, representatives of the colonial state, colonial capital and the British Trades Union Congress (TUC). In the immediate post-First World War period, the armies they led may well have been phantom, but the colonial state and more conservative sections of the British TUC leadership championed the likes of Chowdhury in order to pre-empt the growth of nationalist and communist influence. While the rights of Indian trade unions to organise would be legally protected, the extent and form that organisation took would be heavily controlled and monitored by the colonial state, in consultation with India's leading industrial interests. They were involved in a race against time and were attempting to head off and anticipate future events. Writing in the late 1920s, D. H. Buchanan reviewed the progress of the colonial state in bringing a functioning Indian trade union apparatus into existence:

> Leaders have been developed and have learned something of how to deal with the men, the employers and the government. Besides the experience gained at home, they have come into contact with union leaders of other countries, especially in England and at the international labour conferences.[52]

Despite official encouragement, Indian trade union activists continued to face deep-rooted hostility from the employers, which was attested to in 1921 by the secretary of the Calcutta-based Employees Association:

> There is another important aspect of the question, viz., the unity among the employers in Bengal which is a menace to the economic up-liftment of the workers. The committee is aware of several cases, specially one in Raniganj where 'hukum' went around different factories not to employ 'budmashes' who caused strikes and therefore must starve. In fact strong weapons now exist in the hands of employers not only to lock out but to induce fellow-employers not to engage Union men or strikers. This method is not used wholesale at present, but will be resorted to sooner or later by the Employers Unions and Associations and Chambers of Commerce whose principal asset is exploitation of cheap 'native' labour.[53]

The official attempt to encourage 'responsible trade unionism', as a means of limiting nationalist influence, was also affected by the colonial state's strategy of binding the mill owners and managers into government decision making frame-works within the mill districts. Labour activists commonly faced hostile magis-trates who were often also mill managers, a problem that increased with the growth of the communists during the late 1920s and the move towards a more punitive approach to the 'labour question' by the colonial state. Before this time, jute capital had faced surprisingly little pressure from Indian political groups. During the non-cooperation agitation, Khilifat activists organised volunteer groups and trade unions amongst jute workers, while Khilifat activists were also behind the formation of the Kankinarah Labour Union (KLU) in 1923, but the influence of this union never really extended beyond the local.[54] The record of the nationalists was little better. In 1875, the leading English-language national-ist newspaper in Calcutta, *Amrita Bazar Patrika*, declared, in answer to the rising demands of British manufacturers for Indian factory legislation, that a 'larger death rate amongst our operatives is far more preferable to the collapse of this rising industry.'[55] During the 1900s and early 1920s, nationalists, such as A. C. Banerjee and C. R. Das, were alerted to the political potential of the jute workers, but the wider nationalist movement proved reluctant to use industrial labour as anything more than an auxiliary force in demonstrations.[56] Interest in the 'labour question' amongst bhadralok youth was also minimal at this stage, and the demise of the non-cooperation movement in 1922 saw many young Bengali intellectuals turning towards revolutionary terrorist groups, such as Anushilan Samiti and Juguntar, which showed signs of recrudescence in the mid-1920s.[57] It would not be until the 1930s and the demise of the Civil Disobe-dience campaign that the nationalists' stand-offish attitude towards industrial labour would change, encouraged by the demise of revolutionary terrorism and the formation of the Congress Socialist Party (CSP).[58] Comprising figures such as the former communists Sibnath Banerjee and A. M. A. Zaman, the CSP in Bengal would spearhead a major challenge to the communists in the trade union sphere.[59]

During the 1920s, it was left up to individual 'outsider' activists, who were themselves often nationalists, to bring trade unionism to the jute belt. Conflicts between the Dundee School and Indian workers continued, and would provide the impetus for the formation of a local trade union that grew into a new and militant type of industrial unionism. The Gourepore mill was the scene of some of the worst violence during the 1920–2 labour upsurge and in the early months of 1923, a further strike followed the alleged assault by a Scottish supervisor, a Mr Small, on a sirdar called Ganesh Lall, which resulted in the sirdar's 'severe injury', dismissal and eviction from the mill lines.[60] The subsequent decision by the manager to sack and evict the strikers from their tied accommodation in the mill lines resulted in a procession of 200 workers to the head office of the mill agents in Calcutta (a round trip of 32 miles) in order to publicise their griev-ances. With increasing pressure being exerted on management by workers and an increasingly restive nationalist press, Small was hastily sent back to Scotland. The dismissal of a Scottish supervisor was a rare occurrence, and the episode gave birth to the Gourepore Works Employees' Association in April 1923. Faced with a growing resolve by management to break the new union, workers conducted nine further strikes at mills in the Gourepore area over the course of the following two years, including a protracted and bitter dispute that lasted over three months.[61]

During the cold weather of 1925–6, labour organisation in Bengal received a fillip with the ground-breaking visit of John Sime and Thomas Johnston, at the behest of the Dundee Jute and Flax Workers' Union.[62] By the time of Sime and Johnston's arrival the Gourepore Works Employees' Association had merged with two other local unions, covering the Nuddea and Reliance mills, which gave rise to the formation of the Bhatpara-based Bengal Jute Workers' Association (BJWA).[63] Although the new union was small, with a nominal membership of 3,000 and a paying membership of only 400–500, Sime and Johnston were impressed with its level of organisation, which distinguished it from the other small and 'quite useless' nationalist and Khilifat unions that they encountered.[64] The leaders of the BJWA included Santosh Kumari Gupta, a wealthy barrister's daughter, who became involved in Khilifat and Congress politics in 1921 before gravitating towards labour issues through her involvement in the Bengal monthly newspaper, *Samhati*, which offered a critique of labour conditions in the Bengal jute industry.[65] Sime and Johnston also developed a good working relationship with Kalidas Bhattacharya who they described as 'an able, intelligent workman' who had 'the root of the matter in him.' Bhattacharya, an ex-revolutionary terrorist, had briefly worked in a jute mill before being dismissed and was also involved in the formation of the unions at Gourepore, Nuddea and Reliance mills.[66] Sime and Johnston were particularly anxious to make contact and to establish working relations with trade union activists and leaders who were not influenced by nationalist, Khilifat or communist ideas, and the BJWA seemed to be just such an organisation. As a result, the executive of the JFWU decided to make a grant of £50 to 'push on organisation amongst the Bengal jute workers.'[67] In the months following Sime and Johnston's return to Britain, however, communism started to sink roots in Bengal, and the BJWA came under its growing influence.

The coming of the communists

In 1919, the Third International, or Comintern as it became known, was established to bring about a worldwide workers' revolution. In its early years, however, it primarily functioned as a means of reducing the pressure on the embattled Soviet regime, which was facing a British led foreign military intervention. British intelligence chiefs expected the Soviets to use the Comintern as a means of attacking Britain's 'eastern possessions … and particularly India', a suspicion that was further underlined in December 1919 when a Soviet radio broadcast announced that 'the Russian Communist Party had decided to "take concrete measures to spread Revolution in the East" and that the International was about to establish sections in oriental countries.'[68] The British Raj stepped up security measures as worried colonial officials prepared for the arrival of hordes of soviet agents.

In the event, the fears of colonial officials proved to be largely groundless, as, up to the late 1920s, the progress of the communists in India was minimal, due to the Comintern's repeated failure to properly co-ordinate their intervention. The work in India was initially co-ordinated by M. N. Roy from his bases in Berlin and Paris, but Roy failed to establish a functioning Indian group, despite heavy expenditure. As a result, responsibility for India was given over to the Communist Party of Great Britain (CPGB) in 1924, under the direction of Rajani Palme Dutt who kept in regular contact with the communist full-timers who were sent to India. By 1927–8, these efforts were bringing rewards through the efforts of George Allison and Philip Spratt.[69] Their success stemmed from their ability to coordinate the efforts of Indian communists and socialists who were increasingly attracted to the 'Russian brand' of socialism. A key early contact and recruit in Bengal was Gopen Chakraborty, who, in 1924, was one of the first Anushilan activists to break away from revolutionary terrorism.[70] Chakraborty was first attracted to communist ideas during his incarceration in a detention camp, when he read *The Statesman*. This Calcutta-based newspaper representing British interests was 'abusively fulminating every day against Soviet Russia, particularly Lenin. This convinced us that something really progressive was taking place.'[71] Chakraborty exemplified the self-sacrifice and audacity of the small group of pioneering young bhadralok activists who were attracted to communism. However, their willingness to fight against British imperialism on the basis of working class struggle ran up against potentially far-reaching problems. They had no base or day-to-day contact with the working class, and few, if any, activists possessed even an elementary knowledge of Hindi or Urdu, and were thus cut off from direct contact with the majority of workers within the province. Moni Singh described the almost comical dilemma that he and his comrades faced when they visited the Kessoram cotton mill in 1928;

> Most of the workers … were non-Bengali people from Bihar and UP. The workers began to explain to us in chaste Urdu, why they had gone on strike. It was a language we did not know. Neither did we have any experience of textile mills. I could not follow a single word. Gopen Da had a smattering of Hindi, but even he failed to understand much. Seeing our blank looks, the workers realised that we could follow nothing. They said, 'Come to the Secretary Sahib.' Though called secretary, he was actually the manager. The manager was an educated Marwari gentleman, young in age. We considered it better to see the manager, because we could not really understand the problem at all.[72]

The response to this deep-seated difficulty was typical of the élan and energy of the early Bengali communists. In 1927, Gopen Chakraborty had become a 'machine man' in the Bhatpara jute mill and took a room in the mill bustee, where he lived for nine months before being sacked and blacklisted.[73] This experience, though brief, was far-reaching. A branch of the Bengal Jute Workers Union (BJWU) was established in Bhatpara that subsequently became a communist stronghold and platform for widening communist influence.[74]

The intervention of the communists in Chengail-Bauria, to the south of Calcutta, during a widespread strike in 1928 built on the foundations established at Bhatpara; and this also provided a model for work by leftist groups in the 1930s. Regular and protracted visits to the mill districts enabled the communists to build a base of contacts through the setting up of factory cells and workers' study groups, which were maintained through the establishment of, very often, rudimentary trade union offices that became focal points for workers with grievances against mill management. These, in turn, provided the communists with issues to campaign on through factory gate and bustee meetings. It was a simple but highly effective method of reaching the workers – but not controlling them. Very rarely were membership lists kept by labour activists as these could be seized by the police and agents of jute capital. However, despite the self-sacrifice and high-mindedness of the communist bhadralok, the encounter with the chotalok sparked a sometimes-bitter inner conflict that was highlighted by the experience of a youthful Sibnath Banerjee, who later became a leading figure in the Congress Socialist Party (CSP):

> It might have been in my sub-conscience [*sic*] mind that jute workers repelled me. When I was a student in the school, there was a mill opposite to it and there three ferry-boats drawn by motor launch used to take the workers from Hooghly side and they were so dirty in their clothes and vulgar in their talk that I almost was repelled. I belonged to an intellectual class, though poor but proud of our culture and all that, and this feeling of repulsion, perhaps, was in me.[75]

This frank admission by a leading trade unionist underlines the massive social chasm that separated the bhadralok from the mass of Muslim and low-caste Hindu jute workers. Banerjee was able to overcome his prejudices, but these were often deep rooted amongst men and women from a similar class and caste background, few of whom came in regular contact with industrial workers, or who shared Banerjee's political convictions. The racial hierarchy of colonial Bengal that weighed so heavily on the self-esteem of the bhadralok was paralleled by a bhadralok prejudice towards the jute workers that served as a psychological and cultural barrier in the fight to build a broad-based anti-imperialist movement. In addition, jute workers had to contend with long working hours, a subsistence diet, and tied housing that severely affected their ability to play a meaningful political role outside work hours. Philip Spratt also pointed to a further, and important, difficulty arising from the common practice of early marriage amongst many male jute workers, which he believed discouraged the emergence of working class leaders because young married men were unlikely to risk their jobs by openly facing down management. With few resources at their disposal, the communists were virtually compelled to appoint young middle-class Bengalis as labour leaders and 'party wholetimers', because they could maintain themselves when they worked in the mill districts.[76] Bhadralok activists were able to fall back upon the goodwill and generosity of family and friends in order to recuperate from the rigours of political work, and to shelter from police atten-tion.[77] This was also possible for migrant worker militants, but the family small-holding could not be sustained for long periods without the income from their wages. As a result, it was well nigh impossible for jute workers to maintain full-time political activity without endangering the links with their own communities. The full-time worker militant remained a contradiction in terms against which the communists fought in vain.[78]

Although few if any jute mill workers became full-time political activists, this should not be taken to suggest that worker self-organisation was absent in the mill districts. As in Dundee, many strikes in Bengal that were described as 'spontaneous' were actually carefully planned, although bhadralok labour activ-ists, as well as the colonial state and the employers, often failed to identify the mechanics of this organisation. The mills and the wider mill districts formed a complex matrix of networks, with shifting relationships and alliances between different kin, community, religious and work groups and with other social actors, such as moneylenders, shopkeepers and goondas. During strikes these networks ensured access to credit, and also enabled the establishment of links with other workers in further flung areas of the jute belt.

The influence of these various networks was revealed by the *Report of the Committee on Industrial Unrest* in 1921. In November 1920, following approaches from weavers at the Hooghly mill, who were striking over a demand for an increase in wages, strike action broke out amongst weavers in the Fort William jute mill, who then approached the workers of the Ganges mill in Sibpur. Within a week nearly 30,000 workers in the Howrah mill district were out on strike, and on 2 December 1920 a large assembly of jute workers from local mills gathered in Sibpur bazaar in Howrah in order to discuss a suitable course of action, a meeting, which was also attended by a number of maulvis from Calcutta. Many workers felt that a long-term dispute was out of the ques-tion due to a lack of resources and the meeting broke up inconclusively. The next day a group of strikers from the Ganges mill returned to work and on 5 December another mass meeting at Sibpur decided to end the strike.[79] This brief description brings out some of the essential elements of working class organisa-tion. We see the importance of specific work groups, such as the weavers who, as already shown, played a leading role in the non-cooperation movement, making use of religious networks and connections that went beyond the level of the mill to encompass contacts with other Julaha weavers, and also other Muslim workers and elites from across the Calcutta conurbation and beyond. The extent and effectiveness of these organic forms of working class organisation was rec-ognised by the Australian Comintern agent, J. F. Ryan, who observed that 'in most Unions led by outsiders, much of the real organisation is done by the workers – and the employers know it.'[80] Strike leaders were, though, extremely reticent when it came to identifying themselves openly to management. They were aware of the often contemptuous and racist attitudes of jute mill managers – and indeed Bengali babus – and often welcomed bhadralok offers to represent their grievances. Bhadralok representatives were, in their eyes, sahibs who could often negotiate with mill managers in English – indeed many had a better grasp of Received Pronunciation than some Scottish *Doric*[81] speaking mill managers. This was certainly the experience of Sibnath Banerjee, who described many of the Scottish mill managers with whom he negotiated as 'almost illiterate', and commonly 'embarrassed' by their inability to answer the questions that were put to them.[82]

With the coming of the communists, the Indian labour question became ever more politicised. The influence of more liberal elements within the colonial state was marginalised, leading directly to the Meerut conspiracy case and the utilisation of the full weight of the colonial state against the nascent communist apparatus in Bombay and Calcutta.[83] However, the belief of officialdom and employers that a crackdown would still labour unrest proved to be wildly off the mark as the largest ever movement of jute workers broke out a few weeks following the Meerut round-up.

The Marwaris, the jute wallahs and the 1929 jute strike

With a booming export trade and rising prices, the Bengal jute industry emerged from the First World War in a very strong position, and the IJMA ensured the continuation of high profit levels, even during the post-war depression of 1920–3, through brokering a series of short-time working agreements.[84] The venerable old 'Calcutta hand', D. R. Wallace, reflected the optimism of the 'jute wallahs' in 1927 when he wrote that:

> Markets have now assumed a brighter outlook and the financial position of the mills is such as to put them in a position to weather for all time the fluctuating dangers of markets provided the agents curb their ambitions and the quality of mutual trust prevails in all ranks when knotty points crop up for discussion.[85]

In the event, Wallace's optimism would prove to be misplaced, as British colonial capital was challenged from within the very heart of their citadel. The example set by G. D. Birla and Sarupchand Hukumchand proved to be an inspiration to other Indians, shattering business apartheid within the Bengal jute industry and dispelling the notion that Scotsmen alone could control the world markets for jute. Tensions between the Anglo-Scottish managing agencies and the Indian newcomers were minimal while the fat years continued, but increased from the late 1920s as economic problems started to emerge. G. D. Birla and other Marwari magnates, such as Kessoram Poddar, became leading supporters of and close friends with Gandhi, while many other Indian businessmen supported Congress in a more discreet manner. In 1927, the establishment of the Federation of Indian Chambers of Commerce and Industry (FICCI) created a powerful organisation of Indian businessmen with nationalist sympathies that quickly emerged as a major opponent of the British-dominated Bengal Chamber of Commerce (BCC).[86] Many Calcutta jute wallahs never accepted Birla and

Hukumchand as being a part of the tradition on which the *Romance of Jute* was based, but their antipathy towards the Marwaris was founded on more than mere prejudice. The established British-controlled companies had accumulated substantial reserves that helped in purchasing stocks of raw jute, but new mills needed to borrow for this purpose, thus greatly adding to their costs of production. Their higher fixed costs meant that they had to work at full capacity, which conflicted with the IJMA's long-established support for short-time working agreements.[87] By the late 1920s, the newer, predominantly Indian-owned, 'outside mills' accounted for 6 to 8 per cent of total output in the Bengal jute industry, and established firms responded to this new threat by, often surreptitiously, adding to their own capacity.[88]

On 1 July 1929, the Bengal jute industry was plunged into further turmoil with the ending of the IJMA short-time working agreement, which paved the way for a competitive war between the British managing agencies and the mostly Marwari controlled 'outside mills'. Working hours were raised from 54 to 60 with no increase in wages, while *khoraki*, paid when working hours were reduced and worth 10 per cent of wages, was removed, and weavers' piece rates were manipulated so that they also lost out.[89] A certain amount of labour trouble was always expected during the transition to different shift systems, but workers normally settled down after a few days. Almost on cue, on 5 July strikes broke out at four mills in the Jagatdal-Kankinara area – Alliance, Waverley, Craig and Megna – when the weavers decided to work for no more than 54 hours. During early July, further strikes broke out at Baranagore, a northern suburb of Calcutta, and in the Sealdah-Belliaghata area in east Calcutta. Following a further strike at the Baranagore East and South mills, workers contacted the BJWU, which attempted to intervene in the spreading strike-wave. During late July and early August, thousands of red leaflets printed in Hindi and Urdu were circulated throughout the jute belt, processions were organised, and volunteers wearing red sashes urged workers to join the strike. By 5 August, all bar two of the mills between Naihati, in the far north of the jute belt, and Calcutta were on strike along with most of the mills in the Hooghly district, affecting around 120,000 workers.[90] The size of the dispute was already unprecedented, but the following days witnessed a further escalation and by 15 August it was reported that upwards of 240,000 workers were out. The following day *Amrita Bazar Patrika* reported 'a heavy exodus of strikers ... declaring that they will come back only when their demands will be fulfilled and the BJWU will instruct resumption of work.'[91] However, the control of the union over the strikers was much more limited than this comment suggests, as would be underlined during the course of the negotiations that led to the ending of the dispute.

The IJMA had steadfastly refused to negotiate with the BJWU, which they dismissed as an 'unregistered union' run by 'professional agitators', but the spiralling strike forced them to change tack.[92] Negotiations were, though, conducted, not with the established labour leaders who made up a majority of the central strike committee, but with a minority nationalist element within the committee led by Prabhabati Das Gupta.[93] On 14 August, with the strike still

escalating, the employers agreed to increase wages, to re-introduce *khoraki* payments and to reinstate the old system of bonus payments, which prompted an
orderly return despite the opposition of the majority of the strike committee.[94]
The agreement produced a serious split in the BJWU, and led to fresh walk-outs
by workers in mills such as Howrah and Fort Gloster, who had not joined the
main strike movement, but who were anxious to be included in the strike
settlement.

A note written by the government mandarin, R. N. Gilchrist, in November
1929, pointed to the 'widely believed rumour that the prolongation and extension of the dispute was really due to the intrigues of speculators in the hessian
market.'[95] *Capital* added its voice to the rumour mill, charging Marwari speculators with cancelling contracts for jute goods at unprofitable rates in order to gain
better deals at the higher rates that resulted from the strike.[96] In the coming
months and years such accusations would proliferate – particularly when industrial action was limited to Anglo-Scottish jute mills – and would often implicate
Birla. The 1929 strike was a result of Marwari influence, but not in the way suggested by conspiracy theorists within the IJMA. As we have already seen, the
ending of the working-time agreement, which triggered the strike, was a consequence of the determination of the IJMA to deal with, predominantly Marwari-
controlled, 'interloper' mills.

The political climate in Bengal at this time, allied with Birla's well-known
support for Indian nationalism, ensured that suspicions regarding the Indian
interlopers would strengthen amongst an increasingly paranoid British business
community. Birla became a bogeyman, and his influence was discerned not only
in the jute general strike of 1929 but also in the eruption of the Civil Disobedi-
ence Movement the following year. In June 1930, Edward Benthall, the leading
figure within Bird & Co., argued long and hard with George Schuster of the
Indian government regarding the attitude to be taken towards Birla:

> I explained that the trouble was that Birla had owing to his success in
> wirepulling ... earned the reputation of being able to pull any strings and
> that this gave him a power among Indian businessmen which they did not
> understand and feared, and that therefore they were afraid to oppose him.[97]

In the ensuing years, Benthall's attitude towards Birla changed as he strove to
reconcile Indian and British interests, but these attempts foundered due to the
difficulties created by the depression and particularly the increasing animus that
marked relations between sections of British and Indian jute capital during the
course of the 1930s. As Chapter 7 will demonstrate, these developments would
also have a far-reaching impact on the nature and character of the imperial nexus
of jute.

6   The imperial nexus and labour politics in Dundee during the 1920s

Bhat spoke of the need for a union between the workers of Scotland and India. Scotland in particular, he said, had been hard hit by the competition of low paid Indian labour. Jute workers in Dundee ought not to forget what the transference of capital from Dundee to India meant. In India the raw jute was produced and worked by raw human beings (laughter) docilely working on deliciously low wages, and it was transported at rates about a 1/5 of the transport rates here. Whether by land or sea Indian workers were at the throat of the Scottish workers through the economic manipulation of one set of workers against another.... The division which had existed it had been the policy of all the governments of the earth to make use of in the interests of the capitalists. The message from India was 'Let there be no division'.

(Address by K. S. Bhat, on behalf of the Workers Welfare League of India (WWLI), to the Scottish Trades Union Congress at Edinburgh in April 1922)[1]

When K. S. Bhat addressed the Scottish Trades Union Congress (STUC), a serious economic depression had been spreading for nearly two years, and his plea for linking up the struggles of Indian and British workers drew an enthusiastic response, particularly from delegates representing the Jute and Flax Workers' Union (JFWU).[2] In the immediate post-war years the Indian jute industry had grown at an alarming rate, while a 1919 Trade Board *Report* had also calculated that the cost of producing one ton of British jute goods had increased from twice that in Bengal to three times in three years.[3] The question of 'low-paid Indian labour' was also taken up by the 1922 British Trades Union Congress when a JFWU sponsored resolution calling for a trade union delegation to be sent to the sub-continent was debated and passed.[4] However, it would take nearly five years before the TUC acted on their resolution and, faced with increasing foreign competition and a rising communist challenge, the JFWU leadership took their own initiative.[5] In October 1925, with a state round-up of British communist leaders in progress, it was announced that 'Mr Tom Johnston, MP and Mr J. F. Sime, secretary of the union, left the city on Wednesday, 14th October, en route to India. They will be away until early in the New Year. Their enquiry will be into the working conditions of jute workers which we hope will benefit the workers of Dundee in the future.'[6] The Indian visit was a ground-breaking venture, but it also opened up a major fault-line in Dundee's labour movement, between a social democratic vision of a Labour-empire that promised to use imperial structures to regulate and improve workers conditions and a communist perspective of an international workers revolution that would emerge from the ruins of Empire.

British communists and the colonial question

The communists in Dundee

Engagement with the causes and consequences of imperialism was, though, not a given during the formative period of British communism. At the second congress of the Comintern in 1920, Tom Quelch, a delegate from the British Socialist Party (BSP), caused exasperation when he stated that 'the average English worker would consider it [being required to help anti-colonial movements as] treason'.[7] Quelch also attended the 1921 Comintern congress at Baku where he met M. N. Roy, who attempted to convince the sceptical British delegate 'that there were hopes of Communism being established at least in Bengal.... He based this statement on the ground that Bengal was the brain of India, and religious differences ... are less apparent [there] than elsewhere.'[8] Progress in convincing the British communists of the necessity of establishing organisational links with anti-colonial movements was, however, slow and three years later the British party was upbraided by the Comintern for doing 'as good as nothing' to support nationalist and anti-imperial movements. Even more damning, they had not yet declared 'unequivocally for the separation of the colonies from the British Empire'.[9] The criticisms, though, were being addressed by leading British communists such as R. P. Dutt and Clemens Dutt, both of whom were centrally involved in attempting to develop a coherent theoretical and organisational approach to the issue of British imperialism, along with Shapurji Saklatvala, who became the first communist MP in 1922.[10] In addition, links were established with Indian émigré revolutionaries in Berlin, including M. N. Roy, which led to the creation of the Indian Labour Bureau in 1923.[11]

Despite other differences, British communist theorists agreed with M. N. Roy that India was undergoing a phase of rapid industrialisation endorsed and sponsored by the British imperial state, which became known as the 'decolonisation theory'. For M. N. Roy, the new strategy of British imperialism resulted from the seeming inability of British industry to keep the Indian market supplied with manufactured goods, which, in turn, opened up a position for nascent Indian manufacturers.[12] In effect, British imperialism was seeking to detach the big sections of the Indian bourgeoisie from the country's burgeoning nationalist movement by offering concessions, in the shape of the 1919 Government of India Act. In this way, British imperialism was attempting to pull the nascent Indian bourgeoisie into a role as a junior partner in the exploitation of Indian labour, which in turn would inevitably lead to an intensification of class conflict between an enlarged Indian proletariat and Indian industrial capital.[13] The 'decolonisation theory' markedly differed from the Comintern view that Indian industrial development was being held back by British imperialism.[14] It also contradicted the ideas outlined by Lenin in *Imperialism: the highest stage of capitalism*.[15] While Lenin saw imperialism as bolstering the material condition of the British working class, thus allowing for the emergence of a 'labour aristocracy', M. N. Roy and other communist specialists stressed the negative impact of Indian cheap labour competition for British economic and social development, a position similar to that outlined by the radical liberal J. A. Hobson and also, as we shall see, of Labour's leading spokesmen on imperial issues.

The early agitation and propaganda work of the communists rarely involved anything more than generalised attacks on the iniquities of British imperialism. Bob Stewart, the Scottish party's first full-time organiser, admitted that it was only through the patient encouragement of Mikhail Borodin, a representative of the Comintern who was sent to Britain in 1922 in order to 'get an on-the-spot understanding' of the British communists methods of work, that he came to understand the 'value of international work, international trade union contact [and] international exchange of information ... all of which was very new to me.'[16] Borodin's advice did not go unheeded – in 1923 British intelligence sources reported that 'Bob Stewart, a Communist, has been trying to win over Indian students at Dundee University.'[17] Although nothing seems to have come from this early attempt at international contact work, the communists in Dundee were an increasing source of concern for 'moderate' elements within the city's Labour Party, as well as the British intelligence services.

Bob Stewart attended the Communist Unity Convention of July–August 1920 as one of four delegates from the Socialist Prohibitionist Fellowship and intervened in some of the most important debates.[18] As a young man he had campaigned for the independent labour candidate James MacDonald in 1895, but, due to his early involvement in the Independent Order of Good Templars (IOGT) and the Rechabites, he was attracted to socialist prohibitionism, joining Neddy Scrymgeour's Scottish Prohibitionist Party (SPP) in the early 1900s. In 1908 he was elected as an SPP town councillor, and also acted as Scrymgeour's election agent during the 1908 parliamentary by-election, which was won by Winston Churchill. Tensions had, though, been building between Stewart and his erstwhile political mentor and a 'year or so after the election' he left the SPP because, 'I could no longer stomach the religious prattlings of Scrymgeour and some of his adherents. A number of us broke away and formed the Prohibition and Reform Party.'[19] Stewart quickly became a leading figure within the Communist Party of Great Britain (CPGB). He was the party's first parliamentary candidate in the Caerphilly by-election in 1921, shortly before his appointment as the Scottish party full-timer.[20] His local role following the establishment of the Dundee CP was therefore limited, although the Socialist Prohibitionist Fellowship's Unity Hall became the new party's local headquarters.[21]

The formation of the CPGB marked a major transition towards a new type of British Marxist party. Whereas earlier socialist organisations, such as the SDF and the Socialist Labour Party (SLP), emphasised the role of education and propaganda, reflecting their belief that mass support for socialism would only emerge following a full-blown crises of capitalism, the major focus of the new organisation was on action and full participation in all spheres of working class experience. Gone was the belief that 'reason is the main force of human action' and that socialism would be accepted because of its self-evident 'justice, rationality and wisdom.'[22] Lenin outlined the new method in *Left Wing Communism: an infantile disorder*, which was written and published in 1920. Lenin heavily criticised the purist isolationism of many British Marxists and urged them to 'work by every possible means wherever the masses are to be found', be it 'within unions, societies' or even 'chance gatherings of the common people' including the 'humble tavern', where they should engage with workers in a way that was not patronising or overly-intellectual.[23] Lenin also emphasised the importance of full participation in the Labour Party and parliamentary elections, and succeeded in overcoming the ultra-left and syndicalist instincts of many industrial militants, including Willie Gallagher, a leading figure within the BSP and the Glasgow shop stewards movement. Despite almost complete acceptance of the new methods, the CPGB remained, for the first few years of its existence, a loose federation of 'vague, propagandist territorial groupings'.[24] Although the early British communists had a strong presence within some unions, their industrial work lacked the systematic approach prescribed by Lenin and recommended by the *Report on Organization*, adopted by the CPGB in 1922 in a bid to 'bolshevise' the party.[25]

The early progress of the communists in Dundee was also marked by fit and start. Between August 1920 and February 1921, 69 new members were enrolled, of which only six were female, while the active membership, indicated by attendances at party aggregate meetings, totalled no more than 40.[26] Despite its modest size, the Dundee CP produced an impressive result at the 1922 general election, Willie gathering 5,906 votes. Following the election, Gallagher, the CP's Dundee candidate, 'informed a comrade that "Old Pal Trotsky has sent word across regretting that I did not get in. They say that I *must* get in so it's up to us to see that there's no mistake next time." '[27] While Gallagher did not 'get in' at the following year's general election, the 10,380 votes that were gathered led to hopes that the party was on the verge of a major breakthrough, encouraged by the palpable radicalisation of many jute workers during the bitter Camperdown strike and lock-out that had brought the Dundee jute industry to a standstill earlier that same year.[28] The 1923 election results must have given particular pause for thought for Neddy Scrymgeour. His vote had dropped by nearly 7,000 compared with his breakthrough of the previous year, an indication, perhaps, of the anger felt by many jute workers at his attacks on the JFWU leadership at the height of the Camperdown dispute.[29] Although the 1923 election saw the first minority Labour government take office, the vote for Dundee's Labour candidate, E. D. Morel, fell from 30,292 to 23,343, further indicating that the CP was emerging as a new and potent electoral force in the city.[30]

The Dundee CP was never a mass organisation in membership terms and during its early years a revolving door syndrome was evident with many new recruits slipping out of activity and leaving the party. Despite this, by February 1925 membership was 172, compared with 120 in May 1924, and the party was reaching a widening audience through the distribution of the *Weekly Worker*, sales of which increased from 1,120 at the end of May 1924 to 4,320 by the middle of February 1925.[31] Supporting the communists, however, came at a price. Blacklisting and arrest for petty offences linked to street meetings, fly-posting and strike activities could result in long periods of unemployment, and as a pretext for the withholding of the character references that were necessary in order to secure a tenancy with private landlords. Victimisation was a particular, and ever-present, threat for party members in the smaller industrial towns of Forfarshire. In Arbroath it was reported that 'while the members were prepared to distribute the paper and attend to the trades union and trades council work they were diffident in regards to public propaganda, fearing victimisation.'[32] The only recourse for activists identified as troublemakers, or 'bolshies', was often out-migration in search of work and better prospects. For those who rejected the option of flight but could not keep their heads down, life could become an unremitting struggle, which the experience of an activist such as Mary Brooksbank testifies to. As a communist and jute worker in Dundee's low mills she had to contend with long periods of unemployment as her reputation as a militant became known to the authorities and employers, forcing her to seek work where she could in seasonal and temporary jobs such as fruit canning.[33]

As the CPGB started to shape itself into a more centralised body in the 1920s, tensions sometimes arose when members in Dundee refused to accept party discipline, while the major controversies within communism also took their toll. In May 1925, the emerging split within the Soviet Union that resulted in the marginalisation of Leon Trotsky and the Left Opposition coincided with significant numbers of party members leaving the party.[34] In the early 1930s, Mary Brooksbank would be expelled for denouncing Stalin, and spent the rest of her life as an independent socialist revolutionary with Trotskyist sympathies. In effect, she became a one woman roving class war machine, denouncing employers, the state, labour reformism and stalinist communism alike.[35] Mary Brooksbank was, though, unusual in the level of her commitment: she remained a convinced revolutionary until her death, even visiting Hanoi in 1970 at the age of 73 in order to 'tend the wounded and to rebuild a city being bombed "round the clock" by B52 bombers.'[36] By contrast, most members who dropped out of the CP moved towards involvement in the more mainstream avenues of the labour movement, or else dropped out of politics altogether. For other worker militants, however, the party remained a refuge from a wider society that was often hostile and unforgiving. Indeed, for many it became a veritable world within a world where they could find material and psychological support. The party also provided the opportunity for political education and organisational and leadership responsibilities, which imbued many working class recruits with a newly discovered confidence in their own capabilities. The unremitting attacks on the party throughout the 1920s also acted as a double-edged sword. While some ordinary workers may have been careful to avoid over-close relations with known communists, others were undoubtedly attracted to a party that seemed to stand separate and apart from all the others.

There was, though, another party in Dundee that strove for eminence amongst the ranks of the despised. Whilst very different in many regards, the prohibitionists and communists shared some important characteristics. Both groups were imbued with a deep-seated belief in the desirability and inevitability of political and social transformation. Both parties, too, developed an inner-party culture that was highly distinctive, and which sought to insulate members from the pressures and influences of wider society. Indeed, in July 1919 the SPP had entered into discussions with the Independent Labour Party (ILP) and Bob Stewart's National Prohibition and Reform Party (NPRP) regarding the possibility of forming a Dundee-based communist grouping.[37] The subsequent failure of the SPP to accept the proposal had less to do with any fundamental political disagreements and more to do with the personality and character of Scrymgeour. It is difficult to imagine Scrymgeour being able to work within a party that was bigger than he was, as his often prickly personality would never have been able to maintain the self-discipline and selflessness to the cause demanded by membership of a cadre organisation, such as the CP became in the course of the 1920s.

Both the SPP and the CP failed to develop a large active cadre amongst jute workers, despite having an influence amongst the city's working poor and unemployed that was out of all proportion to their small membership figures. While the SPP had an active membership and leadership that was disproportionately drawn from the lower middle class, particularly amongst shopkeepers, CP membership appeared to be concentrated amongst male skilled workers in engineering, ship-building and the building trades, as well as the postal and transport services, with women, and mill-girls in particular, woefully under-represented.[38] In 1925, CP membership in Dundee stood at 122, but female membership was only 28, although the situation was a little better in the Young Communist League (YCL) where females actually outnumbered males, being nine and eight respectively.[39] However, despite the small number of communist activists in the jute mills, the party became a considerable source of concern to the JFWU leadership.

From 1920 onwards, Dundee's Labour leaders were involved in an increasingly bitter fight with left-wing elements inside the party, including the communists who had, following Lenin's advice, joined Labour in increasing numbers. This was a definitive period for Labour, at a national level and in Dundee. Whereas the party had always functioned as a kind of 'umbrella organisation' for a host of independent groups and parties, the early 1920s saw the first steps being taken in a move away from a federal structure and towards a more centralised form of party structure. The tentative adoption of the geographically based ward system, which cut across the independence of affiliated groups such as the

ILP, enabled the 'moderate' leadership, organised around E. D. Morel and his circle, to create a definitive Labour culture, separate and apart from the local ILP as well as the recently formed CP.[40] By the mid-1920s, the Dundee CP was also starting to shape itself into a more centralised party, encouraged and prodded at every turn by King Street.[41] But it still comprised a confusing mixture of competing personal rivalries and animosities that often spilled onto the pages of the Dundee party's minute book. Friction was common between the adult party and the YCL. Concerns were sometimes expressed regarding the character of some of the younger comrades, which was compounded when the YCL treasurer absconded with funds, and the YCL was banned from using the party hall for the purpose of dances because of the frequency of fist fights and general drunkenness. However, dinner dances and other 'soirees' organised by the adult party were also often ruined by drink and violence, to the extent that leading members were directed to attend party social functions in order to ensure calm. Indeed, such was the concern at the impact of alcohol within the Dundee party that in March 1924, the No. 7 branch sent a resolution to the Local Party Committee (LPC) asking that the next aggregate meeting debate the issue of prohibition.[42]

Despite the antics witnessed when they were at play, the communists were developing an important position within Dundee's political culture. By the end of 1924, in line with the re-organisation proposals of the CPGB, an industrial 'faction' was established, comprising party members within the jute and flax industries. In 1925, communist factory groups were established at the Camperdown and Constable Works, the latter group comprising child and juvenile workers, and an industrial paper for jute workers, *The Picker*, was also produced – albeit irregularly. In addition, the party was conducting work amongst the unemployed through the National Unemployed Workers' Committee Movement (NUWCM, renamed NUWM), and was also starting to reach out beyond the bounds of Dundee, with communist branches being established in Perth, Arbroath and Brechin.[43] The party's horizons were also starting to shift much further eastwards than Arbroath. Shapurji Saklatvala was a regular visitor to the city and in January 1923 he spoke at a crowded meeting on behalf of the WWLI, organised to follow up K. S. Bhat's initiative of 1922, in order to forge links between jute workers in Dundee and Calcutta. He did not mince his words, 'During all these years ... you have called yourself trade unionists. You are nothing of the sort. You are only Dundonians. In the jute trade the men who ought to have been in your union first and foremost were the Bengal growers of jute.'[44] At the same meeting, Saklatavala announced that he intended to 'put himself into communication with Mr E. D. Morel ... and to enlist his aid in this matter.'[45] He was true to his word, but was unceremoniously rebuffed by Morel who immediately wrote to his Dundee agent:

> I send you a copy of a rather peculiar letter I have had from Saklatvala, who I don't trust, and who is a communist. I wonder – who did he see in Dundee? Show it to Sime.

PS Since writing I have got a cutting from the Dundee papers about what he said there: and I have also written to Middleton, copy of which I enclose. I think it is very awkward indeed for a member of the LP – so called – who is really a communist, and says he is, to invade my constituency, and sow the seeds of what, I suppose, is the usual communist propaganda.[46]

Morel's hostility to Saklatvala was a reflection of the threat he felt from the communists' rising influence inside Dundee Labour Party (LP). Morel was a recent convert, having stood twice for the Liberals in Oldham, and was part of a large influx of radical and progressive liberals who joined Labour and the ILP following the First World War, due to growing dismay with official liberalism. Many, including Morel, would go on to play an important part in the marginalisation of more socialist, and communist, ideas and influence within the labour movement.

The 1922 Labour Party conference rejected the attempt by the CPGB to affiliate as an organisation, and also introduced amendments to the party constitution that challenged the, hitherto, undisputed rights of communists to belong to and represent Labour as individual members. Communists were also barred from representing trade unions at the Labour Party conference, while local parties were called upon to exclude communists who had been elected as trade union representatives.[47] These attacks prompted a determined response from the left, and Labour's 1923 conference lifted most of the discriminatory clauses, but insisted that every person elected as a delegate should accept the party constitution.[48] The CPGB continued to press, unsuccessfully, for affiliation and a number of communists were locally endorsed as Labour candidates at the 1923 general election, but were refused national endorsement – including Willie Gallagher whose nomination, despite the opposition of Morel, was supported by the ILP in Dundee.[49]

In February 1924 the issue of India came back to the fore as a result of the minority Labour government's attacks on Indian communists with their initiation of the Cawnpore conspiracy trial.[50] The CPGB responded by launching a defence campaign that was enthusiastically taken up by the communists in Dundee,[51] while the imperial nexus of jute was also beginning to loom ever larger in communist thinking. In early March 1924, M. N. Roy outlined how the evolving strategy of British imperialism affected British workers:

There are three sets of Indian workers whose interests demand an immediate international settlement. They are the lascars, cotton mill workers and jute mill hands. The interests of the British and Indian workers engaged in these three branches of industry are so closely interlinked that the welfare of both demands international cooperation and organisation.[52]

Roy singled out the imperial nexus of jute as an outstanding exemplar of his decolonisation theory, when he charged that 'No British labour leader has paid any attention to the inhuman exploitation of Indian workers in Calcutta jute mills, an exploitation which undercuts the workers in Dundee.'[53] Less than two weeks following the appearance of Roy's article, an internal Dundee Communist Party (CP) document reported that the party's Women's Guild 'were to send to the joint committee of the local jute unions a resolution on the position of workers in the Indian jute industry'.[54] The following month, Saklatvala also pushed for the forging of links between the jute workers of the imperial nexus when he addressed the Scottish TUC on behalf of the WWLI.[55] Saklatavala was now, however, a marked man in the eyes of many trade union leaders and his address seemed to have little impact beyond alerting the communists' opponents inside the labour movement to their growing interest in Indian affairs. As well as attacking the largely illusory threat posed by communism in India, the first Labour government also increasingly utilised state structures and power for the purpose of attacking the more 'home grown' of the species. In May 1924 Sydney Webb reported that 'The Home Secretary was continuously watching all their [the CPGB] proceedings and reporting weekly to the Prime Minister the discoveries of the police spies.'[56] The gathering strikes that marked the early months of the first Labour government did, though, present opportunities for the communists to broaden their base of support amongst trade union and labour militants, and in August 1924 this was given an organisational form with the establishment of the National Minority Movement (NMM).[57] The new grouping, which was designed to bring the left wing minorities of individual trade unions under one umbrella organisation, became an important forum that enabled the wider British labour movement, including communists, to engage with the issue of imperialism. This was underlined in January 1925 at the second NMM conference, which focused on colonialism and its impact on British workers – when the sending of 'propagandists to India' was also discussed.[58]

The NMM was never intended as a communist dominated 'front organisation'. To be effective it had to function as an essential part of the wider British labour movement, by directly engaging with trade union and labour activists. This, though, presented potentially serious problems for the communists in Dundee who were tasked with building links between the jute workers of the imperial nexus. While it was important that this initiative should be recognised as communist inspired, practical measures would have to be discussed and agreed on by the jute trade unions, a broad-based strategy that also meant having to negotiate with the obdurately anti-communist leadership of the JFWU, and particularly John Sime.[59]

The Sime–Johnston visit and the Labour empire

The 'Zinoviev letter' general election of October 1924 witnessed a virtual meltdown in Labour's parliamentary representation, but E. D. Morel bucked the national trend as he was returned with a large majority, which represented a substantial improvement on his disappointing showing at the 1923 general election. However, on 12 November, Morel, whose health had never really recovered from his war-time incarceration, died suddenly from heart disease as he recuperated from the strain of his recent election triumph. His passing was widely mourned by labour movement activists and progressive opinion in Britain and internationally. John Sime, who admired Morel almost to the point of hero-worship, was inconsolable when he learned of his erstwhile comrade's passing. He had been a prime mover behind Morel's selection in 1922, and was again centrally involved in the nomination of a figure who would be a worthy successor to 'the white man with the straight eye' – the moniker bestowed on Morel by tribal chiefs during his pre-war African anti-slavery campaign.

In November 1924, at an internal meeting of the Dundee CP called to prepare for the by-election caused by Morel's untimely death, Bob Stewart noted 'the adroitness' of the Labour Party in selecting Tom Johnston as Morel's successor.[60] Johnston was, indeed, a well-chosen candidate. He had entered parliament in 1922, but had then lost his West Stirlingshire seat at the 1924 general election.[61] During his first stint in Parliament, Johnston had quickly emerged as a leading member of the 'Clydesiders', the group of left-wing Labour MP's that also included John Wheatley and John Maxton, who were also elected in 1922 from the west of Scotland. Johnston was also the editor of *Forward*, the highly regarded Scottish socialist newspaper, and was a keen supporter of prohibition. After a peremptory by-election campaign he easily defeated the only other candidate in the field.[62]

Following his election, Johnston quickly came to the fore as a leading Labour spokesman on imperial and international issues. He was a keen advocate of J. A. Hobson's theory of 'under-consumption', which contended that suppressed consumer demand was a major cause of high unemployment, a problem that Johnston believed was further aggravated by Britain's large war debt.[63] Empire, according to Johnston, added to these problems because the importation of goods produced by cheap labour in the colonies had a detrimental impact on British employment levels and wages.[64] Rather than a 'free market' in the production of 'sweated goods', whether produced at home or abroad, Johnston envisioned a radical policy involving the collective purchasing and marketing of Empire foodstuffs and raw materials, the bulk exchange of surpluses between Britain and Empire countries, and the widespread introduction of cooperative schemes in marketing and distribution. According to Johnston, this policy would end the damaging impact of middlemen and speculators through the development of a socialist policy of 'Imperial preference' that would prohibit the importation of sweated goods from the colonies.[65] The election of Labour governments in the Dominions was seen as the basis for providing greater unity and international cooperation, and Johnston envisioned an Empire under socialist control, with home rule for the colonies and a federated parliament, which he believed 'might be made the greatest lever for human emancipation the world has ever known.'[66] A system of Empire trade would also encourage Indian industrialisation, while British laws would protect workers and peasants and guarantee the rising wages that could be used to buy British consumer goods. Similarly, new industries in the colonies would purchase their machinery from British manufacturers, thus guaranteeing continuing British economic dominance, higher standards of living and low unemployment rates.[67]

Johnston was also instrumental in establishing the Labour Commonwealth Group of MPs, involving figures such as the noted left-winger and founder of the *Daily Herald* George Lansbury, and the Lancashire cotton workers' leader Tom Shaw.[68] Although only ever numbering around 30 active members, the Commonwealth Group proved highly effective at getting resolutions on colonial issues debated and passed at Labour conferences, and also convened several Commonwealth conferences during the 1920s, which brought together labour leaders from the Dominions.[69] Leading figures within the Commonwealth Group, such as Johnston and Shaw, deprecated what they viewed as tiresome communist tub-thumping on the issue of colonialism. For them the Empire was a reality that could not be removed with the wave of a communist apparatchik's wand. Indeed, far from advancing socialism, as the communists argued, the break-up of the Empire, according to Johnston, would create a virtual apocalypse involving 'fresh wars and reconquests, wholesale decimation, fire, slaughter, and a relapse to barbarism'.[70] Britain had a responsibility to the peoples of the Empire who had not yet learned how to govern themselves in a modern, fast-changing world, so rather than pulling it down root and branch, the Empire would be improved and gradually reformed out of existence. For the communists, the policies of the Commonwealth Group confirmed their prediction of a coming together of Labour reformism with the ruling interests of the British and colonial state. Some of those who outlined a vision of a caring, sharing Empire were, after all, enthusiastic communist witch-hunters within the British labour movement, while Tom Shaw was also a leading figure within the International Federation of Trade Unions (IFTU), which was involved in an often desperate, and always dirty, war against communist influence within the international trade union movement.[71]

In February 1925, in the pages of the *Jute and Flax Workers Guide*, Johnston declared that:

> If a capitalist in Dundee were to start a factory in England and pay his labourers a *jeely piece*[72] extra when the Prince of Wales came to the district (whereby Mr Capitalist becomes expectant of a knighthood), the jute workers in Dundee would be on the war path. They would see that fourpenny jute wages in England would soon drag down the miserably low standards in Dundee.
>
> But, if this capitalist opens his factory at Calcutta (as some have already done) and gets his cheap fourpenny-a-day labourers and produces jute bags at a price with which Dundee cannot compete, ought the trade unionists of Dundee to cry 'Hurrah for free imports of the sweated jute bags?'[73]

The article concluded 'that a socialist country would prohibit absolutely the import of sweated goods.'[74] Johnston, though, was not prepared to wait around for the red flag to be hoisted above Whitehall, and in early 1925, alongside John

Wheatley, he succeeded in getting Labour to establish a committee to consider the issue of sweated imports from the colonies.[75] Johnston and Wheatley garnered plaudits for this initiative, but there was a very different response in June 1925 when they sided with Conservative MPs, against the bulk of the Parliamentary Labour Party (PLP), in voting for Imperial Preference. They were sharply rebuked for confusing the issues of sweated goods and Empire by H. N. Brailsford, editor of the ILP newspaper the *New Leader*, who argued for an alternative Labour policy of preference for imports based on labour conditions and not imperial connections.[76]

Earlier that same month, Johnston had been chosen to accompany John Sime as part of a JFWU 'delegation to India to ascertain, as far as possible, the conditions, wages, etc of jute operatives there, and to give them a fillip in Trade Union organisation.'[77] Although the communists in Dundee were responsible for first raising this proposal, it appears that John Sime had effectively seized the initiative.[78] In fact, as soon as the issue was raised within Dundee's joint committee of textile unions, Sime used the status and the votes of his union to insist that the delegation should consist only of himself and Tom Johnston.[79] The communists still attempted to exert their influence when George Rough 'submitted [a] policy which he considered should be carried out by [the] delegation to India', but the initiative had firmly passed into the hands of Sime, and from June 1925 he busied himself with preparations for the forthcoming trip. By one of those twists of fate, the death of Henry Williamson was announced a few days before the pair set off on the long voyage to Bombay.[80] It seemed, with Williamson's passing, that Dundee's trade union movement had finally emerged from an era of *ma-baap* trade unionism towards a broader, international vision that was prepared to take the fight right into the dark heart of British imperialism.

The visit itself was short but eventful. In his memoirs, Johnston described the constant tailing by the CID, the horrific conditions of Bombay's infamous *chawls*[81] and the immense red light area of the city's Grant Road, where prostitutes from every part of the world pleaded for custom behind the bars of cages.[82] The pair also made contact with N. M. Joshi, and were immediately pitched into the midst of a major strike of Bombay cotton workers. Their time in Calcutta was also eventful, and no less shocking. They visited some of Bengal's *bustees*, experiencing at first hand the gut wrenching stench, the swarms of flies and excrement smeared passageways in these breeding grounds for cholera, typhus and bubonic plague.[83] They also condemned the corruption of the sirdars within the Bengal jute industry, who, they argued, had the 'poor workers in the hollow of their hands' through their powers over the recruitment process – a view that would be echoed by subsequent British trade union delegations to India.[84]

While John Sime was in India, the Dundee *Evening Telegraph* detailed, in a sarcastic vein, his unsuccessful attempts to organise a meeting for Scottish supervisors interested in establishing a trade union.[85] In his reply, Sime set out the difficulties he had encountered. The advertised starting time of the meeting had been changed without his consent from 6 pm to 9 pm on a Sunday evening due to the pressure exerted on the venue's management committee by Sir Alexander Murray, a leading spokesman of the Indian Jute Mills Association. Sime blamed this intervention for the smaller than expected turnout, which included a 'disgracefully drunk' shareholder who heckled him throughout the meeting, and who had to be forcefully removed from the hall. He also explained the kind of pressure that was exerted on, the apparently 'contented', supervisors:

> It is not true that the Europeans are contented. They are well under 'control' of the management. When men had to meet us at a late hour at night and we had to pledge and assure them their names would never be mentioned, that there are incidents we know of but cannot mention for fear the men are 'spotted', and that men, whom I know were afraid to give me a handshake for 'auld lang syne' in presence of their managers.[86]

Perhaps not surprisingly, considering the circumstances, Sime's initiative failed. The episode did, though, illustrate the extent to which paternal despotism acted on the Dundee School as well as Indian labour. Although mill foremen and mechanics in Dundee were expected to follow a code of behaviour befitting their status, they were still able to join trades unions in large numbers, despite their employers' often deep-seated antipathy towards workers' combination. Male workers in calendering and tenting were also tightly organised, while mechanics and engineers commonly belonged to the Amalgamated Engineering Union (AEU). Indeed, the extent of trade union membership amongst the Dundee jute industry's 'labour aristocracy' was such that in 1906 *Forward* claimed that 'almost all the foremen and engineers' within the Bengal Jute industry were 'quondom British trade unionists or professed SOCIALISTS'.[87] However, those who chose to don the white suit and solar topee quickly discovered that the relative freedoms and rights that were taken for granted in Juteopolis became little more than a dim memory as soon as they landed on Indian soil.

   The jute mill compounds along the river Hooghly were protected by the visible symbols and order of colonial rule, but they still remained a frontier, miles distant from the imperial centre of Calcutta. This isolation not only increased the ability of colonial capital to control native labour, it also undermined the ability of the Scottish supervisory cadre to resist the control of higher management. Being forced to spend so much time within the bounded universe of the jute mill compound, supervisors rarely escaped the direct or indirect gaze of managerial authority. As British subjects they were, as we saw in Chapter 5, subject to the authority of the jute mill managers to an even greater degree than native labour, which is graphically borne out by the experience of Alex Scott. Shortly after his arrival in 1939, and still unfamiliar with the power of management, he was found by *durwans*[88] trying to sneak over the compound wall of the Baranagore mill at 2 am, after having spent the evening at a locally organised dance. Inevitably, the errant young supervisor was reported and he was summoned to the manager's office for a severe dressing down. Alex was fearful for his job and his future prospects with the firm, as he was well aware that the manager 'could sack you anytime' and 'send you home'.[89] Alex was right to be fearful. If a supervisor transgressed the code of behaviour laid down by management, retribution could be swift, and he would find it very difficult, if not impossible, to secure another position along the Hooghly.

Scottish supervisors in Calcutta were recruited as single young men, and they were officially discouraged from marrying while they were engaged in Indian service. They were also strictly forbidden from entertaining female guests in their rooms and there were few, if any, unmarried British women in the mill areas, while consorting openly with Anglo-Indian or Indian women was simply out of the question, at least within the mill compound. Although ex-jute wallahs were invariably unwilling to discuss the topic of sexual relations, one interviewee did admit, in an aside delivered after the tape-recorder had been turned off, that small groups of Scottish assistants commonly shared the services of concubines or prostitutes, often Anglo-Indian women, who they visited on a rota system at weekends. S. K. Basu (who was employed as the first Indian supervisor at the Gourepore mill in 1950) also remembered that Scottish supervisors 'could do all mischief with [Anglo-Indian] girlfriend, but not marry'.[90]

At the end of the long working day, the club became the major social hub for the Dundee School. It was, in the words of an ex-supervisor, a 'neutral place', where the different grades of European staff, from the assistant on his first term to the manager and assistant manager, mixed together.[91] It was a place to meet, socialise and, most importantly, to drink alcohol. The club, and the alcohol that was its main attraction, fulfilled an important function. Here tempers could be calmed, managerial behaviour justified, and important decisions explained, usually over the ubiquitous 'peg' of whisky and soda. Ceildhs also featured regularly as 'dance nights', organised to bring the clubs of different mills together, and, along with occasions such as St Andrew's and Burns Night celebrations, further encouraged folksy nostalgia and race group bonding. According to Eugenie Fraser:

> One of the most popular events in Calcutta during the cold season was the celebration of St Andrew's Day when the Caledonian Society presented a concert in the New Empire Theatre. The Scots community flocked to it.... There was a fair amount of talent in Calcutta and the singing of Scottish airs brought back a bit of Scotland with a certain nostalgia. At the end of the concert the performers and the audience stood up and joined in singing 'Auld Lang Syne'.[92]

The kind of shortbread-tin nationalism so despised by Scottish nationalist intellectuals, such as Hugh MacDairmid, thrived under the pressures exerted by close confinement, racial segregation and subsidised whisky. An *esprit de corps*, of sorts, was built from these varied and unstable materials, but during the interwar period it would come under increasing pressure.

By the time of the Sime/Johnston visit, the Bengal jute industry provided work for upwards of 1,500 managers, supervisors, mechanics and clerks, underlining the continuing, and increasing, importance of the imperial nexus of jute to the perpetuation of Dundee's labour aristocracy.[93] The Indian jute industry had grown to enormous proportions by the inter-war period, and the major firms were well established, as were the networks of influence that made decisions with regards to recruitment and promotion. It was now much more difficult for the ambitious young mechanic to scale the giddy heights of professional success than it had been for the pioneers of the Dundee School. The wheels of the jute industry moved along a 'weel kent' but rutted road, and advancement required a different kind of personality from that which had nurtured the *romance of jute*. For many, the limit of their ambition was to see out their term of service, and to return home with enough savings to guarantee an early retirement.

The number of 'jute wallahs' returning each year, following service in India, had greatly increased from the pioneering days of the Dundee School. While some were able to retire, or to secure senior positions with Dundee firms, others settled for a 'gaffership' and often irritated workers through their perceived incompetence and 'sticky' attitudes.[94] Tom Clarke, a communist who was wounded while serving in Spain with the International Brigade, worked under an ex-jute wallah in the 1920s who he remembered as a 'bloody fool'.[95] David Phillips also remembered, from his childhood in the 1920s, the resentment that was commonly shown towards the returning jute wallahs:

> The money they earned was little short of fabulous compared to ordinary wages. They were the worker-aristocracy of the jute trade, returning after some years to open a shop or to accept a gaffership. One sometimes heard an odd one who had come back to the mill criticised – 'That ane seems tae think he's still ower the darkies yit.'[96]

From the late 1920s onwards, the 'home' jute industry was convulsed by a developing wave of rationalisation and troubled labour relations, which the return of increasing numbers of jute wallahs only served to intensify.

John Sime may have failed to bring trade unionism to the Dundee School, but events surrounding the Bengal visit did provide him with an opportunity to deal once and for all with the troublesome communist presence within the JFWU, thus revealing the fundamental motivation behind Sime and Johnston's groundbreaking visit to Bengal: it was not the fear of rising Indian competition, but the increasing interest shown by the city's communists in the issue of the imperial nexus of jute that prompted the initiative and turned it into one front in the much wider war of position between labour reformism and communism that was developing at this time.

While preparing for his return to the UK in January 1926, Sime was handed a letter by T. C. Goswami that he had received from George Rough, the communist industrial full-timer in Dundee. Rough had asked Goswami to inform him if Sime and Johnston showed signs of unseemly friendliness towards colonial officials or the jute wallahs.[97] Sime was incensed at this insult to his integrity and launched a furious attack on the communists immediately following his return that ran the very real risk of splitting the JFWU. In March 1926, rowdy scenes were witnessed at the union annual general meeting (AGM), and when derogatory remarks were aimed at the communists by union leaders 'the gathering divided into separate factions, and instead of the business proceeding on the intended lines the "opposition camps" indulged in warm discussions'. The meeting descended into such chaos that no office bearers were elected, and broke up as the 'opposition camps' traded insults. Further animated scenes were also witnessed following the meeting, with crowds of members entering 'into further heated arguments, while a band of women proceeded along Ward Road arm-in-arm and singing lustily.'[98] The fact that the union leaders failed to control the meeting demonstrates the extent of communist influence within the JFWU at this time. They had emerged as a troublesome thorn in the side of the union leadership, and, following the establishment of a communist jute workers' faction, were threatening to extend their base through a more systematic approach to industrial work.

Sime was undeterred by the possibility of open divisions appearing within the union and continued to attack the communists at every available opportunity. The *Jute and Flax Workers Guide* was pressed into service through a continuous stream of vituperative articles ridiculing and goading well-known communist activists, while the anti-communist campaign by 'moderate' elements inside Dundee Labour Party was also stepped up. In May 1927 the *Guide* published details of the continuing efforts by the national Labour leadership to sideline radicalism by undercutting the federal structure of the party through the extension of the ward and constituency form of organisation. Readers were reminded that 'by decision of a LP National Conference, members of any Political Party not affiliated to the LP are *not* eligible for membership of the ward committees.'[99] In October 1928, the JFWU leadership delivered what they hoped would be the coup-de-grace to the communists when a specially convened meeting, again marked by rowdy scenes, banned them from holding office within the union.[100]

In the event, however, developments in the Soviet Union proved to be much more effective at marginalising communist influence than the efforts of British labour and trade union leaders. During 1924–6, the 'Triumvirate', comprising Stalin, Kamenev and Zinoviev, extended their control over the Russian Communist Party following a vicious campaign of attacks on the Left Opposition. In the wake of Trotsky's expulsion from the Politibureau in October 1926, communist policy moved sharply to the left, and in the process opened up a path towards the purging of 'rightist elements' around Bukharin.[101] These changes had a direct and almost immediate impact on international communist strategy, as the Comintern increasingly became a foreign policy instrument in the hands of the newly triumphant clique around Stalin.[102] During July–September 1928, the sixth congress of the Comintern imposed a radical new strategy on its affiliated organisations. In the new view, capitalism had entered a 'Third Period', characterised by the 'severe intensification' of the 'general capitalist crisis', which opened up the possibility for worldwide revolutionary upheaval.[103] The organisational tasks flowing from this political perspective underlined the need to develop a 'united front from below' in order to expose the non-communist workers' movement, and the nationalist bourgeois parties in the colonies, as the real enemies of the workers.[104] The new line – misnamed 'Class against Class' – was a disaster in every country in which it was applied, as communist influence was increasingly marginalised, membership plummeted and independent-minded cadres and non-party sympathisers who questioned the new line were branded as 'revisionists' and 'social fascists'.[105]

Although some communist historians have questioned the extent to which 'Class against Class' was actually implemented by the CPGB, the new line had an almost instant impact in Dundee.[106] In the immediate aftermath of the 1928 decision to ban them from holding office in the JFWU, 88 CP members and sympathisers within the union organised a meeting and issued a 'manifesto to workers in the jute industry on the advisability of affiliating to the Red International of Labour Unions'.[107] The communist initiative was always doomed to failure, and only succeeded in allowing the union leadership to characterise them as splitters and ultra-leftists. The new Comintern line also succeeded in alienating many, formerly sympathetic, left-wing Labour members and trade union activists, and seemed to justify the gathering witch-hunt of communists inside the labour movement.

The adoption of 'Class against Class', with its thoroughgoing intolerance towards so-called 'bourgeois nationalism', also had a dramatic and destructive impact on the nascent communist grouping in Bengal. The shaky alliance represented by the establishment and growth of broader front organisations, such as the Workers and Peasants Party (WPP), fell to pieces as fellow travellers and nationalist sympathisers were branded 'social fascists'. On the eve of the Meerut crackdown in March 1929, the baneful impact of the new line in Bengal was highlighted by Philip Spratt when he wrote that the:

> Bengal WPP events are nothing short of a tragedy. I write in a mood of deep despondency about this; I feel that the work of a year has practically been destroyed. The bulk of the Party members remain but of the active membership, half have gone (they resigned recently, and we gather will form a 'Peoples Party') and what is worse the other half all seem to be paralysed – through sickness, other occupations, or mere slackness.[108]

After a highly promising beginning, the communist advance in Bengal was halted and then reversed during the course of 1929 and 1930.

The failure of the communists not only covered the organisational field, as the decolonisation theory was also found wanting in several key regards. The large-scale expansion of Indian industry, along with the expected revolutionary upheavals, failed to materialise, while it also became increasingly clear that Indian capital was refusing to behave in the way suggested by M. N. Roy's view of them as a *comprador* class, as leading Marwaris, such as G. D. Birla, nailed their colours to the Congress mast.[109] The imperial nexus of jute also proved reluctant to play the central role assigned to it by Roy, as the widespread belief regarding the deleterious effect of Indian 'cheap labour competition' was challenged by Sime and Johnston. During the course of their Indian investigations they discovered that only 'a very small part of the Indian output now competes in the markets of the world with the finer qualities of jute manufactured goods turned out in Dundee',[110] which also meant that there 'was no excuse whatever for ... reducing wages because of Indian competition.'[111] For Sime and Johnston, the 'excuse' of Indian competition was designed to aid the jute barons' case in negotiations between the employers and the Board of Trade over wages, and was a handy bargaining counter with government over questions such as tariff levels. While Dundee's domination of the 'speciality product' markets was being increasingly challenged during the mid 1920s, it came from sources closer to home than the banks of the Hooghly, a development encouraged by changes in British foreign and monetary policy. In 1924, the signing of the Dawes Plan, by France, Britain and the USA, which by insisting on the continuance of largescale reparation payments, encouraged a government-led export drive by German manufacturers who increasingly emerged as serious competitors, particularly in the, formerly Dundee dominated, South American markets.[112] In 1925, the return of sterling to the Gold Standard at the high pre-war parity also had an immediate and damaging impact on British exports, so that while the world economy boomed during the second half of the 1920s, large swathes of the British economy languished.[113]

The return to the Gold Standard increased the prices of Dundee jute products in the export markets, and prompted other European jute producers to join with Germany in a widening assault on the international markets for speciality jute products. As a result, exports of jute yarn, which had been a valuable market for the home industry, grew very little between 1924 and 1928.[114] In April 1928, the Dundee and Forfar jute firm Don Brothers was forced to admit that the 'crash business' in the valuable American market had been lost to Czech, Belgian and US producers with 'no hope of recovery'.[115] Dundee firms responded to these growing threats in time-honoured fashion, by reducing labour costs through a series of Trade Board sanctioned wage cuts.

The lack of progress in Indian industrialisation during the 1920s not only undermined the decolonisation theory, it also dashed the hopes of Tom Johnston and the Labour Commonwealth Group. Indian industrialisation and a large improvement in the purchasing power of the Indian masses was seen as a central element in their vision of a 'Labour Empire'. In truth, the attitude of Labour and the TUC towards the colonial question never amounted to a coherent policy, despite the work of the Labour Commonwealth Group and the British trade union delegations that subsequently followed in the wake of Sime and Johnston. As the 'Roaring Twenties' drew to a close, the British labour movement's engagement with India waxed and waned according to the levels of concern over 'cheap-labour competition', and the extent of nationalist and communist influence on Indian workers. But the onset of world depression in the 1930s brought in its train serious political convulsions across the globe, and India would again become a central issue for the British labour movement. As we shall see in the final chapter, the 'Devil's Decade' would also emerge as a defining period for the imperial nexus of jute, as it faced unprecedented challenges to its integrity and, indeed, to its very existence.

7 The breaking of the Dundee–Calcutta nexus, 1930–40

In May 1930, the Scottish nationalist and journalist William Power visited Dundee, where he had begun his journalistic career many years earlier. He was keen to see how much the city had changed, and was particularly impressed with the new wider roads, and 'housing schemes, in stone, concrete, brick and rough cast, and steel, the homes in the last named materially being painted in various shades of yellow'. He also noted, however, that the 'big profits' had vanished from the city's staple trade and the wages of jute workers had been reduced. Dundee was largely living on 'old money' and had not been able to free itself from the overweening influence of jute. Power lamented that better 'for her, probably had she never seen jute or the Irish'.[1]

In the following years, Dundee's textile interests would grapple with the challenges presented by the world depression and rising foreign competition by turning towards new technology and rationalisation. In the process, thousands of jobs were shed, productivity levels were improved and the spectre of trade union power appeared to have been exorcised. But, by turning towards new technology, the jute barons unwittingly created a double-edged sword that was wielded by Indian competitors as they scaled the 'home' industry's last redoubt in the markets for 'speciality products'. By 1935, the challenge to the Indian Jute Mils Association (IJMA) and their working time agreements from so-called 'outside mills' had grown, as had the Bengal jute industry. The self-same managing agencies that had forced Dundee firms towards the production of 'speciality products' in the 1890s, by capturing a large part of the markets for hessian cloth, now turned towards rationalisation and product diversification in order to lessen the impact of the 'outside mills' in the markets for 'standard' jute goods. The 1930s underlined the linked nature of developments within the imperial nexus of jute, as the rationalisation process impacted on both sets of workers, adding to the wage cuts, short-time and speed-ups that had been their lot since the beginning of the decade. As we shall see, these developments would also have far-reaching consequences for the very nature, and indeed existence, of the imperial nexus of jute.

The depression and rationalisation in Dundee

The worldwide depression that followed the collapse of the New York Stock Exchange in 1929 proved to be far more severe, long lasting and consequential than any previous slump. By 1932, the industrial output of some countries was halved, and in Britain unemployment nearly doubled to 20 per cent and industrial output shrank by 16 per cent, as prices and international trade slumped.[2] While the south of England and the midlands, with their more diversified economies, were spared the worst consequences of the depression, the north of England and the 'Celtic fringe' were devastated. Collapsing prices spelt disaster for Dundee's jute firms, while some of their major European competitors – particularly German producers – were being encouraged towards an export drive by governments keen to boost their foreign currency reserves.

In response, Dundee's leading jute firms sought salvation through rationalisation, and the late 1920s saw the arrival of Taylorist 'bonus schemes' and new high-speed machinery for preparing and spinning: processes that had most benefited from the 'revolutionary design in machinery' effected during and immediately following the First World War.[3] By the end of the 1930s, 39 per cent of spindles were of the high-speed type, which had a major impact on manning levels.[4] In December 1932, at the height of the rationalisation mania, John Sime explained to a correspondent that high-speed machinery enabled 'one person in many cases to attend the number of machines that previously required three persons. In addition auto-doffing on spinning frames ... dispenses with the services of seven to eight young girls to a squad, doffing say 16 frames'.[5] Sime also claimed that 'if the data was at our disposal, it would be found that today the cost of production has been hugely reduced compared with that of ten years ago, in the spinning section of the trade particularly.'[6] Sime's claim proved to be uncannily accurate, as demonstrated by Figure 7.1 (page 174). Between 1930 and 1935, productivity in the British jute industry improved from 4.8 to 7.1 tons per worker per year, while the workforce declined from around 29,000 to around 24,000.[7] During the same period labour costs were reduced from 85 per cent of the total cost of production to 69 per cent.[8]

The 1930s also witnessed a shift in the Dundee jute industry's gender balance, with the percentage of women employed dropping from 63 per cent in 1930 to 54 per cent in 1939.[9] This change was encouraged by the widening introduction of double shifts by employers eager to recoup the costs of new high-speed machinery. With women and juveniles barred from night shift working, men were increasingly recruited, and some employers dispensed with women workers altogether. In 1930, the Angus Jute Works, of Jute Industries Ltd, fitted out an entire mill with high-speed frames. Although managers had intended to employ women spinners on the day shift, the policy was quickly changed because 'it was felt to be unfair to keep men on night shift, and the mill is therefore now being run entirely by male labour.'[10] While some observers approved of the removal of women workers because the new high speed machinery 'required a more highly skilled operative than the older type of organisation',[11] indications that women were better suited are rather more evident. Thus, in September 1933 W. G. Don, of Don Brothers, wrote to the secretary of the Forfar Factory Workers' Union:

We have been trying for the past year or so, to train men to wind cops. Either they cannot, or they will not, attain anything approaching the efficiency of girls doing the same work in our Dundee mill. We therefore, have this morning, dispensed with next weeks' day shift of male cop winders, and we are replacing them with skilled female winders from Dundee, as we have already spent too large a sum in our attempts to train men, and we cannot now afford to spend money training local girls.

We have come to the conclusion that winding is an unsuitable occupation for a man.[12]

The occupations of spinning and weaving had long been the preserve of women workers. It was difficult for male recruits to match the efficiency and speed of female spinners, who were perceived as possessing 'quicker fingers', while earlier attempts to introduce men into power loom weaving had also foundered when new male recruits were unable to master the required techniques.[13]

Although the increase in night-time working undoubtedly encouraged the recruitment of men, women were also increasingly viewed as an unstable element. In response to practices such as 'time cribbing' and the employers' reluctance to provide secure employment terms, women workers often resorted to absenteeism, or moved to other mills in search of better wages and conditions. In 1921 *The People's Journal* noted that:

In Dundee there has always been a large proportion of unsettled workers, drifting in and out of work, and moving from one place to another. As compared to a town like Forfar, the proportion of 'movies' is very large.... In pre-war times Dundee employers regarded in and out workers with fatalistic indifference. When there was a demand for labour managers competed for the drifters, and in dull times the drifters were cleared out. Times have changed, however, and, as working costs have increased, more attention will be given by all employers to the wastage caused by in and out working. The probability is that efforts will be made to weed out workers who cannot be depended upon to work full-time or to carry on in one establishment.[14]

This strategy of 'everyday resistance' through flight, which as we saw in Chapter 2 was also common in Bengal, encouraged the employers to view women workers as a problem that had to be removed, and male adult labour provided a solution to the problem. In effect, the jute barons' perception of the nature of female labour had undergone a complete reversal from the period of the genesis of jute dependency, when women and children had been seen as more docile and flexible than male labour. With escalating rates of male unemployment, there was also a rising crescendo of calls from civic institutions and social reformers to deal with the longstanding and deep-seated problems associated with the large-scale employment of married women, which allowed the new strategy of jute capital to acquire a progressive patina.

Jute capital used the conditions created by depression and the rationalisation process to extend its control over labour. Rationalisation and labour control were actually combined within the same process through the widespread adoption of

Taylorist bonus schemes.[15] One of the most popular 'premium bonus schemes' in Dundee was the Bedaux system, which, according to TUC investigators, had as its main objective the provision of 'an incentive to greater intensity of effort, and to increase output per worker, by offering a monetary bonus, while at the same time bringing about an automatic cutting of the rate per unit, as the output is increased beyond a given standard.'[16] In effect, the more workers produced, the less, in relative terms, they earned. While direct labour received 75 per cent of the bonus payments from excess output, the remaining 25 per cent was shared out between workers and foremen, which effectively meant that workers were paying the foreman to speed them up.[17] The Bedaux system had 'the effect and in some cases the intention of speeding up the individual worker to the greatest possible extent, regardless of his health, comfort and individuality.'[18]

The first instance of a 'bonus scheme' of this type in the Dundee jute industry occurred at the Dens mill in 1927, when an American 'management specialist' was brought in to introduce the new method of working. The *Jute and Flax Workers Guide* acerbically commented that:

> If he is typical of the American specialist ... then American firms have a lot to learn in regard to managing their business.... We have not come across a single operative employed by Messrs Baxter Brothers who have a single complimentary word to say of him.[19]

In the next few years this situation was replicated in mills across the city, and by the end of 1931 the Bedaux system was generating wider concern from trade union organisations in Leicestershire and Lancashire, and at the highest levels of the Trades Union Congress (TUC). Sime was deluged by requests for information, and on Christmas Day in 1931 he wished the Leicestershire hosiery workers' leader, Horace Moulden, 'every success in the fight now being made against the most pernicious form of wage slavery I have ever come across.'[20]

New workload agreements came in the wake of the new machinery and bonus schemes. Employers looked to introduce 'double spinning', where workers were forced to operate two, and in some cases more, of the large new high-speed spinning frames. In 1917–18, an earlier attempt to introduce double spinning had been successfully resisted by the JFWU, while the attempt by Jute Industries Ltd to introduce it at their Camperdown Works had sparked the 1923 general strike and lock-out. Although the strike was defeated and Jute Industries Ltd adopted double spinning, the union was able to prevent a wider-scale adoption of the practice during the 1920s. Conditions during the 1930s were, however, much more favourable for the employers. In 1931, John Sime admitted to a trade unionist, that with:

> over 60% textile operatives idle or on short time, you will realise our difficulty in getting resistance to the reduction [in wages] by stoppage of Works. At the moment, we have trouble with the only firm in Dundee, Messrs Boase Spinning Co. Ltd, working flax canvas, at present, who, 'in the most

friendly manner' arrange with their employees to reduce wages almost to the minimum. You know how these 'friendly talks' are arrived at when the workers meet the Firm's representatives in the office.[21]

By June 1930 unemployment in the Dundee jute industry was 37 per cent, and by September it was 48 per cent. The plight of some of the most desperate amongst the ranks of the unemployed was captured during the bitterly cold January of 1931 when it was reported that in:

> the centre of the city one can see any morning queues of women and children huddled together in the doorways of certain big bakers shops awaiting their opening, so as to obtain a 'bargain' in the way of bread and teacakes which had been left unsold the previous day. Last Saturday a queue had begun to form as early as 3.30 am in the morning at one well-known bakers premises.[22]

Fifty-six per cent of jute workers were unemployed by March 1931, and those still in work were facing escalating attacks on their wages and conditions.[23] In 1926 the translators of Sime and Johnston's *Exploitation in India* had recommended the 'small pamphlet' to the German trade unionists by explaining that no one 'will desire that the conditions which are ruling in India should be introduced in our midst.'[24] By the early 1930s, however, Indian 'conditions' of employment *were* being introduced into the midst of Juteopolis – possibly at the instigation of ex-jute wallahs.[25] In September 1933 John Sime learned that an unpaid volunteer spinner had been working in the Dura mill of James Scott & Sons. Sime was appalled to learn that this was, in fact, 'a regular practice. Automatic machinery is being introduced and "learners" are allowed to work "voluntarily" and for no payment to "get their hands in." '[26] Although the union stoutly opposed these kinds of illegal practices, where they had knowledge of them, the most desperate amongst the swelling ranks of the unemployed were prepared to go to great lengths in order to secure work, even if this meant foregoing wages in order to learn 'on the job'.[27]

Before the depression of the 1930s, the unemployed had commonly sought relief through out-migration, but opportunities were now more limited. The slump in manufacturing and construction was widespread, while the USA, a traditional escape route for Dundee tradesmen, was also restricting immigration.[28] In 1931, the situation for those who could not find an escape route became even more desperate following the formation of the National Government. Almost immediately, national insurance benefits were cut by 10 per cent, while assistance for those who did not qualify for insured benefits was made subject to a household 'means test' that became feared and loathed by those who came under its cold scrutiny, while local councils were also pressured into reducing their levels of Poor Law relief.[29] Within weeks of these changes, Dundee's poor relief system, as in September 1921, was on the verge of breakdown. On 6 and 7 September 1931 the city was re-visited by large-scale riots following the breaking up of a peaceful demonstration in the city centre organised by the communist-dominated National Unemployed Workers Movement (NUWM). The trouble spread to other parts of the city, and resulted in 42 arrests, many of whom were remanded in custody for a week, including the communist candidate Bob Stewart.[30] Fifteen people were treated for injuries, including a pregnant woman who was attacked by baton-wielding police officers when she left her house in the Overgate in order 'to see what all the hullabaloo was about', and a railway-man who was assaulted by police officers while he was making his way to work.[31] Writing many years later, the noted Dundee historian David Phillips still vividly remembered the riots:

> At the age of sixteen, much more interested in meeting girls than in political meetings, my pal and I, out for a walk that evening, stopped dead in our tracks at the end of Dudhope Street at the amazing scenes at the foot of the Hilltown.... Thursday was a hard up night usually, no money for the pictures – but here was three dimensional action to the shrieks of women and children and outraged shouts from men, not forgetting the slithering clatter of horses' hooves on the *cassies*[32] – aye and on the *plennies*[33] as well, as the mounted police flourished their batons at the scattering crowd. One horse actually entered a close, the sound of its hooves suddenly echoingly amplified (there were several reports afterwards of horses pursuing citizens up closes).... A woman caught in the thick of it with her young daughter has since told me of how the only way she could get home up the Hilltown was to dodge as opportunity afforded from close to close with the terrified child.[34]

The conduct of the police during the riots drew protests from Michael Marcus, the city's Labour MP, who had been elected in 1929 following Tom Johnston's decision not to stand, but, perhaps not surprisingly, his demand for an official inquiry fell on deaf ears.[35]

A few weeks after the Albert Square riots, the National Government was resoundingly returned to power and Michael Marcus came third in the two-member Dundee constituency behind Florence Horsburgh for the Conservatives, with Dingle Foot of the Liberal Party topping the poll.[36] The 1931 election was also a disaster for Neddy Scrymgeour. His popularity had always been based on his success in distinguishing himself from Labour, but by 1931 he had become associated with official Labour in the minds of many prospective voters – and paid the price at the polls.[37] Scrymgeour reacted to defeat by lamenting that 'My heart is with the people. I have never deserted them, although they have deserted me'.[38] This was his last election campaign, which also signalled the decline of the SPP as a political force in Dundee. While the Labour and SPP vote virtually collapsed, the communist candidate, Bob Stewart, polled 10,264 votes, over 4,000 votes up on his showing in 1929. With Dundee also returning a Tory as its other MP for the first time in its history, electoral politics in the city appeared to be polarising between the far left and the right. The selection of Florence

Horsburgh, who was re-elected in 1935, turned out to be a canny choice on the part of Dundee's Tories, with many recently enfranchised women seeing her as a plausible alternative to paternalist labourism, in the shape of Scrymgeour as well as Labour, which had promised so much but delivered so little.[39]

In the immediate aftermath of the 1931 debacle, rising disillusion amongst left-leaning Labour and Independent Labour Party (ILP) members saw up to 5,000 joining the CPGB. Communist optimism was further buoyed by the decision of the ILP to disaffiliate from Labour in 1932, leading to a collapse of the party in many parts of Scotland. While Labour fared better in Dundee, it was not until the later 1930s that they recovered their position. The serious divisions inside Labour's ranks, along with the terminal decline of the SPP, increased communist hopes that they could emerge as *the* mass working class party of Dundee. The CPGB grew dramatically in the immediate aftermath of the 1931 election, but most new members quickly drifted away, and those who remained were often the first to be retrenched in depression-hit mills and factories. Communist membership dwindled, and their 'Class against Class' stance continued to sour relations with the wider labour movement.

By the mid-1930s, however, a step-change in the fortunes of Dundee's labour movement was becoming clearly discernible, as a result of tentative economic recovery and an up-turn in industrial action. Progress on the part of the communists was encouraged by the Comintern's adoption of the 'United Front' strategy, in response to Hitler's election in 1933, which effectively ended the party's isolationist stance. In March 1936, the chairman of Dundee Labour Party publicly approved the 'United Front' strategy, following the support given by the communists to Labour candidates during the 1935 general election. In August 1936, the success of the 'new line' in Dundee was further demonstrated when the Powerloom Tenters Society called on Labour 'to encourage and accept the affiliation of all working class organisations', which was seen as a barely concealed attempt to raise 'the question of affiliation of the Communist Party to the Labour Party.'[40] There was, though, very little sign of reconciliation within the JFWU, as was demonstrated in March 1937 when the union AGM decided by a large majority to 'retain the rule that members or supporters of the Communist Party ... or any other allied or similar organisation shall not be eligible to hold office or to represent [the JFWU] at any congress or conference.'[41]

Despite the anti-communism of the JFWU leadership, and some ordinary members who still remembered the bitter intra-union conflict of the 1920s, a unity of sorts was achieved in the fight against fascism in Spain, when the JFWU called on the STUC 'to immediately initiate a campaign to secure the end of the non-interventionist policy of the present government.'[42] Seventy recruits from Dundee joined the International Brigade between December 1936 and October 1938, the highest proportion of any British city, including many local communists and socialists. John 'Patsy' McEwan, a timber yard worker and member of Dundee Young Communist League (YCL), was killed in action in September 1937. In his last letter to his mother McEwan wrote that if 'I don't go and fight fascism, I'll just have to wait and fight it here.'[43] Others went to Spain out of a sense of adventure or to escape the poverty, unemployment and boredom of Depression-era Dundee. Three of the 17 Dundee volunteers who gave their lives in Spain had close links with the jute industry: John Ness, who died at the battle of Ebro in July 1938, had served his apprenticeship as a mechanic at the Larchfield Works and was unemployed at the time of his enlistment; David Samson, who was killed at the battle of Brunete in July 1937, is of particular interest because he had served in the Indian jute mills as a supervisor; John Mudie, reported as missing/killed in action, was listed as a driver and jute worker. Described as one of the 'Incorrigibles', Mudie was a member of the Labour League of Youth. In February 1937 he had been arrested as an alleged deserter and spent the rest of his brief life in Spanish prisons and hospitals before meeting his fate in March 1938 at Belchite-Caspe.[44] The rise of fascism in Europe meant that India became a lesser priority for the Comintern, and the flow of resources and agents to the sub-continent slowed to a trickle. In September 1938, as Neville Chamberlain prepared for his date with destiny at Munich, a young Victor Kiernan set sail for India:

> to see the political scene at closer hand, and with some schemes of historical study. I was the bearer of a lengthy document from the Communist International, which would have been cheering to the British authorities if it had fallen into their hands. Its gist was that Moscow could not campaign at present for legalization of the Indian party; the reason of course was Soviet eagerness for a collective security agreement with Britain.[45]

While the attention of the communists was increasingly dominated by the need to combat the growing threat of fascism, the period just prior to the outbreak of the Second World War witnessed a bold and imaginative attempt by the JFWU to forge direct links with the sub-continent. Faced with government reluctance to protect the 'home' industry, the union responded by securing the selection of Krishna Menon, a leading nationalist and close friend of Nehru, as a Dundee Labour parliamentary candidate. Menon's candidature was, though, revoked in April 1940 by the party's National Executive Committee, thus underlining Labour's ambiguous attitude towards the Indian National Congress (INC) and the issue of Indian independence.[46]

The depression and the Bengal jute industry

In Calcutta, the period immediately following the general strike of 1929 was marked by the rapid onset of depressed trade conditions, and by 1931 hessian exports were at their lowest level since 1912.[47] In June 1930, the IJMA responded by adopting a 54 hour working week and instituting a moratorium on further capital investment, but prices and profits continued to fall, leading to even tougher output restrictions the following month when mills were ordered to close for one week per month, while stringent industry-wide wage cuts were also imposed.[48] The impact on jute workers was all too predictable. The government investigator, A. C. Roy Chowdhury, estimated that 65 per cent of the total monthly expenditure of jute workers was being spent on food, while 76 per cent of families in the mill districts were reported as being in debt, with the average rate of interest on loans taken out by workers being 78 per cent. Chowdhury heard 'much discontented talk on the subject of low wages and lack of accommodation', adding that it:

> was a pitiable sight to watch the Kabuli money-lenders and others sitting outside the gates on pay days and realising their dues. Of recent years the local money-lenders have increased in number and anybody who can spare a few rupees invest it with the coolies because of the high rates of interest.[49]

In March 1931, faced with a continuing slump in prices and profits, the IJMA further limited working hours to 40 per week, sealed 15 per cent of Association looms, abolished multiple shift working, and retrenched 80,000 jute workers. The increasing adoption of the single shift allowed management to 'seed' labour, which was often a euphemism for the widespread removal of workers seen to be of the 'badmash' and 'bolshevik' class. Those workers who managed to keep their jobs complained of attacks on basic rights that had once been taken for granted, as this workers' petition from March 1931 graphically illustrates:

> Again at the time we are working in mills we find ourselves imprisoned as it were, with no liberty even to go to answer the calls of nature. If any of us pressed by [an] urgent call goes out his token is taken away and he is dismissed. If any of our relations in our home happens to fall ill or if any danger befalls any member of our family at the time we are working in Mills, we can not get any information as the gates of Mills are kept closed and no one is allowed to go in or come out. We do not see why this new rule should have been introduced, regarding the closing of gates etc., when for many years in the past the gates were kept open during working hours and there was no trouble whatsoever in the working of mills.[50]

The threat of retrenchment and persistently high unemployment forced worker militants to keep their heads down as competition for available employment increased: 3,241,000 working days were lost in 1929 as a result of jute strikes, but by 1932 this figure had slumped to 650,000, and by 1935 it was only 74,000 days.[51] Despite the institution of successive working time agreements, and the successful offensive against the wages and working conditions of jute mill labour, the integrity of the IJMA, and their working time strategy, was increasingly threatened by the actions of the 'outside mills'. In 1932, the IJMA complained to the Government of Bengal (GOB) that 'if the system of shifts, which is permitted to work in some of the non-Association mills were to become the general practice in all mills, the industry would produce in four months the yardage exported during the whole of last year.'[52] The IJMA attempted to use their authority, backed up by all manner of threats, to prevent the 'outside mills' from increasing production, but in reality there was little that could be done to pull them into line. By 1935, 'outside mills' accounted for over 10 per cent of Indian output, and the increasing number of IJMA firms contemplating withdrawal strongly suggested that this percentage would continue to grow.[53]

With the markets for standard goods becoming saturated, the managing agencies faced mounting calls to open up 'suitable new avenues for the absorption of an expanded outturn in the direction of new outlets of use for their production.'[54] Many leading managing agencies needed little encouragement. Faced with growing competition, and under increasing pressure from colonial government to reform, sections of Anglo-Scottish jute capital were already turning to rationalisation, product diversification and new technology as they sought to establish 'clear blue water' between themselves and 'outside mills'. By 1936, Thomas Duff & Co. was taking orders for heavy hessians for the, formerly Dundee-dominated, South American market,[55] and was also eyeing the linoleum trade as it was seen as 'quite a paying trade at this end, and with cheaper labour it should be all the more so in India.'[56] A representative of Thomas Duff & Co. back in Dundee also noted that:

> there is evidence here that Calcutta is gradually displacing Dundee in several fabrics of special construction. I understand that regular consignments of Tarpaulin are now coming forward from Calcutta, and I have seen samples from Bansberia and Henderson's group of mills which compare very favourably with Dundee manufacture.[57]

The extent of Indian progress was further demonstrated in 1937 when Dundee merchants took delivery of Calcutta-produced linoleum backing for the first time.[58] Bengal mills were also breaking into the market for 'outside widths' of hessian cloth, as demonstrated by this report in *Capital* from September 1938:

> Previously ... it was generally the case that a premium had to be paid on goods made in Calcutta which were termed 'outside widths'. Now the merchant can purchase practically any width from 36 to 54 inches on the same basis as 40 inches.... As to quality, I think I have mentioned before that most consumers prefer Calcutta goods to Dundee goods, owing to the big improvement that has taken place in recent years.[59]

In order for product diversification to work, it was necessary to guarantee a better quality of yarn, which led to the increasing purchase of high-speed preparing and spinning machinery. By 1935–6, jute machinery imports were back to pre-depression levels, amounting to Rs144 lakhs[60] in value.[61] In early 1936, the scale of re-tooling was such that the owners of a Dundee spinning firm complained that they had not received their order for new frames because all 'the makers ... are very busy and some cannot keep up deliveries to the dates promised.'[62] Heavy sales of new machinery continued, and in June 1937 the Leeds-based machinery manufacturers Fairbairn, Lawson, Combe and Barbour (FLCB) declared that orders were 'approximately ten times' greater than the previous year.[63] At FLCB's AGM the following year, the chairman, J. K. Anderson, congratulated the Bengal jute industry for its 'pluck and foresight in purchasing extensive amounts of new and up-to-date machinery'.[64] Between 1934 and 1939 FLCB and the Monifeith-based J. F. Lowe's sold 27,300 spindles to a total of 26 Indian mills, comprising 13 different managing agencies, including the 'big four' of Yule Bros, Bird, Duff and Jardine Skinner.[65] Although only a minority of Bengal jute mills turned towards product diversification, new technology, and other forms of rationalisation, the huge overall scale of the 'Calcutta cutty' ensured that the impact of these developments on the 'home' jute industry would be serious.

Between 1932 and 1939, industrial accidents in the Bengal jute industry more than doubled from 2.9 to 7.5 per thousand workers, with accidents involving weavers more than trebling, from 271 to 879 per thousand.[66] Mill managers commonly blamed this rise on the carelessness of workers, the growing efficiency of factory inspectors and the influence of the Workmen's Compensation Act, which it was felt tempted many workers to fabricate false compensation claims. This view was challenged by the 1935 *Factory Act Report* for Bengal when it noted that the higher rate of 'accidents due to flying shuttles, breaking straps and spindles etc' coincided with machinery being 'worked at considerably higher speeds than previously', before adding that the disproportionate number of weavers included in the accident figures was probably due to:

> the re-starting of 10% of the looms which, under the agreement, were sealed down in 1932. A large number of weavers who have been out of employment for a long time have now been re-employed and it is reasonable to assume that whilst they are settling down and becoming accustomed to operate the looms at the higher speeds, accidents must be more numerous.[67]

The pushing of labour through the speeding up of looms, and other machinery, contributed towards an increase in worker productivity from 2.6 tons a year in

Table 7.1 High speed machinery of different types sold to the Calcutta jute industry, 1934–9

Year	J. F. Low	FLCB	Total
1934	98	75	173
1935	111	202	313
1936	177	88	265
1937	181	482	663
1938	3	31	34
1939	1	227	228
Total	571	1,105	1,676

Source: Compiled from Fairbairn, Lawson, Combe and Barbour Papers, West Yorkshire Library, 365/acc3154/95/5–6, Order Books, India, vols 1 and 2; J. F. Low Papers, Dundee University Archives, MS/89/6/2, Indian Order Books.

1931 to 4.4 tons in 1937, as shown in Figure 7.1. Weavers and spinners were not only being asked to produce more in a shorter time, they were also being pushed to produce better-quality work. As the Calcutta industry moved into new lines of production for the US market, the insistence on quality cloth from powerful buyers such as Bemis Brothers meant that yarn quality had to be high, which placed particular pressure on spinners, who were forced to pay closer attention to their work in order to check for more frequent end breaks. The new frames operated at optimum efficiency only when the best grades of jute were used, but the quality of raw material started to deteriorate in the 1930s.[68] As a result, the output of weavers was affected and their earnings were often reduced even further by fines for shoddy production. During the course of 1937 there were 1,508 fines imposed on weavers at Thomas Duff's Titaghar No. 1 mill, out of a mill-wide total of 1,530, while the situation for weavers at Titaghar No. 2 mill was little better, with 1,156 fines, meaning that there were probably few weavers in these two mills who were not fined.[69] Weavers were also being increasingly dismissed, as pressures grew on Thomas Duff & Co. to improve the quality of their woven cloth. Twenty-three per cent of weavers and 12 per cent of the total workforce at the Angus mill were dismissed during 1935, and in 1936 dismissals were even higher, at 51 per cent and 27 per cent respectively.[70]

In December 1936 the Bengal jute industry was plunged into a period of unprecedented turmoil when Birla announced his intention to quit the IJMA over the issue of restricted working time. Birla began running his mill – one of the largest on the Hooghly – on a multiple shift system, which hugely increased production, while IJMA mills were limited to 40 hours per week. When the leading British managing agency, Gillanders & Arbuthnott, threatened to follow Birla's lead the IJMA announced the cancellation of their working time agreement from 1 March 1937, thus laying the basis for a production war between the IJMA and outside mills.[71] In effect, the strategy of the IJMA 'was to spoil the market so that every mill would be incurring losses. They had strong reserves and wanted to crush out of existence the recalcitrant mills … mostly owned by Indians not long ago [established] and [who] had slender reserves.'[72] The IJMA's declaration of war on 'outside mills', with the dislocation in hours and wages that would come in its wake, stretched the patience of workers to breaking point, and they moved onto the offensive in the most spectacular fashion. Between February and May 1937, over 225,000 jute workers and workers in other industries in the Calcutta conurbation were drawn into a struggle that, at its height, appeared to threaten the very basis of ordered government in Bengal.

The 1937 jute general strike

At the beginning of February 1937, reports of strike action in Howrah started to reach government officials, who were preparing arrangements for the up-coming elections to the re-constituted Bengal Legislative Assembly.[73] These elections included specially created labour constituencies, and Sibnath Banerjee, the official trade union candidate in Howrah, underlined his aim of Labour Swaraj, which prompted an enthusiastic backing at the polls and added to the already excitable atmosphere created by the spreading strikes.[74] The *Congress Socialist* newspaper hailed the electrifying impact of the election, stating that 'success in it has not only created a ferment; it has done something more. It has aroused in [the jute workers] a hope and an expectation and a confidence both in themselves and in the candidates they have sent to the legislature.'[75] In early March, as new disputes flared in the south of the jute belt, comments like this appeared to justify the claims of jute capital that the strikes were politically inspired, and the colonial authorities responded by arresting workers' leaders and imposing orders under Section 144 of the Indian Criminal Code, a legislative catch-all that gave magistrates wide-ranging powers. Despite this measure, fresh strikes continued to break out, thus demonstrating the organisational capability of the jute workers themselves and their independence from those who sought to represent and lead them. In early March 1937, as the strike began to affect the southern portion of the jute belt, the nationalist labour activist Devandranath Sen noted that:

> [T]hese labourers of Budge-Budge wear such a dull, sullen countenance, that it is well nigh impossible for a man not intimately known to them, to entertain any great regard for them, least of all credit them with any great capacity for heroic action of the kind they have done. Even in a meeting, where they become knit together by a sense of collective unity, they evince no great enthusiasm. Not unoften a speaker finds it difficult to hold on, his audience seems so dull and devoid of life.
>
> But when the meeting has been dissolved, and the bulk of the audience has dispersed, some of the workers would be found assembled in small groups, carrying on conversations in an amazingly animated way. They would then be seen arriving at momentous decisions in a strikingly short time and setting to work those out in a still more striking fashion. And strangest of all, these decisions have very often little connection with the speaches (*sic*) they had heard just a few minutes before.[76]

These comments confirm that the 1937 strike was not, as jute capital and the colonial state claimed, a communist conspiracy against ordered government. Contact between the Calcutta-based labour leaders and striking workers was maintained through a network of full-time organisers, such as Devendranath Sen, who were mostly from a bhadralok background. Crucially, however, the strike was spread by workers' leaders who emerged suddenly in the course of the burgeoning dispute, and just as suddenly disappeared – perhaps wisely – back into the mass when it came to an end. Bengali workers provided the initial impetus for the strike, but when the up-country workers in the northern mills were brought into the orbit of the strike, the village link of these workers ensured that it would be protracted. A comparison with the situation facing their counterparts in Dundee further underlines the decisive role the village link played in facilitating the coming together of mass workers' action. As we have seen, the Dundee jute industry also faced a frantic, rationalisation-inspired, upheaval during the

1930s leading to the outbreak of many strikes, but these never took on an industry-wide character despite the repeated urgings of trade union leaders. In March 1936, a 'mass meeting' called by Dundee's four main jute trade unions to build support for a general strike against rationalisation drew a paltry turnout of fewer than 500 jute workers. A leading figure in the JFWU, T. M. Ferguson, admitted that 'in all sincerity it would be most foolish for jute workers to come out in the present state of the market.'[77] The previous, harrowing, experience of the 1923 general strike may also have made many Dundee jute workers very wary about embarking on such a course again. Such was the influence of the jute industry on Dundee that when the 1923 dispute assumed a general character there was barely a family in the city that was not affected. Under these conditions, and without wider support, it had been well-nigh impossible for the movement to maintain itself for an extended period of time.[78] The defeat of the 1923 jute general strike in Dundee was a traumatic experience for activists and ordinary workers alike, and was probably responsible for the conspicuous absence of jute workers from involvement in the 1926 general strike – an issue that led to bitter disagreements within the ranks of the city's communists.[79] It is clear that the jute workers of Dundee, despite their relatively more powerful and well-organised trade unions, were caught more firmly within the web of jute dependency than their Indian counterparts.

Although the 1937 general strike was conducted against the background of the increasing implementation of new working practices and technology, there appears to no specific mention of this in the demands made by workers, or of the central strike committee that was constituted by the labour organisations.[80] However, the response to rationalisation was there in the frequently stated demand for security of service and an end to the practice of arbitrary dismissal by sirdars. According to Devandranath Sen the cause of the strike in the Budge-Budge area was:

> [T]he dismissal of five weavers of the Budge-Budge jute mill employing 5,000 labourers, for their alleged failure to produce the required number of yards per week. That such a small incident, involving only 5 persons, would lead to such a conflagration of the dimensions we are beholding was what none had expected, least of all the mill authorities. They had been pursuing this policy of dismissal, rather merrily and systematically, with no opposition at all, since long time.[81]

The surprise of Devendranath Sen mirrored that of other labour leaders, mill managers, and government officials alike, and reveals a fundamental blindness of these groups towards the real conditions of workers and their concerns. Security of service emerged as the major issue that galvanised jute workers because of the virtual permanent revolution that had been unleashed by the employers during the course of the 1930s. In this regard, the 1937 general strike bears a strong resemblance to the first instance of widespread strike action in the Bengal jute industry during the 1890s, which resulted from the increasing pressures that many recent up-country recruits faced as the Bengal mills sought to break into the Dundee-controlled markets for hessian cloth. The scale and intensity of the 1937 strike was, though, of a completely different magnitude.

Many, if not all, Indian labour historians have, like Devendranath Sen, failed to note the not-inconsiderable contribution of rationalisation to the 1937 general strike. Indeed, it is denied that any kind of meaningful rationalisation process took place at all.[82] In this view, Anglo-Scottish capital – and Marwari capital – were wedded to mercantilism, with little thought for the long term or anything beyond immediate profits. By the early 1930s, there was little doubt that the Bengal jute industry was technically outmoded, and the influential *Barker Report* of 1935 has been widely cited as evidence of this incontrovertible fact.[83] In effect, the *Barker Report* has been unanimously accepted as an obituary for the Bengal jute industry, but the reforms wrought following its publication have never been noted. By the time of the *Report*, many leading jute wallahs were already well aware of the need to move away from the old ways of doing business, which its publication only served to underline. Those Indian historians who do accept that rationalisation took place within the Bengal jute industry see it as a limited process, and as an illustration of the wider failure to transform the nature of the Bengal jute industry as a whole.[84] However, it was not the introduction of new technology by itself that underpinned the transformative strategy of jute capital during the 1930s. Before technological rationalisation could be contemplated on any scale, the problem of high manning levels and low worker productivity had to be tackled, through the mass retrenchments of the early 1930s and the introduction of the single shift system of working, which enabled more efficient supervision. Only when this phase was completed in the mid-1930s were firms confident enough to adopt new technology, a process that was augmented, and indeed encouraged, by product diversification, changes in quality control and in the ways that jute workers were controlled and supervised.[85]

In April 1936, the impact of product diversification and new technology on the jute workers had been flagged up by the sudden outbreak of a violent strike involving 11,000 workers at the huge Hukumchand mill.[86] Although investigations 'failed to elicit any satisfactory explanation' for the strike, it is significant that a major technological overhaul of the mill had only recently been completed.[87] The probable role of new technology in sparking the strike was not noticed, let alone addressed, on this occasion, but during March 1937, as the general strike spread out from the south of the jute belt, 4,000 workers of Wellington Mill struck in protest at the introduction of high-speed spinning frames, and 11 other mills were affected by sympathy strikes, which only ended with the official termination of the general strike on 10 May 1937.[88]

In the period following the general strike, disputes continued to break out throughout the jute belt as managers moved against known worker militants and the pace of rationalisation increased. Most of these strikes were over issues such as retrenchment and the victimisation of worker militants, but the issue of new technology also emerged.[89] This period also witnessed one of the most significant strikes associated with the issue of new technology. The spinners and weavers of Thomas Duff's Angus mill had, as we saw earlier, suffered years of fines and dismissals, and the post-general strike period promised more turmoil as the company geared up for a further wave of rationalisation. In May 1937 senior company figures, in an attempt to marginalise trade union influence within the mill, sanctioned the creation of factory committees, which, however, they quickly lost control of to a workforce emboldened by the still fresh experience of the general strike. Two months later, the committees proved such an effective means of workers' control that the manager of Angus complained that 'the over-seers in charge had practically no say in the running of the mill.'[90] This situation of 'dual power' could not continue indefinitely, and on 16 July the sacking of 104 workers, including many who had served on the factory committees, led to a month-long strike that only ended when the sub-divisional officer of Serampore gave his personal assurance that the dismissals would be thoroughly investigated. Despite this, bad feelings lingered and then intensified, giving rise to further and even more serious trouble.

From August 1937, mill managers along the Hooghly remained untroubled by industrial strife for over three months, but in late November another wave of strikes began, and the issue of 'technological unemployment' again came to the fore. On 26 November, 3,500 workers at the Naihati mill struck work against the introduction of high-speed spinning frames.[91] The following week, an appeal was issued by the Hazinagar branch of the Bengal Jute Workers' Union (BJWU);

> Everywhere the authorities have begun to make reductions. With this end in view they introduced automatic machines, particularly in the spinning department with which machines one man can do the work of four ... the new machines are to be introduced in all the mills in the Calcutta area. This will be in your mills too. Many will lose their jobs.[92]

On 5 December, resolutions were passed at a mass solidarity meeting, recognising 'the assistance rendered to the strikers by the workers of certain other jute mills' and urging the Minister for Labour 'to intervene and to adopt measures against retrenchment by the introduction of machines'. Another resolution called on the newly elected labour representatives of the Bengal Legislative Assembly to 'prepare bills providing for the permanency of service of the workers and counteracting technological unemployment.'[93] A few days later, strikes over the introduction of new technology also broke out at Bird & Co.'s Dalhousie and Northbrook mills, which resulted in the sacking of 260 'troublemakers'. In February 1938 this already familiar pattern was repeated at the Naihati mill when '150 men were not allowed to rejoin their work' following the settlement of the dispute there.[94] This strike wave was a litmus test for the newly formed Bengal Chatkal Mazdoor Union (BCMU), but their attempt to resist new technology and retrenchment failed.[95] The momentum that had been gained from the 1937 general strike had quickly dissipated, and the BCMU's ability to counter the post-strike offensive by jute capital was also affected by their lack of overall organisation, mounting rivalry within their ranks and, as we shall see, by the turn towards a communal labour policy on the part of the newly elected provincial government.

The introduction of new technology in Bengal, as in Dundee, particularly affected women workers, who were concentrated in preparing and sack sewing. Their sometime fierce resistance to the threat of technological unemployment meant that, again like their counterparts in Dundee, they were increasingly regarded as a troublesome presence by many mill managers. This was demonstrated in Titaghar during January 1939 with the mass dismissal of around 1,500 Madrassi workers, including many women, because of the leading role that they had played during the strikes against the introduction of the Bengal Jute Ordinance in September 1938.[96] In sharp contrast to the up-country men, Madrassis migrated in large family groups and settled permanently in the mills districts, with the women commonly finding work in the preparing departments, where they were highly regarded due to their skills as feeders and receivers in carding.[97] In December 1938, the Special Branch received reports that strike leaders had decided 'to recruit 100 "conscious" workers in Titaghur [including women] as secret propagandists in mills in other areas. Miss Sudha Roy who has earned the esteem of the women strikers, in Titaghur, will direct their activities.'[98] Bad feelings continued in the wider Barrackpore area into July 1939, when a serious strike developed at the Shyamnagar mill over the dismissal of Tetri, a female batcher and worker militant. When she was also arrested, rioting broke out and a delegation of workers who had approached the sub-divisional officer for a meeting were lathi-charged by police as they were sitting inside the police compound.[99]

In May 1939, the retrenchment of 500 workers following the renovation of Bird & Co.'s Union North mill also led to angry confrontations between women workers and the mill authorities, which prompted Bankim Mukherjee to call for a 'strike agitation' covering the Bird group of mills. At a rally at Calcutta's Albert Hall, Mukherjee described the mass dismissal as a 'matter of great concern to 1,000s of women workers ... because the same act may be repeated by the owners of other jute mills' and accused the managing agencies of copying 'Hitler's tactics of sending womenfolk back to the home, but not so directly as Hitler has been doing'. At the same meeting, Sibnath Banerjee also astutely connected the retrenchment to the Jute Ordinance, which had 'rendered unemployed over 40,000 jute labourers', thus allowing capital 'to procure cheaper male labour.'[100]

The support for striking and dismissed women workers illustrated by these, by no means isolated, examples challenges Samita Sen's view that the trade unions acquiesced in the removal of women jute workers.[101] For Sen, the general strike of 1937 demonstrated the rising authority and power of the jute trade unions. In its aftermath, strikes were increasingly 'better organised' and 'better led', which enabled trade union leaders to broker agreements that protected the rights of male workers, whilst discriminating against female workers.[102] In reality, the vast majority of jute workers never belonged to a trade union, a situation that had only marginally improved by the late 1930s. Strikes were indeed 'better organised' and 'better led', but this was largely due to the self-organisation of worker militants rather than the minimal organisation, leadership and resources that the trade unions were able to provide. Samita Sen's 'patriarchal bloc' thesis also fails to take into account the clear inability of the bhadralok labour leaders to involve any workers – male or female – in the leadership and direction of the trade unions, and their further failure to mount an effective defence of the jute workers as a whole during the course of the *Devil's Decade.*[103] The 'patriarchal bloc' thesis is dependent on the existence of a powerful and organised trade union movement, but the reality was rather different. The long drawn-out strike of 1937 exacted its toll on the jute workers, as well as on the shattered nerves of jute capital, while new disagreements and serious splits also appeared within the trade union movement. The labour leaders tried without success to repeat the trick they had apparently performed with such ease in February 1937, but they proved unable to sustain an organised movement against the imposition of the Bengal Jute Ordinance in September 1938, or against the declaration of war a year later.

In the immediate aftermath of the 1937 strike, the Communist Party of India (CPI) journal *The New Age* asked, 'What is the cause of this disparity between the spontaneous actions of the masses and the leadership?'[104] The answer that they offered was as disquieting as the question itself: 'the failure of the leadership to keep pace with the masses – was due to their lack of contact with the masses.'[105] This 'lack of contact' meant that the communists had 'entirely underestimated the tempo of the rising struggle in its early stages', when they urged workers to settle with management 'as happily as possible'. As the dispute spread to Budge-Budge, the communists had shifted tack by offering their support to the existing strikes, but they still refused to support the nationalists' call for a general strike because the movement had 'not yet assumed the character of a demand arising out of the mass of the workers themselves.'[106] As a result, valuable time had been wasted, and workers took their own initiative by sending delegations and columns of flying pickets to neighbouring areas. It was only in late April, once the strike had spread to their Barrackpore stronghold, that the communists fully intervened in what was by that time a general strike in full spate. At this moment, the left nationalists, who had first raised the general strike call, came under sustained pressure from the Congress leadership in Bengal, which in turn was being pressed by the INC 'High Command' to present itself as a constitutional opposition within the reformed Bengal Legislative Assembly.[107] As a result, left nationalist leaders started to present the strike as a purely economic struggle and called for its orderly cessation.[108]

The communists benefited from the resulting confusion of the left nationalists, and quickly made their influence felt within the spreading strike. In its aftermath, and despite their many tactical and even strategic errors, the communists were in a more influential position than they had been at any time since the late 1920s. They were tentatively starting to broaden their influence and class composition through a coordinated intervention in industries such as engineering, and in public services such as the trams and the post office. Educated workers were starting to openly identify with the party as their increased profile generated its own momentum.[109]

The immediate post-strike period also witnessed the party's first serious and concerted attempts to address the peasant question in Bengal. Faced with the prospects of mass unemployment and government control of the jute crop, the communists responded by convening a joint conference of jute workers and jute ryots, and communist activists and leaders headed for the rural tracts of Bengal in unprecedented numbers.[110] The communist initiative was taken very seriously by the colonial state, which had never before been faced with a potential coming together of the industrial and agricultural struggles, which only underlined the communists' previous failure to develop a coherent strategy towards the peasant question in Bengal.

The remaking of paternal despotism

The difficulties facing the Bengal labour movement in the wake of the general strike were exacerbated by a resurgence of communalism that threatened to wipe away the minimal gains that had been won in the strike agreement.[111] The 1937 provincial elections produced a coalition government comprising the Krishak Proja Party (KPP) and the Muslim League (ML), but it quickly became a prisoner of arithmetic.[112] The communal nature of seat distribution ensured that Hindus were under-represented, which made the election of a Congress government impossible, while the European community, who were grossly over-represented, were the main beneficiaries.[113] As a result, Bengal's first ever elected government was tied to the apron strings of British capital. In private discussions with jute representatives shortly after being elected, the new Labour Minister, Saheed Suhrawardy, admitted that the 'government were looking to the Europeans to support them in office and in return were definitely anxious to see that they carried the Europeans with them in any measure or policy they may initiate.'[114]

With strikes still ongoing, the provincial government encouraged the establishment of 'white flag' unions as a 'responsible' alternative to those controlled by the 'Reds' and the nationalists. Aided and encouraged by the provincial government and the, initially sceptical, employers, the 'white unions' quickly grew in size and influence, and when they were attacked by the BJWU as *dalal*, or pro-employer, unions, Suhrawardy responded by raising the cry of 'Islam in danger', a development that was viewed with increasing trepidation by leading jute wallahs. According to Chapman Mortimer, a prominent member of the Bengal Assembly's European group:

> the European group ought to have made it abundantly clear to Fazlul Huq and Nazimuddin in March and April last that ... one thing they would not tolerate would be a communal government. Now it is of course too late. It may be retorted that it is obvious that the Europeans would not tolerate a communal government. I am afraid this retort leaves me cold, as the facts of the case are that we are supporting what has become to all intents and purposes a communal government and that we have given clear assurance to Fazlul Huq and Nazimuddin of our continued support.[115]

Despite the jute wallahs' distaste for Suhrawardy, he was only voicing out loud what had always been their unspoken policy, which was demonstrated in Titaghar in the immediate post-strike period when the mass retrenchment of Madrassi workers was followed by widespread accusations that employers were replacing Hindu workers with Muslims.

For Anglo-Scottish capital and the colonial state the 1937 general strike acted as a crossing of the Rubicon. They were forcibly made to realise that the strike was organised by and for the jute workers themselves rather than by manipulative communist and nationalist labour leaders attempting to bend the jute workers to their will. At the height of the strike, a director of Thomas Duff nervously observed that the worker had effectively 'thrown aside any influence Sirdars or Babus may have had over him and thinks he is standing on his own.'[116] The anxiety of jute capital was further heightened when it was learned that many sirdars, both openly and surreptitiously, had gone over to the side of the strikers.[117] Indeed, in large parts of the jute belt the labour control mechanism had almost completely broken down, prompting serious discussions within the British business community regarding the future of the sirdar cadre. However, while the mill owners were keen to break up the sirdar cadre, in order to prevent it from acting as an alternative source of authority, they remained resolutely opposed to its complete removal, as had been demanded by British trade union figures such as Tom Johnston and John Sime as well as Indian labour organisations. Instead, an increasing number of mill managers abolished the post of head sirdar, and pulled the line sirdars 'into the body of the Kirk' through the introduction of pension schemes and other benefits.[118]

In the immediate aftermath of the 1937 strike an increasing number of managing agencies also began recruiting educated Bengalis as supervisors who, it was envisaged, would combine the supervisory role of the sirdar and the technical skills of the Dundee School.[119] Edward Benthall was an early advocate of, what became known as, 'Indianisation', and in August 1937 he explained his support for the new policy to his rather more sceptical brother, Paul:

> I am afraid that having made a promise to Mukherjee I must press for the offering of encouragement to men trained in the Dundee schools. If we can encourage them to go by merely offering them a job, on trial of course, when they return so much the better, but I see no objection myself to giving a small scholarship to show our good faith. If we don't actively support policies like this in the future but merely confine ourselves to words the hollowness of our promises will soon become apparent. Having therefore settled on a policy I am in favour of seeing it through wholeheartedly.[120]

Benthall was seeking to win the trust of Indian business interests in the fight against radical nationalism, as well as the communists, and the 'Indianisation' of the lower grades of supervisory personnel was a possible, and cost effective, means of achieving this goal. However, the new policy was not without its difficulties, which was highlighted in the case of an early Muslim recruit whose progress was being monitored by Paul Benthall:

> As you know Kazini was a very good man in many ways but he has one failing in that he cannot control labour. He admits this himself and attributes it to the fact that he is known to be a Mohammedan, the Hindus distrust him and the Mohammedans all expect him to favour them. I fear we shall always be up against this sort of trouble when we employ Indian overseers in Jute Mills, but some may succeed in overcoming this difficulty.[121]

At this stage, the appointment of Indian overseers within Bird & Co. was very much a rarity, and Kazini was valued because, as an Indian Muslim, 'his presence had a certain political value.'[122] Although the 'Indianisation' policy alienated many amongst the Dundee School, it was never designed with the aim of completely removing them. The number of Indian supervisors increased markedly in the post-independence period, but Scottish managers, mechanics and supervisors remained familiar figures in Indian mills up to the 1960s, when Jim Balfour, who had recently arrived from Arbroath, likened a trip into the centre of Calcutta to walking down Dundee high street, such was the prominence of the *oary* tongue.[123]

The whole period of the 1930s emerges as an extended damage limitation exercise for the jute wallahs. They had to show a deft sleight of hand when attempting to juggle with successive crises, but by 1937 all these crises seemed set to come together. The danger, however, passed, and the resolve of capital, which had been momentarily shaken, returned. The changes to the labour control strategy, comprising the removal of the head sirdar, the introduction of 'white flag' unions, and the Indianisation policy, were augmented by the introduction of labour officers, and new labour recruitment practices. All of these separate changes, when taken together, represented an attempt to reform paternal despotism into a more effective bureaucratised structure that could still worker unrest without giving rise to the development of alternative centres of power within the mill. Paternal despotism was being re-made rather than re-shaped, as many jute wallahs realised that for things to remain the same everything had to change.

The breaking of the imperial nexus of jute

In 1931, with the world economic depression showing few signs of abating, the National Government renounced free trade and decided to protect British industry and commerce within an imperial economic bloc, a far-reaching change in economic policy that was realised in August 1932 with the signing of the Ottawa Agreement. While British negotiators recognised that an imperial free trade zone would lead to an inevitable increase in imports into the UK, they also calculated that the increased sterling balances gained by the Empire countries would make it easier for 'debtor' countries such as India to meet their obligations to the 'mother country'.[124] Samuel Hoare, the secretary of state for India, was also hopeful that Ottawa, by 'bringing India more definitely into the orbit of imperial trade', would reassure the still powerful and increasingly restive Lancashire lobby that there was still a place for it in Indian trade, thus preventing it from allying with Churchill and the die-hard Conservatives in their increasing attempts to wreck any chance of a constitutional settlement of the developing Indian crisis.[125] This provided little comfort for Dundee mill owners, who were well aware that the 18 per cent tariff placed on Indian imports of jute goods would provide them with precious little protection. Ottawa led to a growing conviction within Dundee that the city's jute industry was being used as a bargaining counter in a loaded imperial game, a conviction borne out by Hoare's belief that 'an easier entry into the UK market for some of India's products would help allay the worst fears of Indian businessmen and that the agreement would tend to improve the political atmosphere between the two countries.'[126]

In the event, Ottawa failed to placate both the Lancashire lobby and Indian business interests, while UK consumption of 'home' produced jute goods dramatically improved between 1932 and 1935, as demonstrated by Figure 7.2. However, from 1935 up to the outbreak of war, Dundee's share of the UK market markedly declined as a growing band of Calcutta's leading mills, faced with increasing competition from 'outside mill' in many other markets, eyed the small but profitable 'home market'. Dundee responded by accusing Calcutta of 'dumping', a charge strenuously denied by the chairman of the IJMA, Harry Burn:

> It is unnecessary for me to remind you that Calcutta's increased output during the past two years has been misinterpreted as a competitive attack upon Dundee and has given rise to a strong plea for protection of the United Kingdom market against the influx of jute goods from India. We do not admit the impeachment; the battle which has been fought and which I hope is reaching a close, has been fought in the interests of the industry as a whole including Dundee, though it has taken place on the banks of the Hooghly where the policy of the industry must essentially be determined.[127]

The future of Dundee as a major textile centre was now wholly dependent on decisions taken within the boardrooms of the jute wallahs and the chambers of the IJMA. Underlying these decisions was the imperative of dealing once and for all with the Marwari 'interlopers'.

Although the attitude of these 'jute wallahs' towards the 'outside mills' may seem overly punitive, bearing in mind the small scale of Indian involvement in the Bengal jute industry, the rise of the Marwaris undermined the cohesion and discipline of the IJMA, which was a fatal development for an organisation with a long track record as a cartel-regulating body. The instinctive antagonism of the jute wallahs towards the Marwari newcomers was neither irrational, nor overstated. No class ever leaves the stage of history without a furious struggle, and the Calcutta wallahs were no exception to this rule. The descendants of the pioneer jute wallahs trod the same ground as their venerable ancestors, and benefited from family ties and acquaintance to make their mark in the industry. The leading jute wallahs were not prepared to sacrifice their

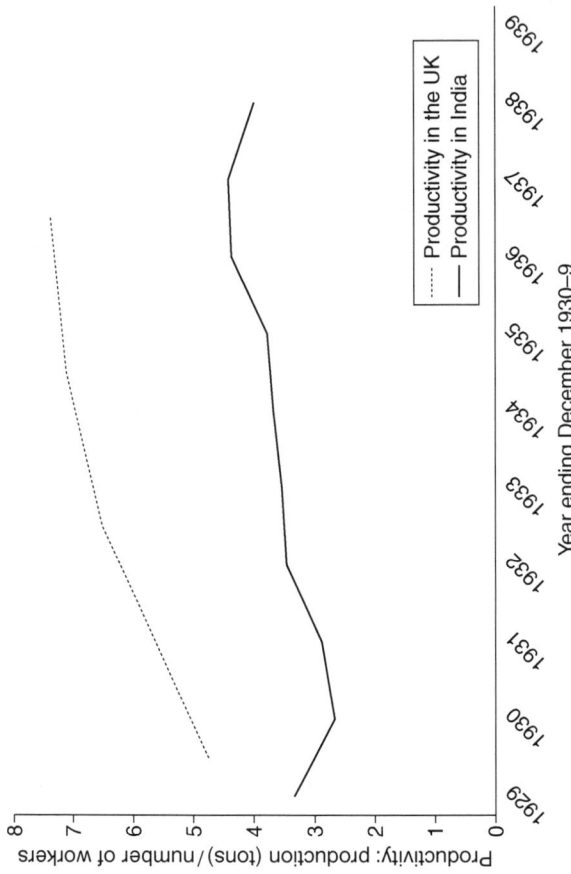

Figure 7.1 Worker productivity in India and the UK, 1929–39.

Year ending	Indian production '000 tons	% of 1929–30 figure	Indian workers	% of 1929–30 figure	Indian productivity tons/worker*	UK production '000 tons	% of 1930 figure	UK workers	% of 1930 figure	UK productivity tons/worker
June	1,141	100	343,257	100	3.32					
December 1930						137	100	28,727	100	4.77
June	815	71	307,676	90	2.65					
December 1931						125	91			
June	795	70	276,810	81	2.87					
December 1932						124	91			
June	907	79	263,442	77	3.44					
December 1933						147	107	22,547	78	6.52
June	907	79	257,175	75	3.53					
December 1934						160	117	23,535	82	6.80
June	968	85	263,739	77	3.67					
December 1935						172	126	24,190	84	7.11
June	1,048	92	277,986	81	3.77					
December 1936						171	125			
June	1,262	111	289,136	84	4.36					
December 1937						179	131	24,239	84	7.38
June	1,347	118	305,785	89	4.41					
December 1938						153	112			
June	1,172	103	295,162	86	3.97					
December 1939			298,967	87		177	129			

Source: Indian workers from A. K. Bagchi (1972) *Private Investment in India*, Hyderabad, p. 277, Table 8.3. All other figures from *Board of Trade Working Party Reports*, 1948: Indian production p. 12, Table 4; UK production p. 10, Table 2; UK workers p. 41, Table 21.

Notes
* Dates for worker numbers are mostly from previous calendar year, while production is measured from July to June.

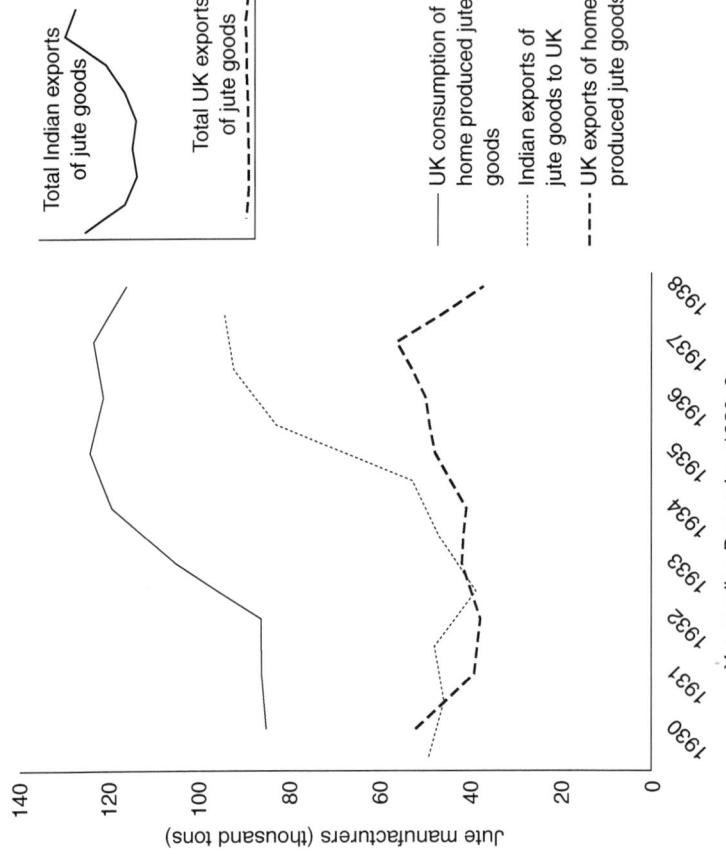

Figure 7.2 Indian exports, UK exports and the UK home market, 1929–38.

Year ending	Indian total exports of jute goods, '000 tons	Indian exports of jute goods to UK, '000 tons	UK exports of home produced jute goods, '000 tons	UK consumption of home produced jute goods, '000 tons
June	945	49	52	85
December 1930				
June	716	46	39	86
December 1931				
June	662	48	38	86
December 1932				
June	685	39	42	105
December 1933				
June	667	47	41	119
December 1934				
June	724	53	48	124
December 1935				
June	834	83	50	121
December 1936				
June	1058	92	56	123
December 1937				
June	1000	94	37	116
December 1938				

Source: *Board of Trade Working Party Reports*, 1948: UK figures p. 10, Table 2; Indian figures p. 12, Table 4.

hard-won bequest without a fight, hence their frenzied reaction to the emergence of the Marwaris.[128]

As the destiny of the imperial nexus of jute was being decided on the banks of the Hooghly, the Dundee jute industry faced up to a fresh onslaught on another front, as European jute industries expanded production. German jute manufacturers were steadily increasing their share of the international markets at Dundee's expense and by 1939 the German jute industry was as large as, if not larger than, the 'home' industry.[129] Faced with consecutive attacks on a number of fronts many feared the writing was on the wall for Juteopolis, while there appeared to be little chance of shaking off the shackles of jute dependency through economic diversification. In February 1936, an ambitious and long-standing plan to span the Tay with a road bridge finally foundered, prompting one acerbic observer to claim that 'if the estuaries of the Forth and Tay were 100 miles nearer London they would have had road bridges fifty years ago.'[130] The failure to attract outside capital and government funding should not, however, have been a problem. By the late 1930s, the nine investment trusts connected with Dundee possessed between them £26 million of reserve capital, but little of this enormous sum was invested locally.[131] If Dundee's economy was going to be re-built in a more balanced and sustainable manner it was unlikely to happen through the efforts of the city's entrepreneurial elites, who were still firmly wedded to jute and foreign investment.

With little chance of economic diversification in the short or medium term, Dundee was virtually compelled to keep faith with its staple industry, and in July 1937 hopes were briefly raised with the opening of new Indo-British trade talks, following increasing dissatisfaction, particularly on the part of Indian politicians and business interests, with the results of the Ottawa Agreement.[132] The Dundee lobby reiterated their longstanding demand for import controls, but this argument was vigorously challenged by the British Jute Goods Association (JGA), which claimed that import controls would merely force the Indian government to retaliate through the imposition of heavy duties on raw jute exports, while jute firms in other parts of Britain 'engaged in the bag making industry will be threatened with extinction, leaving the entire manufacture of jute cloth and bags to be carried out in Dundee, a task which, as the employment and production figures indicate, they cannot undertake.'[133] In September 1936, at a time when there were 1,750 unemployed spinners in the city, it was believed that none had any experience of working automatic spinning frames.[134]

In August 1937, as the increasingly fraught Indo-British trade talks rumbled on and social conditions in Dundee showed signs of further deterioration, Edward Benthall wrote to Harry Burn expressing his growing fear that import controls would be implemented by the British government because 'politically and economically they are much concerned over the prosperity of Dundee.'[135] In the following months, with a new US recession starting to spread, Dundee's grim condition showed little sign of improvement, despite increasing orders for war materials. In February 1938 the Association of Jute Spinners and Manufacturers (AJSM) attempted to pressurise the BBC into withdrawing a radio broadcast on the Dundee jute industry because the 'trade did not take kindly to the form of presentation, particularly the aspect dealing with the hardships in working class homes.'[136] Some relief did come to Dundee with the introduction of the Bengal Jute Ordinance in September 1938, which effectively ended the Bengal production war.[137] In the following months, imports of Calcutta jute goods into Britain slowed, while large government orders for sandbags and other war materials stimulated activity in the city's shipyards and foundries, giving rise to increasing hopes that Dundee's looming social crisis could be averted. What was given with one hand was, though, quickly snatched away by another. In March 1939, the new Indo-British trade agreement was finally announced, and, much to the astonishment of many within Dundee, it included a clause allowing for the free entry of Indian jute goods into Britain. Although the decision prompted the usual furious protests from Dundee, it made perfect sense in terms of British financial and imperial interests to support the Calcutta lobby. After all, the 'home industry' was steadily losing markets to Indian and European competitors, while jute dependency had turned Dundee into an 'industrial cul-de-sac' that both shocked and dismayed observers in equal measure. It was becoming clear that protecting the Dundee jute industry was never part of 'official' thinking and nor was it part of the 'remedy' suggested by 'independent' bodies such as the Scottish Economic Committee.[138] Instead, the focus was on the need for a smaller rationalised 'home' jute industry within a more diversified local economy.[139] Importantly, the revenues of the British as well as the Indian government would be assured in the likely event that the 'Calcutta cutty' extended its growing dominance of world jute production to the speciality goods market. In addition, the 1939 agreement also assuaged Indian economic interests, whilst bolstering the position of British capital in Bengal. The Dundee jute industry was, thus, opened up to the full draft of international competition with the approval of the highest levels of the British imperial state.

During the late 1930s, increasing war preparations gained a momentum, and Britain's centres of heavy industry in the north of England and the Celtic fringe began to show palpable signs of recovery. Juteopolis, however, remained a serious cause for concern. In October 1938, with the ink barely dry on the Bengal Jute Ordinance, the Scottish Economic Committee called the Scottish Secretary of State's attention to the 'disastrous situation developing in Dundee and asked for the most serious consideration of the Government with a view to adopting practicable measures for a remedy.'[140] Remedies, though, were in shorter supply, particularly given the scale and seriousness of urban and social deprivation in Juteopolis. The two-roomed tenement flat remained the city's dominant housing type and, despite the building of new housing schemes during the inter-war period, many working class families still faced atrocious housing conditions. Indeed, Scottish housing conditions were deemed to be so bad that government statisticians developed a more stringent method of classification to measure Scottish overcrowding from that used in the rest of the UK, but not even statistical manipulation could conceal Dundee's shocking housing conditions. In 1933 *The Architects' Journal*, drawing on official government figures, revealed that in only seven, much larger, British cities did more people suffer from overcrowding.[141] With 22,438 persons living over three per room and

60,288 living over two per room, Dundee needed 20,000 more houses in order to eradicate overcrowding. Hull, a major port and industrial centre in Yorkshire, with a very similar population, needed 6,000 houses.[142]

Despite the slow pace of improvement in the city's housing stock, the long-standing problem of infant mortality was dramatically improving: while the rate during 1916–20 was 129 per thousand by 1936–40 it was 77 per thousand.[143] William Burgess, the city Medical Officer, claimed that this improvement resulted from the Corporation's 'direct attack on the infant health problem', but high unemployment and short-time working meant that many women were less likely to be working during the critical periods of late pregnancy and immediately following childbirth, and this undoubtedly had a larger impact than the efforts, worthy though they were, of Dundee Corporation.

Rationalisation opened the industry up to adult male labour and Dundee was no longer so closely associated with child and juvenile labour as it once had been. Notwithstanding the problem of forged birth certificates, which remained a problem up to the eve of the Second World War, the average age of jute workers was creeping upwards.[144] Changes within the jute industry also affected, and reflected, wider social changes within Dundee. From the late 1920s the marriage rate amongst Dundee women began to rise, and during the course of the 1930s it was greater than the other three major Scottish cities. Women were more likely to marry unskilled and semi-skilled men whose chances of long-term employment were less than certain, which in turn meant that married women were more likely to enter the labour market. A common observation of married working women during the inter-war years was that 'one wage was no good to get a decent living'.[145] The depression also witnessed an increase in the ranks of that emblematic figure of Juteopolis, the 'kettle boiler'. With regular work difficult to come by, many unemployed Dundonian men turned to casual work such as decorating, minor repairs and collecting and selling shellfish, which supplemented family income and allowed them to play the role of provider. Where the man was unable to provide it was often the case that the main meal was divided so that 'the person that was working got the beef, and you got the broth'.[146] In 1937, a pioneering documentary film, *Dundee*, strengthened the association between Juteopolis and the 'kettle boiler' in the Scottish imagination;

FIRST MAN: That was a man's job building ships.
FIRST WOMAN: But the women had tae work in the mill.
FIRST MAN: How the hell should they no?
[Shot of men leaving shipyard after work.]
SECOND MAN: All that meant more work for the men, but they still said, 'Marry a Dundee wife and give up work'.
FIRST WOMAN: Aye, marry a Dundee wife and be a kettle boiler.[147]

In a city afflicted by high unemployment for so long it was no social disgrace to be unemployed. Indeed, for some men the advent of unemployment benefits provided an opportunity to embrace a way of life that ridiculed the myth of the

Scottish 'democratic intellect' and the 'work ethic' that it was founded on. The depression-era Dundee street song, *The Bureau*, sung to the tune of *Blackbird Bye Bye*, captured the mixture of resignation and relish felt by some of those caught in the trap of long-term unemployment:

> We're the lads fae the tap o' the hill,
> We never worked and we never will,
> We're on the Broo,
> Just like the lads fae Peddie Street,
> Mention work – We tak tae oor feet,
> We're on the Broo.[148]

Even following the coming of cinema, the dance hall and the 'wireless', the street remained a theatre of dreams, social club, friendly society and organising centre for Dundee's urban poor, and would remain so up until the 1950s. It was a place where gossip was shared and plans were hatched, where problems could be forgotten whilst whiling away the time in penny betting and, for some of the most desperate, the drinking of 'red biddy', a noxious concoction of methylated spirits and cheap wine that could be purchased for a fraction of the cost of beer or whisky. The 'Howff', a medieval churchyard in the centre of Dundee, was a regular gathering place for the 'wretched addicts' and was regularly raided by the police, and it was a common sight to see children 'queuing at "dry-salter" shops at 8am in the morning for meths', before the sale of 'red biddy' and methylated spirits for consumption was outlawed following the parliamentary intervention of Florence Horsburgh in 1937.[149]

The coming of the Second World War improved Dundee's woeful unemployment rates, but local unemployment was 6 per cent in the autumn of 1941, when the national rate had fallen to about 1.5 per cent.[150] Because of the shortage of shipping and the danger of submarine attacks, shipments of raw jute to Dundee declined from pre-war levels and Bengal was called upon to furnish the bulk of war-related jute goods. Industrial production and the demand for jute mill labour in Dundee declined to such an extent that by 1945 only 10,773 of the city's jute workers were employed, compared with 26,172 in 1939.[151] The contraction of the Dundee jute industry during the Second World War freed up labour that could be re-directed towards war work, but Scottish feelings ran high when it was discovered that girls were to be sent south of the border.[152] Convoys of young Dundee women made their way to the south of England and the midlands, where they were allocated work in engineering factories. Encouraged by the higher wages and better working and living conditions, many did not return to Juteopolis, while those who did found that little had changed during their absence, prompting angry denunciations from Dave Bowman, the communist parliamentary candidate for Dundee at the 1945 general election:

> No one has a right to expect that munitions workers who have experienced fairly good conditions such as canteen facilities, good wash-up and private

locker accommodation are to meekly return to the former poor conditions in jute.... It must therefore be understood that if a return of workers to jute is to be effected ... there must be a revolutionary change in the wages and conditions.[153]

Following the Second World War, new foreign-owned industries began operations on the city's outskirts and many jute workers voted with their feet by seeking work in these new light-filled and well-ventilated factories along and off the Kingsway. Now, for the first time, Dundee's mill owners had to compete for recruits with companies who paid higher wages and provided better facilities. In early 1947, with a mounting recruitment crisis in the jute industry, J. Ernest Cox mournfully admitted that 'competition for labour will be acute for many years to come', and that the jute industry would not be able to attract new recruits until it provided better working conditions in the shape of 'canteens, accommodation for clothing and other amenities'.[154] The mill owners responded, and by 1954 there were 17,224 people employed in the jute industry, representing a dramatic improvement from the war years. The modernisation of the preparing and spinning processes was also re-commenced following the wartime hiatus, and automatic looms were introduced. Output improved and in 1954 the 'home' jute industry produced 81,000 tons of piece goods, compared with 59,000 tons in 1948.[155] The jute industry would undergo further crises, but these never impacted on Dundee to the devastating degree that had been regularly experienced during the heyday of Juteopolis. The city had at last managed to break free from the shackles of jute dependency, but its shadow still lingered in the shape of a local economy that relied on a still too-narrow range of industries, thus maintaining the close association between Dundee and high unemployment rates, poor housing conditions, poor health and a lower life expectancy than was the British norm. Indeed, although it is nearly 15 years since the 'bummer' called spinners to their frames for the final time, in December 1998, the shadow of jute dependency lingers still amidst the dashed dreams of urban planners and a continuous procession of so-called 'regeneration' schemes that seem hell-bent on obliterating all that remains vital about *Oary* Dundee.

Conclusion

With the demise of the Soviet Union and the command economies of the 'Eastern bloc' in the early 1990s, the world economy came to be dominated by a 'New World Order', marked by economic liberalisation, globalisation and privatisation. As smokestack industries toppled across the developed world, particularly in Britain and the United States, the power of organised labour seemed to wither in the face of an emerging 'post-industrial society'. For many social scientists, the economic and political changes that marked this period fundamentally undermined the viability of the class narrative and the privileged position given to the working class in the making of history. This changing perspective was encouraged by the increasing influence of post-modernist and post-structuralist theories, particularly within the social science departments of universities in the United States and Britain. Some academics saw themselves as going beyond Marxism, seeing their previous support for it as a necessary but passing phase in the evolution of their intellectual and political thought.

Discourse theory and feminist ideas were particularly influential in undermining the idealised notion of a contained, pure and egalitarian-minded working class, giving rise to a view of class as only one, and not the most important, form of self-expression that people choose to adopt. While this far-reaching 'deconstruction' of class has had positive effects, particularly in the long-overdue recognition that there is no automatic relationship between social structures and political movements, class as a form of social organisation has been reduced to little more than a descriptive category, with dire consequences for the field of labour studies. The wheel, however, is beginning to turn. There are real signs of a resurgence of interest in the labour question in the context of a developing systemic crisis of finance capitalism and the emerging battle over who pays for the crisis. We are now entering the rapids of history, marked by the eruption of the 'Arab Spring' and the mass movements against austerity measures in southern Europe. Still further movements may well be unleashed, particularly within the so-called 'emerging' economic powers of Asia and South America. Incorporating the urban and rural poor and unorganised workers, they may well resemble those investigated in the foregoing pages.

This monograph has been designed to help us look into that future by looking back at the past – at the world created by the forces of industrialisation and imperialism during the nineteenth century. It is the first study, as far as I am aware, that has sought to directly compare the trajectory of development of labour market formation, labour supervision, and the cultures of labour and class formation between two regional economies, one in an imperial country and the other in a colonial state. The interlinked character of the jute industries in Dundee and Calcutta has provided an almost unique opportunity to re-address and re-configure our understanding of the impact of Empire on the process of class formation in the metropolitan context and to critique the findings of labour historians within the field of jute labour studies who have limited the scope of their enquiries to either centre of production.

For many Indian historians, paternal despotism as a mind-set and as a form of management practice was bound up with the colonial context of the Bengal jute industry, thus underlining the intrinsic differences between the experience of industrialisation and class formation in Europe and India. In reality, and as this study has demonstrated, the roots of paternal despotism lay in the major structural revolution that enveloped the Dundee linen industry during the 1830s and 1840s. Its emergence was dependent on the creation and maintenance of a reserve army of labour, which checked rising wages and the ability of workers to resist the often-overweening control of management. We have seen that the rise of the Calcutta jute industry was spearheaded by the emerging Dundee School of engineers, mechanics, foreman and managers, who became the living embodiments of paternal despotism in Calcutta. Accustomed to an apparently unassailable position of authority within the 'home' jute industry, these men were well suited to the demands of managing an industry in a colonial context. Like their fellow Scots in colonial government from an earlier phase in the subjugation of India, the pioneer jute wallahs 'found ... the business of presiding over thousands of unrepresented subjects neither very uncongenial nor particularly unfamiliar.'[1] In effect, the jute mill workers of Dundee and Calcutta struggled against a management cadre drawn from a single source, and which mobilised similar forms of labour control. Paternal despotism as a labour control mechanism was, though, given further impetus through the development of the imperial nexus. Over the years, the working experience of the Dundee School in India encouraged views and attitudes towards Indian jute workers that, in turn, coloured and influenced class relations in Dundee. We thus see the emergence of an interface between the patriarchal form of labour control practised in Dundee and the racialised form of labour control practised in Calcutta, which effectively brought two very different cultures and peoples into a process of dialogic interaction. The jute industries on the banks of the Tay and the Hooghly were intimately connected, and these connections must be noted and understood if we are to properly understand the inner dynamics of either centre.

I am not suggesting that the jute working classes of the imperial nexus were formed in the same way, or in the same image, but when terms such as pre-industrial or colonial are juxtaposed with other terms such as bourgeois or metropolitan this imparts notions of difference that serve to muddy our understanding of the real significance of imperialism and industrialisation. Scottish and Indian jute workers may well have been separated by oceans, culture and history, but paternal despotism was a shared experience, which had a profound impact on the process of class formation in both centres.

By the end of the nineteenth century, the Scottish Juteopolis had become an industrial cul-de-sac *par excellence*, and an intermittent subject of official concern due to appalling social conditions.[2] The Dundee mill girl did not have a long history of artisan and guild organisation to draw upon and there was little evidence of an impulse towards social betterment or accomplishment in the domestic arts. Her life revolved around a hard, often unremitting struggle for existence within the mills and slum areas, such as the Blue Mountain and the 'five middens'.[3] She was more inclined to read penny romances than educational tracts, and seems to have reacted to the widespread contempt of those groups that lay above her in the social hierarchy of Juteopolis with a stubborn refusal to recognise the worth of middle-class notions of respectability. We search in vain for the 'bourgeois subject' that the Subaltern School of writers expects to find in the metropolis. Instead we find a workforce – and the most significant part of Dundee's working class – whose way of life often mocked and shamed the myth of the 'Scottish democratic intellect'.

The emergence of the 'Calcutta cutty', with its vast supply of cheaper workers and its nearness to the source of the raw material, should have been the cue for the marginalisation of the Dundee jute industry, but it actually served to limit the development of other competitor jute industries in countries such as Germany, Belgium, Czechoslovakia and the USA. Jute industries did develop in these countries, and would have an increasing impact on Dundee's export and home markets in the inter-war period, but until this point Calcutta, with its growing dominance in the markets for sacking and later hessian cloth, effectively acted as an umbrella over the head of Dundee. Without the emergence of Calcutta, these countries might well have competed with Dundee jute products through intensive capital investment and product diversification. In the event, the Dundee jute barons responded to their formidable Indian competitor through recourse to the exploitation of their labour resources on the basis of cheap wages. They lobbied the British state on a whole number of issues relating to child working, wages and working conditions, thus guaranteeing the survival of the 'home' jute industry and its increasing dominance of the local economy, which had far-reaching consequences for social conditions within Juteopolis.

Paternal despotism did not, however, go unchallenged. Indeed, the struggle against it became a defining factor in the emergence of the jute working class in both centres. In Dundee, the period between 1885 and 1905 saw industrial struggle on a constantly widening front, but largely in the absence of any kind of formal workers' organisation other than that provided by Henry Williamson's pro-employer and paternalist Manufacturing and Factory Operatives Union (MFOU). The spontaneous strike became a defining characteristic of industrial relations in Dundee, in the context of a developing trade war between Juteopolis and the 'Calcutta Cutty'. Strikes seemed to appear suddenly with the coming of the spring sun. They were not preceded by negotiations and were not ended by written agreements between managers and official workers' representatives, demonstrating, in spectacular style, that it 'is quite possible for a bright awareness of class – or even an explosion of "class hatred" – to occur within a world that is dominated by organisations that have little or no commitment to a doctrine of "class struggle" or to revolution.'[4]

This is even clearer when we turn our attention to developments within the Bengal jute industry, where the large-scale strike movements of the late nineteenth and early twentieth centuries were conducted in the complete absence of any kind of trade union apparatus or centralised form of organisation. While the comparative framework of this study has focused on similarities in the experience of class formation in Bengal and Dundee, we cannot ignore the clearer colonial context within which class formation occurred in Bengal, as it undoubtedly gave an added edge and impetus to the process of class formation. We saw, in Chapters 2 and 5, that ill treatment at the hands of Scottish supervisors was the major cause of some of the most violent and bitter strikes in the Bengal jute industry, which ensured that the fight against 'paternal despotism' became a defining feature in the making of the jute working class in Bengal. The colonial state became acutely aware of the need to limit the potential harm that could be caused by the overreaction of jute mill managers and supervisors to labour disputes, and this reasoning formed the *raison d'être* behind the active efforts of the colonial state to rein in jute mill management during the strike waves of the 1890s and early 1920s.

Despite the heightened antagonism caused by the presence of the Dundee School, they were not, as claimed by many Indian historians, simply the willing soldiers of empire. Neither were they the cheap 'semi-skilled or unskilled recruits' described by Amiya Bagchi.[5] They were, in fact, drawn from the upper sections of the skilled working class in Dundee, with wages and conditions from service in India far in excess of those enjoyed by their counterparts back in Scotland. They were, though, subject to levels of company control, through restrictive contracts and the legal obligations flowing from their position as British subjects working and living in a colony, that would have been totally unacceptable to their lower paid counterparts in Dundee. Coercion as well as privilege was, thus, a hallmark of their often limited time in India and tensions could, and did, break through the employer constructed *esprit de corps* that ruled within the European quarter of the jute mill compounds. Thrust into the alien and often hostile environment of the Bengal jute mill districts, and faced with a workforce that was increasingly influenced by anti-colonial rhetoric, to say nothing of the often overt racism demonstrated by elements within the Dundee School itself, it is little wonder that fear-induced overreaction occasionally took hold, transforming some industrial disputes into serious anti-colonial struggles.

The tumultuous events and experiences that accompanied the re-making of the imperial nexus dramatically re-shaped the 'disposition' or outlook of the jute workers in both centres. Old ideas were churned up and 'traditional' beliefs were invested with new, and often radical, meanings that informed and influenced the strike movements and social struggles of this period. We can see this process at work with regards to popular religious beliefs. Hindu and Islamic reform movements encouraged a wider nationalist, anti-colonial feeling amongst mill workers that directly impacted on industrial relations in Bengal. As we saw in Chapter 2, the attempt by Scottish managers to exclude workers from the celebration of Hindu and Muslim festivals during the 1890s led to the first major strike movements in the history of the Bengal jute industry, and the forging of links between workers of different religions. These developments point to the protean nature of religion, demonstrating the radically different ways in which religious teachings were interpreted and religious organisational forms adapted for very different purposes.

Similar processes were evident in Dundee, where a locally based socialist party, influenced by millenarian Christianity, became a major rival to the Labour Party through a radical and socialist inspired Biblical exegesis. The emergence of the Scottish Prohibitionist Party (SPP) allows us to interrogate 'the stages theory' of teleological development championed by Eric Hobsbawm, which sees no place within the 'mature' industrial economy of late Victorian Dundee for the kind of, apparently backward looking, socialist millenarianism exemplified by the SPP. The rise of socialist millenarianism was dependent on the melding of new ideas and much older, and more local, radical traditions. During the 1840s, a revolutionary socialist impulse was clearly discernible in the fiery denunciations of 'Gradgrind' capitalism made by Dundee's artisan leaders, who drew on influences including Protestant resistance theory and artisan radicalism to create a developing language of class that would later be echoed in the incendiary oratory of Neddy Scrymgeour. Bob Stewart, a leading communist apparatchik and acquaintance of Stalin during the inter-war years, was embarrassed by his early adherence to socialist millenarianism, but he surely had more cause for pride than embarrassment in the realisation that his formative socialist influences drew on local radical traditions that extended much further back in time than November 1917.[6]

The nature of trade unionism in the imperial nexus of jute

As the nineteenth century gave way to the twentieth, the challenge to paternal despotism started to take on a more organised and constitutional form. Labour activists and social reformers saw, in the large-scale movements of the jute workers, the potential power of these largely unorganised workforces. The coming of industrial trade unionism was fiercely resisted by the employers in both centres, who had long shown a deep-seated antipathy towards collective bargaining and workers' combination, and the struggle over trade union rights and recognition became another major factor in the process of working class formation.[7] Writing in the late 1920s, following an investigative trip to India, the eminent American industrialist and writer D. H. Buchanan brought out the fundamental relationship between employers' attitudes and growing workers militancy. He was confident that Indian trade unions had a future, but he was also aware that 'when it comes to a "show-down" and employers find their control questioned, most of them, both British and Indian, falter. Often they insist that they would welcome "proper" trade unions, but that the existing organisations are led by outside self-seekers and trouble-makers.'[8] In Buchanan's opinion, the Anglo-Scottish managing agencies 'were more ready to accept unionism as such but they had less patience with the incipient unionism with which they had to deal, and were often possessed of a lurking fear that this was a blow at something more than factory discipline – at British *izot* (prestige) in India. Indeed, the movement sometimes looked like revolution.'[9] This was also an accurate description of the attitude of the jute barons in Dundee, who also steadfastly refused to accept the legitimacy of trade unions.

Industrial unionism came to the Dundee jute industry in 1906, in the shape of the Jute and Flax Workers' Union (JFWU). The JFWU was a very different kind of organisation than the longer-lived, and *ma-baap*, MFOU, and the attitude of the jute barons towards it was marked by a thoroughgoing hostility that continued through to the end of our period. The new union was led and organised by leaders who underlined the importance of class solidarity founded on trade union membership, collective bargaining and the recognition of the separate and distinct interests of capital and labour. They were reformist by inclination, but were consistently forced down the road of major confrontation with the jute barons, particularly during the early years of the union's existence. In effect, the employers' intolerant attitude towards workers combination only served to bring into being the very kind of trade unions that they feared and despised most. It created combative leaders who also invariably failed to control their membership and to prevent serious, and frequent, outbreaks of so-called 'wild-cat' strikes. In the years prior to the First World War, industrial disputes over limited demands became transformed into full-blown class-based confrontations, and working class militancy became even more pronounced during the war years, encouraged by the general widening out of the industrial struggle and the eruption of rent strikes. In 1916, in the midst of an increasingly serious challenge by wide sections of the industrial workforce in the west of Scotland, the newly established Dundee newspaper, the *Textile Workers' Guide*, made the telling comment, '[w]e do not know whether we have corrupted the Clyde engineers or they us'.[10] The wartime wave of militancy in the Dundee jute industry extended into peacetime, with employers and the local and national state seeking, unsuccessfully, to control regular and protracted strikes and the growing political militancy of the jute workers.

The 'brief heroic age'[11] of jute trade unionism in Dundee would be brought to a juddering halt with the cataclysmic experience of the 1923 general strike and lockout. For the JFWU, the remainder of the inter-war period became a long exercise in damage limitation, as the employers sought to claw back many of the improvements in wages, conditions and bargaining rights that had been won during and immediately following the First World War. The trade union field in the jute industry also became the site of an increasingly bitter conflict between communists and more mainstream labour activists, which underlined the importance of the imperial nexus on the evolution of labour politics in Dundee. While communists were subjected to bans and proscriptions within the British labour movement during the 1920s, their attempts to forge links with workers' organisations in the Bengal jute industry resulted in conflict with the leadership of Dundee Labour Party that turned a divide into a yawning chasm, and paved the way for bans and proscriptions on communist involvement in the JFWU.

For many Indian labour historians, the palpable lack of a functioning trade union apparatus for most of our period points to the failure of trade unionism in Bengal. In Chapter 5 we saw that trade unions in the Bengal mill areas were sometimes mere shells – little more than headed note paper and tin pot leaders of phantom armies, who remained largely isolated from the workers that they sought to represent. Very few trade union leaders were actually workers, and the wider trade union movement was never able to free itself from the fractious politics of Bengal. These are well-rehearsed factors that are seen as drawing the limits, not only of trade union consciousness, but also of the Bengal jute workers' ability to constitute themselves as a working class after the Marxist paradigm. In fact, such absences, or failures are found not only in the Bengal trade union movement. French trade unions have always been historically weak in organisational terms, and also have a 'low propensity' to 'engage in official bargaining terms'.[12] Yet, despite these perceived weaknesses, French trade unions were, and still are, able to mobilise large numbers of workers in strike activity, and are seen as powerful institutions in French civic culture. Furthermore, even the classical model of British trade unionism, against which the failure of trade unionism in Bengal is often measured, showed a pattern of development that was often highly problematic and organisationally limited, as demonstrated by the example of the JFWU.

All of this should not obscure another important difference in the way that trade unionism developed in the two centres of the imperial nexus of jute. Industrial unionism came to Bengal in the late 1920s as a movement spearheaded by a small, but growing, cadre of bhadralok communist activists who looked towards the Soviet Union as an inspiration in their fight against British imperialism. Under these circumstances, industrial relations in Bengal became transformed into a barely concealed and often vicious ideological conflict – a front in the evolving war of movement between the forces of bourgeois democracy and communism, which encouraged closer relations between the colonial state and capital with regards to 'the labour question'. This also had important repercussions for the development of working class consciousness in Bengal during the inter-war period, by facilitating the political solidarity of the jute workers through their experience of the colonial state as an increasingly repressive and antagonistic force during moments of industrial action. Despite this, trade unions were able to sink roots in the Bengal jute industry, and the scope and scale of their activities clearly increased during our period. By the eve of World War Two, trade unions in Bengal had developed their structures and influence, but official trade unionism still remained supplementary to more informal forms of worker organisation and resistance.

The influence of the labour movement in both centres was circumscribed by the material conditions created by jute dependency, and the forging and continuing impact of the imperial nexus of jute. Free time was always at a premium, and appalling wages, living conditions and low educational levels all militated against the development of a meaningful form of associational culture amongst jute workers. However, while jute workers may not have been directly involved in formal politics, they were able to effectively organise shifting blocs with the parties and trade unions that sought their support. The emergence of jute dependency and the imperial nexus of jute also created the basis for the regular eruption of 'wild cat' and mass strikes. In both centres the concentration of mills in specific geographical localities, which was very different from the pattern of industrial organisation in other jute industries, seemed to encourage the development of industry-wide strike action. In Bengal, where the jute workforce numbered hundreds rather than tens of thousands, the mass strike was all the more feared, by colonial officials and capital alike. The 1923 strike and lock-out may well have marked the effective ending of the use of the mass strike in Dundee, but it remained a potent threat in Bengal right up to the end of our period, which points up another major difference in the process of working class formation in the Scottish and Indian contexts. The village link enabled the up-country workers to sustain the 1937 general strike for so long, but without an equivalent means of support and trapped in a jute-dominated local economy, the mill hands of Dundee were effectively ensnared within the web of jute dependency to a much greater extent than the so-called 'peasant-proletarians' of Bengal.

Labour segmentation and class formation in the imperial nexus of jute

For many middle-class commentators, who were deeply influenced by the cult of domesticity that gathered momentum during the Victorian era, the Dundee mill girl represented the antithesis of the ideal female, and the phenomenon of large-scale female employment was viewed as the root of many social evils.[13] Social commentators were particularly scornful of the so-called male 'kettle-boilers' of Juteopolis. Trapped in a one-industry town with few outlets for gainful employment, many unskilled male workers often found themselves unemployed while their wives or partners found work in the city's mills. This 'unnatural domestic situation', as it was described by the travel writer H. V. Morton, was seen to represent everything that was backward and negative about the industrial society spawned by jute dependency. In many households headed by male unskilled workers (often employed in the jute industry), it was also common for children to work, along with the wife or unmarried partner. In these family groups domestic duties tended to be more democratically organised, in contrast to the more patriarchal domestic arrangements within households headed by skilled or middle-class males. In this sense, jute dependency gave rise to a form of household arrangement that anticipated a more modern, progressive division of gender roles within the household – a positive development that is often lost sight of amidst the hand-wringing commentaries of contemporary observers.

Although patriarchy, as a form of labour organisation and control, was undoubtedly present in Dundee, the extent of its influence and power has been over-exaggerated by feminist scholars who have analysed labour relations in Juteopolis. Eleanor Gordon, drawing on the ideas of Sylvia Walby and other feminist labour historians, describes patriarchy as a system of interrelated structures through which men exploit women.[14] The managerial ethos of the Dundee jute industry may well have ordered, segregated, controlled and ultimately exploited the labour of women workers, but patriarchy was never a system of interrelated structures. Male dominance and control of women's paid and domestic work was not the rule within all households, due to the economic independence of many female workers, and the power of patriarchy was further undermined by the widespread development of female-headed households.

Also found wanting is the claim by Eleanor Gordon that the jute trade unions were involved in a 'patriarchal bloc' with managers and employers that aimed to bolster the position of male workers at the expense of their female counterparts. This study has demonstrated that the failures of Dundee's trade unions stemmed from the conditions that they operated in, and there is no evidence of a patriarchal bloc between male managers and workers. There were many unskilled male workers who earned lower wages than the better paid female workers, such as weavers, while the major trade union encompassing jute workers, despite having a male general secretary, was remarkable for the extent to which it involved women members at the highest levels of decision and policy making. Eleanor Gordon also claims that resistance and organisation amongst Dundee's mill workers showed fundamental differences along gender lines, with male workers wedded to constitutional forms, and women workers embracing less structured forms, personified by spontaneous strikes and demonstrations. This study has demonstrated that male workers, both young and old, were also involved in less organised and spontaneous forms of protest, which were encouraged by the way the industry functioned and the fact that it was geared to, often volatile, international markets. Under these circumstances, the element of surprise was absolutely essential for guaranteeing any chance of success in strike action.

The situation facing the women workers of the Bengal jute industry was very different from that of their counterparts in Dundee. They were a more marginal group, in social and numerical terms within the Indian jute workforce, and were often described as comprising many widows of mainly Bengali origin, and, aside from sack sewing, they were spread throughout the mill in a variety of generally menial tasks. As a more marginal group, they were in a vulnerable position, particularly within the northern up-country dominated mill towns of the Calcutta jute belt, where they often formed temporary marriages with up-country male workers. The colonial view of these 'marital arrangements', which bears a striking resemblance to the elite view of marital and household arrangements in Dundee, has been the target of recent forays by Indian feminist writers.[15] The work of Samita Sen, in particular, has provided a detailed examination of the lives and struggles of female jute workers in Bengal, but Sen, who is adept at pointing to the contradictory character of 'elite' and colonial discourses regarding the women workers of the Bengal jute industry, reproduces some of these self-same, elite assumptions in her own writing. According to Sen the nature of the relationship between married male and unmarried or widowed female workers was more akin to a patron-client relationship, as existed between sirdars and workers. Female workers were treated as little more than cash cows, and were completely dependent on the protection of male workers, who often discarded them when they were of no further use. There was no room or opportunity in these 'temporary marriages' for an emotional bond or sexual love, only a kind of 'contract', neither recognised in law, nor respected by the male beneficiaries of the earnings, the energy and the bodies of the female workers.[16] What we are left with is a crude picture that corresponds to the colonial and bourgeois stereotype of male workers as innately violent, sexual predators, and of women workers as powerless subjects without any effective agency of their own. In the context of a highly patriarchal culture where few women jute workers had strong family and kinship links within the mill districts, it is undoubtedly the case that many of these women were in a deeply vulnerable position, but we should not over-exaggerate the weakness of their position. As demonstrated in Chapter 7, working women in the Bengal jute mills were capable of defending themselves and of organising collectively in their own interests. It is also clear that male mill workers often came to their assistance following allegations of mistreatment at the hands of Scottish supervisors or sirdars, undermining Sen's claim, following Gordon, that a 'patriarchal bloc' existed in Bengal. Indeed, as Chapters 2 and 5 have demonstrated, the issue of the mistreatment of women and child workers became a symbol, not only of capitalist exploitation, but also of colonial misrule, which triggered some of the most serious and violent phases of industrial unrest in the history of the Bengal jute industry. Disputes involving women workers were more likely to be taken up by the Indian press and nationalist movement, where the figure of suffering Indian womanhood became a potent means of organising resistance to British owned enterprises, and even to British rule itself.[17]

The workforce of the imperial nexus of jute was not only segmented along the lines of gender. In both centres, workers were drawn from different ethnicities and religions, which in the essentialist or reductionist view should preclude any possibility of their coming together and acting in class ways. This study has demonstrated that diversity was actually a crucial precondition towards the development of militant mass action. We have seen that jute workers in Dundee were drawn from different sources, including the Scottish Highlands and the north-east of Scotland, and particularly from Ulster. Ethnic and religious tensions between Scots Protestants and Irish Catholics were common in Dundee during the 1830s and 1840s, but by the later nineteenth century were far less evident. Unlike west and central Scotland, Dundee did not experience the same degree of Ulster Protestant immigration, and the city did not witness the rise of the Orange Order to nearly the same extent. In Dundee, the high points of Irish

Catholic in-migration occurred during the 1870s and 1880s, which coincided with the eruption of unprecedented levels of industrial struggle. Thereafter rates of in-migration slowed, and by the early years of the twentieth century had almost completely halted. By the inter-war period the different elements of Dundee's working class were starting to come together and meld through inter-ethnic household formation, and shared economic and social interests. Although Dundee had by this time become synonymous with working class militancy and socialist politics, the industry-wide strikes that marked the period of the re-making of the imperial nexus were conspicuous by their absence, particularly following the traumatic defeat of the 1923 jute strike.

While women have long been the main concern of historical studies of the Scottish Juteopolis, children have rarely figured as major actors in their own right. In contrast, this study has demonstrated that the half-timers and adolescent workers within Dundee's preparing sheds and spinning mills played a central role in the forging of the city's distinctive working class culture. These child workers came overwhelmingly from households headed by unskilled male workers, many of whom were also jute workers; and the wages that the children earned were absolutely essential to household sustainability. As a result, the half-timers became important economic actors within the mill districts, and any threat to their income through wage cuts or dismissal could, and did, spark serious and often widespread responses from adult workers, as evidenced by the eruption of industry-wide strikes during the 1890s and 1900s. Some of these children, many no older than 10 or 11 years old when they began their working lives, would also become the adult workers who looked towards the prohibitionists and communists during the inter-war period; and some, such as Bob Stewart and Mary Brooksbank, would become the leaders and activists of militant class-based forms of socialism that challenged the hegemonic intentions of the Labour Party in Dundee.

The imperial nexus of jute demonstrated the fundamental impact of Empire on economic development, working class formation and the evolution of wider social relations in Dundee. Individual entrepreneurs, shareholders, managers and supervisors all benefited from the 'coal face of Empire', particularly as the Scottish seams bore less and less, but Empire also produced a low-paid, unhealthy and increasingly pugnacious working class. While Juteopolis may emerge as an 'extreme case' in this regard, we should not forget that the 'home' jute industry was only one part of a wider Scottish economy that kept the forces of Empire on the move and armed to the teeth, so that the story of the rise and fall of the imperial nexus of jute represents only one chapter in a larger narrative of the Scottish, and indeed British, working class experience of Empire that still remains to be told.

Glossary

Babu (also baboo)	Bengali clerk
Badmash (also budmash)	hooligan
Banian	traders who acted as agents for the managing agents
Busti (also bustee)	slum
Bazaar	market
Bhadralok	lit. gentleman
Bleaching	the procedure of improving the whiteness of cloth
Bobbin	a tapered barrel for holding rovings or yarns
Boxwallah	British businessman or merchant
Brahmo Samaj	reformist Hindu religious group
Budli (also badli)	temporary workers
Bummer	mill whistle in Dundee
Burlap	term applied in the United States to coarser plain cloth made from single yarns
Burra babu	head clerk
Chhotolok (also Chotalok)	lit. the small people
Cop	a form or package of yarn such as is spun on a spindle
Count	a number indicating the mass per unit length or the length per unit mass of yarn
Crore	10,000,000
Cut	a length of cloth
Calender	a finishing process involving the cleaning of cloth
Dasturi	customary right
Dundee School	Scottish supervisors, engineers and managers who were employed in the Bengal jute mills
Durwan	gatekeeper
Fatka	lit. bubble, referring to the Calcutta futures jute market
Gherao	riot or disturbance
Godown	warehouse
Goonda	ruffian or thug

Gunny/gunnies	coarse jute cloth
Halflin (also Halfling)	child worker in jute industry
Half-timer	children whose day was divided between work in the jute industry and education
Hartal	strike
Hessian	single-warp jute cloth
Insaf	sense of honour
Izzat (also izot)	honour
Jamedar (also Jamadar)	guard
Julaha	caste of Muslim weavers
Kabuli	Pathan moneylender
Kettle-boiler	an unemployed man in Dundee who carried out domestic duties whilst his partner or wife worked
Kistiwallah	moneylender
Kutcha	second class or lower grade
Lakh	100,000
Lathi	stick used for self-defence
Ma-baap	lit. mother-father
Madrassis (also Madrassees)	lit. of Madras
Maund	unit of weight, about 82lbs
Mazdoor (also Mazdur)	labourer or manual worker
Midden	a rubbish tip
Mistri	workman; skilled or leading hand
Panchayat	traditional village council
Oary	dishevelled, untidy or out of place; also refers to the working class Scots dialect spoken in Dundee
Orra hand	spare worker
Piece	a length of fabric
Piecer	normally a child worker who was responsible for fixing the loose ends dropped by the spinner
Pucca	higher grade or first class
Puja	festival
Ryot	peasant
Sahib	boss; often used to refer to British managers and supervisors, but also used by jute workers to refer to the bhadralok
Salami	gift given to a superior
Shifter	normally a child worker who replaced full bobbins for empty ones in the spinning process
Sirdar (also sardar)	lit. headman or chief; foreman in Bengal jute mills
Sliver	an assemblage of fibres in rope form without twist
Swaraj	self-rule
Tenter	a workman employed to tune loom
Twill	a type of woven fabric characterised by a pattern of diagonal lines

Twist	the winding together of fibres in order to give added strength to yarn
Warp	threads arranged lengthways in a fabric
Weft	threads arranged widthways in a fabric
Zamindar	landlord

Notes

Introduction

1 Hugh MacDiarmid, 'Dundee', p. 190, in Lewis Grassic Gibbon and Hugh MacDiarmid, *Scottish Scene*, London, 1934, pp. 189–94.

2 Old Scots name for a poet.

3 This was the title of James Thomson's epic poem and grim ode to his native city of Glasgow, which Herman Melville described as a 'modern book of Job'. It would also be the title of a later poem by Rudyard Kipling. For further details see Tom Leonard, *Places of the Mind: the life and work of James Thomson*, London, 1993.

4 Gordon Stewart, *Jute and Empire: the Calcutta jute wallahs and the landscapes of Empire*, Manchester, 1998, p. 4.

5 See Michael J. Piore, 'The Technological Foundations of Dualism and Discontinuity', in Suzanne Berger and Michael J. Piore, *Dualism and Discontinuity in Industrial Societies*, Cambridge, 1980, pp. 57–65.

6 See Charles Sabel, *Work and Politics: the division of labor in industry*, Cambridge, 1989, pp. 44–5.

7 For a discussion of the impact of home charges on Indian economic development see B. R. Tomlinson, *The Economy of Modern India, 1860–1970*, Cambridge, 1993, pp. 13–14. See also Tom Kemp, *Historical Patterns of Industrialisation*, Harlow, 1993, pp. 135–6.

8 See CSAS, Benthall Papers, Box 13, Edward Benthall to Paul Benthall, Confidential PO, 17 September 1937.

9 These studies include, Ranajit Das Gupta, *Labour and Working Class in Eastern India: studies in colonial history*, Calcutta, 1994; Arjan De Haan, *Unsettled Settlers: migrant workers and industrial capitalism in Calcutta*, Rotterdman, 1994; Samita Sen, *Women and Labour in Colonial India: the Bengal jute industry*, Cambridge, 1999; Parimal Ghosh, *Colonialism, Class and a History of the Calcutta Jute Mill-hands, 1880–1930*, Hyderabad 2000; Subho Basu, *Does Class Matter? Colonial capital and workers' resistance in Bengal, 1890–1937*, New Delhi, 2004. For a recent and insightful appraisal of the field of Indian jute labour studies see Subho Basu, 'The Paradox of the Peasant Worker: re-conceptualizing workers' politics in Bengal 1890–1939', in *Modern Asian Studies*, 42, 1, 2008, pp. 47–74.

10 Gordon Stewart, op. cit.

11 See Edward W. Said, *Orientalism*, London, 1978.

12 The *Subaltern* project, which came to prominence during the late 1980s and 1990s, attempted to marry the Marxist labour history of Edward Thompson with the 'postmodernist' ideas of Edward Said, Jacques Derrida and Michel Foucault so as to uncover the previously hidden worlds of India's subaltern classes. In more recent times, however, the project has come under sustained criticism for its almost exclusive concern with a more literary style of investigation based on discourse theory. For an

effective critique of the Subaltern School see Sumit Sarkar, 'The Decline of the Subaltern in *Subaltern Studies*', in, Sumit Sarkar, *Writing Social History*, New Delhi, 1997, pp. 82–109. See also D. A. Washbrook, 'Orients and Occidents: colonial discourse theory and the historiography of the British Empire', in R. W. Winks (ed.), *The Oxford History of the British Empire*, vol. v, Oxford, 1998, pp. 597–611. We should note, too, the recent work by David Cannadine, which is centrally concerned with putting 'the history of Britain back into the history of empire, and the history of the empire back into the history of Britain'. Cannadine, though, is more concerned with how the British elites perceived and imagined empire than he is with the working-class experience of imperialism. See David Cannadine, *Ornamentalism: how the British saw their Empire*, New York, 2001, p. xx. See also Andrew Thompson, *The Empire Strikes Back? The impact of imperialism on Britain from the mid-nineteenth century*, Harlow, 2005.

13 Jute was widely referred to as the *golden fibre* by the late nineteenth century due to the fortunes made by the leading manufacturers in Dundee and Calcutta as well as its lustrous hue following retting.

14 The Camperdown mill, owned by Cox Brothers, was, until the emergence of the Calcutta jute industry in the late nineteenth century, the largest jute mill in the world and dominated the local economy and society of Lochee, which lay to the west of Dundee. Champdany was owned by James Findlay & Co. and was situated to the north of Calcutta on the Howrah side of the Hooghly.

15 Dipesh Chakrabarty, *Rethinking Working Class History: Bengal 1890–1940*, Princeton, 1989. Chakrabarty's thesis has been challenged by many scholars who have followed him, but his view of the nature of capital relations remains influential.

16 Ibid., p. 170.

17 Dipesh Chakrabarty, *Provincializing Europe*, Princeton, 2000, p. 4.

18 It seems that leading personnel within the IMF and the European Bank share J. S. Mill's views on the inability of southern Europeans to govern themselves, as, at the time of writing, these organisations are demanding the appointment of unelected banking officials in Greece and Italy in order to oversee 'structural adjustment' policies designed (rather optimistically) to counteract the widespread financial crisis that is engulfing southern Europe.

19 John Stuart Mill, *Principles of Political Economy*, Boston, 1848, pp. 319–20.

20 Lit. mother-father.

21 Dipesh Chakrabarty, *Rethinking Working Class History*, p. 3.

22 See Frederick Engels, *Condition of the Working Class in England in 1844*, London, 1936, pp. 287–8. Similar legislation to the New Poor Law Act was brought into law in Scotland in 1845.

23 See 4 Geo. VI, c. 34 (1823). 'An Act to enlarge the Powers of Justices in determining Complaints between Masters and Servants', in R. H. Campbell and J. B. A. Dow (eds), *Source Book of Scottish Economic and Social History*, Oxford, 1968, p. 189.

24 The four girls later complained that 'Mr William Baxter, Messrs Carmichael and Bruce, our manager and overseer, were with the judges when we entered the court, stood by them while we were examined, and our master talked in low whisper[s] to the judges before we received sentence.' See House of Commons Library, Public Petitions, Appendix to the Thirteenth Report of the Select Committee, 1846, p. 148.

25 See William Dodd, *The Labouring Classes of England: especially those concerned in AGRICULTURE AND MANUFACTURES*, Fairfield, 1976, p. 93. This is a republication of a tract originally published in Boston, USA, 1848. For a compelling discussion of the debates between British abolitionists and pro-slavery advocates in the USA see Domenico Losurdo, *Liberalism: a counter history*, London, 2011, pp. 12–14, 47–8, 56–8.

26 Socialist League Archives, F274, International Institute of Social History, Amsterdam, quoted in J. D. Young, *Women and Popular Struggles*, Edinburgh, 1985, p. 120. See also A. A. Bulley and M. Whitley, *Women's Work*, London, 1894, pp. 99–100.

27 The 1842 March to Forfar was sarcastically dubbed the 'Pilgrimage of Folly' by James Myles, a bookseller and former Chartist. See his characteristically acerbic description of events in James Myles, *Rambles in Forfarshire*, Dundee, 1850. For Leslie C. Wright, the march to Forfar was 'a pathetic affair well named "The Pilgrimage of Folly"'. See Leslie C. Wright, *Scottish Chartism*, Edinburgh, 1953, p. 150. In similar fashion J. T. Ward described it as a 'tragi-comic march of a ragged group of Chartists to Forfar'. See J. T. Ward, *Chartism*, London, 1973, pp. 163–4. A recent study has, however, sought to achieve a more balanced view see Malcolm Chase, *Chartism: a new history*, Manchester, 2007. For a recent study that focuses on Scottish Chartism see W. Hamish Fraser, *Chartism in Scotland*, Pontypool, 2010.

28 For a fascinating and insightful analysis of the rise and fall of the revolutionary working class challenge during the period of early British industrialisation see John Foster, *Class Struggle and the Industrial Revolution: early industrial capitalism in three English towns*, London, 1974. For a critique of Foster's views see Gareth Stedman Jones, *Languages of Class: studies in English working class history, 1832–1982*, Cambridge, 1983.

29 Enid Gauldie (ed.), *The Dundee Textile Industry, 1790–1885: from the papers of Peter Carmichael of Arthurstone*, Edinburgh, 1969, p. 61.

30 Although the hand hacklers were undermined by mechanisation, they made their way into the English language, the term heckling being directly derived from their reputation for political disputation. The noted nineteenth century Scottish lexicographer John Jamieson defined the use of the term heckle in its verb form as to '*come o'er the heckle pins*, to be severely examined'. See John Johnstone (ed.), *Jamieson's Dictionary of the Scottish Language*, Edinburgh, 1846, p. 330.

31 Peter Carmichael, the manager of Baxter Brothers Dens Mill and a senior partner within the firm, was responsible for the mechanisation of key processes in the linen industry, many of which were designed to overcome problems associated with industrial disputes. His first attempt to mechanise hackling, for example, occurred in 1827 during a serious strike of hacklers, and he was still inventing machines designed to dispense with troublesome workers as late as 1873, when he designed 'an apparatus' for use in the calendaring department 'which presses and does the tying up in a manner superior to what was ever done by hand'. See Enid Gauldie, op. cit., pp. 62–3, 211.

32 See D. A. Washbrook, 'Progress and Problems: South Asian economic and social history c. 1720–1860', *Modern Asian Studies*, 22, 1 (1988) p. 90,.

33 See Victor Kiernan, *Imperialism and its Contradictions*, London, 1995, p. 57. The Permanent Settlement granted a perpetual private property right in revenue collection to the zamindars of Bengal. In the early nineteenth century the colonial state granted the zamindars with 'formidable powers of extra-economic coercion, including distraint and eviction, to enable them to extract rent from the peasantry and regularly remit revenue to the government.' See Sugata Bose and Ayesha Jalal, *Modern South Asia*, Padstow, 1999, pp. 69–70.

34 Quoted in Rajani Palme Dutt, *India Today*, Calcutta, 1992, p. 120. During the seventeenth century there were 120 big cities and 3,200 townships in India. The largest cities included Agra, which 'in the days when it contained the court' had a population of 660,000. Dacca and Patna each had populations of 200,000, while the population of Surat was also estimated at 200,000 in 1700. Irfan Habib concluded that 'Such data suggest that the fixing of the ratio of urban to the total population of the country at 15 : 100 is not unreasonable; and from what we know of the depopulation of the towns in the nineteenth century, it is unlikely that this ratio was exceeded until the twentieth century.' See Irfan Habib, *The Agrarian System of Mughal India, 1556–1707*, New Delhi, 1999, pp. 83–4.

35 See D. A. Washbrook, 'Progress and Problems', pp. 57–96. See also Crispin Bates, *Subalterns and the Raj: South Asia since 1600*, London, 2007, pp. 80–93.

36 Abed Ali Mian, *Desh Shanti*, Gantipara, Rangpur, 1925, quoted in Sugata Bose, *Peasant Labour and Colonial Capital: rural Bengal since 1770*, New Delhi, 1993, p. 59.

37 See Ajan De Haan, op. cit., p. 73. See also Dipesh Chakrabarty, *Rethinking Working-Class History*, pp. 102–5.

38 For a discussion of internal migration patterns in Germany see Mary Nolan, 'Economic Crisis, State Policy, and Working Class Formation in Germany, 1870–1900', pp. 367–9, in Ira Katznelson and Aristide R. Zolberg, *Working Class Formation: nineteenth century patterns in western Europe and the United States*, Princeton, 1986, pp. 352–97. For a discussion of French patterns of migration see Alain Couttereau, 'Working Class Cultures, 1848–1900', pp. 139–42, in ibid. pp. 111–57.

39 See Sharon Stichter, *Migrant Laborers*, Cambridge, 1985, pp. 184–90.

40 For example, in a recent work, William Knox draws on Gordon's work to claim that spontaneous strikes were especially prevalent amongst women jute workers because they 'found ad hoc organisation more in keeping with their dual workplace and domestic roles than formal associations.' See W. W. Knox, *Industrial Nation: work, culture and society in Scotland, 1800–Present*, Edinburgh, 1999, p. 158. The influence of Gordon's work is also apparent in a very recent article by Valerie Wright, 'Juteopolis and After: women and work in twentiety century Dundee', in Jim Tomlinson and Christopher A. Whatley (eds), *Jute No More: Transforming Dundee*, Dundee, 2011, pp. 132–63.

41 See Eleanor Gordon, *Women and the Labour Movement in Scotland, 1850–1914*, Oxford, 1991, esp. pp. 12–13. For the wider influence of these views on British labour historiography see M. Savage and A. Miles, *The Remaking of the British Working Class, 1840–1940*, London, 1994, pp. 39–40; Neville Kirk, *Change, Continuity and Class: labour in British Society, 1850–1920*, Manchester, 1998, pp. 218–19.

42 See Charles Sabel, op. cit., pp. 18–19.

43 See Ira Katznelson, 'Working-Class Formation: constructing cases and comparisons', in Ira Katznelson and Aristide E. Zolberg (eds), op. cit. pp. 3–45.

44 See ibid., p. 15. For a defence of Marxist structuralism see G. A. Cohen, *Karl Marx's Theory of History: a defence*, Oxford, 2000, esp. pp. 73–9.

45 Ira Katznelson, op. cit., p. 16.

46 Ibid., p. 18.

47 Ibid., p. 20.

48 *Oary* is the distinctive Dundee rendering of the Scots word *orra*, and is used to describe the working class dialect of Dundee. Gary Robertson and Mark Thomson have applied the term to describe the vibrant and distinctive '*Oary*' poetry of Tribal Tongues, a group of Dundonian Rap poets. See Gary Robertson, *Pure Dundee*, Glasgow, 2007; Mark Thomson, *Bard fae thi Building Site*, Edinburgh, 2007. The word also has a number of other meanings, the most common being 'of persons or things spare, unoccupied; also meaning, extra, odd or superfluous'. See Mairi Robinson, *The Concise Scots Dictionary*, Aberdeen, 1985, p. 455. In the jute and linen industries *orra*, or spare, workers were employed during busy periods to provide relief to hard-pressed production workers.

49 J. P. Day, 'The Jute Industry in Scotland During the War', p. 272, in David T. Jones, Joseph F. Duncan, H. M. Conacher and W. R. Scott (eds), *Rural Scotland During the War*, Oxford, 1926, pp. 267–307.

1 The making and re-making of the Dundee-Calcutta nexus, 1840–1900

1 This refers to Birkmyre and Brothers who controlled the Hastings mill, the pioneering Indian producer of burlap cloth.

2 D. H. Nicoll, *Ten Years of Conflict and Mrs Juteburgh*, in *Character Sketches:*

modern trade battles, ten years conflict and Mrs Juteburgh, Dundee (undated), p. 141.

3   Of St Mary's, Dundee's medieval parish church.

4   A coarse fabric used in the manufacture of bagging.

5   See 'Tam O' Shanter: A Tale', in Andrew Noble and Patrick Scott Hogg (eds), *The Canongate Burns: the complete poems and songs of Robert Burns*, Edinburgh, 2001, p. 263. A 'cutty sark' is a short shirt.

6   A Scottish board of manufacturing and fisheries was established in 1727. Almost half its budget went to the linen industry for the foundation of spinning schools, improved looms and the appointment of inspectors.

7   Originally a cloth of plain weave made from coarse linen in the province of Hanover, osnaburg cloth was successfully copied by weavers in the Arbroath area in the late 1730s, and quickly became a staple product of the Forfarshire linen industry. See Sir John Sinclair, *The Statistical Account of Scotland, 1791–99*, vol. xiii, Wakefield, 1976, p. 253.

8   C. A. Oakley (ed.), *Scottish Industry*, London, 1953, p. 3.

9   Though less than 50 per cent of the value, reflecting the coarse nature of the county's products. See Henry Hamilton, *The Industrial Revolution in Scotland*, Oxford, 1932, pp. 108–9.

10   G. Jackson and K. Kinnear, *The Trade and Shipping of Dundee, 1780–1850*, Dundee, 1991, p. 18.

11   See Henry Hamilton, op. cit. The 1833 Factory Act stipulated that no child under nine years of age should be employed in textile mills and factories, and that no children between the ages of nine and 13 should be employed without a schoolmaster's certificate showing that the child had attended school for at least two hours per day, thus creating the half-time system whereby the working day of child workers was divided between the workplace and the schoolroom. In 1844, the age at which children could be employed was reduced from nine to eight, which was justified on the grounds that their working hours were reduced to six and a half per day from a 48 hour working week, and that they now received three hours schooling per working day. See Edmund and Ruth Frow, *The Half Time System in Education*, Manchester, 1970, pp. 11–17.

12   The rise of mechanised flax spinning also had a dramatic impact on Ulster's cotton industry with a large scale transfer of capital, labour and enterprise from cotton to flax occurring during the early 1830s. See Phillip Ollerenshaw, 'Industry, 1820–1914', p. 70, in Liam Kennedy and Phillip Ollerenshaw, *An Economic History of Ulster, 1820–1939*, Manchester, 1985, pp. 62–109.

13   Quoted in Jonathan Bardon, *A History of Ulster*, Belfast, 1992, p. 267. Thomas perished during the Irish Famine.

14   Brenda Collins, 'The Origins of Irish Immigration to Scotland in the Nineteenth and Twentieth Centuries', in Tom Devine, *Irish Immigrants and Scottish Society in the Nineteenth and Twentieth Centuries*, Edinburgh, 1991, p. 9.

15   Census figures quoted in William Walker, *Juteopolis: Dundee and its textile workers, 1885–1923*, Dundee, 1979, p. 114.

16   See Chapter 3 for further discussion of this issue. For the emergence of the labour aristocracy in Britain during this period see John Foster, *Class Struggle and the Industrial Revolution: early industrial capitalism in three English towns*, London, 1974. For a discussion of the development of patrimonialism in the Lancashire cotton industry see Michael Savage, *The Dynamics of Working-Class Politics: the labour movement in Preston, 1880–1914*, Cambridge, 1987, pp. 64–101.

17   See William Walker, op. cit., pp. 121–2.

18   *Dundee Advertiser*, 16 July 1841.

19   From the Sanskrit word, *goni*, meaning 'a sack'. *Tat* was also a commonly used Hindi word for coarse sacking. See William Crooke (ed.) *Hobson-Jobson: a glossary of colloquial Anglo-Indian words and phrases*, New Delhi, 1994, p. 403.

20 Alexander J. Warden, *The Linen Trade, Ancient and Modern*, London, 1864, pp. 50–1.
21 Ibid.
22 Ibid., p. 60. It is often claimed that it was the introduction of whale oil, a valuable by-product of Dundee's whaling industry, which provided the crucial breakthrough for softening the jute fibre, but vegetable oil was used for the same purpose in Bengal, and by the inter-war period was widely perceived as being a better softening agent.
23 Tow is a waste product comprising the short fibres produced in the heckling or combing process when preparing linen and hemp for spinning. See I. E. P. Menzies and D. Chapman, 'The Jute Industry', p. 235, in H. A. Silverman (ed.), *Studies in Industrial Organisation*, London, 1946.
24 See A. J. Warden, op. cit., p. 77.
25 Figures computed from ibid., pp. 648–52.
26 British Association, *Handbook and Guide to Dundee and District*, Dundee, 1912, p. 85.
27 David J. Jeremy, 'Lancashire and the International Diffusion of Technology', in Mary B. Rose (ed.), *The Lancashire Cotton Industry: a history since 1700*, Preston, 1996, pp. 210–38.
28 D. R. Wallace, *The Romance of Jute: a short history of the Calcutta jute mill industry, 1855–1927*, London, 1928, p. 10.
29 *Banians* were Hindu traders, predominantly from Gujarat, who acted as agents for the managing agencies during the nineteenth century. See *Hobson-Jobson*, p. 63.
30 The rise of the Marwaris in Bengal is discussed in Chapter 5.
31 D. R. Wallace, op. cit., pp. 34–5.
32 For a discussion of the development of the Bombay industry see Rajnarayan Chandavarkar, *The Origins of Industrial Capitalism in India: business strategies and the working classes in Bombay, 1900–1940*, Cambridge, 1994, pp. 21–72.
33 Quoted in Amales Tripathi, 'Indo-British Trade between 1833 and 1847 and the Commercial Crisis of 1847–8', p. 288, in A Siddiqi (ed.), *Trade and Finance in Colonial India, 1750–1860*, Delhi, 1995, pp. 265–90.
34 N. K. Sinha, 'Indian Business Enterprise: its failure in Calcutta, 1800–1848', in *Bengal Past and Present*, Diamond Jubilee Number, 1967, p. 120.
35 This term refers to the period, from the 1770s to the 1830s, when the governance of Scotland was dominated by the Dundas family headed by Henry Dundas, 1st Viscount Melville (1740–1811), and his son Robert, 2nd Viscount Melville (1771–1851). See Michael Fry, *The Dundas Despotism*, Edinburgh, 1992, pp. 1–2.
36 For an illuminating account of Dundee involvement in the EIC see Andrew MacKillop, 'Dundee, London, and the Empire in Asia', in C. McKean, B. Harris and C. Whatley (eds), *Dundee: Renaissance to Enlightenment*, Dundee, 2009, pp. 160–86.
37 Olive and Sydney Checkland, *Industry and Ethos: Scotland 1832–1914*, Edinburgh, 1989, p. 159.
38 See ibid., pp. 159–61.
39 R. S. Rungta, *Rise of Business Corporations in India, 1851–1900*, Cambridge, 1970, pp. 58–9.
40 See Omkar Goswami, *Industry, Trade and Peasant Society: the jute economy of eastern India, 1900–1947*, Delhi, 1991, pp. 12–16.
41 Alongside Duff's and Andrew Yule, the other two were Bird & Co. and Jardine Skinner & Co.
42 A. J. Warden, op. cit., p. 81.
43 See D. R. Wallace, op. cit., p. 36.
44 R. S. Rungta, op. cit., p. 58.
45 Marwari and Bengali merchant capital did, however, establish trading connections with China at this time due to their involvement in trading commodities such as

opium. See C. M. Turnbull, *A History of Singapore, 1819–1988*, Oxford, 1992, pp. 37–41.

46 See Morris D. Morris, 'The Growth of Large-Scale Industry to 1947', pp. 580–1, in D. Kumar and M. Desai, *The Cambridge Economic History of India*, vol. 2: *c*.1757–1970, Cambridge, 1989, pp. 553–677.

47 By 1925, only 28 per cent of the managerial cadre in the Bombay industry were described as 'Europeans', although they were concentrated in the higher positions. See D. H. Buchanan, *Capitalistic Enterprise in India*, New York, 1934, pp. 210–11.

48 The Baranagore mill was erected by the Borneo Company in 1859, and was the first British registered company in the Calcutta jute industry. See D. R. Wallace, op. cit., p. 15.

49 Ibid., p. 22.

50 Headman or jobber.

51 A Bengali clerk.

52 *Dundee Year Book 1894* (hereafter referred to as *DYB*), p. 103.

53 See *Report of the Royal Commission on Labour in India* (hereafter referred to as *RCLI*), London, 1931, vol. v, part 1, p. 209.

54 As observed in 1911, 'Calcutta itself contains but few factories, only three jute mills and two jute presses lying within its limits.' See E. Gait, C. G. H. Allen, H. F. Howard, *Imperial Gazetteer of India: Bengal*, vol. 1, New Delhi (n.d., probably 1910 or 1911), reprinted in 1984, p. 403.

55 In the early 1900s, the labour investigator, B. Foley observed that up-country workers in Bengal often preferred employment in the northern mills because of the greater availability of company-built mill lines. He further admitted that 'it would be perfectly impossible ... to present the advantages to be derived from employment in industrial and commercial centres if the employee is to live in some of the bustis which exist in Howrah.' See GOB, B. Foley, *Report on labour in Bengal*, Calcutta, 1906.

56 See P. S. Lokanathan, *Industrial Organisation in India*, London, 1935, p. 115.

57 T. Woodhouse and A. Brand, *A Century's Progress in Jute Manufacture, 1833–1933*, Dundee, 1934, p. 38.

58 A. K. Das Gupta, 'Jute Industry: how it works', p. 95, in *Textile India*, 1953.

59 This lip or sign language was still widely practised in the late 1970s in the jute mills of Arbroath, where it was observed by the author. Sign language and lip reading would be used by the women workers to warn of the approach of a foreman or manager, and when the foreman entered the section the women would look as busy as possible.

60 See Dundee Oral History Committee, Barrasie Court History Group, *Work or Want*, Dundee (undated).

61 See DUA, Records of Don Brothers, MS 100/I/9/6, 'Rules to be observed by workers employed by Don Brothers, Buist & Co. Ltd'.

62 See final chapter for further details.

63 Odyssey interviews, quoted in Gordon, op. cit., p. 157.

64 See *Reports of Transactions of National Association for the Promotion of Social Science*, 1863, p. 804. In 1866, weavers were earning 13s compared to the 9s 6d they were earning in 1861, while spinners' wages rose by 40 per cent between 1851 and 1866, from 6s to 10s. See B. Lenman, C. Lythe and E. Gauldie, *Dundee and its Textile Industry, 1850–1914*, Dundee, 1969, Appendix III, pp. 106–7.

65 Lenman, Lythe and Gauldie, op. cit., p. 67.

66 See W. H. Marwick, *Economic Development in Victorian Scotland*, New York, 1973, p. 187.

67 Ibid., p. 149.

68 The extent to which this period amounted to a 'Great Depression' has been challenged by some historians. See S. B. Saul, *The Myth of the Great Depression, 1873–1896*, Tiptree, 1972.

69 Between 1866 and 1871, weavers' wages fell from 13s to 9s 3d and those of spin-ners fell from 10s to 8s 6d. See Lenman, Lythe and Gauldie, op. cit., Appendix III, pp. 106–7.

70 The Dundee strike wave was part of a broader international labour upsurge, while strike activity was also stimulated by the passing of the Criminal Law Amendment Act of 1871, which gave British trade unions new rights and some degree of legal protection.

71 See *Peoples Journal*, 14 October 1922.

72 *Dundee Advertiser*, 5 January 1872.

73 In June 1872, the *International Herald* published a list of the 24 British societies affiliated to the International, including branches in Dundee, Glasgow and Aber-deen. See H. Collins and C. Abramsky, *Karl Marx and the British Labour Move-ment*, London, 1965, n.1, p. 252. In 1869, the IWMA received correspondence from Dundee Trades Council desiring 'information as to the aims of the associ-ation and how they might assist in the good works', and from the Dundee Working Men's Association, which originated in 1864 when it emerged out of a Garibaldi Reception Committee set up to host the, failed, visit of the popular Italian leader to Dundee. There is no indication that these organisations affiliated to the IWMA, but it is likely that individual members of both organisations played a role in establishing the IWMA in Dundee. See Mike Arnott, 'A History of Dundee Trades Union Council: The Victorian Era', unpublished manuscript draft (n.d.), p. 2. I am grateful to Mike Arnott for making this manuscript avail-able to me.

74 Lenman, Lythe and Gauldie, op. cit., p. 71.

75 Ibid.

76 Oliver Graham, op. cit., pp. 68–9.

77 *DYB 1885*. Mill and factory extensions, as well as new works, were made possible by improvements in the town's water supply, which were completed in 1872, allow-ing new mills to be built away from traditional sites alongside streams and burns. See W. H. K. Turner, 'The Evolution of the Pattern of the Textile Industry within Dundee', *Transactions of the Institute of British Geographers*, 1952.

78 See *DYB 1885*, p. 33.

79 It is sometimes wrongly supposed that the investment trust was a Dundee invention but the first, the Foreign and Colonial, was founded in London in 1868. See N. McKendrick and J. Newlands, *'F&C': a history of the Foreign and Colonial Invest-ment Trust*, London, 1999. See also J. Newlands, *Put Not Your Trust in Money: a history of the investment trust industry from 1868 to the present day*, London, 1997. I am grateful to John Bradfield for drawing my attention to these two sources.

80 Following a crisis in railway securities as a result of over-expansion in the 1870s, many Dundee investment trusts shifted towards cattle ranching.

81 The Oregon and Washington Trust Investment Company Ltd was established in 1873, and was followed in 1876 with the foundation of the Dundee Mortgage and Trust Investment Company and the Dundee Land Investment Company. See B. Smith, *Robert Fleming 1845–1933*, Haddington, 2000, pp. 48–9.

82 See Dave Bowman, *Future of Jute*, Dundee, 1945, p. 6.

83 Lowdon was an assistant to James Bowman Lyndsay, who had lit his study with electricity as early as 1835 and who had also pioneered wireless telegraphy between 1853 and 1859. See Bruce Lenman and Enid Gauldie, 'The Industrial History of the Dundee Region from the Eighteenth Century to the Early Twentieth Century', pp. 171–2, in S. J. Jones (ed.), *Dundee and District*, Dundee, 1968, pp. 162–74.

84 DCA, Dundee Chamber of Commerce Archives (hereafter referred to as DCC), Report of Annual Meeting, March 1880.

85 Even these figures are likely to be an underestimate. See B. Lenman and K. Donald-son, 'Partners' Incomes, Investment and Diversification in the Scottish Linen Area,

1850–1914', p. 3, in *Business History* (13–14), 1971–2, pp. 1–18. See also John Gilbert, *A History of Investment Trusts in Dundee, 1873–1938*, London, 1939.

86 'Alpargatas', *The Bulletin of the British Community Council in the Argentine Republic*, April 1965, vol. x, 8.

87 *DYB 1885*, p. 28.

88 Arbroath Library, Newspaper Cutting Book, Miscellaneous, vol. 1, unnamed newspaper cutting, July 22 1897, 'Tom Mann In Arbroath'. Mann, along with many other leading socialists, was a regular visitor to the north-east of Scotland. In 1889, he was invited to stand as Dundee's independent labour candidate, but was forced to decline due to his involvement with the London dock strike.

89 For figures see *The Encyclopaedia Britannica*, New York, vol. xv, 1911, p. 606.

90 D. R. Wallace, op. cit., p. 26.

91 See DCA, DCC, Report of Annual Meeting, March 1885.

92 D. R. Wallace, op. cit., p. 38.

93 Ibid., p. 95.

94 William Smith, the marketing manager of the Shyamnagar jute mill company, was instrumental in opening up new markets. He had served his commercial apprenticeship with Cox Brothers in Lochee. See ibid., p. 36.

95 Ibid., pp. 42–4.

96 This view is shared by all writers within the field of study, to a greater or lesser extent.

97 D. R. Wallace, op. cit., p. 47.

98 DCA, DCC, Annual Report, March 1885.

99 The MFOU was initially open only to women at a fee of 3d and weekly dues of 1d. Williamson had developed a taste for the 'labour question' in the 1870s when he intervened in a six-week strike of Forfar flax workers who were protesting against a 5 per cent reduction in wages. The strike ended, at his prompting, when workers accepted a 3.5 per cent wage reduction. See Eleanor Gordon, *Women and the Labour Movement in Scotland, 1850–1914*, Oxford, 1991, p. 124.

100 *People's Journal*, 14 October 1922.

101 *Arbroath Guide*, 10 November 1888. Williamson had been asked to come to Arbroath during the 'Great Strike', which led to mass demonstrations of up to 2,000 of the town's jute and flax workers, in order to establish a branch of the MFOU. Although a union was successfully established, divisions quickly emerged when Williamson played the gender card, through the exclusion of male trade unionists from local leadership positions, in his attempts to marginalise critics of his overbearing leadership style. Growing resentment at Williamson's *ma-baap* attitude to ordinary members led to the establishment in 1889 of the Forfarshire Federal Union of Textile Workers (FFUTW), with branches in Brechin and Forfar, encompassing almost half of these towns' textile workers. In stark contrast to the MFOU, the FFUTW was not averse to challenging the employers on controversial issues, as when they proclaimed their support for the ending of the half-time system.

102 *DYB 1894*, p. 113.

103 Ibid., p. 112. At this time, the rupee was worth 1s 1d.

104 In 1870 the exchange rate of the rupee against sterling stood at around 2s, but by 1881–2 it was 1s 8d and by 1894–5 it had further fallen to 1s 1d. See Index Number of Indian Prices, 1861–1918, 1919, p. 18, cited in Rungta, op. cit., p. 127.

105 For Calcutta wage details see *DYB 1887*, p. 123. Some Dundee weavers in double loom working were earning up to 20s per week, although their cost of living was far in excess of their Indian counterparts. For details of Dundee wage rates see Lenman, Lythe and Gauldie, op. cit., Appendix III, p. 106.

106 Dundee had a legally enforced 56-hour working week at this time. In Calcutta, following the introduction of electric lighting and multiple shift working, a working week of up to 80 hours was common. By 1895, the average wage of a weaver in Bengal was Rs4.75 per week, or around 5s (at the new exchange rate of R1 to 1s

1d.). The weekly wage of a Dundee weaver was thought to be around 11s per week. For Indian figures see GOB, *Prices and Wages in India*, 35th Issue, Table 23 (17), cited in Ranajit Das Gupta, *Labour and Working Class in Eastern India: studies in colonial history*, Calcutta, 1994, p. 335. For Scottish figures see Lenman, Lythe and Gauldie, op. cit., Appendix III, p. 106.

107 For figures detailing the movement in the price of raw jute see *Capital*, 29 October 1914.

108 *DYB 1894*, p. 120.

109 T. Woodhouse and A. Brand, op. cit., p. 95.

110 *DYB 1894*, p. 122.

111 See British Association, *Handbook and Guide to Dundee and District*, Dundee, 1912, pp. 84–5.

112 This is particularly marked in the work of Dipesh Chakrabarty. See *Rethinking Working-Class History*, Princeton, 1989, pp. 186–219. See also A. De Haan, *Unsettled Settlers: migrant workers and industrial capitalism in Calcutta*, Calcutta, 1996, pp. 238–43.

113 We should not, however, draw too much of a distinction between 'floating' and 'permanent' labour in either centre, as continuous employment could never be taken for granted.

114 *DYB 1894*, p. 121.

115 Adams to Secretary, GOB, General Dept, 14 September 1909, General Dept, Misc. Progs. A. January 1910, quoted in Parimal Ghosh, *Colonialism, Class and a History of the Calcutta Jute Mill Hands, 1880–1930*, Hyderabad, 2000, p. 90.

116 D. H. Buchanan, op. cit., p. 369.

117 *Report of the Textile Factories Labour Commission*, London, 1907, p. 12.

118 Ibid., p. 83.

119 B. Foley, op cit., p. 10.

120 Ibid.

121 *DYB 1894*, p. 120.

122 See British Association, *Scientific Survey of Dundee and District*, London, 1939, pp. 84–5.

123 This represented a substantial development of the earlier 1881 Act. The new act barred the employment of children under the age of 9 years, and no person could be employed as an adult until certified to be over 14 years of age. A child could not be employed for more than seven hours, while women could not be employed for more than 11 hours. The working day for women and children also had to fall between 5am and 8pm, which effectively prohibited them from night work. See J. C. Kydd, *A History of Factory Legislation in India*, Calcutta, 1920, p. 65.

124 Quoted in R. S. Rungta, op. cit., p. 76.

125 Quoted in Gordon Stewart, op. cit., p. 68.

126 *DYB 1896*. Between 1894 and 1895 alone, imports of jute and flax increased by 45,000 tons and 8,000 tons respectively.

127 Ibid.

128 Ibid.

129 By 1910–11, the Indian balance of payments surplus of around £29 million helped towards the annual payment of so-called 'home charges', which were supposed to cover the cost of the India Office, as well as the pay, pensions, leave allowance and training costs of British military and civil personnel based in India. By the early twentieth century, the annual cost of these 'home charges' was around £17 million. Britain also benefited from the transfers of profits by British merchants as well as 'invisible' charges for services such as shipping, banking, and insurance. In addition, the depreciating value of India's currency between the 1870s and 1890s also increased the real burden of India's payments to Britain. See Sugata Bose and Ayesha Jalal, *Modern South Asia: history, culture, political economy*, New Delhi, 1999, pp. 99–100.

130 *DYB 1896*, p. 93.

131 While many of these 'special fabrics' were quite simple in structure, others were more complicated. Brussels and Wilton carpets were the most elaborate commodity produced in Dundee, but 'considerable ingenuity and taste' was also 'displayed in connection with other types of carpets and rugs.' See British Association, op. cit., pp. 281–2.

132 By 1939, the UK linoleum industry, concentrated in and around the Fife town of Kircaldy, controlled 60 per cent of the world export trade. See Sir Robert Spencer-Nairn, 'Linoleum', pp. 10–13, in C. A. Oakley (ed.), *Scottish Industry*, Edinburgh, 1953, p. 12.

133 See Lenman, Lythe and Gauldie, op. cit., p. 68.

134 *Dundee Advertiser*, 2 April 1896.

135 It should be noted, however, that the cheapness of Calcutta-produced 'standard' jute goods also impacted on the price levels that Dundee manufacturers could charge for more specialised jute goods.

136 *Dundee Advertiser*, 6 December 1874.

137 Lenman and Donaldson, op. cit., pp. 6–7.

138 J. R. Benvie, *A Benvie Chronicle*, Dundee, 1998, pp. 127–35.

139 Phyllis Dean and W. A. Cole, *British Economic Growth 1688–1959*, Cambridge, 1967, p. 207.

140 Figures from David Lennox, op. cit.

141 Phyllis Dean and W. A. Cole, op. cit.

142 Figures from David Lennox, op. cit.

143 Lenman, Lythe and Gauldie, op. cit., pp. 35–6.

144 Although the import of raw jute into Dundee almost doubled from 1885 to 1905, the numbers employed within the industry increased by only 12½ per cent, underlining the substantial growth in worker productivity during this time.

145 William Walker, op. cit., p. 93.

146 See Graham Smith, 'The Making of a Woman's Town: household and gender in Dundee, 1890–1940', unpublished Ph.D. thesis, University of Stirling, 1996, chapter entitled 'The Male Headed Household', pp. 18–19. This draft was given to me by the author, and was not consecutively numbered. All page references, therefore, refer to the chapters cited.

2 The coming of the up-country men: labour conditions and class formation in the Bengal jute industry, 1875–1910

1 Nestor, the King of Pylos in Greece, was the oldest and most experienced of the chieftains who went to the siege of Troy. See E. Cobham Brewer, *The Dictionary of Phrase and Fable*, New York, 1978, p. 884.

2 *Dundee Year Book 1894* (hereafter referred to as *DYB*), Dundee, 1895, p. 95.

3 See Dipesh Chakrabarty, *Rethinking Working-Class History: Bengal 1890–1914*, Princeton, 1989, especially pp. 164–70.

4 L. S. S. O'Malley, *24 Parganas District Gazetteer*, Calcutta, 1914, p. 83.

5 GOI, *Report of the Indian Factory Labour Commission of 1908*, vol. ii, London, 1909, *Evidence*, Parliamentary Paper, 1909, vol. 63, witness no. 192, p. 278, quoted in Ranajit Das Gupta, *Labour and Working Class in Eastern India: Studies in Colonial History*, Calcutta, 1994, p. 21.

6 GOI, *Report of the Indian Factory Commission*, Calcutta, 1891, p. 76, quoted in S. D. Punekar and R Varickayil (eds), *Labour Movement in India, Documents: 1891–1917*, vol. ii: Factories, New Delhi, 1990, p. 135.

7 Ibid., p. 136. Midnapore, along with Bankura, had long furnished the Bengal mills with labour, and would continue to do so into the 1930s and beyond. See GOI, *Report of the Royal Commission for Labour in India* (hereafter referred to as *RCLI*), London, 1931, vol. v., pt. i, pp. 4–5.

8 Letter from Indian Jute Mills Association to Bengal Chamber of Commerce (hereafter referred to as BCC), appended to *Report of the Bengal Chamber of Commerce of 1890–1.*

9 NAI, Home Judicial, No. 36 of January 1880, quoted in Ranajit Das Gupta, op. cit., p. 320.

10 John Hume (ed.), *Early Days in a Dundee Mill, 1819–1823*, Dundee, 1980, p. 20.

11 Meaning not fully grown, this old Scots term was commonly used to refer to half timers employed in the Dundee textile industry.

12 Bob Stewart, *Breaking the Fetters: the memoirs of Bob Stewart*, London, 1969, p. 15.

13 A. J. Warden observed of 'hasheesh' that 'in the Hindoo economy this serves as a substitute for malt, the favourite intoxicating liquor called banga or bhang, being produced from it.' See A. J. Warden, *The Linen Trade, Ancient and Modern*, London, 1864, p. 42. Warden also informs us incorrectly that the word gunny is derived from the Hindi word ganja. In fact, it is derived from the Sanskrit word goni, 'a sack', and the Hindi word gon meaning 'a sack or sacking'. See William Crooke (ed.), *Hobson-Jobson: a glossary of colloquial Anglo-Indian words and phrases*, New Delhi, 1994, p. 403.

14 *DYB 1894*, p. 98.

15 The entertainment given to a visitor, or a gift given to those who apply for it, on the last day of the year. See John Johnstone (ed.), *Jamieson's Dictionary of the Scottish Language*, Edinburgh, 1846, p. 343.

16 Although a full complement of 'hands' was eventually forthcoming, production was down fully a quarter on what Brown had expected. He also felt it necessary to have the main gate locked at nine o'clock, and not re-opened until the day hands arrived, in order to 'prevent pilfering'. John Hume (ed.), op. cit., p. 48.

17 DCL, Lamb Collection, 1, 8 January 1918. During the New Year celebrations of 1939, east met west in the crowd of over 12,000 that thronged Dundee's City Square when two 'lascar seamen . . . joined in the jollifications. Perhaps they knew not what they were celebrating, but their antics – stimulated by having wined well rather than wisely – kept others in good spirits.' See DCL, Lamb Collection, 2 January 1939. Lascar seamen on the *Juters* were often Bengali, drawn from Sylhet in modern day Bangladesh.

18 A corruption of the Hindi word tari. Toddy was fermented from the sap of the tar or Palmyra, and also of other palms, such as the date and the coco-palm. See *Hobson Jobson*, p. 927, which also points to the introduction of the word into Scots usage in the eighteenth century.

19 Toddy shops were licensed by the government and sold 'very intoxicating' 'native liquor' at two pice per glass or 32 glasses for a rupee. See *DYB 1894*, p. 98.

20 Ibid.

21 WBSA, GOB, Gen. Misc. Nos. 1–2 of October 1876, *Annual Administrative Report for Bengal of 1875–6*.

22 The Scots term ratten is in turn derived from the Gaelic word radan meaning rat. See A. Warwick (ed.), *Chambers Scots Dialect Dictionary*, Edinburgh, 1911, p. 445. See also *Jamieson's Scottish Dictionary*, p. 523.

23 NAI, Home, Judicial, No. 218 of September, 1883, Pt. A, quoted in R. Das Gupta, op. cit., p. 328.

24 NAI, Home. Judicial. No. 36 of January 1880, quoted in ibid., p. 323. This form of resistance through flight was also commonly experienced in Dundee during the same period.

25 *Report of the Indian Factory Commission*, p. 77.

26 Ibid.

27 In 1890, the IJMA complained that while English workers had a 'highly disciplined regularity of attendance' at the workplace Indian workers 'come and go in a manner . . . which would reduce English manufacturers to despair.' Letter from BCC to GOB, 10 April, 1890, appended to *Report of the Bengal Chamber of Commerce of 1890–1*.

28 For a discussion of circular migration in Bengal see Haraprasad Chattopadhyay, *Internal Migration in India: a case study of Bengal*, Calcutta, 1987.

29 The Julahas were a caste of Muslim weavers, whose position within the Bengal jute industry is investigated later in this chapter.

30 *Selections from the Records of Government, North-Western Provinces*, pt. xi. Allahabad, 1864, art. Iv, 'Information regarding the Slackness of Demand for European Cotton Goods', p. 151, quoted in Gyan Pandey, *The Construction of Communalism in India*, Delhi, 1990, p. 73.

31 Waterman who supplied water to households.

32 *Selections from the Records of Government, North-Western Provinces*, p. 151, quoted in Gyan Pandey, op. cit., p. 73.

33 With the notable exception of centres such as Benares and to a lesser extent Azamgarh. See 'Reports on the Condition of the Lower Classes of the Population of India', letter no. 2420/vii-49, from Collector, Ghazipur to Commissioner, Benares Division, 10 April 1888, para 17, quoted in Gyan Pandey, op. cit., p. 74.

34 G. A. Grierson, *Notes on the District of Gaya*, Calcutta, 1893, p. 95, quoted in ibid., p. 77.

35 For details of figures see Ranajit Das Gupta, op. cit., p. 51, n. 41.

36 See ibid., pp. 22–5.

37 The extent to which the jute industry influenced Bengal's demographic development is further demonstrated by the decline in the proportion of women to men in the province between 1872 and 1911, from 992 to 945 per thousand. See GOI, *Census of India 1921*, vol. v, part 1, Calcutta, 1923, p. 111.

38 See Arjan De Haan, *Unsettled Settlers: migrant workers and industrial capitalism in Calcutta*, Calcutta, 1994, p. 73.

39 See Dipesh Chakrabarty, op. cit., pp. 102–5.

40 Ranajit Das Gupta observed that 'the actual wage rates were arrived at by taking into account the conventional or prevailing subsistence in the rural areas. In the observations and discussions on wage rates made by the employers, conventional subsistence was the usual point of reference.' See Ranajit Das Gupta, op. cit., p. 233.

41 DUA, Thomas Duff Papers (hereafter referred to as TDP), MS 86/V/7/18, PO Letters to Calcutta, Mason to MacDonald, 6 November 1936.

42 Gyan Pandey, op. cit., pp. 60.

43 See GOB, S. H. Freemantle, *Report on the Supply of Labour in the UP and in Bengal*, Delhi, 1906, p. 53. Large-scale riots and disturbances accompanied official efforts to contain outbreaks of plague and 'Burdwan fever' in Calcutta during the late nineteenth and early twentieth centuries.

44 Gyan Pandey, op. cit., p. 102.

45 *Census of India*, 1921, vol. v, Bengal, pt. ii, Table xxii, pt. iv.

46 Kinship links were also important in gaining access to employment in the Dundee jute mills. See pp. 69–70 for further details.

47 GOB, B. Foley, *Report on Labour in Bengal*, Calcutta, 1906, p. xxii. This move towards a patrimonial form of recruitment may well have been encouraged by the increasing adoption of the shift system.

48 *RCLI*, vol. v, p. 283.

49 See Indrajit Gupta, *Capital and Labour*, Calcutta, 1953, p. 43, and interview with Saroj Bandophadyay, 10 April 1996.

50 See Subho Basu, *Does Class Matter? Colonial capital and workers' resistance*, New Delhi, 2004, pp. 74–113.

51 By 1929, mills in Bengal were also, by some margin, the largest in India, with an average workforce of 3,635, compared with 1,150 in cotton. See P. S. Lokanathan, *Industrial Organisation in India*, London, 1935, p. 112.

52 For the Indian ratio see *RCLI*, vol. v, part I, London, 1931, p. 299. For Dundee figure, see DUA, MS 15/46, 'Wage Records of an Unidentified Jute Mill, 1860–2'.

According to ex-jute mill workers, this proportion had not altered much by the end of our period. See interview with Betty Taylor, 20 February 1997.

53 Interview with Saroj Bandophadhyay, 10 April 1996.

54 During a visit to the Telinapara area, in June 1996, a number of mosques were pointed out to me as being named after local sirdars who had provided funding for their construction.

55 Interview with Saroj Bandopadhyay, 10 April 1996.

56 B. Foley, op. cit., p. 11.

57 I. L. Tripathi was employed as a chemist involved in research and development work by Birla's and was visiting the mill when this incident happened. Tripathi visited Dundee to study at the Dundee Technical College during 1945–47. He eventually turned his back on research and development and became a jute mill manager and rose high within the Birla firm. Interview with I. L. Tripathi, 6 August 1996.

58 GOB, Bulletin of Industries and Labour, No. 14, A. T. Weston, *Factory Construction in Bengal*, Calcutta, 1921, p. 27.

59 See Subho Basu, op. cit., pp. 50–1.

60 See WBSA, GOB, Com Dept, Com Branch, April 1923, B 77, Appendix B, interview with Mr Malish of Beliaghata Jute Mill, cited in ibid., p. 51.

61 See ibid.

62 See pp. 191–2 for a more extended discussion of these household structures.

63 Hugh Fraser, 'Folksong from Eastern Bengal', *Journal of Asiatic Society of Bengal*, 52, 1883, pp. 7–8, quoted in Anand Yang, *The Limited Raj: agrarian relations in colonial India, Saran District, 1793–1920*, Delhi, 1989, p. 198.

64 Quoted in Gyan Pandey, op. cit., pp. 78–9.

65 See *RCLI*, vol. v, pt. 1, p. 279.

66 GOB, Commerce Dept, April 1930, No 9, quoted in Panchanan Saha, *History of Working Class Movement in Bengal*, New Delhi, 1978, p. 15.

67 Parimal Ghosh, *Colonialism, Class and a History of the Calcutta Jute Mill Hands 1880–1930*, Hyderabad, 2000, p. 1.

68 See Ranajit Das Gupta, op. cit., p. 61.

69 Literally 'small people' and referring to lower caste Bengalis.

70 Ranajit Das Gupta, op. cit., p. 64.

71 Sugata Bose, *Peasant Labour and Colonial Capital: rural Bengal since 1770*, Cambridge, 1993, pp. 52, 80, 112.

72 Ibid., pp. 52, 63.

73 See Mike Davis, *Late Victorian Holocausts: El Nino, famines and the making of the Third World*, London, 2001, for a compelling study of the link between El-Niño and the development of capitalist relations of production in the colonial world in the late nineteenth century.

74 Sugata Bose, op. cit., p. 52.

75 The 'Young Bengal' movement was established by Henry Derozio, a teacher at the Hindu College in Calcutta, in 1818. The group embraced westernising notions, and derided 'irrational' Indian customs. The Brahmo Samaj, which was established by Rammohum Roy in the 1820s, campaigned against caste, idolatry and sati. See Sugata Bose and Ayesha Jalal, *Modern South Asia: history, culture, political economy*, New Delhi, 1998, pp. 80–2.

76 For an account of the 'Blue Mutiny' see Blair B. Kling, *The Blue Mutiny: the indigo disturbances in Bengal 1859–1862*, Philadelphia, 1966.

77 The words of Seton Kerr, a former Foreign Secretary of the British Raj, quoted in Jawaharlal Nehru, *The Discovery of India*, New Delhi, 1995, p. 326.

78 Quoted in Anil Seal, *The Emergence of Indian Nationalism: competition and collaboration in the later nineteenth century*, Cambridge, 1968, p. 214.

79 See Rudyard Kipling, *The Jungle Book and Other Stories*, London, 1924. See also Niraud C. Chaudhuri, *Thy Hand Great Anarch: India 1921–1951*, London, 1987, p. 672.

80 Ranajit Das Gupta, op. cit., p. 65.
81 *DYB 1894*, p. 93.
82 Between 12 and 15 Scottish overseers were employed in each mill.
83 See GOB, Judl. Police Progs, January 1896, *Pratt Report*, cited in Arun Mukherjee, *Crime and Public Disorder in Colonial Bengal*, Calcutta, 1995, p. 273.
84 Ibid.
85 *Pratt Report*, quoted in Ranajit Das Gupta, op. cit., p. 351.
86 GOB, *Factory Act Report for 1895*, Calcutta, 1896.
87 Ibid.
88 *Indian Factory Labour Commission*, London, 1908, Evidence, vol. ii, Witness No. 176.
89 Kankinarah would continue as a centre of trade unionism with the Kankinarah Labour Union keeping an organised presence into the 1920s. The Mohammedan Association was not the first instance of reform work being carried out amongst jute workers. In 1870, Sasipada Banerjee, a leading figure within Brahmo Samaj, founded a Workingmen's Club at Baranagore, as well as a journal that covered labour matters, *Bharat Sramajeebi*, in 1874, along with an institute for workers, which was established in 1876 and was still active in 1906.
90 For a description of the 'Talla riots' see Ranajit Das Gupta, op. cit., pp. 375–8; Subho Basu, op. cit., pp. 121–5.
91 Quotation from *Rabindra Rachanabali* (Collected Works of Rabindranath), Calcutta, 1961, vol. xii, p. 961, quoted in Ranajit Das Gupta, op. cit., p. 402, n. 278.
92 WBSA, GOB, Judl. (Police), September 1897, Report by Messrs Begg Dunlop & Co., pp. 83–4.
93 *The Englishman*, 21 April 1896, quoted in Subho Basu, op. cit., p. 123.
94 Cited in Subho Basu, op. cit., p. 123.
95 'One following evil courses'. See *Hobson Jobson*, p. 122.
96 Ruffian or thug.
97 D. H. Buchanan, op. cit., p. 308.
98 *Times of India*, 25 September 1905.
99 GOB, *Jute Industry Tribunal Report*, Calcutta, 1947, p. 142.
100 The 'world view' theory was developed by Charles Sabel who describes it as the 'set of fears and hopes, visions of success and failure: an intuition of possibilities that define at once our ambitions and our sense of social honor.... The set of hopes and fears, together with the map of the social world that it establishes, is called a world view.' See Charles Sabel, *Work and Politics: the division of labor in industry*, Cambridge, 1989, p. 11.
101 Amy Bridges observes that whilst the theory of the moral economy 'is often offered as a "precapitalist" social phenomenon ... certain kinds of values associated with Thompson's moral economy persist well past the period he writes about.' See Amy Bridges, 'Becoming American: the working classes in the United States before the Civil War', p. 180, in Ira Katznelson, *Working Class Formation: nineteenth-century patterns in Western Europe and the United States*, Oxford, 1986, pp. 157–97.
102 See the discussion of workers' honour and labour disputes in Anthony Cox, 'Paternal Despotism and Workers' Resistance in the Bengal Jute Industry, 1920–1940', unpublished Ph.D. thesis, University of Cambridge, 1999, pp. 160–1.
103 See the discussion of the meaning and significance of these terms in Subo Basu, op. cit., pp. 60–1.
104 See the quotation at the beginning of this chapter.
105 GOB, *Bengal Administration Annual Review*, 1895–6.
106 For further details see Subho Basu, op. cit., pp. 118–126.
107 GOI, Home Dept (Police), Progs, June 1898, 133, notes dated 16 April by H. Luson.
108 Strike figures computed from *Bengal Factory Act Reports* and *IJMA Reports* from 1894 to 1897.

109 Quoted in Bose and Jalal, op. cit., p. 117.
110 See ibid., pp. 118–21.
111 *Amrita Bazar Patrika*, 17 October 1905.
112 Ibid., 18 December 1905.
113 GOB, Home Public Progs A, June 1906, n. 75, quoted in Sumit Sarkar, op. cit., p. 228.
114 See Arun Mukherjee, op. cit., Appendix VII, pp. 272–9.
115 See Sumit Sarkar, op. cit., pp. 233–4.
116 See ibid., pp. 234–7.
117 *DYB 1894*, p. 99.
118 GOI, Home Dept (Police), Prgs, June 1898, 133, notes dated 16 April, by H. Luson.
119 For figures, see Ranajit Das Gupta, op. cit., p. 46, Appendix A.
120 For a discussion of the role of diversity in working class formation see Charles Sabel, op. cit., pp. 14–20.
121 I am paraphrasing Charles Sabel, see ibid., p. 15.

3 The imperial nexus and the making of Juteopolis, 1875–1910

1 Juter refers to the ships, part of an extensive port fleet, that carried the cargoes of jute from Bengal.
2 A trading smack with raised hatches: derived from the old Scots, *Bat*, meaning boat. See John Johnstone (ed.), *Jamieson's Dictionary of the Scottish Language*, Edinburgh, 1846, p. 37.
3 Much.
4 The distinctive Dundee pronunciation of onions.
5 Whelks.
6 Mary Brooksbank, *Sidlaw Breezes*, Dundee, 1991, p. 60. The song is sung to the tune of 'The Ball of Kirriemuir'.
7 Mary Brooksbank, *No Sae Lang Syne: a tale of this city*, Dundee, 1971, p. 25.
8 Knew.
9 A ship that carries flax fibre: derived from the Angus term Hamit or 'Hamit-linjet, flax–seed which has been raised at home'. See *Jamieson's Scottish Dictionary*, p. 310.
10 Derived from the Scots 'to Liver', meaning 'to unload; applied to ships': from the French word livr-er meaning to deliver. See ibid., p. 413. The word probably refers to smaller cargo vessels involved in the coastal trade.
11 Mary Brooksbank, *No Sae Lang Syne*, p. 25.
12 Or pucka. This Hindi word has a number of meanings, but generally refers to a 'permanent' or 'substantial' quality. Within the jute trade, the word referred to pucca bales that weighed 400 lb. Indian mills were supplied with 360 lb. bales of kutcha, meaning raw or uncooked, jute, which were of a poorer quality. See William Crooke (ed.) *Hobson-Josbson: a glossary of colloquial Anglo-Indian words and phrases*, New Delhi, 1994, p. 734.
13 Mary Brooksbank, *No Sae Lang Syne*, p. 25.
14 Ibid.
15 See Censuses of Scotland and Great Britain, 1881–1911. Figures for 1851 taken from L. J. Saunders, *Scottish Democracy, 1815–1840: The Social and Intellectual Background*, London, 1950, p. 400, fn.3.
16 DCL, Lamb Collection (hereafter referred to as LC), 278/5.
17 For details of all 1901 employment figures see David Lennox, 'Working Class Life in Dundee, 1878–1905', unpublished Ph.D. thesis, St Andrews University (n.d., prob. 1906), Appendix, Table 129.
18 The closure of Gourlay's yard in 1908 had a dramatic impact on the output of Dundee's shipbuilding industry. While 22,100 tons of shipping was launched in 1907–8,

the following year the gross tonnage launched in Dundee was 7,912 tons, before dropping to 5,592 tons in 1910. See British Association, *Handbook and Guide to Dundee and District*, Dundee, 1912, p. 295.

19 Around 1900, Stewart returned to the Gourlay yard where he 'got a job on the building of the *Discovery*, the ship which took Captain Scott on the National Antarctic expedition.' See Bob Stewart, *Breaking the Fetters: the memoirs of Bob Stewart*, London, 1967, pp. 25, 31–2.

20 John Hume (ed.), *Early Days in a Dundee Mill, 1819–1823*, Dundee, 1980, p. 38.

21 By the eve of the First World War there was 69 mills in Bengal, with each mill employing between 15–20 Scottish personnel. See S. R. Deshpande, *Report of an Enquiry into Conditions of Labour in the Jute Mill Industry in India*, Delhi, 1946, p. 6.

22 Interview with Alex Scott, 13 September 1996.

23 The young time-served mechanic would also commonly complete one year's further employment as an 'improver'.

24 Interview with Alex Scott, 13 September 1996.

25 Interview with Alfred Tosh, 25 September 1996.

26 Interview with Alistair Martin, 25 June 1998.

27 Interview with Alex Scott, 13 September 1996.

28 Committee on Industry and Trade, *Factors in Industrial Efficiency and Commercial Efficiency: being part I of a survey of industries*, London, 1927, p. 211.

29 William Walker, *Juteopolis: Dundee and its textile workers, 1885–1923*, Dundee, 1979, p. 91.

30 Ibid.

31 Ibid.

32 Board of Trade, *Earnings and Hours of Labour, Textile Trades in 1906*, London, 1909, p. lvi, cited in ibid., pp. 91–2.

33 The cost of living comprised rents and the price of fuel and food. With London taken as 100, the index number of rents and prices in Dundee was 99. See Board of Trade, *Cost of Living of the Working Classes in the UK*, London, 1907, p. xxxviii, cited in ibid.

34 B. S. Rowntree, *Poverty: a study of town life*, London, 1902, p. 110. See also Eric Hobsbawm, *Labouring Men: studies in the history of labour*, London, 1976, pp. 286–7.

35 Bob Stewart, op. cit., p. 11. The midden was situated in the back courtyards of the tenements where household waste and 'night soil' was deposited to be collected by scavengers or 'scaffies' employed by Dundee Corporation.

36 Eric Hobsbawm, op. cit., pp. 286–7.

37 *Dundee Year Book, 1885*, Dundee, 1886, pp. 32–3.

38 The Census of Scotland and Great Britain, 1891, cited by Graham Smith, 'The Making of a Woman's Town: household and gender in Dundee, 1890–1940', unpublished Ph.D. thesis, University of Stirling, 1996, chapter entitled 'Poverty, Child Labour and Family Duty', Fig. 4.5, p. 11.

39 DCA, Records of Dundee Chamber of Commerce (hereafter referred to as DCC), MS GD/CC, 7, p. 208.

40 Ibid., p. 251.

41 W. A. Graham, *The Linen, Jute and Hemp Industries in the United Kingdom With Notes on the Growing and Manufacture of Jute in India*, US Dept of Commerce, Washington D.C., 1913, p. 113, cited in Gordon Stewart, op. cit., p. 69.

42 William Walker, op. cit., pp. 255, 267, 266.

43 See Chapter 1 for John Leng's attitude towards this issue.

44 *Dundee Advertiser*, 13 November, 1903.

45 DCA, Wages Records of the Victoria Spinning Company 1894–8, MS GD/Mns 105/1/3.

46 Mary Brooksbank, *No Sae Lang Syne*, pp. 6–7.

47 'The Day I Sarted Among the "Shiftin-Wifies"'. Article signed by J.A.E.M in, *Evening Telegraph*, 5 November 1970.
48 Ibid.
49 Exemptions to under-age children for work in the jute industry could be given if their families could prove that their need was exceptional.
50 Barassie Court History Group, *Work or Want*, Dundee, 1996, p. 4.
51 Cited in William Walker, op. cit., p. 82.
52 *Annual Report of the Chief Inspector of Factories and Workshops*, 1909, London, 1910, p. 158.
53 See D. R. Wallace, *The Romance of Jute: a short history of the Calcutta jute mill industry, 1855–1927*, London, 1928, pp. 89–90.
54 See Barassie Court History Group, op. cit.
55 Young workers in Dundee also sought other avenues, outside the jute industry, where they could earn wages, such as work in the home sewing sacks or making up greeting cards for Valentine's, or work as messengers and paper sellers. See Graham Smith, op. cit., chapter entitled 'Poverty, Child Labour and Family duty', p. 15.
56 James Rollo, *A Century's Record of Ecclesiastical Life in Dundee*, Dundee, 1902, p. 68.
57 In 1911, only 8 per cent of Dundee's proprietors owned more than 200 tenancies, the largest owned 1 percent of house property in the city and the top five owners between them controlled only 4 per cent. Property investment companies were not significant (as was also the case in Glasgow) and controlled just over 3 per cent of all tenancies. See J. K. Young, 'From "Laissez-Faire" to "Homes fit for Heroes": housing in Dundee, 1868–1919', vol. ii, University of St Andrews, 1991, unpublished Ph.D. thesis, p. 302.
58 See A. Dickson and J. H. Treble, *People and Society in Scotland*, vol. iii, Edinburgh, 1992, pp. 183–4.
59 The Dundee Social Union was formed in 1887 in order 'to improve the housing conditions in Dundee'. For further details see Dundee Social Union (hereafter referred to as DSU), *Report on Housing and Industrial Conditions in Dundee*, Dundee, 1905, p. vii.
60 W. S. Churchill to H. A. L. Fisher, 18 November 1922, quoted in Martin Gilbert, *Winston S. Churchill*, vol. iv, London, 1975, p. 890.
61 Bob Stewart, op. cit., pp. 10–11.
62 Ibid.
63 Ibid.
64 Figures taken from Lenman, Lythe and Gauldie, op. cit., Appendix I, table a, p. 103.
65 Alex Wilkie was also elected as one of the first Labour MPs in Scotland at the 1906 general election following a campaign that highlighted the need for housing reform.
66 DSU, op. cit., p. vi.
67 Followed by Jorasanko (202), Jorabagan (201), and Moocheepara (199). See *Imperial Gazetteer of India: Provincial Series, Bengal*, vol. i, New Delhi, 1984, p. 400.
68 DSU, op. cit., p. viii.
69 See Anthony Wohl, *Endangered Lives: public health in Victorian Britain*, London, 1983, p. 305.
70 *Imperial Gazetteer of India*, p. 400.
71 Ibid., p. viii.
72 Whilst there was no compulsory registration of births in India, Thomas Johnston and John Sime, during their fact-finding mission to Bengal in 1925–6 on behalf of the Dundee Jute and Flax Workers' Union, met an old man in a bustee adjoining a jute mill who claimed that 'half the babies born ... died'. The Director of Public Health for Bengal also declared, in 1923, that 'half the children die before they reach ten years of age.' See Tom Johnston and John Sime, *Exploitation in India*, Dundee, 1926, p. 12. A. A. Purcell and J. Hallsworth, who visited India on behalf of the

British TUC in 1927, acerbically noted that 'altogether, 545,000 children died in [Bengal in] 1926 at ages which the Director [of Public Health] considered far below what might be termed any economic value.' See A. A. Purcell and J. Hallsworth, *Report on Labour Conditions in India*, London, 1927.

73 Anthony S. Wohl, op. cit., p. 13.

74 Ibid., p. 13.

75 City & Royal Burgh of Dundee, Licensing (Scotland) Act, 1903, Printed Notices published of those convicted and circulated in Police District, Notices from 10 April 1905 to January 1906. I am grateful to Dougie Bissell, the proprietor of the Balmore Bar, Stobswell, for allowing me to consult these records.

76 See 'Forty-third Annual Report of the Local Government Board, for 1913–14, Supplement, "Third Report.... Infantile Mortality"', pp. 12ff, quoted in Anthony S. Wohl, op. cit., p. 350, fn. 91.

77 In the twenty years from 1861 to 1881, Dundee's population increased from 91,664 to 142,154. By contrast, between 1891 and 1911 the population only showed a small increase, from 155,998 to 165,004.

78 DSU, op. cit., p.xii.

79 Eleanor Gordon, *Women and the Labour Movement in Scotland, 1850–1914*, Oxford, 1991, p. 285.

80 Ibid.

81 Ibid., pp. 286–7.

82 See Michelle Barrett, *Women's Oppression Today*, London, 1980. See also Michael Savage's discussion of patriarchy in *The Dynamics of Working Class Politics: the labour movement in Preston, 1880–1940*, Cambridge, 1987, pp. 50–1, 228, fn. 1.

83 Gareth Stedman Jones, *Languages of Class: studies in English working class history, 1832–1982*, Cambridge, 1983, pp. 66–7.

84 See C. M. M. MacDonald, *The Radical Thread: political change in Scotland. Paisley politics, 1880–1924*, East Linton, 2000, p. 150. See also W. W. Knox, *Hanging by a Thread: the Scottish cotton industry, c.1850–1914*, Preston, 1995, pp. 17–27.

85 Mary L. Walker, 'Work among Women', in British Association, *Handbook and Guide to Dundee and District*, Dundee, 1912, p. 69.

86 C. M. M. MacDonald, op. cit., pp. 151–2.

87 M. L. Walker, op. cit., p. 69.

88 For 1891 figures see Graham Smith, op. cit., chapter entitled 'The Female Headed Household', p. 3. His research suggests that each of Dundee's five districts contained the same proportion of female headed households, although Lochee, with the 'largest jute works in the world may have encouraged a larger proportion of female heads'. For 1904 figures see DSU, op. cit., p. 17.

89 Mary Walker, op. cit., p. 74.

90 Graham Smith, op. cit., p. 7.

91 Ibid., p. 10.

92 This is a view that is particularly evident in the work of Eleanor Gordon. See Eleanor Gordon, op. cit., p. 157.

93 Ibid., p. 7.

94 Mary Walker, op. cit., pp. 74–5.

95 Graham Smith, op. cit., pp. 3–4.

96 Carl Chinn, *They Worked all their Lives: women of the urban poor in England*, Manchester, 1988, p. 162.

97 Graham Smith, op. cit., p. 11.

98 Ibid.

99 For figures see ibid., chapter entitled 'The Male Headed Household', p. 5.

100 Ibid.

101 Ibid., p. 16.

102 In Edinburgh, 20 per cent of all marriages were registered as 'irregular', while in Glasgow it was 12 per cent and in Aberdeen almost 8 per cent. See Kenneth M. Boyd, *Scottish Church Attitudes to Sex, Marriage and the Family, 1850–1914*, Edinburgh, 1980, p. 159.

103 See G. Desmond Greaves, *The Life and Times of James Connolly*, London, 1976, p. 30.

104 H. V. Morton, *In Search of Scotland*, London, 1939, p. 106. First published in 1929, this book went through no fewer than 25 editions by 1939.

105 Lenman, Lythe and Gauldie, op. cit., p. 66.

106 See Thomas Ferguson, *Scottish Welfare, 1864–1914*, Edinburgh, 1958, p. 222. See also DSU, op. cit. The Dundee pie, pronounced 'peh' locally, has a hard crust pastry shell and is filled with minced meat, of often varying quality. The development of mincing machines in the 1870s allowed their easy preparation and they quickly became a popular 'treat', along with fish and chips, for many working class families. They still remain very popular today, as evidenced by the snaking columns of hungry customers that daily queue during lunch, or dinner time as it is called in Scotland, outside Dundee's bakers shops.

107 DSU, op. cit.

108 A 'piece' is a slice of bread.

109 See *Report of the Royal Commission on Poor Laws and Relief of Distress* (Scotland) 1909, vol. xxiii, Appendix.

110 The Dundee calculations were deduced from a sample of 722 workers whose average age was 18.9 years.

111 *Report of the Indian Factory Labour Commission*, London, 1909, Minute of Dissent by Dr T. M. Nair.

112 Ibid.

113 DSU, op. cit.

114 George Barnes, *From Workshop to War Cabinet*, 1923, p. 20, quoted in Eric Hobsbawm, op. cit., p. 46. Jute manufacturing was established in Barrow-in-Furness during the 1870s, which largely accounts for the close links between the two areas. By the early years of the twentieth century there was also a proliferation of official schemes to encourage emigration.

115 The information regarding the temporary migration of my great grandparents was told to me by my great aunt who accompanied her parents to the USA in the first years of the twentieth century as a very young girl. The family were employed in a jute mill on the eastern seaboard, but subsequently moved to Canada, and then returned to Scotland at the outbreak of the First World War so that my great grandfather could join the Royal Navy.

116 Bruce Lockhart, *My Scottish Youth*, Glasgow, 1937, p. 132.

117 David Lennox, op. cit., Appendix, Table 283.

118 See Charles W. J. Withers (ed.), *Burt's Letters from the North: as related by Edmund Burt*, Edinburgh, 2005.

119 See Charles W. J. Withers, *Urban Highlanders: highland-lowland migration and urban Gaelic culture, 1700–1900*, East Linton, 1998, p. 234.

120 During the late eighteenth century Scotland was reckoned to be one of the most literate societies on earth, despite a relative dearth of formal educational opportunities for the urban poor in towns and cities. Dundee, with its tradition of radical Protestantism and large numbers of literate hand loom weavers, hacklers, and wrights, played its full share in this plebeian and artisan flowering of Scottish autodidact culture.

121 See L. C. Wright, *Scottish Chartism*, Edinburgh, 1953, pp. 152–3.

122 Successful and highly literate individuals did emerge from the low mills and half-time schools of Dundee, including the notable example of Mary Slessor who went from Baxter's weaving shed in east Dundee to West Africa where, during the

1870s and 1880s, she found world-wide fame as a missionary. Bob Stewart and Mary Brooksbank are other notable examples of how the half-time system acted as a finishing school for some of the finest minds produced by Juteopolis, but this should not deflect from the poor state of schooling open to the majority of the city's working class children.

123 See D. Lennox, op. cit., Table 252, 'Occupations of Chief Groups of Adult Readers in Lending Department of Dundee Free Library, 1885–6'.

124 From the old Scots word for a cabbage patch, the term was applied to a group of Scottish writers who exploited a sentimental and romantic image of small town Scottish life, with much use of the vernacular. J. M. Barrie, from the Forfarshire textile town of Kirriemuir, was amongst the leading exponents of *kailyard* literature.

125 The different musical traditions of the Scots and Irish could give also rise to occasional tensions. Liz Falconer, my great aunt, recounted a family story from the first years of the twentieth century, in which she explained that migrant Scots and Irish workers to the USA, whilst generally getting along in a tented encampment adjoining a newly built jute mill on the eastern sea board, had very different musical tastes. Quarrels would occasionally erupt over arrangements for the use of the sole wooden building within the encampment, which was used for musical and dance evenings at the weekend. As a result, different evenings had to be set aside for each community to organise their own social events and there was little cultural interaction between the two groups.

126 Mary Brooksbank, *No Sae Lang Syne*, p. 3.

127 See Nigel Gatherer, *Songs and Ballads of Dundee*, Edinburgh, 2000, pp. 82, 92.

128 See Mary Brooksbank, *Sidlaw Breezes*.

129 The oary tongue still thrives today in the vibrant and distinctive *Oary* poetry practised by 'Tribal Tongues'. See Gary Robertson, *Pure Dundee*, Glasgow, 2007 and Mark Thomson, *Bard fae thi Building Site*, Edinburgh, 2007.

130 The 'hull' refers to the Hilltown, a textile suburb that overlooked the old town.

131 This song was sampled by Martyn Bennet in his experimental, and acclaimed, album *Grit* in 2003, under the title *Nae Regrets*. Bennet in his album notes remarked that 'Annie, from Dundee, was about 4′ 10″ with a voice, not of an angel, but of the power of a small PA system. I often heard her unmistakable voice in noisy pubs enthusiastically accompanied by as many as thirty musicians. There was something about her that reminded me of Edith Piaf.' See the album, Martyn Bennet, *Grit*, Real World, 2003.

132 See David Phillips, *Lichty Nichts Omnibus*, Dundee, 1981, p. 105.

133 Bob Stewart, op. cit., p. 20.

134 City & Royal Burgh of Dundee, Licensing (Scotland) Act, 1903, Printed Notices circulated in Police District, Notices from 10 April 1905 to January 1906.

135 Ibid.

136 David Lennox, op. cit., Table 286, 'Proportion of Licenses and Arrest for Drunkenness to Population in each of the three Principal Towns in Scotland'.

137 See DSU, op. cit., p. xv.

138 Bob Stewart, op. cit., p. 20.

139 City & Royal Burgh of Dundee, Licensing (Scotland) Act, 1903, Notices from 10 April 1905 to January 1906.

140 D. A. Lennox, 'The Evolution of Race in Forfarshire', p. 643, in British Association, *Handbook and Guide to Dundee and District*, Dundee, 1912, pp. 626–664.

141 See James E. Fraser, *From Caledonia to Pictland: Scotland to 795*, Edinburgh, 2009, pp. 47–8. It is believed that the creators of Scotland's monumental standing stones drew their inspiration from body art, embroidery and jewellery. For a discussion of the history and meaning of the standing stones see Lloyd and Jenny Laing, *The Picts and the Scots*, Stroud, 2001, pp. 90–9, 106–111. The claim that tattooing in Angus endured as a continuous cultural practice from the Roman period should be treated

with caution, but this stray comment is, nevertheless, highly suggestive and cannot be completely discounted without further research.

142 See Clare Anderson, '*Godna:* Inscribing Indian Convicts in the Nineteenth Century', p. 102, in Jane Caplan, *Written on the Body: the tattoo in European and American history*, London, 2000, pp. 102–118. I am grateful to Professor Ian Duffield for drawing my attention to this book.

143 'Under the influence of civilisation tattooing is losing its ethnological character, and has become, in Europe at least, an eccentricity of soldiers and sailors, and of many among the lower and often criminal classes of the great cities.' See *Encyclopaedia Britannica*, vol. xxvi, New York, 1911, p. 452.

144 Havelock Ellis, *The Criminal*, London, 1890, p. 103, cited in James Bradley, 'Body Commodification? Class and Tattoos in Victorian Britain', p. 139, in Jane Caplan (ed.), op. cit., pp. 136–156.

145 The electric tattoo machine was not invented until 1891, by Samuel O'Riley in New York, which strongly suggests that tattoos were still being applied manually by needle and, probably, Indian ink. See www.vanishingtattoo.com (accessed 5 July 2011).

4 Working class militancy and labour politics in Juteopolis, 1885–1923

1 David Lowe, *Souvenirs of Scottish Labour*, Glasgow, 1919, pp. 5–6. Following his arrival, Lowe became a leading figure behind the establishment of the Labour Party in Dundee.

2 Michael Dyer, *Capable Citizens and Improvident Democrats: the Scottish electoral system, 1884–1929*, Aberdeen, 1996, p. 22, Table 2.

3 See John Kemp, 'Red Tayside? Political Change in Early Twentieth Century Dundee', p. 153, in L. Miskell, C. A. Whatley and B. Harris (eds), *Victorian Dundee: image and reality*, Dundee, 2000, pp. 151–69.

4 *Dundee Advertiser*, 20 October 1890, quoted in ibid., p. 155.

5 It is likely that IWMA activists were involved in the campaigns for shorter working hours and trade union formation, but it is difficult to gauge the extent of their influence on organisations in Dundee such as the Trades Council and the Factory Acts Association. The IWMA played an important role in raising the demand for the eight-hour day in 1866, and in keeping alive the idea of international socialism within a constricted British labour movement, otherwise wedded to craft unionism and close cooperation with liberalism. The IWMA was also instrumental in establishing the Reform League, which, though envisaged as a vehicle for independent working-class representation when it was formed in 1865, quickly came under middle class and liberal influence. For the role of the IWMA in the British labour movement see H. Collins and C. Abramsky, *Karl Marx and the British Labour Movement*, London, 1965, pp. 62–71.

6 DCL, Joe Handy, 'The Rise of Labour in Dundee, 1885–1910', unpublished manuscript, Dundee, 1979.

7 The SDF was founded in 1883 by H. M. Hyndman, a wealthy businessman who made a Damascene conversion to Marxism when he read *Kapital* in the early 1880s. Marx and Engels' mistrust of Hyndman became an open antipathy following the publication of Hyndman's *England for All*, a barely disguised plagiarism of *Kapital*. Hyndman's chauvinism was revealed when he justified his failure to acknowledge the influence of Marx by arguing that British people would not accept ideas produced by foreigners.

8 See Desmond Greaves, *The Life and Times of James Connolly*, London, 1976, p. 35. William Morris founded the SLL after leaving the SDF in 1884. Though smaller than the SDF, the SLL was a pole of attraction to more free-thinking socialists who

were becoming increasingly impatient with Hyndman's domineering personality. In 1890, the SLL in Scotland merged with the SDF.

9 See David Lowe, op. cit., pp. 24–5.
10 See Desmond Greaves, op. cit., p. 31. Despite failing to provide evidence to the contrary, William Walker dismisses Greaves claim that there were two SDF branches in Dundee. See Walker, *Juteopolis: Dundee and its textile workers*, Dundee, 1979, p. 244.
11 See William Walker, op. cit., p. 249.
12 Ibid.
13 A very recent article has also challenged Walker's dismissive attitude towards the SDF, see Kenneth Baxter and William Kenefick, 'Labour Politics and the Dundee Working Class *c*.1895–1936', in Jim Tomlinson and Christopher A. Whatley (eds), *Jute No More; Transforming Dundee*, Dundee, 2011, pp. 193–4. See David Lowe, op. cit., pp. 89–91.
14 The phrase is taken from Stuart Macintyre, *A Proletarian Science: Marxism in Britain, 1917–1933*, London, 1986, p. 225.
15 Dundee Trades Council was conspicuous by its absence. Although the Trades Council successfully fielded two 'labour' candidates at the 1890 Municipal elections, neither was connected with Dundee's independent labour movement. David Lowe described Dundee Trades Council as a 'feckless body' on the issue of independent working class representation. See David Lowe, op. cit., p. 69.
16 Joe Handy, op. cit.
17 Ibid.
18 These churches comprised 12 Church of Scotland, seven Free Church, five Roman Catholic and six Episcopalian. See H. Henderson, 'Religious Life', p. 634, in J. M. Jackson (ed.), *The Third Statistical Account of Scotland: the city of Dundee*, Arbroath, 1979, pp. 632–77. The two Chartist churches that were established in Dundee in the 1840s, along with the Labour Church that was active in the 1890s, are conspicuous by their absence from this otherwise comprehensive list.
19 For the 1851 figures, which are taken from that year's Census of Scotland, see Callum Brown, *Religion and Society in Scotland since 1701*, Edinburgh, 1997, p. 58. For 1891–1901 figures see David Lennox, 'Working Class Life in Dundee, 1975–1905', unpublished Ph.D. thesis, St Andrews University (n.d., probably 1906), Appendix, Table 255.
20 William Walker, op. cit., p. 143.
21 These groups were established in 1835 and 1847 respectively.
22 See Chapter 7.
23 See William Walker, op. cit., p. 25.
24 See John D. Kemp, 'Drink and the Labour Movement in Early Twentieth Century Scotland: with particular reference to Edwin Scrymgeour and the Scottish Prohibitionist Party', unpublished Ph.D. thesis, University of Dundee, 2000, p. 147.
25 William Norrie, *The Life of James Scrymgeour*, Dundee, 1887, p. 31.
26 See John D. Kemp, 'Drink and the Labour Movement', p. 147.
27 Ibid., p. 156.
28 Ibid., p. 229.
29 See *Ritual, Constitution and Songs of the Scottish Prohibition Party*, quoted in ibid., p. 230.
30 Ibid., p. 232.
31 See Fig. 5 in ibid., p. 234. The other Scottish branches were, Arbroath, Auchtermuchty, Kirkcaldy, Paisley, Perth and Strathkinness.
32 *Scottish Prohibitionist*, 30 April, 1912.
33 See William Walker, op. cit., pp. 353–4.
34 Eric Hobsbawm, *Primitive Rebels: studies in archaic forms of social movements in the 19th and 20th centuries*, Manchester, 1978, p. 143.

35 Ibid., p. 142. Although there was an active Labour Church in Dundee, the nature of its relationship with the SPP is not clear.
36 Ibid., p. 145.
37 William Walker, op. cit., p. 63.
38 Ibid., p. 65.
39 Ibid. See also Norman Cohn, *The Pursuit of the Millennium: revolutionary millenarians and mystical anarchists of the middle ages*, London, 1957.
40 William Walker, op. cit., p. 66.
41 This phrase is, of course, taken from Karl Marx.
42 J. D. Kemp, 'Drink and the Labour Movement', p. 259.
43 Ibid., p. 261.
44 See later in this chapter for a critique of Eleanor Gordon's view of the fatalism of mill-girl culture.
45 For a description of the strike see Stephen Humphries, *Hooligans or Rebels? An oral history of working-class youth, 1889–1939*, Oxford, 1995, pp. 95–105.
46 See *Dundee Advertiser*, 9 October 1889.
47 Stephen Humphries, op. cit., p. 97.
48 See the description of the strike in William Walker, op. cit., pp. 166–170.
49 Ibid., p. 167.
50 *Dundee Advertiser*, 26 August 1895.
51 See *Dundee Advertiser* for 3 and 6 March 1906.
52 The NFWW grew out of the Women's Trade Union League, founded by Emma Paterson in 1874 to promote female trade unionism. When MacArthur became secretary of the League in 1903, and in 1906 she federated the unions supported by it to the NFWW.
53 See Mary Agnes Hamilton, *Mary MacArthur: a biographical sketch*, London, 1925, p. 51.
54 See Stuart MacIntyre, op. cit., p. 17.
55 Daniel De Leon, a Dutch-born American revolutionary socialist, founded the Socialist Labour Alliance in 1895, and merged it with the International Workers of the World (IWW) in 1905. He was centrally involved in developing syndicalism as a theory and as an important international movement that advocated the seizure of industry by syndicates of workers through a revolutionary general strike. Syndicalist ideas had a deep impact on the development of trade union organisation in France, Italy, the US and Australia. Tom Mann became the leading British proponent of syndicalism, which also exerted an influence on Scottish worker militants such as Willie Gallagher.
56 See Raymond Challinor, *The Origins of British Bolshevism*, London, 1979, p. 49.
57 See Eleanor Gordon, *Women and the Labour Movement in Scotland, 1850–1914*, Oxford, 1991, pp. 196–7.
58 William Walker, op. cit., p. 304.
59 Ibid.
60 See *City Echo*, December 1911, quoted in ibid.
61 See William Walker, op. cit., pp. 305–6.
62 By the time the pistols and ammunition arrived, the strike had come to an end. Letter dated 7 March 1912, from R. Burbidge, managing director of Harrods to Cox Brothers, Lochee. I am grateful to Tom Black for providing me with a copy of this letter.
63 William Walker, op. cit., p. 307.
64 Emma Wainwright, 'Gender, Space and Power: discourses on working class women in Dundee's jute industry, c. 1870–1930', unpublished Ph.D. thesis, University of St Andrews, 2002, p. 156.
65 Ibid., p. 184.
66 For the full text of the song see Mary Brooksbank, *Sidlaw Breezes*, Dundee, 1991, p. 59.
67 Ibid., p. 58.
68 See T. M. Devine, *The Scottish Nation, 1700–2000*, London, 1999, pp. 319–20.

While the 1870s and 1880s witnessed some growth in Orange Order membership in Dundee, this was from a very small base.

69 Although the women's suffrage movement exerted some influence inside Dundee Labour Party, and succeeded in getting two candidates elected on to Dundee Parish Council, Leah Leneman has, rather reluctantly, admitted that 'working-class involvement is difficult to prove.' See Leah Leneman, 'Dundee and the Women's Suffrage Movement: 1907–1914', p. 93, in Christopher A. Whatley (ed.), *The Remaking of Juteopolis, Dundee circa 1891–1991*, Dundee, 1992, pp. 80–96.

70 See Nathan Abrams, *Caledonian Jews: a study of seven small communities in Scotland*, Jefferson, 2009, pp. 76–7.

71 See C. Whatley, D. B. Swinfen and A. Smith, *The Life and Times of Dundee*, Edinburgh, 1995, p. 171.

72 DCL, Obituary Notices for 22 January 1934 and 15 February 1979.

73 The Fourth Battalion was spared on this occasion when, at the very last moment, a senior officer arrived and gave the order to stand down. See Bob Burrows, *Fighter Writer: the eventful life of Sergeant Joe Lee, Scotland's forgotten war poet*, Derby, 2004, p. 76.

74 J. P. Day, 'The Jute Industry in Scotland during the War', in David T. Jones, Joseph F. Duncan, H. M. Conacher and W. R. Scott (eds), *Rural Scotland During the War*, London, 1926, p. 276.

75 Figure from Board of Trade, *Labour Gazette*, quoted in G.D.H. Cole, *Labour in War Time*, London, 1915, p. 119.

76 J. P. Day, op. cit., p. 276.

77 See Bob Stewart, *Breaking the Fetters: the memoirs of Bob Stewart*, London, 1967, p. 53.

78 Dundee also experienced a major rent strike in 1912.

79 See *Courier and Argus*, 25 September 1915.

80 See *People's Journal*, 16 October 1915.

81 Ibid., 23 October 1915.

82 See Ann Petrie, *The 1915 Rent Strike: an east coast perspective*, Dundee, 2008, p. 52.

83 Ibid., p. 33.

84 The Fourth Battalion had been in action at Neuve Chapelle and Festubert by this time.

85 The British death toll at Loos was over 60,000, compared with around 30,000 German losses. It is estimated that 4,213 Dundee men were killed during the First World War, which represents an attrition rate for the city of more than 1:43, compared with Glasgow's rate of 1:57. For figures see Trevor Royle, *The Flowers of the Forest: Scotland and the First World War*, Edinburgh, 2007, p. 285.

86 Mary Brooksbank, *No Sae Lang Syne*, Dundee, 1971, p. 6. Mary was later jailed for 40 days for her part in a local anti-war demonstration at the first Armistice Day celebrations.

87 *Peoples Journal*, 27 November 1915.

88 *Dundee Advertiser*, 9 October 1915.

89 See *Forward*, 23 October 1915 and 27 October 1915, cited in Ann Petrie, op. cit., p. 54.

90 This is the Scottish term for the agents of landlords.

91 See Ann Petrie, op. cit., p. 55.

92 J. K. Young, 'From "Laissez-Faire" to "Homes fit for Heroes": housing in Dundee, 1868–1919', unpublished Ph.D. thesis, vol. i, University of St. Andrews, 1991, p. 377.

93 *Report of the Committee to Enquire into the Circumstances Connected with the Alleged Recent Increases in the Rental of Small Dwelling Houses in Industrial Districts in Scotland*, London, 1915, 'Minutes of Evidence', 2 November 1915, p. 61.

94 Ibid.
95 Figures cited in William Walker, op. cit., p. 330.
96 *Peoples Journal*, 27 November 1915.
97 J. K. Young, op. cit., pp. 381–2.
98 See *Report of the Committee to Enquire into the Circumstances Connected with the Alleged Recent Increases in the Rental of Small Dwelling Houses in Industrial Districts in Scotland*, London, 1915.
99 J. K. Young, op. cit., p. 362.
100 Ibid., p. 383.
101 Ibid.
102 DUA, Cox Brothers Archive, Letterbook, letter dated 3 April 1916, from the Director to the Competent Military Authorities.
103 *Textile Workers' Guide* (no. 2), April 1916.
104 William Walker, op. cit., p. 187.
105 Figures cited in ibid.
106 The six day long Etaples mutiny, of September 1917, involved up to 100,000, British, Australian and New Zealand, troops, in the weeks leading up to the Passchendale offensive. William Allison and John Fairley interviewed two Dundonians who were involved in the mutiny, including Joe Perks who joined the army after being sacked as a jute worker for whistling. For further details see William Allison and John Fairley, *Toplis: the monocled mutineer*, London, 1979, pp. 57–67.
107 See DCA, Records of the Association of Jute Spinners and Manufacturers (hereafter referred to as AJSM), 'Report of Joint Meetings between representatives of the Employers and Trade Unions', 30 August to 12 September 1918.
108 Oliver Graham, 'The Dundee Jute Industry, 1828–1928', unpublished Ph.D. thesis, University of St Andrews, 1928, pp. 126–7.
109 See *Dundee Advertiser*, 24 December 1919.
110 DCA, AJSM, Minutes of Wages and Hours Sub-Committee, 6 August 1919, letter of 24 July 1919, from F. L. M. McGrady to AJSM.
111 Ibid., Minutes of Wages and Hours Sub-Committee, 6 August 1919.
112 Oliver Graham, op. cit., pp. 130–1.
113 See *People's Journal*, 23 July 1921.
114 Ibid.
115 Ibid.
116 DCA, Records of Dundee Corporation, *Dundee Public Health Report*, 1922, pp. 164–5.
117 Ibid.
118 *Peoples Journal*, 13 August 1921.
119 Ibid., 27 August 1921.
120 Ibid.
121 During the pre-war period E. D. Morel came to international prominence due to the leading role he played in the campaign against slavery in the Congo, which resulted in abolition in 1913. Following the outbreak of war he became involved, along with Ramsay MacDonald, Charles Trevelyan and Norman Angell, in founding the anti-war organisation, the Union of Democratic Control. Morel also broke with the Liberal Party at this time and joined the Independent Labour Party. In 1917, Morel was imprisoned for six months for a trivial offence under the Defence of the Realm Act, which had serious consequences for his long-term health.
122 See DCL, LC, 7–9 September 1921.
123 See Ian Levitt, *Poverty and Welfare in Scotland, 1890–1948*, Edinburgh, 1988, pp. 111–120.
124 The new combine, which employed around 13,000 workers, represented most of Dundee's leading jute firms, including Cox Brothers, Gilroy and Sons, J. & A. D. Grimond and Harry Walker & Sons. See DCL, LC, 8, Monday 5 February 1923, p. 80.

125 During the dispute, Jute Industries declared profits of £606,224 for the previous year's trading.
126 *Jute and Flax Workers Guide*, March 1923.
127 Cited in T. Paterson, *Churchill: a seat for life*, Dundee, 1980. This prophecy was popularly referred to by many who lived through this period as 'Churchill's curse', which I was first made aware of by my grandfather, an Arbroath engineer who took part in anti-Churchill demonstrations. I also remember my grandfather, on more than one occasion, describing Churchill as 'the pig'.
128 Whereas 33.7 per cent of registered electors voted for left candidates in Glasgow in 1922, the total in Dundee was 48.7 per cent. See William Walker, op. cit., pp. 439–86.
129 DCA, JFWU Records, Union letter book no. 2, fo. 574, Sime to Mrs Finch, 21 Nov. 1922.
130 *Scottish Prohibitionist*, 12 March 1921, quoted in William Walker, op. cit., p. 470.
131 *Dundee Catholic Herald*, 21 October, 1922, quoted in ibid., p. 474.
132 DCL, LC, 8, 14 May 1923.
133 Ibid.

5 Challenging the jute wallahs: non-cooperation, communism and the Marwaris, 1918–30

1 NAI, GOI, Home (Poll), 1926, F.244/26-Poll, 'European Association and Spence Case at Gourepore Mill'.
2 See CSAS, E. W. Holland Papers, 'Bengal: The Last Twenty Five Years of British Rule', July 1975. Holland was in charge of the committal proceedings in the Spence case. See also *Jute and Flax Workers Guide*, June 1926.
3 J. P. Day, 'The Jute Industry in Scotland during the War', in David T. Jones, Joseph F. Duncan, H. M. Conacher and W. R. Scott (eds), *Rural Scotland During the War*, London, 1926, p. 287.
4 NAI, Home (Poll) A, September 1918, N.20, quoted in Suranjan Das, *Communal Riots in Bengal, 1905–1947*, Delhi, 1991, p. 61.
5 See Irfan Habib, *The Agrarian System of Mughal India, 1556–1707*, Oxford, 1999, pp. 49–50 fn.77.
6 The khatris, who originally hailed from UP, established a powerful position in Burra Bazar, but following the emergence of the Marwaris they, like the Bengalis, were increasingly marginalised. See A. K. Bagchi, *The Evolution of the State Bank of India*, vol. ii, New Delhi, 1997, p. 91, fn. 2.
7 Indian Central Jute Committee, *Report on the Marketing of Jute*, Final Report, Calcutta, 1941, p. 89.
8 Calcutta Jute Baled Association, Report of the Committee 1912–13, Calcutta, 1913, p. 3, quoted in Omkar Goswami, *Industry, Trade, and Peasant Society: the jute economy of eastern India, 1900–1947*, New Delhi, 1991, p. 85.
9 *Capital*, 16 January 1930.
10 Hindi word for a groom.
11 Suranjan Das, op. cit., pp. 62–3.
12 The Khilifat movement developed as a direct result of the harsh peace treaty imposed on the Ottoman Empire following the First World War. Khilifatists demanded that the Turkish Sultan, or Khalifa, must retain control over the Muslim sacred places, and that he must have sufficient territory to enable him to defend the Islamic faith and that the Jazirat-ul-Arab (Arabia, Syria, Iraq and Palestine) must remain under Muslim sovereignty. See Sumit Sarkar, *Modern India, 1885–1947*, Basingstoke, 1992, p. 195.
13 IOL, GOI, L/P&J/3810/18, Kerr to Home Secretary of GOI, No. 3319 P-D of September 1918.

14 *Indian Daily News*, 27 July 1918, quoted in Suranjan Das, op. cit., p. 64.
15 For a description of the riots see Suranjan Das, op. cit., pp. 66–72. See also Subho Basu, *Does Class Matter? Colonial capital and workers' resistance in Bengal, 1890–1937*, New Delhi, 2004, pp. 157–162.
16 These were amongst the individuals who signed the Urdu leaflet published in order to build support for the banned protest meeting of 8 September. Other elite Muslims included merchants from the area around the Nakhoda mosque, one of the main organising centres of the protest, and Mohammed Daud, a prominent lawyer and president of the Indian Seamen's Anjuman.
17 Suranjan Das, op. cit., pp. 74–5.
18 Subho Basu, op. cit., p. 160.
19 Ibid.
20 Passed by the Imperial Legislative Council in March 1919 in the face of opposition from all non-official Indian members, the Rowlatt Act introduced a system of special courts and detention without trial for the mere possession of written materials deemed to be seditious. It was an attempt to make wartime limitations on civil liberties permanent and to pacify white opinion, which had been growing increasingly fearful of terrorist outrages and rising anti-British feelings.
21 See Crispin Bates, *Subalterns and the Raj: South Asia since 1600*, London, 2007, pp. 124–30.
22 This was the term given to the organising committee established by the Non-cooperation movement. The term satyagraha was used by Gandhi to describe non-violent coercion (literally 'truth force' or 'soul force').
23 These figures are calculated from strike reports given in the GOB, *Report of the Committee on Industrial Unrest*, Calcutta, 1921 and the 'Monthly Reports on Industrial Disputes' issued by the GOB for 1922.
24 Six of these assaults were on European staff, one on a Gurkha guard and one on a mill clerk. See ibid.
25 Ibid. There was also a similar dispute involving a Scottish supervisor in the Kessoram cotton mill in Bengal, when staff demonstrated following his transfer to Madras.
26 See CSSC, MCC, quoted in Parimal Ghosh, *Colonialism, Class and a History of the Calcutta Jute Millhands, 1880–1930*, Hyderabad, 2000, p. 99.
27 GOB, *Report of the Committee on Industrial Unrest*, p. viii.
28 Ibid., pp. xiii–ix.
29 See GOB, *Report of the Committee on Industrial Unrest* and the 'Monthly Reports on Industrial Disputes' issued by the GOB for 1922. No fewer than eight out of the 19 disputes involving supervisory staff, along with four cases of alleged assault, occurred in the central mills.
30 According to one estimate, of 557,000 Scots who enlisted, 26.4 per cent perished in combat, compared with an average death rate within the British Army of 11.8 per cent. Only Turks and Serbs suffered greater fatalities. See Niall Ferguson, *The Pity of War*, London, 1998, p. 298. This estimate has recently been challenged by Trevor Royle who claims that around 150,000, of his much higher Scottish enlistment estimate of 700,000, were killed in action. However, this still produces a very high death rate of 21.4 per cent. See Trevor Royle, *The Flowers of the Forest: Scotland and the First World War*, Edinburgh, 2007, p. 284.
31 Quoted in Niall Ferguson, op. cit., p. 384.
32 During some of the worst examples of industrial unrest, the Scottish supervisors withstood sieges in the last redoubt of the managers' office, which invariably contained secret doorways and safe passageways. In 1937, the first labour officer, appointed by Bird & Co., within the Bengal jute industry was provided 'with an office in Titagurh bazaar on a piece of Kinnison land with an unobtrusive and private means of entry through the back into Titagurh compound in case at any time a hasty retreat becomes desirable.' See CSAS, Benthall Papers, Box 13, Paul Benthall to Edward Benthall, 20 September 1937.

33 WBSA, GOB, Political Dept (Political), File No 307, 1920, 'Note by Ronaldshay', 1 December 1920.

34 Ibid.

35 Ibid., 'Use of Auxiliary Force in Suppressing Disturbances and Grouping of Mills in Defence Schemes', Serial No 1, Calcutta, 27 November 1920, p. 3.

36 WBSA, GOB, Political Dept (Political), April 1921, 'Memo from Lt. Gen. H. Hudson, Adjutant General in India, to all General Officers Commanding Districts and Divisions', p. 1.

37 Ibid., p. 1.

38 Ibid., p. 5.

39 Calculated from figures given in WBSA, GOB, Political Dept (Political), File No. 307, 1920, 'Auxiliary Force Membership in Jute Mills', pp. 1–5.

40 See Ranajit Das Gupta, *Labour and Working Class in Eastern India: studies in colonial history*, Calcutta, 1994, pp. xvi–xxii; Dipesh Chakrabarty, *Rethinking Working-Class History*, Princeton, 1991, pp. 14–65; Subho Basu, op. cit., pp. 74–113; Parimal Ghosh, op. cit. pp. 105–64.

41 The main recommendations of the Commission included to investigate, '(a) whether new openings for the profitable employment of Indian capital in commerce and industry can be indicated; (b) whether, and if so, in what manner, Government can usefully give direct encouragement to industrial development.' See *Report of the Indian Industrial Commission*, Calcutta, 1919, p. 25.

42 See A. G. Clow, *State and Industry*, New Delhi, 1928, p. 13.

43 GOB, *Report of the Committee on Industrial Report*, p. 5.

44 Ibid., p. 3.

45 Ibid., p. 9.

46 *Reports from Commissioners*, vol. vii, 1917–8, 'Committee of Enquiry into Industrial Unrest', No. 8 Division – Scotland, p. 3.

47 This visit is discussed later in this chapter and in Chapter 6.

48 Despite the advent of the Government of India Act, the issue of working-class representation was still a largely theoretical question, and it would not be until 1937 that an identifiable working-class electorate was brought into being. Even then, the scope of the franchise was still very limited.

49 The ILO was set up in 1919, as a subsidiary body of the League of Nations, in order to regulate labour conditions amongst member states. Progress was monitored by regularly convened international labour conferences. Following the inaugural 1919 Washington conference, the Government of Bengal was urged by Delhi to increase its factory inspectorate, and the scope of the Indian Factory Acts was also widened. See A. G. Clow, op. cit., p. 141.

50 See *Forward*, 30 December 1928.

51 The Bombay-based N. M. Joshi was the highest profile Indian trade unionist of this period. He attended the international labour conference in 1919, where he put up a rather dismal resistance during an argument on working hours with the IJMA representative, Sir Alexander Murray. See IOL, GOI, Dept of Industries, P/11096, 'ILO Conference on the 48 Hour Week Question', Appendix 4, 13 November 1919, 'Statement by Mr Joshi'. Joshi also served on the Indian Legislative Assembly, and entered into a bitter conflict with the communists within the All India Trades Union Congress (AITUC) that led to a damaging split in 1929.

52 See D. H. Buchanan, *Capitalistic Enterprise in India*, London, 1966, p. 430.

53 See GOB, Comm Dept (Comm), File No 1-T-7, Prgs Nos 32–51, Registration and Protection of Trade Unions, August 1922, letter from the Secretary of the Employees Association to the Secretary of GOB, Commerce Dept, 25 November 1921, p. 2. The Employees Association, which was established in 1919, represented around 6,000 mainly Bengali clerical workers.

54 Of 349 Non-Cooperator volunteers arrested in the first week of January 1922 no less

than 123 were described as 'millhands'. See Sumit Sarkar, op. cit., p. 219. K. C. Roy Chowdhury became president of the KLU following the death of Abdul Mazid in 1923.

55 *Amrita Bazar Patrika*, 2 September 1875.

56 C. R. Das was, along with Tilak, the most significant and radical nationalist leader during the early twentieth century. His prestige was such that his, relatively late, approval of Gandhi's Satyagraha strategy virtually guaranteed its approval by the, otherwise sceptical, nationalist movement in Bengal. During the early 1920s, Das was involved in labour organisation at Kharagpur railways works, the Assam–Bengal railways, the Assam tea gardens, the steamship companies and the Calcutta tramways. He was also appointed as President of the AITUC in 1923.

57 The Aunishilan Samiti was formed in Calcutta in 1902 and carried out 'revolutionary' terrorist activities such as the assassination of colonial officials and 'traitors', as well as *dacoities* to raise funds. Their small membership was overwhelmingly drawn from the Bengali upper-castes and they were right wing in their political orientation while Juguntar was regarded as more left wing. For further details see S. N. Mazumdar, *In Search of a Revolutionary Ideology*, Calcutta, 1979.

58 The Congress Socialist Party was formed on the eve of the All-India Congress Committee meeting in Patna in May 1934. The group comprised about a hundred delegates from different parts of India and elected Jayaprakash Narayan as its secretary. For further details see A. K. Chaudhuri, *Socialist Movement in India: the Congress Socialist Party 1934–1947*, Calcutta, 1980.

59 See later in this chapter for details of Sibnath Banerjee. Zaman came to prominence in communist circles in the aftermath of the Meerut conspiracy case, but broke from the party in the early 1930s. He was elected as a labour representative to the Bengal Legislative Assembly in 1937, and also served as a President of the Bengal Provincial Trades Union Congress. In 1939, he broke from the CSP and joined the Forward Bloc of Subhas Chandra Bose. He remained influential in labour circles in Titaghar until the late 1940s.

60 See *Jute and Flax Workers Guide*, October 1923.

61 See Sime and Johnston, *Exploitation in India*, Dundee, 1926, p. 17.

62 The course and consequences of this visit are investigated in the following chapter.

63 A few months following its formation, the new union was re-named the Bengal Jute Workers' Union (BJWU).

64 Sime and Johnston, op. cit., p. 15.

65 David Petrie (ed.), *Communism in India, 1924–7*, Calcutta, 1972, p. 315.

66 Sime and Johnston, op. cit., p. 15.

67 See JFWU Prints Books, 1906–36, letter to Mr W. M. Citrine, Acting Secretary, TUC, dated 2 April 1926 and letter to Mrs Santosh K. Gupta, dated 31 August 1926.

68 See Ashoke Kumar Mukhophadhyay (ed.), *India and Communism: secret British documents*, Calcutta, 1997, p. 93. This is a compilation of reports by the Indian Intelligence Bureau from the early part of the inter-war period, which was originally published in 1933.

69 George Allison, a Lancashire engineer and CPGB member, went to India in April 1926, where he helped to establish a number of labour unions. He was arrested in January 1927 and sentenced to 18 months' 'rigorous imprisonment' for passport violations. Spratt, a graduate of Downing College, Cambridge, arrived in India in December 1926 posing as a representative of a firm of booksellers and worked mainly in Calcutta. He was arrested in 1929 and became one of the leading figures in the Meerut conspiracy trial.

70 In 1924 Chakarborty was sent to Moscow by the Anushilan leadership, who saw the USSR as a potential ally and supplier of arms. On his return, he organised a breakaway from Anushilan, and was involved in the formation of the Young Comrades League, which Phillip Spratt worked closely with following his arrival in Bengal. See David Petrie (ed.), op. cit., p. 130, 243, 285.

71 Quoted in Gautum Chattphadhyay, *Communism in Bengal*, New Delhi, 1970, pp. 127–8.
72 See Moni Singh, *Life is a Struggle*, New Delhi, 1988, p. 21. My thanks to Subho Basu for alerting me to this source.
73 Gautum Chattophadyhay, op. cit., p. 135.
74 'From Bhatpara, we now spread out – to Jagatdal, Titagurh, Kankinara, and so on. We also crossed the Ganges and went to Chandernagar, giving birth to the famous Gondalpara Workers' Union.' See ibid.
75 NMML, Oral History Transcripts, 'Interview with Sibnath Banerjee', pp. 38–39.
76 Interview with Ranen Sen, 21 April 1998.
77 In 1937, the Bengali communist activist Ranen Sen fell seriously ill and was ordered to return to his parental home in order to recover, an arrangement that was considered normal during this time, due to the party's lack of resources. See ibid.
78 A notable exception to the rule appears to be A. M. A. Zaman who was reputed to have come from a working class background and to have been, at some point, a jute worker in the Hooghly mill. But, as with so much else regarding Zaman, his background is shrouded in some mystery. Ranen Sen believed that Zaman was an agent of the colonial state. See ibid.
79 GOB, *Report of the Committee on Industrial Unrest*, p. xxxv.
80 CSSC, MCC, PT 527 (2), 'Paper on Organization by J. Ryan' (undated).
81 The name commonly applied to the dialect of north-east Scotland.
82 NMML, Oral History Transcripts, 'Interview with Sibnath Banerjee', p. 41A.
83 The Meerut conspiracy case was inaugurated following the arrest of leading labour and communist activists in Bombay and Calcutta in March 1929. The trial lasted for over five years. For further details see Pramita Ghose, *Meerut Conspiracy Case and the Left-Wing in India*, Calcutta, 1978.
84 Between 1922 and 1925 alone, the value of exports increased from Rs400 to 600 million. See A. Z. M. Iftikhar-ul-Awwal, *The Industrial Development of Bengal, 1900–1939*, New Delhi, 1982, pp. 176–7.
85 D. R. Wallace, *The Romance of Jute: a short history of the Calcutta jute mill industry, 1855–1927*, London, 1928, p. 94.
86 See Claude Markovitz, *Indian Business and Nationalist Politics, 1931–39: the indigenous capitalist class and the rise of the Congress Party*, Cambridge, 1985, pp. 21–2.
87 *Capital*, 19 September 1929, p. 691.
88 Omkar Goswami, op. cit., pp. 104–6.
89 See Ranajit Das Gupta, op. cit., p. 470.
90 For a description of the strike see ibid., pp. 470–8.
91 *Amrita Bazar Patrika*, 14 August 1929. The demands put forward by the union included an 8 hour working day, a minimum wage of 8Rs per week, annual leave with salary and paid maternity leave.
92 DUA, TDP, MS 86/V/7/15, PO Letters to Calcutta, Thomas Duff & Co to Laird, 28 August 1929.
93 Most of the labour leaders were associated with the communist-sponsored Workers and Peasants Party. Prabhabati Das Gupta was from a wealthy, high-caste background and had studied in the USA before returning to Calcutta in 1926. The following year she was involved, alongside communist activists such as Muzaffar Ahmad, in establishing a trade union for scavengers, in which she became the organising secretary, earning her the epithet *Dhangar Ma*, or mother of scavengers. For further details see Tanika Sarkar, *Bengal 1928–1934: the politics of protest*, Delhi, 1987, p. 52. See also, NMML, 'Interview with Prabhabati Das Gupta'.
94 This was also demonstrated in August 1928 during the long-running Lillooah workshop strike when workers distanced themselves from their established leftist trade union leaders and turned to the moderate trade unionist C. F. Andrews in order to

negotiate a settlement on their behalf. For further details see Gautum Chattopadhyay, op. cit., p. 317.

95 WBSA, GOB, Commerce Dept (Comm), L881, No. 5418 Com, Report on Industrial Disputes in Bengal for September 1929, 7 November 1929, p. 3.

96 *Capital*, 8 August 1929.

97 CSAS, Benthall Papers, Edward Benthall to Paul Benthall, 7 June 1930.

6 The imperial nexus and labour politics in Dundee during the 1920s

1 See *Jute and Flax Workers Guide* (hereafter referred to as *Guide*), April 1922.

2 The JFWU interest in this question was already of long standing. They had first raised the 'Indian textile issue' at the STUC in 1908. For further details see *Guide*, September 1927.

3 Production costs in Dundee increased from £25 to £45 between 1916 and 1919, while costs in Bengal during the same period had increased from £12 to £15. See Board of Trade, *Report of the Departmental Commission Appointed to Consider the Position of the Textile Trades after the War*, London, 1918.

4 See *Guide*, September 1922. This was not the first time that this question had been raised with the TUC. In 1911, a group of trade unionist associated with the General Federation of Trade Unions (GFTU), which included the JFWU as an affiliate, discussed the matter of organising Indian factory workers. However, when GFTU activists took the issue to the TUC's Parliamentary Committee they were informed that nothing could be done 'without a mandate from Congress'. See UWA, TUC Papers, MSS 292/20/1, Parliamentary Committee Minutes, March 1911–December 1912, minute of meeting dated 24 April 1911.

5 A TUC delegation was finally despatched to India in 1927. For further details see A. A. Purcell and J. Hallsworth, *Report on Labour Conditions in India*, London, 1928.

6 *Guide*, October 1925.

7 John Callaghan, 'The Communists and the Colonies: Anti-imperialism Between the Wars', p. 5, in Geoff Andrews, Nina Fishman and Kevin Morgan (eds), *Opening the Books: essays on the cultural history of the British Communist Party*, London, 1995, pp. 4–23. The BSP was the direct descendant of the Social Democratic Federation. It was formed in 1912 when the SDF merged with a number of ILP branches, and claimed an initial membership of 40,000, but by 1914 it was down to 13,755, with the majority being inactive. The BSP would provide the bulk of membership of the British Communist Party following its formation in 1920. See Raymond Challinor, *The Origins of British Bolshevism*, London, 1977, p. 121.

8 'Indian Revolutionaries and the Bolsheviks', Deposit No, 53, June 1921, p. 41, in Subodh Roy (ed.), *Communism in India: unpublished documents, 1919–1924*, Calcutta, 1994, pp. 40–4.

9 John Callaghan, 'The Communists and the Colonies', p. 6.

10 Saklatavala, a former member of the Independent Labour Party (ILP), represented Battersea and was also associated with the WWLI. See Mike Squires, *Saklatvala: a political biography*, London, 1990, p. 60.

11 John Callaghan, op. cit., p. 8.

12 Although the British communists disagreed with Roy's perspective that rapid industrialisation would lead to the gradual dismemberment of the British Empire.

13 Manabendra Nath Roy, *India in Transition*, p. 341, in Sibnarayan Ray (ed.), *The Selected Works of M. N. Roy*, vol. 1, 1917–1922, Oxford, 1987, pp. 183–377.

14 Disagreements were, however, tolerated at this stage, and it would not be until 1928 that the CPGB was forced into line with Comintern policy. M. N. Roy had famously opposed Lenin's report on the national question at the 1920 Comintern congress without facing recriminations, but he was expelled from the Comintern in 1929 on

charges including the central role he had played in advancing the theory of decolonisation. See Sibhnarayn Roy, op. cit., vol. 3, pp. 259–71.

15 Although written in 1916, this pamphlet was not widely known in Britain until the late 1920s when an English language edition was first published. See V. I. Lenin, *Imperialism: the highest stage of capitalism*, Peking, 1975.

16 Bob Stewart, *Breaking the Fetters: the memoirs of Bob Stewart*, London, 1967, p. 121. Borodin would later become the main political advisor to the Goumindang in China and, along with M. N. Roy, would be held responsible for the events that led to the destruction of the Chinese CP at the hands of Chiang Kai-shek. See Alexander Pantsov, *The Bolsheviks and the Chinese Revolution, 1919–1927*, Richmond, 2000.

17 IOL, J. & P. (S) 7847, 'Summary of Information: Indian Communists', 17 May 1923, 'Connections in England and other Countries', in Subodh Roy (ed.), op. cit., p. 111.

18 The Communist Unity Convention involved 160 delegates from the BSP, the Left Wing Committee of the ILP, the Communist Unity Group (CUG), the Socialist Labour Party, the Guild Communists, the Herald League, and Bob Stewart's Socialist Prohibitionist Fellowship. See James Klugman, *History of the Communist Party of Great Britain: formation and early years, 1919–1924*, Southampton, 1968, pp. 38–9.

19 Bob Stewart, op. cit., p. 48. The Prohibition and Reform Party changed its name to the Socialist Prohibition Fellowship following the end of Stewart's prison sentence, for his anti-war activities, in April 1919. See ibid., p. 85. William Walker caustically observed that, 'Stewart has his dates and his sentiments quite wrong. In 1910 he was still a member of Prohibition Party given to singing the praises of Scrymgeour and to commending the "principles of religion which had stood in all time."' See William Walker, *Juteopolis: Dundee and its textile workers*, Dundee, 1979, p. 66.

20 Stewart polled 2,592 votes, compared to the 13,699 votes won by the victorious Labour candidate Morgan Jones. See J. Klugmann, *History of the Communist Party*, p. 184.

21 See NMLH, Dundee Communist Party Records (hereafter referred to as DCPR), CP/LOC/SCOT/1/7, 1920–1 Minute Book.

22 Eden and Cedar Paul, *Creative Revolution: a study of communist ergatocracy*, London, 1920, p. 36, quoted in Stuart Macintyre, *A Proletarian Science: Marxism in Britain, 1917–1933*, London, 1986, p. 193.

23 See Lenin, *Left Wing Communism: an infantile disorder*, London, 1920, pp. 37, 77.

24 See J. Klugmann, op. cit., p. 200.

25 See Stuart Macintyre, op. cit., pp. 188–97.

26 See NMLH, DCPR, op. cit.

27 GOI, Home Pol., F 99, 1923, 'Report on the Revolutionary Organizations in the UK', p. 10.

28 For details of the strike see Chapter 4.

29 Scrymgeour launched a bitter attack on Sime and the JFWU leadership through the local press, for calling solidarity action in support of the Camperdown strikers. He also conducted ballots of jute workers at two SPP organised public meetings, in order to gauge the extent of their support for the JFWU's actions. The first public meeting was poorly attended but still produced a vote of 27 to 18 in favour of strike action. The second meeting in Lochee was much larger and ended in uproar when Scrymgeour was heckled and informed, in no uncertain terms, that he could 'never fill Mr Sime's shoes'. For further details of this episode see William Walker, op. cit., pp. 500–2.

30 For election results see J. M. Jackson, *The Third Statistical Account of Scotland: Dundee*, Arbroath, 1979, pp. 302–3.

31 NMLH, DCPR, op. cit., minute of Local Party Committee (hereafter referred to as LPC), 29 May 1924 and 16 February 1925.

32 See ibid., minute of LPC, 26 May 1925.

33 See Mary Brooksbank, *No Sae Lang Syne: a tale of this city*, Dundee (n.d.).

34 Sixteen members were removed from the books in May 1925 alone. See DCPR, op. cit., minute of LPC, 16 February 1925 and 19 May 1925 respectively.

35 Letter by Hamish Henderson to Ewan MacColl, 9 January 1969, quoted in Timothy Neat, *Hamish Henderson: poetry becomes people, 1952–2002*, Edinburgh, 2009, p. 217.

36 Ibid., p. 103.

37 See J. D. Kemp, 'Drink and the Labour Movement in Early Twentieth Century Scotland: with particular reference to Edwin Scrymgeour and the Scottish Prohibitionist Party', unpublished Ph.D. thesis, University of Dundee, 2000, pp. 263–4.

38 According to local CP members who were active at the time this would remain a problem into the 1930s. See interview with Tom Clarke, 10 October 1998 and interview with Norman Barrie and Charlie McCusker, 11 October 1998.

39 NMLH, DCPR, op. cit., minute of LPC, 16 June 1925.

40 The correspondence between Morel and his Dundee agent demonstrates the importance that they attached to this aspect of party work. See LSE, E. D. Morel Papers (hereafter referred to as EDMP), F 2/1/8. For further details of E. D. Morel's conversion to the Labour Party see Chapter 4, fn. 121.

41 The headquarters of the CPGB.

42 Taking their cue from the stance of the national party on the issue of prohibition, the LPC decided that 'no action be taken in regard to the proposed debate.' See NMLH, DCPR, minute of LPC, 6 March 1924.

43 Ibid., minutes of LPC meetings for 1924–5.

44 DCL, LC, 8, Monday, 22 January 1923.

45 Ibid.

46 LSE, EDMP, F 2/1/8, Saklatvala to Morel, 24 January 1923.

47 James Klugman, op. cit., p. 313.

48 Ibid., pp. 313–4.

49 Ibid., p. 314.

50 The first, minority, Labour government was elected in December 1923. For details of the Cawnpore conspiracy trial see Sir David Petrie (ed.), *Communism in India, 1924–27*, Calcutta, 1972, pp. 55–65.

51 See NMLH, DCPR, minutes of LPC meetings of 25 May and 5 June 1924.

52 *Vanguard*, 1 March 1924, p. 337, in G. Adhikari (ed.), *Documents of the History of the Communist Party of India: vol. 2, 1923–5*, New Delhi, 1982, pp. 334–40.

53 Ibid., p. 338.

54 NMLH, DCPR, minute of LPC, 13 March 1924.

55 *Annual Report of Scottish Trades Union Congress*, April 1924, cited in Mike Squires, op. cit., p. 166.

56 See *Weekly Worker*, 2 and 9 May 1924, quoted in James Klugmann, op. cit., p. 276.

57 The initiative for the establishment of the NMM came from the Comintern and the Red International of Labour Unions (RILU), following Mikhail Borodin's 1923 visit to investigate the extent and effectiveness of communist work within the British trade unions. For further details of the origins and progress of the NMM see Roderick Martin, *Communism and the British Trade Unions 1924–1933: a study of the National Minority Movement*, Oxford, 1969.

58 Following the conference, an aggregate meeting of the Dundee party was convened at which George Rough, the local industrial organiser and a leading figure in the calender workers' union, was asked about the progress that had been made in sending propagandists to India. See NMLH, DCPR, minute of aggregate meeting, 2 February 1925.

59 Discussions regarding the sending of a delegation to India were coordinated by the joint textile committee of trade unions, comprising the JFWU, the Manufacturing

and Factory Operatives Union, the Dundee Powerloom Tenters' Society and the Dundee and District Calender, Linoleum and Dye Workers' Union.

60 NLHM, DCPR, minute of special aggregate meeting, 24 November 1924.
61 For biographical details of Tom Johnston see Graham Walker, *Thomas Johnston, Manchester*, 1988. See also Russell Galbraith, *Without Quarter: a biography of Tom Johnston*, Edinburgh, 1995.
62 Tom Johnston won with 22,973 votes, compared with E. D. Simon's vote of 10,234. See J. M. Jackson, op. cit.
63 For a discussion of Hobson's 'under-consumption theory' see Graham Walker, op. cit., pp. 59–60. See also J. A. Hobson, *Imperialism: a study*, London, 1988. This work first appeared in 1902 and had a profound impact on Lenin, although he firmly rejected Hobson's theory of under-consumption. See Anthony Brewer, *Marxist Theories of Imperialism: a critical survey*, London, 1989, pp. 116–29.
64 Graham Walker, op. cit., pp. 63–4.
65 Ibid.
66 Ibid., p. 67.
67 See Partha Sarathi Gupta, *Imperialism and the British Labour Movement, 1914–1964*, London, 1975, pp. 105–113.
68 Tom Shaw, a former Lancashire textile worker, was secretary of the Northern Counties Textile Federation and a Labour MP. He was also joint secretary of the Labour and Socialist International (the Second International) between 1923–5. For biographical details see ibid., p. 409.
69 Graham Walker, op. cit., pp. 67–8.
70 *Forward*, 26 July 1924, quoted in ibid., p. 66.
71 On the issue of the 'Battle between Red International of Labour Unions (RILU) and Amsterdam' see NMLH, DCPR, minute of industrial aggregate, 19 May 1925.
72 Scots rendering of jam sandwich.
73 *Guide*, February/March 1925.
74 Ibid.
75 See Graham Walker, op. cit., p. 69.
76 See *New Leader*, 26 June 1925, cited in ibid.
77 DCA, JFWU Records, Prints book 1906–36, letter from John Sime to Thomas Johnston MP, 5 June 1925.
78 In 1926, at the height of the so-called 'Spying Letter' controversy, John Sime claimed that the Indian visit was first mooted during discussions with E. D. Morel in 1921. However, there is no evidence of this anywhere in the Morel Papers, and as late as June 1923 Morel was having his speeches to jute workers written for him by his agent and was apparently ignorant of the situation within the industry. See LSE, EDMP, F2/1/8, Ogilvie to Morel, letter dated 22 June 1923. The 'Spying Letter' controversy is dealt with later in this chapter.
79 In early May 1925 the communists in Dundee learned that the 'Joint Committee [of textile unions] had not yet decided whom they should send to India', although the 'general impression was that it should be [a] representative from the unions.' Two weeks later it was reported that 'J. F. Sime had been nominated for [the] delegation to India, the [joint] committee having decided that unions should call meetings to consult members on this question.' See NMLH, DCPR, minutes of LPC meetings, 12 May and 26 May 1925.
80 See *Dundee Advertiser*, 30 October 1925.
81 This word has the same meaning as the Bengali term *bustee*, which refers to slum housing.
82 See Tom Johnston, *Memories*, London, 1952, pp. 67–81.
83 See John Sime and Tom Johnston, *Exploitation in India*, Dundee, 1926, p. 12.
84 Shortly following the Sime/Johnston visit, Tom Shaw conducted his own visit to India. See Tom Shaw, *Report of Investigations into the Conditions of Indian Textile*

Workers, Ashton-under-Lyme, 1927. In 1927 the TUC also finally honoured their conference decision of 1922 by sending an official delegation to India. See A. A. Purcell and J. Hallsworth, *Report on Labour Conditions in India*, London, 1928.

85 *Evening Telegraph*, 30 December 1925.

86 *Guide*, January 1926, p. 2.

87 For quote see DCA, JFWU Records, Prints Book 1906–1936, 'The British Exploitation in India', in *Forward* (n.d., probably 1906).

88 Gatekeeper.

89 Interview with Alex Scott, 13 September 1996.

90 Interview with S. K. Basu and N. S. Basu, 21 June 1996.

91 Interview with Alex Scott, 13 September 1996.

92 See Eugenie Fraser, *A Home by the Hooghly: a jute wallah's wife*, Edinburgh, 1994.p. 25.

93 Sime and Johnston claimed that 900 Dundee men were employed in the Bengal jute mills, but this appears to be a considerable under-estimate. See Sime and Johnston, op. cit., p. 3. In 1929, the *Dundee Free Press* claimed that 3,000 Dundee men were employed in the Calcutta jute mills, a figure that appears to be very high. See *Dundee Free Press*, 18 October 1929. In 1929, there were around 90 jute mills in Bengal, with each mill employing 15–20 'European' personnel.

94 Interview with Mrs Ralph Morrison, 28 July 1996. The phrase was used to describe the perceived snobbishness of employees of Thomas Duff & Co. Ltd.

95 Interview with Tom Clarke, 10 October 1998.

96 David Phillips, *Hud Yor Tongue! further writings in the Dundee dialect*, Arbroath, 1964, p. 22.

97 See *Guide*, October 1927.

98 *Peoples Journal*, 27 March 1926.

99 *Guide*, May 1927.

100 See DCA, JFWU Records, minute of meeting held on 23 October 1928.

101 See Marcel Liebman, *Leninism under Lenin*, London, 1985, pp. 417–49.

102 See Kevin McDermott, 'The History of the Comintern in the light of new documents', in Tim Rees and Andrew Thorpe (eds), *International Communism and the Communist International, 1919–43*, Manchester, 1998, pp. 31–41.

103 Writing in 1936, as Stalin moved towards the final annihilation of the internal opposition to his bureaucratic regime, C. L. R. James acerbically observed that the 'first period was the period which had ended in 1924 [with the defeat of the German Revolution], the second period had ended with the defeat in China, now had begun the third and final period. The Social Democracy, who had been the chief friends in the second period, were now the chief enemy in the third. The same Social Democracy, the same parties, the same men, were yet to become, as they still are today, even better friends than in 1925–7.' See C. L. R. James, *World Revolution 1917–1936: the rise and fall of the Communist International*, New Jersey, 1993, pp. 307–8.

104 Noreen Branson, *History of the Communist Party of Great Britain, 1927–1941*, London, 1985, p. 27.

105 Ibid., p. 28.

106 Nina Fishman maintains that 'Class against Class' was only partially implemented in Britain, where the presence of Harry Pollit and Johnny Campbell 'constituted a significant political counterweight to the Young Turks [Comintern nominated loyalists] and enabled Party members who agreed with them to ignore Class against Class and continue to function as loyal trade unionists.' See Nina Fishman, *The British Communist Party and the Trade Unions, 1933–1945*, Aldershot, 1995, pp. 34–35. However, in a detailed examination of recently released Comintern documents, Keith McDermott has concluded that Pollit and Campbell's opposition was ultimately to no avail as the 'British Party, like all others, were compelled to pursue the ruinous policies of the "Third Period".' See Keith McDermott, op. cit., p. 33.

107 *Guide*, October 1928.
108 CSSC, MCC, P-527(1), P. Spratt to C. P. Dutt, 14 March 1929.
109 Indeed, between 1921 and 1931 the proportion employed in Indian industry actually fell from 10.49 per cent to 9.7 per cent. See Vera Anstey, *The Economic Development of India*, London, 1939, Table VI, p. 522.
110 Sime and Johnston, op. cit., p. 4.
111 *Peoples Journal*, 23 January 1926, p. 13.
112 For details of the background and consequences of the Dawes Plan see James Klugmann, op. cit., pp. 287–90.
113 The British recession of this period also prompted a government-sponsored offensive against wage levels.
114 See *Capital*, 18 December 1930.
115 DUA, MS 100/1/2/7, Don Brothers Letterbook, 1927–1934, Letter from Don Brothers Ltd to Messrs W.B. Fenton & Co., 12 April 1928. 'Crash' referred to fabrics used for towelling and sometimes made from a mixture of fibres.

7 The breaking of the Dundee–Calcutta nexus, 1930–40

1 *Daily Record and Mail*, 14 May 1930.
2 See Sidney Pollard, *The Development of the British Economy, 1914–1990*, Sevenoaks, 1992, pp. 111–12.
3 WYLA, Records of Fairbairn, Lawson, Combe and Barbour (hereafter referred to as FLCB), WYL365/acc.2371/81D, typed manuscript entitled, 'Brief History of the Developments in Jute Machinery', dated 28 October 1946, p. 10.
4 See Jute Trade Board, *Working Party Report*, London, 1948, p. 31.
5 DCA, Jute and Flax Workers' Union Records (hereafter referred to as JFWU), GD/JF/5/4, Letterbook Out 1931–6, John Sime to Mr Shaw, 31 December 1932.
6 Ibid.
7 See *Working Party Report*, Table 22, Employment in the British Jute Industry, p. 43.
8 See *Jute Review*, November 1939, p. 5.
9 See *Working Party* Report, Table 22, Employment in the Dundee Jute Industry, p. 42.
10 DCL, LC, 20, p. 17.
11 See Isabel Menzies and Dennis Chapman, 'The Jute Industry', p. 248, in H. A. Silverman (ed.), *Studies in Industrial Organization*, London, 1946.
12 DUA, Don Brothers Records, MS/100/1/2/7, Letterbook 1927–34, William Don to Secretary of Forfar Factory Workers' Union, 1 September 1933.
13 Graham Smith, 'The Making of a Woman's Town', household and gender in Dundee', Ph.D. thesis, University of Stirling, 1996, chapter entitled 'Change and Continuity in Employment and Household', p. 7.
14 *The People's Journal*, 2 July 1921.
15 Frederick Winslow Taylor was an American specialist in so-called 'scientific management' whose ideas gained increasing influence, particularly following the dramatic success of Henry Ford's application of Taylorist principles to the mass production of automobiles. See Craig Littler, *The Development of the Labour Process in Capitalist Societies*, London, 1982.
16 UWA, TUC Records, MSS 292/112/4, Private and Confidential, TUC General Council, Research Dept, 'Bedaux System of Payments by Results', Memorandum, 19 December 1932, p. 1. The Bedaux system was the brainchild of Charles Bedaux, a French immigrant to the USA, who, as well as being a close friend of the Duke of Windsor, became an advisor to the Nazi and the Vichy regimes. For further details of Charles Bedaux see C. Hardwick, *Time Study in Treason: Charles E Bedaux: patriot or collaborator*, Chelmsford (undated).
17 UWA, TUC Records, *The Bedaux Report*, London, 1933.

18 Ibid.
19 *Jute & Flax Workers Guide*, April 1927, p. 4.
20 DCA, JFWU Records, Letterbook Out, J. F. Sime to Mr H. Moulden, Secretary, Amalgamated Hosiery Union, 92 Rutland Square, Leicester, 25 December 1931. At this time, the Hosiery Workers' Union was involved in a long-running conflict with the Wolsey Hosiery Company, one of the largest firms in the East Midlands. In mid-January 1932, Moulden declared that 'he hoped the last breath would go out of his body before he was prepared to negotiate on the Bedaux system'. See Littler, op. cit., pp. 118–28.
21 DCA, JFWU Records, Letterbook Out, 1931–6, J. F. Sime to Miss Frew, 11 March 1931.
22 *Dundee Free Press*, 30 January 1931.
23 DUA, Records of Association of Jute Spinners and Manufacturers (hereafter referred to as AJSM), *AJSM Annual Report*, 1933, Appendix I, 'Unemployment Figures – Jute Industry'.
24 *Jute and Flax Workers Guide*, September 1926.
25 The ex-jute wallahs would have been well aware that trainee workers in the Calcutta mills commonly relied on their families to support them during their period of training; see pp. 46–7.
26 DCA, JFWU, Letterbook Out, John Sime to Mr Gibson, Trade Board Inspectorate, 22 September 1933. Sime also uncovered many instances where 'qualified' weavers were still being paid at the 'learner' rate following the end of their training period.
27 At the time of writing, the increasing use of 'interns' in the professions and of unpaid 'trainee' labour in unskilled occupations has become an increasing cause for concern in Britain.
28 See Graham Smith, op. cit., Chapter 10, 'Change and Continuity in Employment and Household', pp. 17–18.
29 See Ian Levitt, *Poverty and Welfare in Scotland 1890–1948*, Edinburgh, 1988, p. 136.
30 While women were reported to have taken a prominent role in the disturbances, only one woman, Mary Brooksbank, was arrested. See *Dundee Free Press*, 25 September 1931.
31 Ibid., 30 September 1931.
32 Large rectangular cobbles that served as a road surface. Many roads in Dundee were laid with wooden cassies, particularly on roads leading from the city's docks to some of the larger jute mills, in order to lessen the risk of sparks setting alight to the highly inflammable consignments of baled jute when they were being transported by horse and cart.
33 Flat paving.
34 David Phillips, *The Hungry Thirties: Dundee between the wars*, Dundee, 1981, p. 67.
35 See *Dundee Free Press*, 30 September 1931.
36 J. M. Jackson, *Third Statistical Account of Scotland*, Arbroath, 1979, p. 321.
37 Scrymgeour retired from politics and died 'almost forgotten, in 1947'. See ibid.
38 Quoted in ibid., p. 320.
39 Florence Horsburgh, the granddaughter of a Cupar solicitor and an Edinburgh advocate, was awarded an MBE for welfare work during the war and became the first woman cabinet minister. See ibid.
40 DCL, LC 34.
41 Proceedings at the AGM were reported as being 'of a stormy nature' with 'alleged communists being shouted down when they attempted to speak'. See ibid.
42 Ibid.
43 See Dundee Trade Union Council, *Dundee and the Spanish Civil War: the contribution of a city and its people*, Dundee, undated.

44 While in police custody, Mudie was interviewed as a potential witness to an inquiry into the suspicious death of the Scottish ILP leader Bob Smillie, which may also raise doubts as to the official Republican description of him as 'an undesirable and a drunk', his alleged desertion and the circumstances surrounding his death.

45 Victor Kiernan, 'The Communist Party and the Second World War – Some Reminiscences', in *South Asia* 10, no. 2, December 1987, pp. 61–73, quoted in Victor Kiernan/Harvey J. Kaye (ed.), *Imperialism and its Contradictions*, London, 1995, p. 7.

46 For details of the controversy surrounding the selection and de-selection of Menon see Marika Sherwood, 'Krishna Menon, Parliamentary Labour Party Candidate for Dundee, 1939–40', in *Scottish Labour History*, vol. 42, 2007.

47 IJMA, Circular Files, Letter between secretaries of IJMA and GOB, Commerce Dept, March 1932, p. 1.

48 Ibid., Circular File 1930–1931, No. 65-D.

49 GOB, Commerce Dept, A. C. Roy Chowdhury, *Report on an Enquiry into the Standard of Living of Jute Mill Workers in Bengal*, Calcutta, 1930.

50 WBSA, GOB, Poll Dept, Poll Branch, D/O No. 126 Con, Petition, to the District Magistrate, Alipore, 24 Parganas, 23 March 1931

51 IJMA, Circular Files, 1937–8, 'Industrial Disputes in India 1928–1937', p. 9.

52 Ibid., Revised Draft of IJMA letter to the Secretary of the Government of Bengal, March 1932, p. 2.

53 See *IJMA Report, 1932*, p. 16.

54 *Capital*, 4 March 1936.

55 DUA, Thomas Duff Papers (hereafter referred to as TDP), MS 86/V/7/24, PO Letters from Calcutta, Air Mail from G. L. Yule to Messrs W. W. Ispahani, 30 October 1937.

56 Ibid., MS 86/V/7/18, PO Letters to Calcutta, 25 August 1936, p. 57.

57 Ibid., MS 86/V/7/33, 26 October 1937, p. 3.

58 See Isabel Menzies and Dennis Chapman, op. cit., pp. 250, 253.

59 See *Capital*, 1 September 1938.

60 A lakh is 100,000.

61 See *Times of India Yearbook, 1937–8*, Bombay, vol. xxiv, p. 772.

62 *Capital*, 14 February 1936.

63 WYLA, Fairbairn, Lawson, Combe and Barbour Papers (hereafter referred to as FLCB), File No. 365/acc2371/69, 1934–45, AGM, 30 June 1937, p. 7. The trading profit of FLCB for 1937 amounted to £110,909, a massive increase of £78,972 on the previous year's trading.

64 Ibid., Verbatim Report, OGM, held at Chamber of Commerce, Leeds, 29 June 1938, pp. 9–10. These figures do not include purchases from the second largest jute machinery manufacturing firm, Mackie's of Belfast.

65 The other managing agency houses comprised Barry & Co., Begg-Dunlop, James Findlay, George Hynd, Heilgers, Mackinnon Mackenzie and MacLeods. The figures for machinery are calculated from the order books of J. F. Low and FLCB. In Dundee, the total number of high-speed spindles amounted to 71,184. See *Working Party Report*, p. 34.

66 See WBSA, GOB, *FAR* for relevant years.

67 GOB, *FAR 1935*, p. 15.

68 The deterioration in the quality of raw jute during the 1930s followed from the gathering crisis in the jute growing tracts of eastern Bengal. As ryots, who were faced with declining prices, stepped up the cultivation of jute, merchants were increasingly accused of 'watering' jute, while inferior grades of fibre were commonly found to have been mixed up with higher grades within the same bale. See GOB, *Report of the Bengal Jute Enquiry Committee* (Finlow Committee), Calcutta, 1934, vol. 1, pp. 80–5.

69 DUA, TDP, MS 86/V/8/8 [6], Manager's Report to the Directors (hereafter referred to as MRD) of Titaghar Mill Company, 1937, p. 133. In stark contrast, no fines were imposed on spinners, which was probably due to their much lower earnings.

70 See ibid., MRD for Angus Mill Company, 1936, MS 86/V/8/6/1; MRD, Angus Mill, 1935, MS 86/V/8/7/1; MRD, Shyamnagar North, 1935, MS 86/V/8/7/2.

71 See IJMA, *Report 1937*, p. 4.

72 GOB, *Report of the Bengal Jute Enquiry Committee* (Fawcus Committee), Calcutta, 1939, Note by Sibnath Banerjee, p. 119.

73 The elections resulted from the limited electoral reforms that came in the wake of the 1935 Government of India Act, which R. P. Dutt acerbically observed 'was commonly treated in British expression as a virtual realisation of self-government', and that its 'unanimous rejection by Indian opinion ... was often regarded with surprise as unreasonable even by many who normally hold liberal democratic views when they are dealing with other than colonial peoples.' See R. P. Dutt, *India Today*, Calcutta, 1992, p. 502.

74 Sibnath Banerjee was the official candidate of the All India Trades Union Congress (AITUC).

75 *Congress Socialist*, 20 February 1937.

76 Ibid., 13 March 1937.

77 DCL, LC, 13 March 1936.

78 For an examination of the 1923 strike and lockout see Chapter 4.

79 See NMLH, DCPR, minute of aggregate meeting, 24 May 1926.

80 This committee was established at the beginning of the strike and comprised the candidates elected from the 'labour constituencies' at the provincial elections. These included the congress socialists Sibnath Banerjee and A. M. A. Zaman, and the communist supporters Niharendu Dutt Mazumdar and Bankhim Mukherjee, along with Suresh Banerjee, a Gandhian syndicalist and anti-communist who was close to both Gandhi and G. D. Birla.

81 *Congress Socialist*, 13 March 1937.

82 For Dipesh Chakrabarty, the 'anachronistic nature of the industry – the trading mentality that guided its economic policies and technological choices – was to have a profound influence on the history of the labor force it created, especially in matters of discipline, authority, and, consequently, workers' protest as well.' This view has influenced many subsequent studies of the Bengal jute industry. See Dipesh Chakrabarty, *Rethinking Working-Class History: Bengal 1890–1940*, Princeton, 1989, p. 64. See also Omkar Goswami, *Industry, Trade and Peasant Society: the jute economy of eastern India, 1900–47*, Delhi, 1991.

83 In 1934, S. G. Barker, a British textile scientist, was invited by the IJMA to conduct an investigation into the technological and scientific shortcomings of the Bengal jute industry. His subsequent report called for a thoroughgoing overhaul of the industry's technology and diversification into finer-grade products. See S. G. Barker, *Report on the Scientific and Technical Development of the Jute Manufacturing Industry in Bengal*, Calcutta, 1935. According to Chakrabarty, 'Barker's Report came twenty years too late. And probably too suddenly, given the slow, nineteenth century reflexes of the industry.' See Dipesh Chakrabarty, op. cit., p. 44.

84 See Samita Sen, *Women and Labour in Colonial India: the Bengal jute industry*, Cambridge, 1999, pp. 118–21; Subho Basu, *Does Class Matter?: Colonial capital and workers' resistance, 1890–1937*, New Delhi, 2004, pp. 238–43.

85 By describing the introduction of new technology as a phase I do not mean to suggest that the rationalisation process was centrally planned or orchestrated. The developments of the 1930s should be viewed as part of a long-term process that was interrupted by the coming of the Second World War, and which was subsequently taken up after independence and brought to a conclusion around 1960.

86 Following the Hukumchand strike, trouble also broke out at the massive Anglo-Indian mill complex involving up to 12,000 workers. The neighbouring Gourepore and Naihati mills also witnessed labour trouble over the issue of new technology following the official termination of the 1937 general strike.

87 See *Capital*, 16 April 1937, p. 599. The leading jute wallah and director of Thomas Duff, Sir Alexander Murray, had visited the mill in January 1936, and admitted that the 'layout and buildings compare favourably with anything I have ever seen and reflects great credit on Craig Anderson and other machinery makers' representatives who were present in force and they certainly had something to show off. The latest spinning frames have just been installed but are not yet all started up.' See DUA, TDP, MS 86/V/7/32, Letters of Alexander Murray, 20 January 1936, pp. 1–2.

88 The Wellington strike became particularly serious following the arrest of the labour leader A. M. A. Zaman. See WBSA, GOB, Home Dept (Pol), File No. 484/37, Weekly Report on Industrial Disputes (hereafter referred to as WRID), 13 March 1937.

89 Forty-six women workers resorted to a week-long 'stay in strike' in June 1937, 'in support of their demand for an increase in their numbers and wages' at the Belvedere mill, where the installation of high-speed preparing machinery had led to retrenchment.

90 DUA, TDP, MS 86/V8/8[1], MRD, Angus Mill, 1937, p. 54.

91 WBSA, GOB, WRID, 26 November 1937, pp. 2–3.

92 See CSAS, BP, Box XIV, Copy of 'Appeal from Jute Mill Workers of Calcutta: Strike War in the Hazinagar Jute Mill', 28 November 1937.

93 WBSA, GOB, WRID, 11 December 1937, pp. 1–2.

94 WBSA, GOB, Commerce Dept, File No. 1978-Com, Monthly Report on Industrial Disputes for January 1938, 23 February 1938, pp. 1–2.

95 The BCMU took the place of the All Bengal Jute Workers' Union and included 27 affiliated branches. For further details see Nirban Basu, *The Working Class Movement: a study of the jute mills of Bengal, 1937–1947*, Calcutta, 1994, pp. 122–3.

96 The Ordinance was introduced by the Government of Bengal in the face of widespread instability within the jute industry. Its main clauses included a limitation on working time to 45 hours per week for mills with more than 175 looms and 72 hours per week for mills with 175 looms or fewer, while mills were also prohibited from installing new looms. These changes led to a large retrenchment programme and widespread wage cuts.

97 The Madrassi migrants arrived in Calcutta in the early 1900s from the districts of Ganjam, Vizianagram and Vizayapattam. The skills of Madrassi women in carding were still being extolled by other jute workers as recently as March 1996, as I discovered during a visit to Shyamnagar mill in Titaghar.

98 GOB, Records of Special Branch (hereafter referred to as SB), SW521/38 BCMU, Report No. 182, General Jute Strike, 8 December 1938.

99 GOB, SB, SW572/38, Jute Workers' Union, Press Cutting from *Hindusthan Standard*, 4 August 1938.

100 GOB, SB, SW 629, Report No. 259, 12 May 1939.

101 According to Samita Sen, employers 'used the trade unions and the male workers' fears of unemployment to undermine women's hold over their jobs.' See Samita Sen, *Women and Labour in Colonial India*, pp. 93, 235. The claim that trade unions operated an institutionalised bias against women workers is much more plausible for the post-independence period. For further details see Leela Fernandez, *Producing Workers: the politics of gender, class, and culture in the Calcutta jute mills*, Philadelphia, 1997, pp. 39–40.

102 Sen writes that male 'workers were progressively unionised, especially towards the general strike of 1937. Strikes had begun to be less violent, increasingly better organised, better led and often reached the negotiating table.' See Samita Sen, op. cit., p. 220.

103 See ibid., pp. 213–48.
104 *The New Age*, August 1937.
105 Ibid.
106 Ibid.
107 See pp. 170–1 of this chapter for a discussion of the significance, and consequences, of the 1937 provincial elections.
108 I have looked at this facet of the strike at greater length in 'Paternal Despotism and Workers Resistance', Fellowship Dissertation, Trinity College, Cambridge, 1997, pp. 265–8.
109 Party membership, however, remained very small: in 1938, an internal party document estimate put the all-India membership at only 1,500, made up overwhelmingly of intellectuals. See Asiatic Society, Calcutta, Comintern Papers, RAR 226, 495/20/288/18–35, 'The Situation in India', by J. R. Campbell, 22 December 1938.
110 See WBSA, GOB, Pol Dept, Poll, File No. 68, 1937, 'Action in Connection with Communist Activity'.
111 The agreement included the full recognition of trade unions and a pledge that the employers would investigate the wages issue and the role of sirdars and overseers in appointments and dismissals. See *Amrita Bazar Patrika*, 8 May 1937.
112 The KPP was a secular and radical peasant party with a strong base of support amongst the predominantly Muslim peasantry of Bengal. The centrepiece of their election programme included the demand for the abolition of the zamindari system without compensation, immediate rent reductions and the introduction of compulsory and free primary school education. Their programme was widely supported by the left in Bengal and also by the All-India Kisan Sabha.
113 The breakdown of seats following the elections were; KPP 35, Muslim League 40, Congress 60, Independent Muslims 41, Europeans 25, Independent Scheduled Caste Groups 23 and Independent Caste Hindus 14.
114 CSAS, BP, Box 12, Undated Note, 'For Partners Only: Strictly Private'. Edward Benthall expressed his pleasant surprise at the pro-British business attitude of the Ministry, stating that 'he would hardly know there had been a change in government'. See ibid., Air Mail Letter from E. C. Benthall, 23 August 1937.
115 Ibid., Chapman Mortimer to Edward Benthall, 29 August 1937.
116 DUA, TDP, MS 86/V/7/4, PO Letters, 10 June 1937, p. 14.
117 This was particularly marked in the post-strike period when jute mill management was attempting to limit the powers of the sirdar. See SB, File No. SW 521/38, Bengal Chatkal Mazdoor Union, Report of CL 115, 16 November 1939. This details a meeting between CPI activists and a group of sirdars of the Ganges mill, which was called in order to investigate the possibility of organising a strike in the mill.
118 Despite these reforms, it would be many years before head sirdars were eliminated from the industry, and their removal did not emerge as the panacea envisaged by many proponents. See S. N. Sen and T. Piplai, *Industrial Relations in the Jute Industry in West Bengal (A Case Study)*, Calcutta, 1968, pp. 50–60.
119 I. L. Tripathi, who we met in chapter two, was recruited as a mill supervisor during this time.
120 CSAS, BP, Box 12, PO Letters, Edward Benthall to Paul Benthall, 'Jute Mill Labour', 21 August 1937.
121 Ibid., Paul Benthall to Edward Benthall, 18 August 1937.
122 Ibid., Edward Benthall to Paul Benthall, 29 August 1937. Bird & Co.'s 'scheme of apprentices' involved the recruitment of six Anglo-Indian youths at the Clive and Lansdowne mills. See DUA, TDP, MS 86/V/7/24, PO letters from Calcutta, Murray to Mason, 30 September 1937, pp. 1–2.
123 Interview with Jim Balfour, 13 September 1996.
124 See Basudev Chatterji, *Trade, Tariffs and Empire: Lancashire and British policy in India, 1919–1939*, Delhi, 1992, pp. 70–1.

125 Hoare to Willingdon, 19 February 1932, Templewood MS, I, quoted in Claude Markovitz, *Indian Business and Nationalist Politics: the indigenous capitalist class and the rise of the Congress Party*, Cambridge, 1985, p. 51.

126 Ibid.

127 *Jute Monthly*, April 1938.

128 For a different view see Gordon Stewart, *Jute and Empire: the Calcutta jute wallahs and the landscapes of Empire*, Manchester, 1998, pp. 147–91.

129 In 1937, exports of Dundee-made piece goods to Argentina were outstripped for the first time by German sales. See *Capital*, 17 November 1938, p. 702. It was estimated that the German jute industry contained around 9,600 looms in 1939, compared with Dundee's total of around 8,500; however, the German estimate was inflated by the inclusion of the Czech and Austrian jute industries. See *Working Party Report*, Table 5, p. 13.

130 Hoare Belisha, the Minister of Transport, announced that government financial backing, amounting to 85 per cent of the estimated cost of £2.1 million, was being withdrawn because the scheme did 'not possess sufficient justification to warrant a grant from the Road Fund'. See David Phillips, op. cit., p. 101. Work on a road bridge eventually began in 1963.

131 See John Gilbert, *Investment Trusts in Dundee*, London, 1939.

132 While Britain had given preferences on Indian goods worth about £47 million, they had received preferences on British exports to India worth about £55 million at 1928–9 prices. At the 1937 talks, the Indian delegation argued that more Indian goods should be granted preferential status. See Basudev Chatterji, op. cit., pp. 52–6, 66–74.

133 The 38 per cent increase in 'home' production that would be needed 'in order to cover the requirements of consumers' was, according to the JGA, an unattainable target for the home industry. See NAI, Purshomtamdas Papers, 'Memorandum by the UK Jute Goods Association: Ottawa Agreement with India', September 1937, p. 5.

134 This figure included 1,500 female spinners and 250 male spinners. The total number of unemployed jute workers was 6,378, comprising 4,222 female and 2,156 male workers. See ibid., Appendix, Dundee Labour Exchange Unemployed Figures for the Jute Trade, 21 September 1936.

135 CSAS, BP, Box 12, PO Letter, E. Benthall to H. Burn, 5 August 1937. During 1937, the unemployment rate in Dundee was around 22 per cent, while the UK average was 11 per cent. See J. M. Jackson, 'Economic Life: a general survey', p. 101, in J. M. Jackson (ed.), *The Third Statistical Account of Scotland: the city of Dundee*, Arbroath, 1979, pp. 97–104.

136 See *Jute*, February 1938, p. 3. The programme was eventually broadcasted in March 1939.

137 The Ordinance was quickly followed by an influx back into the IJMA, and by January 1939 IJMA membership covered 96 per cent of the Indian industry.

138 The Scottish Economic Committee involved leading academics, businessmen and civil servants, and was established by the National Government in an attempt to promote Scottish economic diversification. See Tom Devine, *The Scottish Nation, 1700–2000*, London, 2000, pp. 326–7.

139 In 1942 the wartime government announced that Dundee had been chosen as a 'Special Development Area', which meant that it was to be given preferential treatment with regards to foreign inward investment in the post-war period.

140 *Jute Monthly*, October 1938.

141 The seven cities that had more overcrowding comprised Glasgow, Liverpool, Leeds, Manchester, Birmingham, Sheffield and Edinburgh. See *The Architects' Journal*, 26 October 1933, p. 426.

142 Ibid.

143 During 1936–40 the Scottish infant mortality rate was 76 while in England and Wales it was 55. See DCA, TC/SF/18, Corporation of Dundee, W. L. Burgess, 'Notes on the Report of a Sub-committee of the Scientific Advisory Committee on Infant Mortality in Scotland', 1944, p. 3.

144 See Graham Smith, op. cit., chapter 10, 'Change and Continuity in Employment and Households'.

145 Ibid.

146 See Dundee Oral History Project, 020/A/1.

147 The film was produced by Scottish Films Productions. Quoted in Graham Smith, op. cit., chapter entitled 'Change and Continuity in Employment and Households'.

148 In Nigel Gatherer, *Songs and Ballads of Dundee*, Edinburgh, 2000, p. 93. There are two recorded versions of this song in Dundee, but it is probable that there were other versions in Scotland during the depression, as there is a rhyme that still exists in Glasgow that goes, 'I'm Buffalo Bill fi Maryhill, I've never worked an' I never will.'

149 See DCL, LC35, 22 April 1937.

150 Figures quoted in Angus Calder, *The People's War: Britain 1939–1945*, London, 1999, p. 322.

151 Figures quoted in *Working Party Report*, p. 42.

152 Angus Calder, op. cit., p. 333.

153 Dave Bowman, *Future of Jute*, Dundee, 1945, p. 7.

154 Quoted in *Capital*, 20 February 1947.

155 For figures see J. M. Jackson, op. cit., p. 112.

Conclusion

 1 Linda Colley, *Britons: forging the nation, 1707–1837*, London, 1996, p. 139.

 2 The pioneering Labour activist David Lowe explained, with some justification, that the Dundee slums 'were said to be the worst in Europe.' See David Lowe, *Souvenirs of Scottish Labour*, Glasgow, 1919, p. 24.

 3 The Blue Mountain was a slum area in the west end of Dundee, and was demolished in the 1920s. The five middens in the Hilltown area was a group of tenements that housed a large number of jute workers and their families. It was colloquially referred to as the 'five shities', and local legend has it that if you addressed a letter in this manner, it would unfailingly reach its destination.

 4 Aristide R. Zolberg, 'How Many Exceptionalisms?', p. 413, in Ira Katznelson and Aristide R. Zolberg (eds), *Working-Class Formation: nineteenth century patterns in western Europe and the United States*, Princeton, 1986, pp. 397–457.

 5 A. K. Bagchi, *Capital and Labour Redefined: India and the Third World*, New Delhi, 2002, p. 186.

 6 See Bob Stewart, *Breaking the Fetters: the memoirs of Bob Stewart*, London, 1967, pp. 25, 48.

 7 This antipathy pre-dated the industrial revolution and was shared by leading figures of the Scottish Enlightenment, including Adam Smith, who railed against those people 'of the same trade' who seldom met together, 'even for merriment and diversion, but the conversation ends in a conspiracy against the public, or in some contrivance to raise prices.' See Adam Smith, *The Wealth of Nations*, Harmondsworth, 1986, p. 232.

 8 D. H. Buchanan, *Capitalistic Enterprise in India*, London, 1996, p. 430.

 9 Ibid.

10 *Textile Workers' Guide* (no. 2), April 1916.

11 This quote was used by William Walker to describe the short period 'which had begun in the last year of the war, and the failure of the [1923] strike ended that age for ever'. See William Walker, *Juteopolis: Dundee and its textile workers, 1885–192*, Dundee, 1979, p. 486.

12 Even at the height of their power, the combined membership of the main French trade union federations encompassed only 20 per cent of the working population in 1978. See Durand Dubois and Seguin Erbes, 'The Contradictions of French Trade Unionism', p. 72, in Colin Crouch and Alessandro Pizzorno, *The Resurgence of Class Conflict in Western Europe Since 1968*, vol. 1, Basingstoke, 1978, pp. 53–100.

13 The long-standing criticism of working mothers by the Church of Scotland originated with what visiting investigators witnessed in the city during the late nineteenth century. See Kenneth M. Boyd, *Scottish Attitudes to Sex, Marriage and the Family 1850–1914*, Edinburgh, 1980, p. 164.

14 See Eleanor Gordon, *Women and the Labour Movement in Scotland, 1850–1914*, Oxford, 1991, pp. 285–286.

15 See Samita Sen, *Women and Labour in Late Colonial India: the Bengal jute industry*, See also Leela Fernandez, *Producing Workers: the politics of gender, class, and culture in the Calcutta jute mills*, Philadelphia, 1997.

16 See Samita Sen, op. cit., pp. 209–212, especially, p. 210. 'Young women, especially very young women, seem to have been targeted for rape and abduction. Older women too were subjected to physical harassment by the men with whom they lived, local toughs and the police in mill neighbourhoods and *bazars*.... They [the female jute workers] may have sought physical and economic protection in relatively stable and long-term marriages. However, they remained at the unequal end of these relationships.'

17 The great rallying call of Indian nationalism, 'Bande Mataram', or 'I bow to thee Mother', written by the Bengali poet Bankim Chattopadhyah, was a potent symbol of the close association forged between the notion of the Indian feminine ideal and Indian nationalism.

Bibliography

Government records

West Bengal State Archives, Calcutta

Commerce Department Commerce Branch.
Commerce Department Labour Branch.
General Department Miscellaneous Branch.
General Proceedings.
Home Department (Confidential) Police Branch.
Home Department (Confidential) Political Branch.
Political Department Police Branch.

Office of the Deputy Commissioner, Special Branch, Home (Police) Department, Government of West Bengal, Lord Sinha Road, Calcutta

Confidential Records.

Delhi, National Archives of India

Home Department Political Branch.

London, India Office Library

Judicial Department.
Overseas and Industries Department.

Private papers

Asiatic Society, Calcutta

Comintern Papers.

Centre of Social Sciences, Calcutta

Meerut Conspiracy Proceedings.

Centre of South Asian Studies, Cambridge

Benthall Papers.
Holland Papers.

City of Dundee Archives

Records of the Corporation of Dundee.
Dundee Chamber of Commerce Papers.
Dundee and District Jute and Flax Workers' Union Papers.
James A. Scott Ltd, Calcutta Correspondence Papers.

Dundee Central Library

Dundee Directory (various years covering 1875–1939).
Dundee Oral History Project Transcripts.
Lamb Collection, consisting of reports of societies, institutions and newspaper cuttings.
Obituary notices.
Edwin Scrymgeour Papers.

Dundee University Archives

Association of Jute Spinners and Manufacturers Papers.
Baxter Brothers Records.
Personal and business papers of Peter Carmichael of Arthurstone.
Cox Brothers Ltd Papers.
Records of Don Brothers, Buist & Co.
Thomas Duff & Co. Papers.
A. & S. Henry & Co. Papers.
James F. Low & Co. Ltd Papers.
Low and Bonar Ltd Papers.
Records of Victoria Spinning Co. Ltd.

IJMA Library, Calcutta

Circular Files, 1931–50.

India Office Library, London

Linlithgow Papers.
Lothian Papers.
Zetland Collection.

London School of Economics

Dingle Foot Papers.
E. D. Morel Papers.

National Library of Scotland, Edinburgh

Personal and family papers of George Dott.
Tom Johnston Papers.

National Library of Ireland, Dublin

James Connolly Papers.

National Museum of Labour History, Manchester

Records of Dundee Communist Party.

Nehru Memorial Museum and Library, New Delhi

A. C. Banerjee Papers.
All India Congress Committee Papers.
B. C. Roy Papers.
N. M. Joshi Papers.
Purshomttamdas Thakurdas Papers.
Transcript of Interview with Parabhabati Das Gupta.
Transcript of Interview with Sibnath Banerjee.

University of Warwick Archives

Records of British Trades Union Congress.

West Yorkshire Library and Archives, Leeds

Records of Fairbairn, Lawson, Combe and Barbour & Co. Ltd.

Reports and gazeteers

Annual Report on the Administration of the Bengal Presidency (for various years).
Annual Report of the Association of Jute Spinners and Manufacturers, Dundee (1918–40).
Annual Report of the Bengal Chamber of Commerce (for various years).
Annual Report of the Chief Inspector of Factories and Workshops, London (1910–39).
Annual Report of the IJMA, Calcutta (1910–50).
Annual Report on the Operation of the Factories Act in Bengal, Calcutta (1910–40).
Annual Report on the Police Administration of the Town of Calcutta and its Suburbs, Calcutta, 1923.

S. G. Barker, *Report on the Scientific and Technical Development of the Jute Manufacturing Industry in Bengal*, Calcutta, 1935.

Bengal Unemployment Enquiry Committee, 1922–24, Calcutta, 1925.

Board of Trade, Labour Department, *Annual Reports on Strikes and Lockouts in the United Kingdom*, London (1888–1914).

Census of India 1911, vol. v, Calcutta, 1923.

Census of India 1921, vol. v, parts 1 and 2, Calcutta, 1923.

Census of Scotland (1851–1931).

City & Royal Burgh of Dundee, Licensing (Scotland) Act, 1903, Notices from 10 April 1905 to January 1906.

A. C. Roy Chowdhury, *Report on an Enquiry into the Standard of Living of Jute Mill Workers in Bengal*, Calcutta, 1930.

Committee on Industry and Trade, *Factors in Industrial Efficiency and Commercial Efficiency: Being Part I of a Survey of Industries*, London, 1927.

Committee on Industry and Trade, *Survey of Textile Industries*, London, 1928.

Committee of Inquiry into Industrial Unrest, *Reports from Commissioners*, vol. xii, 1917–18, No. 8 Division, Scotland.

Committee on Production, *Arbitration Proceedings between the Scottish Council of Textile Trades and Various Firms and Associations*, Glasgow, 1917.

S. R. Deshpande, *Report of an Enquiry into the Family Budgets of Industrial workers in Howrah and Bally*, Delhi, 1946.

Dundee Corporation, *Dundee Public Health Report* (various years).

Dundee Social Union, *Report on Housing and Industrial Conditions in Dundee*, Dundee, 1905.

B. Foley, *Report on Labour in Bengal*, Calcutta, 1906.

S. H. Freemantle, *Report on the Supply of Labour in the United Provinces and in Bengal*, Delhi, 1906.

E. Gait, C. G. H. Allen and H. F. Howard, *Imperial Gazetteer of India: Bengal*, New Delhi (n.d., probably 1910 or 1911), reprinted in 1984.

Sir William Wilson Hunter, *The Imperial Gazetteer of India*, London, 1887.

Indian Central Jute Committee, *Report on the Marketing of Jute and Jute Products*, Calcutta, 1941.

Indian Factory Labour Commission, London, 1908.

Jute Industry Tribunal Report, Calcutta, 1947.

Jute Trade Board, *Working Party Report*, London, 1948.

H. C. Kerr, *Cultivation of and the Trade in Jute in Bengal: The Bengal Jute Commission*, Calcutta, 1874.

Ministry of Labour, *Reports of Commissioners*, London, 1926.

L.S.S. O'Malley, *24 Parganas District Gazetteer*, Calcutta, 1914, p. 83.

Report of the Bengal Jute Enquiry Committee (Finlow Committee), Alipore, 1934.

Report of the Bengal Jute Enquiry Committee (Fawcus Committee), Alipore, 1939.

Report of the Committee to Enquire into the Circumstances Connected with the Alleged Recent Increases in the Rental of Small Dwelling houses in Industrial Districts in Scotland, London, 1915.

Report of the Committee on Industrial Unrest, Calcutta, 1921.

Report of the Departmental Commission Appointed to Consider the Position of the Textile Trades after the War, London, 1918.

Report of the Jute Enquiry Commission (Aiyangar Commission), Delhi, 1954.

Report of the Royal Commission on Labour in India, London, 1931, vols i, v, and xi.

Report of the Royal Commission on Poor Laws and Relief of Distress (Scotland) 1909, vol. xxiii.
Report of the [Indian] *Textile Factories Labour Commission*, London, 1907.
Return of the Rate of Wages in the Minor Textile Trades of the United Kingdom, London, 1890.
Review of the Trade of India (Annual), Delhi, 1917–40.
Royal Commission on Labour, *Final Report*, London, 1894.

Interviews

Saroj Bandophadhyay, Shyamnagar, 10 April 1996.
A. R. Chaudhuri, 12 June 1996.
S. K. Basu and N. S. Basu, Calcutta, 21 June 1996.
S. C. Roy, Calcutta, 2 August 1996.
I. L. Tripathi, Budge-Budge, 6 and 12 August 1996.
Doug Crockatt, Arbroath, 21 August 1996.
Mrs Ralph Morrison, Fife, 28 August 1996.
Alex Scott, Broughty Ferry, 13 September and 3 October 1996.
Jim Balfour, Carnoustie, 13 September 1996.
Alistair Martin, Arbroath, 24 September 1996.
Alfred Tosh, Fife, 25 September 1996.
Betty Taylor, Arbroath, 20 February 1997.
Ranen Sen, Salt Lake, Calcutta, 21 April 1998.
Tom Clarke, Dundee, 10 October 1998.
Charlie McCusker, Dundee, 11 October 1998.
Norman Barrie, Dundee, 11 October 1998.

Newspapers and journals

Amrita Bazar Patrika
Arbroath Guide
Arbroath Herald
Bulletin of Indian Industries and Labour
Capital
City Echo
Congress Socialist
Daily Herald
Daily Record and Mail
Daily Worker
Dundee Advertiser
Dundee Courier
Evening Telegraph
Forward (India)
Forward (Scotland)
Ganavani
International Press Correspondence
Jute and Canvas Review
Labour Monthly

Langal
Peoples Journal
Textile Workers Guide
Thackers Yearbook
The Communist
The Dundee Year Book
The Eastern Economist
The Jute and Flax Workers' Guide
The New Age
The Piper O' Dundee
The Prohibitionist
The Statesman
The Times
The Times of India
Times of India Yearbook
Tocsin

Select bibliography of books, pamphlets and theses

Nathan Abrams, *Caledonian Jews: a study of seven small communities in Scotland*, Jefferson, 2009.

G. Adhikari (ed.), *Documents of the History of the Communist Party of India: vol. 2, 1923–5*, New Delhi, 1982.

Mohiuddin Ahmad, *Essentials of Colloquial Hindustani for Jute Mills and Workshops*, Calcutta, 1947.

W. Allison and J. Fairley, *Toplis: the monocled mutineer*, London, 1979.

Clare Anderson, '*Godna*: Inscribing Indian Convicts in the Nineteenth Century', in Jane Cuplan, *Written on the Body: the tattoo in European and American History*, London, 2000, pp. 102–18.

Geoff Andrews, Nina Fishman and Kevin Morgan (eds), *Opening the Books: essays on the cultural history of the British Communist Party*, London, 1995.

Vera Anstey, *The Economic Development of India*, London, 1939.

Mike Arnott, 'A History of Dundee Trades Union Council: the Victorian era', unpublished manuscript draft (n.d.).

A. Z. M. Iftikhar-ul-Awwal, *The Industrial Development of Bengal, 1900–1939*, New Delhi, 1982.

Amiya Bagchi, *Private Investment in India, 1900–1939*, New Delhi, 1972.

Amiya Bagchi, *The Evolution of the State Bank of India*, vol. ii, New Delhi, 1997.

Amiya Bagchi, *Capital and Labour Redefined: India and the Third World*, New Delhi, 2002.

Jonathan Bardon, *A History of Ulster*, Belfast, 1992.

Michelle Barrett, *Women's Oppression Today*, London, 1980.

J. Basu, *Documents of the Communist Movement in India*, vols i–vi, Calcutta, 1993.

Nirban Basu, *The Working Class Movement: a study of jute mills of Bengal, 1937–1947*, Calcutta, 1994.

Subho Basu, *Does Class Matter? Colonial capital and workers' resistance in Bengal, 1890–1937*, New Delhi, 2004.

Subho Basu, 'The Paradox of the Peasant Worker: re-conceptualizing workers' politics in Bengal 1890–1939', in *Modern Asian Studies*, 42, 1, 2008, pp. 47–74.

Crispin Bates, *Subalterns and the Raj: South Asia since 1600*, London, 2007.

Kenneth Baxter and William Kenefick, 'Labour Politics and the Dundee Working Class *c*.1895–1936', in Jim Tomlinson and Christopher A. Whatley (eds), *Jute No More: Transforming Dundee*, Dundee, 2011, pp. 191–220.

J. R. Benvie, *A Benvie Chronicle*, Dundee, 1998.

Suzanne Berger and Michael J. Piore, *Dualism and Discontinuity in Industrial Societies*, Cambridge, 1980.

Sugata Bose, *Peasant Labour and Colonial Capital: rural Bengal since 1770*, New Delhi, 1993.

Sugata Bose and Ayesha Jalal, *Modern South Asia*, Padstow, 1999.

Dave Bowman, *Future of Jute*, Dundee, 1945.

Kenneth M. Boyd, *Scottish Church Attitudes to Sex, Marriage and the Family, 1850–1914*, Edinburgh, 1980.

Noreen Branson, *History of the Communist Party of Great Britain, 1927–1941*, London, 1985.

Anthony Brewer, *Marxist Theories of Imperialism: a critical survey*, London, 1989.

D. Bremner, *Industries of Scotland: their rise, progress and present condition*, Edinburgh, 1869.

E. Cobham Brewer, *The Dictionary of Phrase and Fable*, New York, 1978.

British Association, *Handbook and Guide to Dundee and District*, Dundee, 1912.

British Association, *Scientific Survey of Dundee and District*, London, 1939.

Mary Brooksbank, *No Sae Lang Syne: a tale of this city*, Dundee, 1971.

Mary Brooksbank, *Sidlaw Breezes*, Dundee, 1991.

Callum Brown, *Religion and Society in Scotland since 1701*, Edinburgh, 1997.

D. H. Buchanan, *Capitalistic Enterprise in India*, New York, 1934.

A. A. Bulley and M. Whitley, *Women's Work*, London, 1894.

Bob Burrows, *Fighter Writer: the eventful life of Sergeant Joe Lee, Scotland's forgotten war poet*, Derby, 2004.

John Callaghan, *Rajani Palme Dutt: a study in British Stalinism*, London, 1993.

Angus Calder, *The People's War: Britain 1939–1945*, London, 1999.

David Cannadine, *Ornamentalism: how the British saw their Empire*, New York, 2001.

R. H. Campbell and J. B. A. Dow (eds), *Source Book of Scottish Economic and Social History*, Oxford, 1968.

Jane Caplan (ed.), *Written on the Body: the tattoo in European and American history*, London, 2000.

Peter Carmichael, *Reminiscences*, Dundee, 1880.

Dipesh Chakrabarty, *Rethinking Working-Class History: Bengal 1890–1940*, Princeton, 1989.

Dipesh Chakrabarty, *Provincializing Europe*, Princeton, 2000.

Dipesh Chakrabarty and Ranajit Das Gupta, 'Some Aspects of Labour History in Bengal in the Nineteenth Century: two views', *Occasional Paper No. 40*, Centre for Studies in Social Sciences, Calcutta, 1981.

Raymond Challinor, *The Origins of British Bolshevism*, London, 1979.

Rajnarayan Chandavarkar, *The Origins of Industrial Capitalism in India: business strategies and the working classes in Bombay, 1900–1940*, Cambridge, 1994.

Rajnarayan Chandavarkar, 'The Making of the Working Class: E. P. Thompson and Indian history', *History Workshop Journal*, 43, 1997, pp. 177–96.

Malcolm Chase, *Chartism: a new history*, Manchester, 2007.

Basudev Chatterji, *Trade, Tariffs and Empire: Lancashire and British policy in India, 1919–1939*, Delhi, 1992.

Gautum Chattopadhyay, *Communism in Bengal*, New Delhi, 1970.

Haraprasad Chattopadhyay, *Internal Migration in India: a case study of Bengal*, Calcutta, 1987.

A. K. Chaudhuri, *Socialist Movement in India: the Congress Socialist Party 1934–1947*, Calcutta, 1980.

Niraud C. Chaudhuri, *Thy Hand Great Anarch: India 1921–1951*, London, 1987.

Olive and Sydney Checkland, *Industry and Ethos: Scotland 1832–1914*, Edinburgh, 1989.

Carl Chinn, *They Worked All Their Lives: women of the urban poor in England*, Manchester, 1988.

A. G. Clow, *State and Industry*, New Delhi, 1928.

G. A. Cohen, *Karl Marx's Theory of History: a defence*, Oxford, 2000.

Norman Cohn, *The Pursuit of the Millennium: revolutionary millenarians and mystical anarchists of the middle ages*, London, 1957.

G. D. H. Cole, *Labour in War Time*, London, 1915.

Linda Colley, *Britons: forging the nation, 1707–1837*, London, 1996.

H. Collins and C. Abramsky, *Karl Marx and the British Labour Movement*, London, 1965.

Patricia Collins, 'Brothers Under the Sun: British trade unions and the Indian labour movement in the inter-war period', in *Scottish Labour History*, 28, 1993, pp. 30–47.

Anthony Cox, 'Rationalisation and Resistance: the imperial jute industries of Dundee and Calcutta, 1930–1940', Fellowship Dissertation, Trinity College, Cambridge, 1997.

Anthony Cox, 'Paternal Despotism and Workers' Resistance in the Bengal Jute Industry, 1920–1940', unpublished Ph.D. thesis, University of Cambridge, 1999.

William Crooke (ed.) *Hobson-Jobson: a glossary of colloquial Anglo-Indian words and phrases*, New Delhi, 1994.

Colin Crouch and Alessandro Pizzorno, *The Resurgence of Class Conflict in Western Europe Since 1968*, vol. 1, Basingstoke, 1978.

Suranjan Das, *Communal Riots in Bengal, 1905–1947*, Delhi, 1991.

A. K. Das Gupta, 'Jute Industry: How it Works', in *Textile India*, 1953.

Ranajit Das Gupta, *Labour and Working Class in Eastern India: studies in colonial history*, Calcutta, 1994.

Sobhanlal Datta Gupta, *Comintern, India and the Colonial Question, 1920–37*, Calcutta, 1980.

Mike Davis, *Late Victorian Holocausts: El Nino famines and the making of the Third World*, London, 2001.

Phyllis Dean and W. A. Cole, *British Economic Growth 1688–1959*, Cambridge, 1967.

Tom Devine (ed.), *Irish Immigrants and Scottish Society in the Nineteenth and Twentieth Centuries: proceedings of the Scottish Historical Studies conference, University of Strathclyde, 1989/90*, Edinburgh, 1991.

Tom Devine, *The Scottish Nation, 1700–2000*, London, 2000.

A. Dickson and J. H. Treble, *People and Society in Scotland*, vol. iii, Edinburgh, 1992.

William Dodd, *The Labouring Classes of England: especially those concerned in agriculture and manufactures*, Fairfield, 1976.

Ian Donnachie, Christopher Harvie and Ian S. Wood (eds), *Forward! Labour politics in Scotland 1888–1988*, Edinburgh, 1989.

Dundee Oral History Committee, Barrasie Court History Group, *Work or Want*, Dundee (n.d.).

Walter Duncan and Goodricke Ltd, *The Duncan Group: being a short history of Duncan*

Brothers & Co. Ltd, Calcutta and Walter Duncan & Goodricke Ltd, London 1859–1959, London, 1959.

Rajani Palme Dutt, *India Today*, Calcutta, 1992.

Michael Dyer, *Capable Citizens and Improvident Democrats: the Scottish electoral system, 1884–1929*, Aberdeen, 1996.

The Encyclopaedia Britannica, New York, 1911, vols xv and xvi.

Frederick Engels, *Condition of the Working Class in England in 1844*, London, 1936.

Niall Ferguson, *The Pity of War*, London, 1998.

Thomas Ferguson, *Scottish Welfare, 1864–1914*, Edinburgh, 1958.

Leela Fernandez, *Producing Workers: the politics of gender, class, and culture in the Calcutta jute mills*, Philadelphia, 1997.

Nina Fishman, *The British Communist Party and the Trade Unions, 1933–1945*, Aldershot, 1995.

John Foster, *Class Struggle and the Industrial Revolution: early industrial capitalism in three English towns*, London, 1974.

Eugenie Fraser, *A Home by the Hooghly: a jute wallah's wife*, Edinburgh, 1994.

James E. Fraser, *From Caledonia to Pictland: Scotland to 795*, Edinburgh, 2009.

W. Hamish Fraser, *Chartism in Scotland*, Pontypool, 2010.

Edmund and Ruth Frow, *The Half Time System in Education*, Manchester, 1970.

Michael Fry, *The Dundas Despotism*, Edinburgh, 1992.

Russell Galbraith, *Without Quarter: a biography of Tom Johnston*, Edinburgh, 1995.

Nigel Gatherer, *Songs and Ballads of Dundee*, Edinburgh, 2000.

Enid Gauldie (ed.), *The Dundee Textile Industry, 1790–1885: from the papers of Peter Carmichael of Arthurstone*, Edinburgh, 1969.

Pramita Ghose, *Meerut Conspiracy Case and the Left-Wing in India*, Calcutta, 1978.

Parimal Ghosh, *Colonialism, Class and a History of the Calcutta Jute Millhands, 1880–1930*, Hyderabad, 2000.

John Gilbert, *A History of Investment Trusts in Dundee, 1873–1938*, London, 1939.

Martin Gilbert, *Winston S. Churchill*, vol. iv, London, 1975.

R. N. Gilchrist, *Labour and the Land*, Calcutta, 1932.

Eleanor Gordon, *Women and the Labour Movement in Scotland, 1850–1914*, Oxford, 1991.

Omkar Goswami, *Industry, Trade and Peasant Society: the jute economy of eastern India, 1900–1947*, Delhi, 1991.

Oliver Graham, 'The Dundee Jute Industry, 1828–1928', Ph.D. thesis, St Andrews University, 1928.

G. Desmond Greaves, *The Life and Times of James Connolly*, London, 1976.

Ranajit Guha, *Elementary Aspects of Peasant Insurgency in Colonial India*, New Delhi, 1992.

Indrajit Gupta, *Capital and Labour*, Calcutta, 1953.

Partha Sarathi Gupta, *Imperialism and the British Labour Movement, 1914–1964*, London, 1975.

Arjan De Haan, *Unsettled Settlers: migrant workers and industrial capitalism in Calcutta*, Rotterdman, 1994.

Irfan Habib, *The Agrarian System of Mughal India, 1556–1707*, New Delhi, 1999.

Henry Hamilton, *The Industrial Revolution in Scotland*, Oxford, 1932.

Mary Agnes Hamilton, *Mary MacArthur: a biographical sketch*, London, 1925.

C. Hardwick, *Time Study in Treason: Charles E Bedaux, patriot or collaborator*, Chelmsford (n.d.).

H. Henderson, 'Religious Life', in J. M. Jackson (ed.), *The Third Statistical Account of Dundee: the City of Dundee*, Arbroath, 1979, pp. 632–77.

Eric Hobsbawm, *Labouring Men: studies in the history of labour*, London, 1976.

Eric Hobsbawm, *Primitive Rebels: studies in archaic forms of social movements in the 19th and 20th centuries*, Manchester, 1978.

J. A. Hobson, *Imperialism: a study*, London, 1988.

Stephen Howe, *Anti-colonialism in British Politics: the left and the end of Empire, 1918–1964*, Oxford, 1993.

John Hume (ed.), *Early Days in a Dundee Mill, 1819–1823*, Dundee, 1980.

Stephen Humphries, *Hooligans or Rebels? An oral history of working-class youth, 1889–1939*, Oxford, 1995.

Chris Hunt (ed.), *William McGonagall: collected poems*, Edinburgh, 2006.

G. Jackson and K. Kinnear, *The Trade and Shipping of Dundee, 1780–1850*, Dundee, 1991.

J. M. Jackson (ed.), *The Third Statistical Account of Scotland: the city of Dundee*, Arbroath, 1979.

C. L. R. James, *World Revolution 1917–1936: the rise and fall of the Communist International*, New Jersey, 1993.

David J. Jeremy, 'Lancashire and the International Diffusion of Technology', in Mary B. Rose (ed.), *The Lancashire Cotton Industry: a history since 1700*, Preston, 1996, pp. 210–38.

Tom Johnston, *Memories*, London, 1952.

Tom Johnston, *The History of the Working Class in Scotland*, Wakefield, 1974.

Tom Johnston and John Sime, *Exploitation in India*, Dundee, 1926.

John Johnstone (ed.), *Jamieson's Dictionary of the Scottish Language*, Edinburgh, 1846.

David T. Jones, Joseph F. Duncan, H. M. Conacher and W. R. Scott (eds), *Rural Scotland During the War*, Oxford, 1926.

Stephanie Jones, *Merchants of the Raj: British managing agency houses in Calcutta yesterday and today*, Basingstoke, 1992.

S. J. Jones (ed.), *Dundee and District*, Dundee, 1968.

Ira Katznelson and Aristide R. Zolberg, *Working Class Formation: nineteenth century patterns in Western Europe and the United States*, Princeton, 1986.

J. H. Kelman, *Labour in India*, London, 1924.

John D. Kemp, 'Drink and the Labour Movement in Early Twentieth Century Scotland: with particular reference to Edwin Scrymgeour and the Scottish Prohibitionist Party', unpublished Ph.D. thesis, University of Dundee, 2000.

Tom Kemp, *Historical Patterns of Industrialisation*, Harlow, 1993.

Liam Kennedy and Phillip Ollerenshaw, *An Economic History of Ulster, 1820–1939*, Manchester, 1985.

William Kennefick, *Red Scotland! The rise and fall of the radical left, c.1872 to 1932*, Edinburgh, 2007.

Victor Kiernan/Harvey J. Kaye (ed.) *Imperialism and its Contradictions*, London, 1995.

Rudyard Kipling, *The Jungle Book and Other Stories*, London, 1924.

Neville Kirk, *Change, Continuity and Class: labour in British society, 1850–1920*, Manchester, 1998.

Blair B. Kling, *The Blue Mutiny: the indigo disturbances in Bengal 1859–1862*, Philadelphia, 1966.

James Klugman, *History of the Communist Party of Great Britain: formation and early years, 1919–1924*, Southampton, 1968.

W. W. Knox, *Hanging by a Thread: the Scottish cotton industry, c.1850–1914*, Preston, 1995.

W. W. Knox, *Industrial Nation: work, culture and society in Scotland, 1800–present*, Edinburgh, 1999.

J. C. Kydd, *A History of Factory Legislation in India*, Calcutta, 1920.

Lloyd and Jenny Laing, *The Picts and the Scots*, Stroud, 2001.

Leah Leneman, 'Dundee and the Women's Suffrage Movement: 1907–1914', in Christopher A. Whatley (ed.), *The Remaking of Juteopolis, Dundee circa 1891–1991*, Dundee, 1992, pp. 80–96.

Sir John Leng, *Letters from India and Ceylon including the Manchester of India, the Indian Dundee and the Calcutta Jute Mills*, Dundee, 1896.

V. I. Lenin, *Imperialism: the highest stage of capitalism*, Peking, 1975.

V. I. Lenin, *Left Wing Communism: an infantile disorder*, London, 1920.

V. I. Lenin, *Predictions on the Revolutionary Storms in the East*, Peking, 1970.

Bruce Lenman, *An Economic History of Modern Scotland*, Hamden, 1977.

Bruce Lenman and Enid Gauldie, 'The Industrial History of the Dundee Region from the Eighteenth Century to the Early Twentieth Century', in S. J. Jones (ed.), *Dundee and District*, Dundee, 1968, pp. 162–74.

Bruce Lenman, Charlotte Lythe and Enid Gauldie, *Dundee and its Textile Industry, 1850–1914*, Dundee, 1969.

Bruce Lenman and Kathleen Donaldson, 'Partners' Incomes, Investment and Diversification in the Scottish Linen Area, 1850–1914', p. 3, in *Business History* (13–14), 1971–2, pp. 1–18.

David Lennox, 'Working Class Life in Dundee, 1878–1905', unpublished Ph.D. thesis, St Andrews University (n.d., prob. 1906).

David Lennox, 'The Evolution of Race in Forfarshire', in British Association, *Handbook and Guide to Dundee and District*, Dundee 1912.

Tom Leonard, *Places of the Mind: the life and work of James Thomson*, London, 1993.

Ian Levitt, *Poverty and Welfare in Scotland 1890–1948*, Edinburgh, 1988.

Marcel Liebman, *Leninism under Lenin*, London, 1985.

Craig Littler, *The Development of the Labour Process in Capitalist Societies*, London, 1982.

Bruce Lockhart, *My Scottish Youth*, Glasgow, 1937.

P. S. Lokanathan, *Industrial Organisation in India*, London, 1935.

Domenico Losurdo, *Liberalism: A Counter History*, London, 2011.

David Lowe, *Souvenirs of Scottish Labour*, Glasgow, 1919.

Hugh MacDiarmid, 'Dundee', in Lewis Grassic Gibbon and Hugh MacDiarmid, *Scottish Scene*, London, 1934, pp. 189–94.

C. M. M. MacDonald, *The Radical Thread: political change in Scotland. Paisley politics, 1885–1924*, East Linton, 2000.

Stuart Macintyre, *A Proletarian Science: Marxism in Britain, 1917–1933*, London, 1986.

N. McKendrick and J. Newlands, *'F&C': a history of the Foreign and Colonial Investment Trust*, London, 1999.

Andrew MacKillop, 'Dundee, London, and the Empire in Asia', in C. McKean, B. Harris and C. Whatley, *Dundee: Renaissance to Enlightenment*, Dundee, 2009, pp. 160–86.

Claude Markovitz, *Indian Business and Nationalist Politics, 1931–39: the indigenous capitalist class and the rise of the Congress Party*, Cambridge, 1985.

Roderick Martin, *Communism and the British Trade Unions 1924–1933: a study of the National Minority Movement*, Oxford, 1969.

W. H. Marwick, *Economic Development in Victorian Scotland*, New York, 1973.

N. Mazumdar, *In Search of a Revolutionary Ideology*, Calcutta, 1979.

John Stuart Mill, *Principles of Political Economy*, Boston, 1848.

Martin J. Mitchell (ed.), *New Perspectives on the Irish in Scotland*, Edinburgh, 2008.

Morris D. Morris, 'The Growth of Large-Scale Industry to 1947', in D. Kumar and M. Desai, *The Cambridge Economic History of India*, vol. 2: c. 1757–1970, Cambridge, 1989, pp. 553–677.

H. V. Morton, *In Search of Scotland*, London, 1939.

Arun Mukherjee, *Crime and Public Disorder in Colonial Bengal*, Calcutta, 1995.

Ashoke Kumar Mukhophadhyay (ed.), *India and Communism: secret British documents*, Calcutta, 1997.

James Myles, *Rambles in Forfarshire*, Dundee, 1850.

Timothy Neat, *Hamish Henderson: poetry becomes people, 1952–2002*, Edinburgh, 2009.

Jawaharlal Nehru, *The Discovery of India*, New Delhi, 1995.

J. Newlands, *Put Not Your Trust in Money: a history of the investment trust industry from 1868 to the present day*, London, 1997.

D.H. Nicoll, *Character Sketches: modern trade battles, ten years conflict and Mrs Jute-burgh*, Dundee (n.d.).

Andrew Noble and Patrick Scott Hogg (eds), *The Canongate Burns: the complete poems and songs of Robert Burns*, Edinburgh, 2001.

William Norrie, *The Life of James Scrymgeour*, Dundee, 1887.

C.A. Oakley (ed.), *Scottish Industry*, HMSO, 1953.

Gyan Pandey, *The Construction of Communalism in India*, Delhi, 1990.

Alexander Pantsov, *The Bolsheviks and the Chinese Revolution, 1919–1927*, Richmond, 2000.

T. Paterson, *Churchill: a seat for life*, Dundee, 1980.

Ann Petrie, *The 1915 Rent Strike: an east coast perspective*, Dundee, 2008.

David Petrie (ed.), *Communism in India, 1924–27*, Calcutta, 1972.

David Phillips, *Hud Yor Tongue! Further writings in the Dundee dialect*, Arbroath, 1964.

David Phillips, *The Hungry Thirties: Dundee between the wars*, Dundee, 1981.

David Phillips, *Lichty Nichts Omnibus*, Dundee, 1981.

Michael Piore, *Birds of Passage: migrant labor and industrial societies*, Cambridge, 2008.

Karl Polanyi, *The Great Transformation: the political and economic origins of our time*, London, 1957.

Sidney Pollard, *The Development of the British Economy, 1914–1990*, Sevenoaks, 1992.

Bernard Porter, *The Absent-Minded Imperialists: empire, society, and culture in Britain*, Oxford, 2006.

S. D. Punekar and R Varickayil (eds), *Labour Movement in India, Documents: 1891–1917*, vol. ii: Factories, New Delhi, 1990.

A. A. Purcell and J. Hallsworth, *Report on Labour Conditions in India*, London, 1927.

Sibnarayan Ray (ed.), *The Selected Works of M. N. Roy* (3 volumes), Oxford, 1987.

Tim Rees and Andrew Thorpe (eds), *International Communism and the Communist International, 1919–43*, Manchester, 1998.

Gary Robertson, *Pure Dundee*, Glasgow, 2007.

James Rollo, *A Century's Record of Ecclesiastical Life in Dundee*, Dundee, 1902.

Mary B. Rose (ed.), *The Lancashire Cotton Industry: a history since 1700*, Preston, 1996.

B. S. Rowntree, *Poverty: a study of town life*, London, 1902.

Subodh Roy (ed.), *Communism in India: unpublished documents, 1919–1924*, Calcutta, 1994.

Tirthankar Roy, 'Sardars, Jobbers, Kanaganies: the labour contractor and Indian economic history', in *Modern Asian Studies*, 42, 5, 2008, pp. 971–98.

Trevor Royle, *The Black Watch: a concise history*, Edinburgh, 2006.

Trevor Royle, *The Flowers of the Forest: Scotland and the First World War*, Edinburgh, 2007.

R. S. Rungta, *Rise of Business Corporations in India, 1851–1900*, Cambridge, 1970.

Charles Sabel, *Work and Politics: the division of labor in industry*, Cambridge, 1989.

Panchanana Saha, *History of Working Class Movement in Bengal*, New Delhi, 1978.

Edward W. Said, *Orientalism*, London, 1978.

Sumit Sarkar, *Modern India, 1885–1947*, London, 1989.

Sumit Sarkar, *The Swadeshi Movement: 1903–1908*, New Delhi, 1994.

Sumit Sarkar, *Writing Social History*, New Delhi, 1997.

Tanika Sarkar, *Bengal 1928–1934: the politics of protest*, Delhi, 1987.

L. J. Saunders, *Scottish Democracy, 1815–1840: the social and intellectual background*, London, 1950.

S. B. Saul, *The Myth of the Great Depression, 1873–1896*, Tiptree, 1972.

Michael Savage, *The Dynamics of Working-Class Politics: the labour movement in Preston, 1880–1914*, Cambridge, 1987.

M. Savage and A. Miles, *The Remaking of the British Working Class, 1840–1940*, London, 1994.

Anil Seal, *The Emergence of Indian Nationalism: competition and collaboration in the later nineteenth century*, Cambridge, 1968.

Samita Sen, *Women and Labour in Colonial India: the Bengal jute industry*, Cambridge, 1999.

S. N. Sen and T. Piplai, *Industrial Relations in the Jute Industry in West Bengal (A Case Study)*, Calcutta, 1968.

Tom Shaw, *Report of Investigations into the Conditions of Indian Textile Workers*, Ashton-under-Lyme, 1927.

Marika Sherwood, 'Krishna Menon, Parliamentary Labour Party Candidate for Dundee, 1939–40', in *Scottish Labour History*, vol. 42, 2007.

H. A. Silverman (ed.), *Studies in Industrial Organisation*, London, 1946.

Sir John Sinclair, *The Statistical Account of Scotland, 1791–99*, vol. xiii, Angus, Wakefield, 1976.

Moni Singh, *Life is a Struggle*, New Delhi, 1988.

N. K. Sinha, 'Indian Business Enterprise: its failure in Calcutta, 1800–1848', in *Bengal Past and Present*, Diamond Jubilee Number, 1967.

Adam Smith, *The Wealth of Nations*, Harmondsworth, 1986.

B. Smith, *Robert Fleming 1845–1933*, Haddington, 2000.

Graham Smith, 'The Making of a Woman's Town: household and gender in Dundee, 1890–1940', unpublished Ph.D. thesis, University of Stirling, 1996.

Mike Squires, *Saklatvala: a political biography*, London, 1990.

Gareth Stedman Jones, *Languages of Class: studies in English working class history, 1832–1982*, Cambridge, 1983.

Bob Stewart, *Breaking the Fetters: the memoirs of Bob Stewart*, London, 1967.

Gordon Stewart, *Jute and Empire: the Calcutta jute wallahs and the landscapes of Empire*, Manchester, 1998.

Sharon Stichter, *Migrant Laborers*, Cambridge, 1985.

Roger Stuart, 'The Formation of the Communist Party of India, 1927–1937: the dilemma of the Indian left', unpublished Ph.D. thesis, Australian National University, 1978.

Andrew Thompson, *The Empire Strikes Back? The impact of imperialism on Britain from the mid-nineteenth century*, Harlow, 2005.

Jim Tomlinson and Christopher A. Whatley (eds), *Jute No More: transforming Dundee*, Dundee, 2011.

T. A. Timberg, *The Marwaris*, New Delhi, 1978.

Mark Thomson, *Bard fae thi Building Site*, Edinburgh, 2007.

B. R. Tomlinson, *The Economy of Modern India, 1860–1970*, Cambridge, 1993.

Trades Union Congress, *The Bedaux Report*, London, 1933.

Amales Tripathi, 'Indo-British Trade between 1833 and 1847 and the Commercial Crisis of 1847–8', p. 288, in A Siddiqi (ed.), *Trade and Finance in Colonial India, 1750–1860*, Delhi, 1995, pp. 265–90.

C. M. Turnbull, *A History of Singapore, 1819–1988*, Oxford, 1992.

W. H. K. Turner, 'The Evolution of the Pattern of the Textile Industry within Dundee', in *Transactions of the Institute of British Geographers*, 1952.

Emma Wainwright, 'Gender, Space and Power: discourses on working class women in Dundee's jute industry, *c.*1870–1930', unpublished Ph.D. thesis, University of St Andrews, 2002.

Graham Walker, *Thomas Johnston*, 1988.

Mary L. Walker, 'Work Amongst Women', in British Association, *Handbook and Guide to Dundee and District*, Dundee, 1912.

William Walker, *Juteopolis: Dundee and its textile workers, 1885–1923*, Dundee, 1979.

D. R. Wallace, *The Romance of Jute: a short history of the Calcutta jute mill industry, 1855–1927*, London, 1928.

J. T. Ward, *Chartism*, London, 1973.

Alexander J. Warden, *The Linen Trade, Ancient and Modern*, London, 1864.

A. Warwick (ed.), *Chambers Scots Dialect Dictionary*, Edinburgh, 1911.

D. A. Washbrook, 'Progress and Problems: South Asian economic and social history *c.*1720–1860', *Modern Asian Studies*, 22, 1, 1988, pp. 57–96.

D. A. Washbrook, 'Orients and Occidents: colonial discourse theory and the historiography of the British Empire', in R. W. Winks (ed.), *The Oxford History of the British Empire*, vol. v: Historiography, Oxford, 1999.

Mark Watson, *Jute and Flax Mills in Dundee*, Tayport, 1990.

A. T. Weston, *Factory Construction in Bengal*, Calcutta, 1921.

C. A. Whatley (ed.), *The Remaking of Juteopolis: Dundee c.1891–1991*, Dundee, 1992.

C. A. Whatley, D. B. Swinfen and A. Smith, *The Life and Times of Dundee*, Edinburgh, 1995.

C. A. Whatley and B. Harris (eds), *Victorian Dundee: image and reality*, Dundee, 2000.

Charles J. Withers, *Urban Highlanders: highland-lowland migration and urban Gaelic culture, 1700–1900*, East Linton, 2000.

Charles J. Withers (ed.), *Burt's Letters from the North: as related by Edmund Burt*, Edinburgh, 2005.

Anthony Wohl, *Endangered Lives: public health in Victorian Britain*, London, 1983.

T. Woodhouse and A. Brand, *A Century's Progress in Jute Manufacture, 1833–1933*, Dundee, 1934.

Leslie C. Wright, *Scottish Chartism*, Edinburgh, 1953.

Valerie Wright, 'Juteopolis and After: women and work in twentieth-century Dundee', in Jim Tomlinson and Christopher A. Whatley (eds.), *Jute No More: transforming Dundee*, Dundee, 2011, pp. 132–63.

Anand Yang, *The Limited Raj: agrarian relations in colonial India, Saran District, 1793–1920*, Delhi, 1989.

J. D. Young, *Women and Popular Struggles*, Edinburgh, 1985.

J. K. Young, 'From "Laissez-Faire" to "Homes fit for Heroes": housing in Dundee, 1868–1919', 2 volumes, unpublished Ph.D. thesis, Univesity of St. Andrews, 1991.

Index

Page numbers in **bold** denote figures.

Workers Welfare League of India (WWLI) 139, 141, 228n10
working costs, comparison of, in Dundee and Calcutta jute industries 31, 35, 133, 205n104, 228n3
Workmen's compensation Act (India) 162
World War One – *see* First World War
World War Two 181, 236–7n85

Yorkshire 180
Young, J.K. 104–5

Young Bengal 51, 210n75
Yule, Andrew, & Co. 20, 22, 60, 162, 202n41

Zaman, A.M.A 125, 226n59, 227n78, 236n80, 237n88
zamindari system/ zamindars 199n33, 238n112; *see also* landholding systems, landlordism/landlords, Permanent Settlement